Quilt

COLLECTIONS

Quilt
COLLECTIONS

A Directory for the United States and Canada

Compiled by
Lisa Turner Oshins

with State Commentaries by
Barbara S. Bockman

ACROPOLIS BOOKS LTD.
WASHINGTON, D.C.

Library of Congress Cataloging-in-Publication Data
Oshins, Lisa Turner, 1954–
   Quilt collections in the United States and Canada.

   Bibliography: p.
   Includes index.
   1. Quilts—United States—Directories. 2. Quilts—
Canada—Directories. I. Title.
NK9112.O85   1987   026'.74697'02573   87-17455
ISBN 0-87491-845-6
ISBN 0-87491-844-8 (pbk.)

Cover Credits

(Front cover photo) Patchwork quilt hand stitched and donated by Cub Scout Pack #867 of Franconia, Virginia, 1976, courtesy of the Gerald R. Ford Museum/Library, National Archives and Records Administration, Grand Rapids, Michigan.

(flap photo of the author) Photo by Reid S. Baker, Library of Congress.

(back cover photo, top) "Bird of Paradise" bride's quilt. Maker unknown, from New York State, 1858–63. Courtesy of the Museum of American Folk Art, New York, New York.

(back cover photo, bottom) Quaker Friendship Quilt, from the Phillips Family, Bucks County, signed and dated 1845. Courtesy of The Mercer Museum, Bucks County Historical Society, Doylestown, Pennsylvania.

Quilt Collections: A Directory for the United States and Canada was designed by Chris Borges, Art Director; Pamela Moore and Beth Judy, artists.

State commentaries copyright © 1987 by ACROPOLIS BOOKS LTD. The balance of this publication is in the public domain.

ACROPOLIS BOOKS, LTD.
Alphons J. Hackl, Publisher
Colortone Building, 2400 17th St., N.W.
Washington, D.C. 20009

Printed in the United States of America by
COLORTONE PRESS
Creative Graphics, Inc.
Washington, D.C. 20009

Attention: Schools and Corporations
ACROPOLIS books are available at quantity discounts with bulk purchase for educational, business, or sales promotional use. For information, please write to: SPECIAL SALES DEPARTMENT, ACROPOLIS BOOKS LTD., 2400 17th ST., N.W., WASHINGTON, D.C. 20009

Are there Acropolis Books you want but cannot find in your local stores?
You can get any Acropolis book title in print. Simply send title and retail price, plus $2.00 for the first copy, $1.00 for each additional copy to cover mailing and handling costs. District of Columbia residents add applicable sales tax. Enclose check or money order only, no cash please, to:

ACROPOLIS BOOKS LTD.,
2400 17th St., N.W.,
WASHINGTON, D.C. 20009.

FOREWORD

Quilts may be simply "Something to Keep You Warm," as was suggested by the exhibition title for Roland Freeman's fine collection of Mississippi Afro-American quilts, but they are certainly objects of our affection as well. Thus the last decade has been warmed by a profusion of quilt exhibits, quilt films, quilt books, and quilting activities and programs throughout the United States and Canada. Perhaps we may call this profusion a "renaissance." But if it is not a renaissance, that is because the generation before ours, though less inclined to public display, was equally committed in its own way to quilts as an artistic form. In fact, quilting has been popular for generations in America, earning through its versatility, its expressivity, and its tenacity the right to be called one of America's finest flowerings in the realm of folk art.

Happily, it can be reported that the art of the quilt is in no danger of dying out in North America. No alarm need be sounded for the salvaging of quilts or quilting. What *does* seem to be needed is a deeper historical and cultural understanding of quilting. A process of reflection about the art, history, and social function of quilts is well under way today. But many questions remain to be answered, many facets need more thorough and careful exploration. How widespread is quilting? Are there regional or ethnic preferences in fabric, pattern, stitchery, or function? Can we arrive at a reasonably specific and documentable early history of quilting? How much of quilting is family and community tradition, and how much popular style with influences from magazines and pattern books? Can we describe adequately the aesthetic systems underlying the various quilt patterns and styles? How have commercial marketing and distribution affected the tradition of quilting? What do quilts tell us about women in America? About civilization generally? Questions abound where quilts are concerned, and much study and reflection are in order.

Perhaps one reason that research and reflection have lagged a bit behind the actual practice of quilting is that resources for studying quilts are not easily located. Much of the relevant literature has appeared over the years in various popular publications that are not reliably found in libraries. And the quilts themselves are not easy to find, especially in the quantity and with the accompanying documentation that is necessary for serious comparative study. As we received more and more quilt inquiries at the American Folklife Center, we realized that we could not tell people where to find either quilts or quilt-related publications, documents, and expert resources. It is a good rule of thumb that research is always stimulated by a shared, accessible data base. Thus when Lisa Oshins of our staff expressed a particular interest in the subject of quilts, we resolved to commit her to a questionnaire survey in order to locate and describe public resources in the United States and Canada for the study of quilting. She augmented the initial questionnaire results with hundreds of personal letters and telephone calls, and she made appearances at conferences and conventions of quilters, quilt scholars, and quilt lovers. Thanks to her unstinting devotion to the project, we can now share this directory with countless others. We trust that, as these resources are more widely tapped in the future, both the art of quilting and our understanding of it will be enriched.

Alan Jabbour, Director
American Folklife Center
The Library of Congress

PREFACE

From September 1985 through June 1987, the American Folklife Center conducted a survey in the United States and Canada to locate and describe collections and documentation of quilts in museums, archives, libraries, universities, corporate offices, and other public institutions. Questionnaires were sent to 2,700 institutions and 1,224 replied. Seven hundred forty-seven reported collections of more than five quilts or large documentary holdings. Three hundred thirty reported no quilt holdings. One hundred forty-seven reported owning five or fewer quilts or smaller documentary collections. More than twenty-five thousand quilts were tabulated from survey questionnaires. The resulting data are available to researchers at the Library of Congress in the American Folklife Center's research facility, the Archive of Folk Culture.

This directory of public quilt-resource collections in the United States and Canada has been compiled for three groups: quiltmakers, quilt researchers, and quilt afficionados. It not only offers listings of where quilts can be seen and studied but also provides the locations of secondary resources such as patterns and instructions, diaries, journals, letters, taped interviews, photographs, illustrations, paintings, advertisements, video recordings, and films.

"N.B." (nota bene) listed after the brief descriptions of the collections indicates material regarded by the reporting institution as its most significant holding or the highlight of its quilt collection. Telephone numbers, days and hours of operation may change, so they should be verified. Since many of the institutions do not exhibit quilts on a continuous basis, it is prudent to call or write in advance of a visit to confirm planned exhibitions and museum hours. Most of the institutions require advance appointments for special viewing or studying.

Although the directory is not yet a comprehensive compilation, we believe it is the most complete directory now available. The American Folklife Center would be grateful for updates, additions, or corrections to the directory. Please write to the Quilt Collections Survey, American Folklife Center, Library of Congress, Washington, D.C. 20540.

ACKNOWLEDGMENTS

The American Folklife Center at the Library of Congress wishes to express its gratitude to the many individuals and institutions that so generously contributed time and expertise to this project. Our list of questionnaire recipients was sent to state folk cultural coordinators and state historic preservation offices. Mailing lists were also sent to officers/coordinators of state quilt documentation projects for their comments: Marianne Woods and Michele Newton, Arkansas; Helen Gould, California; Marge Kerr, Colorado; Kim Burdick, Delaware; Barbara Brackman, Kansas; Marsha MacDowell, Michigan; Bettina Havig, Missouri; Frances Best, Nebraska; Poppy Sanks and Ellice Ronsheim, Ohio; Jeannette Lasansky, Pennsylvania; Bets Ramsey and Merikay Waldvogel, Tennessee; Kay Hudec, Texas; and Hazel Carter, Virginia.

This book would not have been possible without the valuable and able assistance of the staff of the Folklife Center and help provided by other divisions of the Library and friends in the larger community. Ray Dockstader, deputy director of the Center, initiated the directory in the fall of 1984. Special thanks go to Doris M. Craig and Christina Hughes for assistance in mailing the questionnaires and making follow-up telephone calls to institutions, and to Brett Topping for establishing editorial guidelines. Consultant Barbara Fertig and Center folklorist Peter Bartis helped devise the questionnaire and the final format of the entries, and Karen Moses read the manuscript and offered suggestions. Jan Stiny added to the development of the questionnaire. James Hardin, Folklife Center editor, reviewed the introductory material. For help in researching photographs, special thanks are due Carl Fleischhauer, Judith Gray, and Ann Dancy of the Center and Beverly Brannan of the Library's Prints and Photographs Division. Many of the Farm Security Administration photographs that Carl Fleischhauer and Beverly Brannan located are reproduced for the first time. Barbara Humphrys of the Library's Motion Picture, Broadcasting, and Recorded Sound

Division and Lois Korzendorfer, fine arts specialist of the General Reading Room, also deserve special thanks.

Mary Cross of Portland, Oregon, quilt historian and survey coordinator for the Quilt Historian Research Network, began conducting in 1983 a voluntary survey of national resources available for textile researchers. Her help to the directory project has been immense. We also thank the individual network members, many of whom are also members of the American Quilt Study Group, for sharing their findings: Karoline (Karey) Bresenham, Katy Christopherson, Diana Church, Berniece Clelland, Patricia Cox, Inez Dillon, Mary Dillon, Helen Ericson, DeAnna L. Gehant, Flavin Glover, Cathy Grafton, Nancy Halpern, Laurel Horton, Darlene Kronschnabel, Jean Ray Laury, Millie Leathers, Judith Lopez, Sandra Metzler, Suellen Meyer, Hellen Monday, Pat Nickols, Julie Powell, Bets Ramsey, Ann Reimer, Tonia Sledd, Dorothy Stish, Odette Teel, Ann Wasserman, Sue Ellen White, Joyce Whittier, and Dorothy B. Williams. In addition, we would like to thank Sandi Fox and Nora Pickens for conducting research for elusive and obscure terms in the glossary.

Barbara S. Bockman, quiltmaker and editor, read the manuscript and wrote the glossary and state commentaries with dedication and enthusiasm. Another note of thanks is due LeeEllen Friedland for editing and proofreading.

CONTENTS

Introduction _____ 12

THE UNITED STATES __ 16

Alabama _____ 17
Alaska _____ 18
Arizona _____ 19
Arkansas _____ 21
California _____ 23
Colorado _____ 32
Connecticut _____ 35
Delaware _____ 40
District of Columbia _____ 42
Florida _____ 46
Georgia _____ 48
Hawaii _____ 49
Idaho _____ 51
Illinois _____ 52
Indiana _____ 59
Iowa _____ 63
Kansas _____ 73
Kentucky _____ 78
Louisiana _____ 80
Maine _____ 82
Maryland _____ 85
Massachusetts _____ 88
Michigan _____ 94
Minnesota _____ 99
Mississippi _____ 104
Missouri _____ 106

Montana _____ 109
Nebraska _____ 111
Nevada _____ 114
New Hampshire _____ 115
New Jersey _____ 116
New Mexico _____ 122
New York _____ 123
North Carolina _____ 146
North Dakota _____ 149
Ohio _____ 151
Oklahoma _____ 157
Oregon _____ 159
Pennsylvania _____ 163
Rhode Island _____ 171
South Carolina _____ 172
South Dakota _____ 175
Tennessee _____ 176
Texas _____ 180
Utah _____ 190
Vermont _____ 191
Virginia _____ 194
Washington _____ 198
West Virginia _____ 201
Wisconsin _____ 202
Wyoming _____ 205

CANADA —————— 207

Alberta ———————— 208

British Columbia ————— 209

Manitoba ——————— 210

New Brunswick ————— 211

Nova Scotia ——————— 213

Ontario ———————— 214

Quebec ———————— 221

Saskatchewan —————— 222

Quilts in Collections
Questionnaire ——— 224

Appendix 1:
Quilt Documentation Projects in the United States and Canada ——————— 227

Appendix 2:
Selected Listing of Regional, National, and International Quilt Associations —————— 230

Appendix 3:
Conservation —————— 231

Glossary ——————— 232

Filmography ————— 236

Selected Bibliography — 239

List of Participating
Institutions ————— 244

INTRODUCTION

Needlework ability and ways of providing warmth are basic to the trilogy of domestic necessities: food, clothing, and shelter. For many women, sewing and quiltmaking also began as traditional expressive cultural crafts learned by imitation. And thus quilts have come to document in a visual and tactile way our shared heritage.

Besides their principal use as bedcovers, quilts have been called into service for many purposes: pioneers carried them in their covered wagons and cowboys slept on quilted bedrolls called "suggans." Quilts have been thrown over tobacco to keep it moist in sheds, wrapped around car engines to keep them warm and dry, hung as room dividers, and tacked up as insulation over drafty windows. They have been stored in car trunks to be available as additional traction in mud or snow, and used to pad furniture in moving vans.

Quilts have often marked life's rites of passage or associations: birth, friendship, betrothal, marriage, and death. Families in need have received quilts as part of community help. Quilt raffles continue to raise funds for schools and institutions. Youngsters preparing to leave home for colleges or jobs may well pack a quilt made for the occasion. Quilts have commemorated political elections, the Centennial, the Bicentennial, and the Statue of Liberty celebration. The Red Cross, aid societies, auxillaries, and religious groups made quilts for soldiers during the Crimean, Civil, and Spanish-American Wars, and the two world wars. They have been made for political protest and to promote the cause of peace.

Despite the popular notion that quilts are sewn from used pieces of scrap material, most modern quilts and many historical ones have been made from carefully selected and specially purchased fabrics. But some patchwork quilts are veritable symbols of thrift and economy, testimonials to the phrase "waste not, want not." Pieced Memory quilts, Charm, Signature, Autograph, and Friendship quilts, and crazy quilts made from left-over clothing fabric are tributes to the frugal quiltmaker's scrap bag and to the sharing tradition among quilters. Other materials used in quilt construction range from feed sacks to clothing and upholstery scraps. A popular nineteenth-century book, *The American Frugal Housewife* by Lydia Maria Child (sixteenth edition, 1835), offered the following advice:

> The true economy of housekeeping is simply the art of gathering up all the fragments, so that nothing is lost. I mean fragments of *time,* as well as *materials.* Nothing should be thrown away so long as it is possible to make any use of it, however trifling that use may be; and whatever be the size of a family, every member should be employed either in earning or saving money. . . . In this point of view, patchwork is good economy. It is indeed a foolish waste of time to tear cloth into bits for the sake of arranging it anew in fantastic figures; but a large family may be kept out of idleness, and a few shillings saved, by thus using scraps of gowns, curtains, &c.[1]

A quilt consists of three layers: a top; a middle layer of batting made from cotton, wool, old quilts, blankets, or, lately, synthetics; and a backing, either pieced together or a single large piece of fabric such as muslin. The top, which gives the quilt its distinctive look, is made by sewing predetermined small sections together, *piecework;* by sewing down onto a solid ground an applied *(appliqué)* design; or by quilting a plain or solid expanse of fabric with elaborate stitchery, *whole-cloth.* A trapunto or corded quilt has stuffed designs in relief. Occasionally the three layers are held together by tying them at regular intervals. Otherwise the layers are bound together by tiny running stitches laid down in a prescribed manner. The stitches either echo the pieced or appliqué design, or introduce a new design across the face of the top. These *quilting* stitches transform the three layers into a quilt, and many quilters strive for even, minute stitches that are as well-formed on the back as on the top.

Six thousand patchwork patterns and pattern variations have been identified.[2] There are perhaps as many appliqué patterns, but they have not been cataloged. In some instances the name of the same pattern varies from region to region and individual to individual. For example, the pattern called Endless Chain is also called Job's Tears, Slave Chain, Texas Tears, Rocky Road to Kansas, or Kansas Troubles.[3]

Quilts are now recognized as socially, historically, and artistically valuable and are being conserved and exhibited in a wide range of venues throughout United States and Canada. Always popular items at agricultural fairs, quilts are shown at expositions, festivals, and special annual exhibitions such as the Quilt National in Athens, Ohio. Indeed, quilts are now just as likely to be found in fine art museums as at county fairs. One hallmark twentieth-century exhibition was from the collection of Jonathan Holstein and Gail van der Hoof at the Whitney Museum of American Art in New York City in 1971, where once and for all quilts attained status as a valid and important visual art. Jonathan Holstein recently noted the changing perception of quilts:

The emphasis on the visual aspects of quilts over their other intrinsic qualities, a position which characterized the Whitney exhibition and others, was a necessary step in freeing quilts from their bedspread/craft/mythology baggage. It wasn't long, however, before scholars realized that, as a result of this emphasis, quilts' relevance to social history was being neglected.[4]

A look at the Library of Congress collections shows that there has been a tremendous surge of interest in quilting and the history of quilts since the early 1970s. Before 1968 sixty or seventy books on quilts could be found at the Library. Since then, over four hundred books have been added, ranging in subject from "how to quilt" to historical and social analyses.

The scope of quilt-related Library of Congress subject headings is wide. Books, journals, magazines, and additional sources that discuss quilts and quiltmaking may be found under different headings: folk art, folk crafts, handicrafts, folklore, American studies, material culture, popular culture, women's studies, daily life (in the American home and farm), antiques and collectibles, decorative arts, fiber arts, needlework, and textiles.[5] Under the subject heading "patchwork" are titles for plays, travel guides, and novels, and computer software for designing quilts.

Today quilts and their documentation are preserved in an astonishing number of public and private collections. A number of surveys have revealed important information to quilters and scholars (see Appendix 1). Statewide, county, and provincial quilt documentation projects are spontaneously cropping up across the United States and Canada. The Kentucky Quilt Project led the way in 1982 by documenting quilts made in Kentucky from 1800 to 1900. The project also introduced the quilt-day concept as a means of interviewing quilt owners around the state. Quilts were brought to meetings held at various locations, photographed, and their social history documented on questionnaire forms. The quilt's date, social history, the types of materials used in its making, and other pertinent details were carefully recorded. Katy Christopherson of Louisville, Kentucky, who collaborated on the Kentucky Quilt Project, has since held workshops on how to conduct a state quilt search and has served as a consultant to other statewide projects. A number of the state quilt projects are publishing books and mounting exhibitions and have made formal arrangements to house the results in state historical societies, state museums, or university archives.

In addition to the state projects, a number of organizations and associations promote quilting and foster quilt research (see Appendix 2). According to Michael Kile, publisher of the Quilt Digest Press, there are approximately 225,000 members of 1,500 quilt guilds.[6] Many journals and magazines on quilting publish information about upcoming exhibitions, symposia, and other related activities.

Lisa Turner Oshins
Program Specialist
American Folklife Center

NOTES

1 Lydia Maria Child, *The American Frugal Housewife* (Boston: Carter, Hendee, & Co., 1835), 3. *See also* Lynn A. Bonfield, "The Production of Cloth, Clothing and Quilts in 19th Century New England Homes," *Uncoverings 1981,* 1982:77.

2 Lecture by Barbara Brackman, Bucknell University, Lewisburg, Pennsylvania, June 1987, author and publisher of *An Encyclopedia of Pieced Quilt Patterns,* 8 vols. (Lawrence, KS: Prairie Flower Publishing, 1979).

3 Patsy Orlofsky and Myron Orlofsky, *Quilts in America* (New York: McGraw-Hill Book Company, 1974), 247.

4 Jonathan Holstein, "The Whitney and After . . . What's Happened to Quilts," *The Clarion,* (Spring/Summer 1986), 83.

5 Beverly Gordon, *Domestic American Textiles: A Bibliographic Sourcebook* (Pittsburgh, PA: Center for the History of American Needlework, 1978), 13.

6 "Quilting Comes Into Its Own as an Art," *New York Times,* 20 August 1987.

The United States

ALABAMA

Victorian crazy quilts are numerous.

The Birmingham Museum of Art

2000 8th Avenue North
Birmingham, Alabama 35203
(205) 254-2566

Tuesday–Saturday, 10:00 A.M.–5:00 P.M.; Sunday, 2:00–6:00 P.M.
The Museum has collected eighteen nineteenth century southern and Alabama quilts. Two predate 1820. Most are pieced crazy quilts. Black-and-white quilt photographs and other information on quilts are also available.
NB: Stuffed appliqué on silk taffeta quilt made in Selma, Alabama "for the war effort" c. 1861.
Study Services: Written permission from the curator of decorative arts for access to textile storage area or to review survey findings. Reading room, work tables, photocopy facilities, accession cards/files, and microscope; photo prints and slides.
Public Services: The Museum is conducting a decorative arts survey for Alabama in conjunction with the quilt documentation project of the Artist-in-Education Program of the Alabama State Council on the Arts and Humanities.

Alabama Department of Archives and History

624 Washington Avenue
Montgomery, Alabama 36130
(205) 261-4361

Weekdays, 8:00 A.M.–5:00 P.M.; weekends, 9:00 A.M.–5:00 P.M.
Approximately twenty nineteenth century regional quilts which are not fully cataloged.
Study Services: Access to the stored collections is by prearrangement only; write to the curator of collections. Reading room, work tables, accession cards/files, photocopy facilities and microscope.

Landmarks Foundation of Montgomery

310 North Hull Street
Montgomery, Alabama 36104
(205) 263-4355

Weekdays, 8:00 A.M.–5:00 P.M.; Saturday, 10:00 A.M.–3:00 P.M.; Sunday, 1:30–3:30 P.M.
There are fifteen patchwork, appliqué, silk, and velvet crazy quilts from central Alabama plus eight quilt patterns. Six of the quilts can be dated between 1821 and 1900. Quilts are on continuous display.
NB: 1856 appliqué quilt with Bible verses, names and date written in ink.
Study Services: Contact the curator in advance. Reading room, accession cards/files, and books/journals, photo prints and slides.
Public Services: Quilting demonstrations at seasonal festivals.

Scottsboro-Jackson Heritage Center

208 South Houston Street
Scottsboro, Alabama
(205) 259-2122

Mailing Address:
P.O. Box 53
Scottsboro, AL 35768

Hours not provided.
Six to twelve Appalachian quilts are of regional and traditional patterns.
Study Services: Written request required. Reading room, photocopy facilities, work tables, accession cards/files, and books/journals.
Public Services: Traveling exhibition series, class tours, and workshops.

Pike Pioneer Museum

U.S. Highway 231 North
Troy, Alabama
(205) 566-3597

Mailing Address:
Route 3, Box 342
Troy, AL 36081

Weekdays, 10:00 A.M.–5:00 P.M.; Sundays, 1:00–5:00 P.M.
Approximately thirty southeast Alabama quilts; fifteen are from Pike County. Collection is

predominantly late nineteenth century; about five are post-1900. Quilts are on continuous exhibition.

NB: Silk and velvet quilt with elaborate embroidery; tintype of quiltmakers.

Study Services: Contact director for access. Work tables and accession cards/files; photos available from the Birmingham Museum of Art, Decorative Arts Survey.

Public Services: Special tours pre-arranged.

Archives of American Minority Cultures

Special Collections
Gorgan Main Library
University of Alabama
Tuscaloosa, Alabama
(205) 348-5512

Mailing Address:
P.O. Box S
Tuscaloosa, AL 35487-9784

Weekdays, 8:00 A.M.–5:00 P.M.; Thursday evenings, 6:00–10:00 P.M.

There are two interviews (with slides) taped in 1980 and 1981: one is the annual Freedom Quilting Bee, Gee's-Bend, Alabama (thirty-one slides); the other features quiltmakers from an Alabama family (thirty-eight slides).

Study Services: Call in advance to verify that sound and viewing equipment are available. Reading room, work tables, accession cards/files, subject index, books/journals, photocopy facilities. Archives of American Minority Cultures Special Collections contains Alabama Collection, rare book room, historical manuscripts collection, and university archive; slides available through audio-visual department.

ALASKA

Although the Union's biggest state does not yet boast large public collections, there is a vital quilting community actively at work.

*Anchorage Museum of History and Art
121 West Seventh Avenue
Anchorage, Alaska
(904) 264-4326

Mailing Address:
P.O. Box 196650
Anchorage, AK 99519-6650

*Pratt Museum
3779 Bartlett Street
Homer, Alaska 99603
(907) 235-8635

*Alaska State Museum
395 Whittier Street
Juneau, Alaska
(907) 465-2901

Mailing Address:
Pouch FM
Juneau, AK 99603

*Tongass Historical Museum
629 Dock Street
Ketchikan, Alaska 99901
(907) 225-5600

*Carrie M. McLain Memorial Museum
200 East Front Street
Nome, Alaska
(907) 443-2566

Mailing Address:
P.O. Box 53
Nome, AK 99762

Birmingham, Alabama, February 1937. The Eargle Family moving into their new house at the Gardendale Homesteads. Photo by Arthur Rothstein, negative number LC-USF34-5961-D. Courtesy of the Farm Security Administration Collection, Prints and Photographs Division, Library of Congress.

*Clausen Memorial Museum
Second and F Street
Petersburg, Alaska
(907) 772-3598

Mailing Address:
P.O. Box 708
Petersburg, AK 99833

*Collections of two to four quilts.

ARIZONA

Public institutions offer a wide range of study resources in addition to many fine examples of antique and contemporary quilts.

Fort Verde State Historical Park
Off Interstate 17
Camp Verde, Arizona
(602) 567-6251

Mailing Address:
P.O. Box 397
Camp Verde, AZ 86322

Daily, 8:00 A.M.–5:00 P.M.
A collection of eight handsewn quilts. Continuous exhibition of quilts.

Arizona Friends of Folklore Archive
Northern Arizona University
Liberal Arts Building, Room 319
Flagstaff, Arizona
(602) 523-4420 English Department

Mailing Address:
P.O. Box 5705
Northern Arizona University
Flagstaff, AZ 86011

By appointment.
Approximately 250 slides, national in scope, of quilts and quiltmakers.
Study Services: By appointment. Reading room, work tables, and photocopy facilities; copies of slides available through Media Center.

Arizona Costume Institute of the Phoenix Art Museum
1625 North Central
Phoenix, Arizona 85016
(602) 257-1880

Tuesday, 10:00 A.M.–5:00 P.M.; Wednesday, 1:00–5:00 P.M.; Sunday, 1:00–5:00 P.M. Collection of eight quilts: four from New England, two from Virginia and Maryland, and two from Kentucky. Two are appliqué and six are piecework. Two date prior to 1820, four from 1821 to 1900, and two from 1901 to 1940.

Sharlot Hall Museum
415 West Gurley
Prescott, Arizona 86301
(602) 445-3122

Tuesday–Saturday, 9:00 A.M.–5:00 P.M.; summer: 10:00 A.M.– 4:00 P.M.; winter: Sunday, 1:00–5:00 P.M.
Thirty-six quilts are primarily from the nineteenth century to pre-World War II. Quilts are on continuous display.
Study Services: Written or telephoned request, at least two weeks in advance. Reading room, work tables, accession cards/files, photocopy facilities, microscope, books/journals; prints made from negatives.
Public Services: Tours.

Tempe Historical Museum
3500 South Rural Road
Tempe, Arizona
(602) 966-7253

Mailing Address:
P.O. Box 27394
Tempe, AZ 85282

Tuesday–Saturday, 10:00 A.M.–4:30 P.M.
Thirty-two quilts, of which sixteen can be dated: nine from the late nineteenth century, four from post-1900, and three contemporary. The collection is national in scope. Quilts are occasionally on exhibit.

NB: Bicentennial Signature quilt.
Study Services: Write to staff. Work tables and accession cards/files.

University Art Collections
Arizona State University
Tempe, Arizona 85287
(602) 965-2874

Weekdays, 8:00 A.M.–5:00 P.M.
Ten American quilts date from 1830 to 1974. The majority is nineteenth century. Anonymously made quilts include Feather Star, Diamond, a hexagonal pattern crib quilt, Star quilt, a Nine Patch Presentation quilt with hand-written sayings and messages with trapunto work, and an appliqué Flower Garden.
NB: Star of Bethlehem Civil War period crib quilt and a c. 1870 Pine Tree quilt by Mrs. Amos (Louisa) Price of Berks County, Pennsylvania; Tulip Tree quilt c. 1830 by Mrs. William Walker of Pittsfield, Massachusetts; and 1974 embroidered crazy quilt and sham in brightly colored velvet by Helen Stice.
Study Services: Make written request to registrar. Work tables and accession cards/files; photo prints.

Arizona Historical Society
949 East Second Street
Tucson, Arizona 85719
(602) 628-5774

Monday–Saturday, 10:00 A.M.–4:00 P.M.; Sunday, 12:00–4:00 P.M.
Eighty quilts gathered from the southwest and Kentucky, mostly patchwork and some appliqué and embroidered work. Quilt patterns represented include: Tri-tulip, crazy quilt, Log Cabin, star, Stairstep, Diamond, Prairie Star, Harvest Sun, Pineapple, Washington Pavement, Dresden Plate, Streak o'Lightning, Sunburst, Drunkard's Path, framed medallion, Rising Star, Crossroads, Love Knot, Star of Bethlehem, Ohio Star, Triple Irish Chain, Oak Leaf and Reel. Forty-five quilts can be dated: one prior to 1820, thirty-three between 1821 and 1900, and eleven post-1900.
Study Services: Make written request giving

credentials and outline of research. Reading room, work tables, accession cards/files, photocopy facilities, and microscope; black and white photo prints, and color slides.
Public Services: Tours and lectures on quilts and quiltmaking offered in conjunction with classes at the University of Arizona.

Fremont House Museum
151 South Granada Avenue
Tucson, Arizona
(602) 622-0956

Mailing Address:
P.O. Box 2588
Tucson, AZ 85702-2588

Wednesday–Saturday, 10:00 A.M.–4:00 P.M.
A collection of five nineteenth century quilts. One is a genealogy quilt. Catalog card information provided by donors. The quilts are on continuous exhibition.

The Southwest Folklore Center at the University of Arizona
1524 East Sixth Street
Tucson, Arizona 85721
(602) 621-3392

Weekdays, 8:00 A.M.–12:00 P.M., 1:00–5:00 P.M.
The Center contains approximately 300 slides illustrating quilts from several ethnic traditions in southern Arizona: Afro-American, Piman, Apache, and Mormon. The ten quilts from the Center's exhibition "Geometry in Motion: Afro-American Quilters from Pinal County Arizona" are expected to become part of one of the University of Arizona's museums.
Study Services: By appointment with the director. Reading room, work tables, accession cards/files, photocopy facilities, and microscope.
Public Services: Traveling exhibition service.

ARKANSAS

Regional quilts representing many techniques and patterns are exhibited.

The Castle and Museum at Inspiration Point
U.S. Highway 62, 5.5 Miles West
Eureka Springs, Arkansas 72632
(501) 253-9462

Mid-April to October 31: daily, 9:00 A.M.–5:00 P.M.
Approximately fifty quilts dating from the early 1900s to the present are on continuous exhibition.
Public Services: Photographs may be taken.

The University Museum
University of Arkansas
Fayetteville, Arkansas 72701
(501) 575-3456

Monday–Saturday, 9:00 A.M.–5:00 P.M.; Sunday, 1:00–5:00 P.M.
Approximately 250 quilt blocks and photographs from Arkansas quilters are part of a collection assembled by folklore classes between 1964 and 1965. Five northwest Arkansas piecework, appliqué, and embroidered quilts are dated: two from the Territorial period, two pre-Civil War, and one post-1900. Also included are four interviews and transcribed oral history tapes.
Study Services: Contact museum curator in advance. Reading room, work tables, accession cards/files, photocopy facilities, and microscope.

Old Fort Museum

320 Rogers Avenue
Fort Smith, Arkansas 72901
(501) 783-7841 or 783-7848

Winter: Tuesday–Saturday 10:00 A.M.–5:00
P.M.; Sunday, 1:00–5:00 P.M. Summer: daily,
9:00 A.M.–5:00 P.M. Office: weekdays, 8:00
A.M.–5:00 P.M.
Of twenty-nine quilts five are from Arkansas,
one from Tennessee, and one from Kentucky
or Indiana. There are Victorian crazy quilts,
Log Cabin, one Pineapple, one Ships at Sea,
and several Flower Garden quilts. Twelve date
from the nineteenth century. There is also a
photo of a Texas quilting bee.
Study Services: Contact the collections manager for appointment.
Public Services: Exhibitions are rotated. Quilt
workshops offered.

Arkansas Post County Museum

U.S. Highway 165 South
Gillett, Arkansas
(501) 548-2634

Mailing Address:
P.O. Box 436
Gillett, AR 72055

Wednesday–Saturday, 9:30 A.M.–4:00 P.M.; Sunday, 1:00–4:00 P.M.
Ten handsewn nineteenth century quilts made
by local women. Eight are pieced and two are
embroidered. Quilts are continuously on exhibition.
Study Services: By permission from the director. Reading room, work tables, and accession
cards/files.

Arkansas Territorial Restoration

3rd and Scott Streets
Little Rock, Arkansas 72201
(501) 371-2348

Monday–Saturday, 9:00 A.M.–5:00 P.M.; Sunday,
1:00–5:00 P.M.
Thirty primarily nineteenth century Arkansas
quilts and several from other southern states:
five white-on-white, one appliqué, twenty-four

pieced quilts. Unpublished documentation includes correspondence by quiltmakers and
detailed handwritten notes on quiltmaking.
Contemporary quilts are on continuous exhibition.
NB: Concentration of pre-1870 Arkansas
quilts.
Study Services: Write or phone request to
view quilts. Reading room, work tables, accession cards/files, photocopy facilities, microscope (binocular), and twenty volumes of
books/journals; photo prints and slides.
Public Services: Workshops have been offered
in conjunction with exhibitions.

Old State House Museum

300 West Markham Street
Little Rock, Arkansas 72201
(501) 371-1749

Monday–Saturday, 9:00 A.M.–5:00 P.M.; Sunday,
1:00–5:00 P.M.
Fourteen regional pieced quilts from Ashley,
Clark, Saline, and White counties; others from
Iowa, North Carolina, and possibly Wisconsin.
Four date from the nineteenth century and
two are post-1900.
Study Services: By prior request only. Reading
room, work tables, accession cards/files, pho-
tocopy facilities, and books/journals.
Public Services: Textile conservation work-
shop offered.

Rogers Historical Museum

322 South Second Street
Rogers, Arkansas 72756
(501) 636-0162

Tuesday–Friday, 12:00–4:00 P.M.; Saturday,
10:00 A.M.–4:00 P.M.
Seventeen pieced and three crazy quilts from
the region: one Appalachian, six from the Arkansas Ozarks, and one from southern Arkansas. Twelve quilts date from the nineteenth
century, eight from the twentieth century.
Also available are photo prints and slides of
quilts in private collections researched by museum staff.

NB: Film in the collection, *Quilts in Women's Lives.*
Study Services: By appointment with museum staff. Accession cards/files, and books/journals.
Public Services: Conservation training.
Publications: Luster, Michael. *Stitches in Time: A Legacy of Ozark Quilts* (1986).

Siloam Springs Museum

112 North Maxwell Street
Siloam Springs, Arkansas
(501) 524-4011

Mailing Address:
P.O. Box 1164
Siloam Springs, AR 72761

Wednesday—Saturday, 12:00—5:00 P.M.
Twenty-one piecework quilts in various patterns are from Arkansas and the Midwest: five from Arkansas, one from Kansas, one from Illinois, and two from Missouri; others of unknown provenance. Four crazy quilts, and four appliqué quilts. Twenty-eight quilt patterns/instructions also available.
NB: 1859 Whig Rose appliqué quilt.
Study Services: Contact director. Work tables and accession cards/files. Photo reproductions may be available in the future.
Public Services: Special quilt exhibitions.

Shiloh Museum

118 West Johnson Avenue
Springdale, Arkansas 72764
(501) 751-8411 or 751-6986

Tuesday—Saturday, 10:00 A.M.—5:00 P.M.; June—October: Sunday, 1:00—5:00 P.M.
Twenty piecework quilts are from northwest Arkansas, one quilt from Indiana, and one from Ohio.
NB: Woven wool quilt top, dyed and woven by maker. A 1978 Springdale Centennial quilt made by the Business and Professional Women's Club.
Study Services: Permission of director and registrar required. Work tables, accession cards/files, photocopy facilities, and books/journals.

Facilities to photograph and print photographs of quilts as needed.
Public Services: Periodic exhibits and discovery box for school groups.

Arkansas State University Museum

Arkansas State University
State University, Arkansas
(501) 972-2074

Mailing Address:
P.O. Box 490
State University, AR 72467

Weekdays, 9:00 A.M.—4:00 P.M. Weekends, 1:00—4:00 P.M.
The collection of seventy-five quilts and coverlets from the seventeenth century to the present comes mainly from northeast Arkansas and represents a wide range of techniques. Quilts are on continuous exhibition.
Study Services: By advance appointment. Reading room in library, work tables, accession cards/files, books/journals, and photocopy facilities.
Public Services: Tours, classes, and workshops offered during quilt exhibitions.

Woodville, California. February 1942. Farm Security Administration farm workers' community. Carding surplus cotton which will be used to make quilt batting. Photo by Russell Lee, negative number LC-USF34-71801-D. Courtesy of the Farm Security Administration Collection, Prints and Photographs Division, Library of Congress.

CALIFORNIA

*As diverse as the state itself. Califor-
nia quilts in public collections span
the generations from pioneer gold-
rush days to those of contemporary
quilters.*

Kern County Museum

3801 Chester Avenue
Bakersfield, California 93301
(805) 861-2132

Weekdays, 8:00 A.M.—5:00 P.M.; Saturday, Sunday, and holidays, 10:00 A.M.—5:00 P.M.
Sixty-seven local family quilts. One is Amish.
Twenty-three date from the nineteenth century and forty-four, post-1900.
Study Services: By appointment with museum
staff. Reading room, work tables, accession
cards/files, photocopy facilities, and books/
journals.
Public Services: Demonstration of quilting
techniques on Tuesday mornings. Quilt exhibits.

Robert H. Lowie Museum of Anthropology

University of California, Berkeley
103 Kroeber Hall
Berkeley, California 94720
(415) 642-3681

By appointment only.
Six quilts, most machine pieced and quilted,
from the first half of the twentieth century.

Butte County Historical Society

Pentz Road
Chico, California 95926
(916) 877-9165

Lillian Parker, Curator
5827 Wildwood Lane, #3
Paradise, CA 95969

Hours not provided.
Fifteen quilts are of varying techniques.
Twelve can be dated from the nineteenth cen-
tury. Three are contemporary. Many quilts in
the collection were made on wagon trains
during westward migration.
NB: Ocean Wave variation dated 1859.
Study Services: Contact curator in advance.
Photo print reproductions are available.

State of California Department of Parks and Recreation

Bidwell Mansion State Historic Park
525 Esplanade Avenue
Chico, California 95926
(916) 895-6144

Daily, 10:00 A.M.—5:00 P.M.
Twenty-five quilts are from Chico residents of
1865 to 1900. Quilt patterns include Jack in
the Pulpit variation, Double Nine Patch, Kansas Star, Interlaced Lattice Blocks, Barrister's
Block, Log Cabin in Courthouse Steps, Barn
Raising, and Straight Furrows variations;
flower and leaf design, five star diamond pattern, wool Steeple Chase similar to Millwheel
design, Double Wedding Ring, wool Grandmother's Flower Garden, Nine Patch with
eight pointed star, crazy quilts, Triple Irish
Chain variation, Star of Bethlehem, appliqué
Flower Basket, and Broken Baskets. Quilts are
on continuous display.
NB: Concentration of Log Cabin variations and
crazy quilts. Velvet, satin, taffeta and silk Victorian crazy quilt; silk Cigar Band Log Cabin
Sunshine and Shadow variation. Cigar Bands
still labeled with brand names, c. 1890, made
in Durham, Butte County, California.
Study Services: By appointment only. Records
and photographs are used as much as possible

to avoid excessive handling of quilts. Work tables, accession cards/files, photocopy facilities; photo reproductions.
Public Services: Tours of the mansion with quilts on display. Workshops on conserving quilts and other old items. Interpretive slide program.

Ferndale Museum
Shaw and Third Streets
Ferndale, California
(707) 786-4466

Mailing Address:
P.O. Box 431
Ferndale, CA 95536

Wednesday–Saturday, 11:00 A.M.–4:00 P.M.;
Sunday, 1:00–4:00 P.M.
Five handsewn quilts, notably a local Heritage and a Signature quilt.

San Joaquin County Historical Museum
11793 North Micke Grove Road
Lodi, California
(209) 368-9154

Mailing Address:
P.O. Box 21
Lodi, CA 95241

Wednesday–Sunday, 1:00–5:00 P.M.; Office: weekdays, 8:00 A.M.–5:00 P.M.
In the collection of fifty-two quilts about thirty-six are piecework, seven pieced and embroidered, six appliqué. One quilt each of the following techniques: trapunto, decorative quilting, and printed whole-cloth.
NB: Flower Basket Signature quilt made in 1859 by a woman from New Hampshire on her way west.
Study Services: Make appointment, must work with a staff member. Reading room, work tables, accession cards/files, photocopy facilities, and books/journals.
Public Services: Occasional exhibitions.

Rancho Los Cerritos Museum
4600 Virginia Road
Long Beach, California 90807
(213) 424-9423

Wednesday–Sunday, 1:00–5:00 P.M.
Forty to fifty primarily American quilts: piecework and appliqué from the nineteenth century with a concentration in crazy quilts.
NB: Crazy quilts; and Postage Stamp patchwork.
Study Services: Contact curatorial staff for appointment. Reading room, accession cards/files, and photocopy facilities.
Public Services: Occasional exhibitions; quilt shows in conjunction with local quilt guilds.

Art of the Plains Indians
25852 Westwind Way
Los Altos Hills, California 94022
(415) 948-9448

By appointment.
One hundred fifty predominantly handsewn contemporary quilts by Sioux, Gros Ventre, Assiniboin, Cree, and Mandan Hidatsa. Unpublished personal narratives by quiltmakers; diaries/journals, interviews/oral history tapes.
NB: Motifs inspired by nature and unique to above cultures. Concentration in Plains Indians Morning Star quilts.
Study Services: Contact Florence Pulford, owner and collector. Photo prints and slides available.
Public Services: Lectures at colleges and museums regarding the Plains Indians' culture and its influence on their quiltmaking. Quilts lent for exhibitions.

American Quilt Research Center
The Los Angeles County Museum of Art
5905 Wilshire Boulevard
Los Angeles, California 90036
(213) 857-6083

Hours by appointment only during regular weekday museum hours: Tuesday–Friday, 10:00 A.M.–5:00 P.M.
Center will open in 1988; printed material available on request. Collection is national in

scope, now includes over 100 quilts, and is making additional important acquisitions. The archival material is being assembled and will include: quilt patterns, personal narratives by quiltmakers, taped oral histories, research papers, and other unpublished documentation. All techniques and principal patterns are represented. The bulk of the collection dates from 1820 to 1875.

NB: Baltimore Album child's quilt, and several important eighteenth century pieces. An extensive collection of eighteenth and nineteenth century quilted garments and accessories.

Study Services: Reading room, work tables, accession cards/files, a specialized library of quilt related publications, and access to the Department of Costumes and Textiles Library of 4,000 volumes of books and journals, collection of eighteenth and nineteenth century printed cotton dresses; photocopy facilities, and microscope; photographic reproductions of quilts are being developed.

Public Services: One and two day symposiums are planned. A biennial international symposium for museum professionals, scholars, and students will be held.

Publications: Plans an active program of publications, books, catalogs, and monographs.

Historical Society of Centinela Valley
7634 Midfield Avenue
Los Angeles, California 90045
(213) 649-6272

Sunday and Wednesday, 2:00–4:00 P.M.
Twelve American quilts: four from the nineteenth century, eight from the twentieth century.

NB: 1840 Bear Paw quilted with homespun linen thread.

Study Services: By appointment.

Public Services: Annual exhibit.

Los Angeles County Museum of Natural History
900 Exposition Boulevard
Los Angeles, California 90007
(213) 744-3354

Tuesday–Sunday, 10:00 A.M.–5:00 P.M.; Closed Mondays, Thanksgiving, Christmas, and New Year's Day. Curatorial staff available weekdays, 8:00 A.M.–5:00 P.M.

Twenty-nine nineteenth century quilts and eight from 1901 to 1940 exhibit a broad range of provenances and techniques. Two quilts each from California, Ohio, and Illinois; one each from Texas, Missouri, Minnesota, Pennsylvania, and Kentucky. Techniques include piecework, appliqué, whole-cloth, and white-on-white with stuffed work. There are six crazy quilts, three Log Cabins, and one Yo-Yo. Several on long-term display in American history exhibits.

Study Services: Request through curator; access by appointment. Reading room, accession cards/files, photocopy facilities, microscope, and fifty volumes of published books/journals; photo prints.

Museum of Cultural History
University of California at Los Angeles
405 Hilgard Avenue
Los Angeles, California 90024
(213) 825-4361

Office: weekdays, 8:00 A.M.–5:00 P.M.; Museum: Wednesday–Sunday, 12:00–5:00 P.M. Upon completion of the new building the name of the museum will change to Fowler Museum of Cultural History. Collection is primarily of quilts from Kutch, in Gujarat, India. There are six American quilts.

Madera County Historical Society

Yosemite Avenue
Madera, California
(209) 673-0921

Mailing Address:
P.O. Box 478
Madera, CA 93639

Weekends, 1:00–4:30 P.M.; or by appointment.
Collection includes fourteen piecework, three
appliqué, and six crazy quilts with embroi-
dery. Seven quilts date from the nineteenth
century. Quilts are on continuing exhibition.
NB: Madera County history quilt, Bicentennial
Madera County Ethnic quilt.
Study Services: Write in advance. Accession
cards/files; photo prints.
Public Services: Tours by appointment.

John Muir National Historic Site

4202 Alhambra Avenue
Martinez, California 94553
(415) 228-8860

Daily, 10:00 A.M.–4:30 P.M. Closed Thanksgiving, Christmas, and New Year's Day.
Six quilts used as part of the furnishings of the
house.

American Quilt Study Group

105 Molino Avenue
Mill Valley, California 94941
(415) 388-1382

Weekdays, 9:00 A.M.–5:00 P.M.
Three unpublished research papers and 1,000
published books and/or journals on quilts and
quilting may be seen by appointment. Accession cards/files, and photocopy facilities.

McHenry Museum

1402 I Street
Modesto, California 95354
(209) 577-5366

Tuesday–Sunday, 12:00–4:00 P.M.
Thirty-four quilts of various patterns and techniques.

Sierra Historic Sites Association

Oakhurst, California
(209) 683-6570

Mailing Address:
P.O. Box 451
Oakhurst, CA 93644

Tuesday–Saturday, 1:00–3:00 P.M.; Sunday,
1:00–4:00 P.M.
In the collection of thirteen quilts one is from
Arizona and one from Arkansas. Eight are
piecework, three Victorian crazy quilts, and
two appliqué. The majority of the collection
dates from the 1930s; three are nineteenth
century, nine are post-1900, and one is contemporary. Quilts are on continuous display.
NB: Bicentennial quilt highlighting local history.
Study Services: Contact curator or registrar.
Reading room, accession cards/files, historical
research library, and photocopy facilities.
Public Services: Annual quilt exhibition of
those in the collection and others on loan
from the community.

The Oakland Museum

1000 Oak Street
Oakland, California 94607
(415) 273-3402, Information
(415) 273-3842, History

Wednesday–Saturday, 10:00 A.M.–5:00 P.M.;
Sunday, 12:00–7:00 P.M.
Approximately 130 regional California quilts,
nineteenth century to contemporary. California quilts include two Afro-American quilt
tops, two quilts made by children, two
Church quilts from Oakland, one Eastern Star
quilt from Berkeley, and one League of
Women Voters contemporary quilt from Oakland. Techniques include: twenty crazy quilts
with embroidery, two white-on-white, one Yo-
Yo, one nineteenth century whole-cloth
printed to look like piecing. Quilts are rotated
periodically, displayed continuously.
NB: Selection of sample blocks and pieces.
One dates 1848, the year gold was discovered
in California.
Study Services: Access is quite limited. Re-

quests received three months ahead of time will be considered. Quilt information in assembled binder. Photographic prints can be made. Reproductions available: one exhibition poster, one postcard of a crazy quilt detail. Reference works: many period magazines: e.g. *Godey's, McCalls, Needle Craft, Delineator*, and others.

Public Services: Gallery tours with docents; special quilt sharings; movie programs about quilts; lectures; changing exhibitions; classes; fairs.

Publications: Frye, L. Thomas, editor. *American Quilts: A Handmade Legacy* (1981).

Pasadena Historical Society
470 West Walnut Street
Pasadena, California 91103
(818) 577-1668

By appointment.
Eleven piecework and one chintz appliqué quilt are regional quilts from the nineteenth century.

Study Services: Contact curator by letter or by phone (818) 577-1660. Limited space, work tables, photocopy facilities, and microscope.

Public Services: Periodic exhibits.

Redding Museum and Art Center
1911 Rio Drive
Redding, California
(916) 225-4155

Mailing Address:
P.O. Box 427
Redding, CA 96099

Tuesday–Sunday, 12:00–5:00 P.M.
Collection of eighteen quilts and ten pieced tops includes eleven quilts from northern California, one from Iowa, one New England crazy quilt. There are piecework, appliqué, small and regular size crazy quilts, one Yo-Yo, and one trapunto and appliqué. Seven quilts date nineteenth century, and ten are from the twentieth century.

Study Services: By appointment. Reading room, work tables, accession cards/files, books/journals, photocopy facilities, and microscope.

Public Services: Docent-led tours of special quilt exhibits.

Riverside Municipal Museum
3720 Orange Street
Riverside, California 92501
(714) 787-7273

Tuesday–Friday, 9:00 A.M.–5:00 P.M.; weekends, 1:00–5:00 P.M.
Approximately thirty-six quilts predominantly from the nineteenth century, and nearly all from the Midwest or East Coast. One contemporary quilt was made by local middle school students. Techniques include piecework, appliqué, and white-on-white. The collection is currently being re-cataloged.

NB: Six-Pointed Star, c. 1840, of ninety-five different cotton prints. A dozen quilts, 1828 to 1900, from the same New Hampshire and Massachusetts extended family.

Study Services: Appointments must be made with curator of history. Work tables, accession cards/files, and books/journals. Photocopy facilities and microscope in another building. Five or six of the quilts are photographed; slides available.

The Ruben Salazar Library
Sonoma State University
Rohnert Park, California 94928
(707) 664-2161

September–May: Monday–Thursday, 8:00 A.M.–10:00 P.M.; Friday, 8:00 A.M.–5:30 P.M.; Saturday, 9:00 A.M.–5:00 P.M.; Sunday, 1:00–6:00 P.M.

California Folklore Miscellany (bound unpublished papers from folklore classes, call number GR110.C122 L51), and microfilm collection.

Study Services: Walk-in basis.

Monterey County Historical Society

333 Boronda Road
Salinas, California
(408) 757-8085

Mailing Address:
P.O. Box 3576
Salinas, CA 93912

Weekdays, 9:00 A.M.–5:00 P.M.
Collection of sixteen undocumented quilts; approximately three from the nineteenth century, twelve date after 1900.
Study Services: Verbal request during working hours. Reading room, work tables, accession cards/files, and photocopy facilities.

Calaveras County Museum and Archives

30 North Main Street
San Andreas, California
(209) 754-4203

Mailing Address:
Government Center
San Andreas, CA 95249

Daily, 10:00 A.M.–4:00 P.M.
Eight handpieced quilts c. 1821 to 1940 may be seen by request.

Museum of San Diego History

Casa de Balboa
Balboa Park
San Diego, California
(619) 232-6203

Mailing Address:
P.O. Box 81825
San Diego, CA 92138

Tuesday–Sunday, 10:00 A.M.–4:00 P.M.
Sixty predominantly pieced quilts of unknown provenance, probably brought to San Diego. Thirty-nine pieced quilts, ten appliqué including some in original patterns, fourteen embroidered crazy quilts, one is a Centennial, one Yo-Yo, and four or five miniature doll quilts. Some quilts are marked with dates: one 1821, one prior to 1821; approximately forty-one are nineteenth century, sixteen post-1900; two contemporary.

NB: 1850s quilt made by Juana Machado, original appliqué showing Anglo influences on Californians. Tree of Life made for 1933 Chicago World's Fair, and an unusual early "64 patch" quilt with one-fourth inch blocks.
Study Services: Appointment with curatorial office. Reading room, work tables, accession cards/files, photocopy facilities, and books; photo prints from negatives.
Public Services: Programs offered in conjunction with exhibits.

Bankamerica Corporation Art Program

560 Davis Street, 2nd Floor
San Francisco, California
(415) 622-1265

Mailing Address:
P.O. Box 37000
San Francisco, CA 94137

Weekdays, 8:30 A.M.–5:00 P.M.
Forty quilts that date primarily from 1901 to 1940; nine date from the nineteenth century. Twenty-five were made by Amish, four by Mennonites. Twenty are from Ohio, ten from Pennsylvania, seven from Indiana, and one each from Hawaii and New York. Thirty-eight are pieced, and two are appliqué.
Study Services: By appointment with art program staff. Work tables, accession cards/files, books/journals, and photocopy facilities; slides, and prints made from negatives.
Public Services: Tours of exhibitions, classes, workshops offered occasionally.
Publications: Acquisition brochures.

Esprit de Corp.

900 Minnesota Street
San Francisco, California 94107
(415) 648-6900

Weekdays, 9:00 A.M.–5:00 P.M.
Corporate collection of approximately 250 Amish and ten Mennonite quilts: piecework, appliqué, and one white-on-white. Most date from 1901 to 1940. Quilts on continuous exhibition. One-hundred books/journals on quilts and quilting.
Public Services: Self-guided tours for groups of

six or less; on weekends, curator-led tours for groups of up to thirty-five.
Publications: Small catalog/guide with twenty-seven color plates and descriptions of 250 quilts. A large format book, due for publication in the fall of 1987, will catalog the entire collection.

The Fine Arts Museums of San Francisco
M. H. de Young Memorial Museum
Golden Gate Park
San Francisco, California 94118
(415) 221-4811

Wednesday–Sunday, 10:00 A.M.–5:00 P.M.
Approximately thirty-five American quilts include piecework, appliqué, embroidered, stuffed work, whole-cloth, and printed whole-cloth. There are descriptions and photographs of each quilt.
NB: Amish pieced Chinese Coins, 1925. Appliqué and pieced Churn Dash with signatures, c. 1875.
Study Services: Appointment in advance. Study photos in binder. Reading room, work tables, accession cards/files, thirty-five books/journals, photocopy facilities, and microscope; photo prints and slides.

Levi Strauss and Company
1155 Battery Street
San Francisco, California
(415) 544-6000

Mailing Address:
P.O. Box 7215
San Francisco, CA 94120-6901

By appointment.
Twenty-three nineteenth and twentieth century quilts on display throughout the Levi's Plaza complex: twenty pieced and three appliqué. Provenances include: Indiana, Indiana Amish, Kansas Amish, Missouri, Ohio Amish, Pennsylvania, Pennsylvania Amish, Pennsylvania Dutch, Pennsylvania Mennonite, and Rhode Island.
Public Services: Occasional group tours. Contact art curator (415) 544-6117.

American Museum of Quilts and Related Arts
766 South Second Street
San Jose, California 95112
(408) 971-0323

Tuesday–Saturday, 10:00 A.M.–4:00 P.M.
Collection of ninety-four quilts in the following techniques and patterns: piecework, appliqué, crazy quilt, Log Cabin, Yo-Yo, and stuffed white-on-white. Of those that have been identified twenty-two date nineteenth century, forty-seven post-1900, and twenty-seven are contemporary. Quilts are on continuous exhibition.
NB: White-on-white stuffed quilt; Royal Hawaiian Flag quilt.
Study Services: Make appointment with collections manager and director. Reading room, work tables, accession cards/files, 150 books and journals, and photocopy facilities; slides.
Public Services: Tours of monthly exhibits; classes on quiltmaking. Workshops are offered periodically.

San Luis Obispo County Historical Society Museum
696 Monterey Street
San Luis Obispo, California 93401
(805) 543-0638

Wednesday–Sunday, 10:00 A.M.–4:00 P.M.
Collection includes nineteen regional quilts and a scrapbook of 1930s and 1940s newspaper quilt patterns. There are eight pieced, five crazy quilts with fancy embroidery, five appliqué. Thirteen are nineteenth century, six postdate 1900. Quilts are on continuous exhibition.
NB: Crazy quilt of fabrics from First Ladies' Inaugural gowns.
Study Services: By prior appointment. Reading room, and photocopy facilities; photo prints can be made.
Public Services: Tours of special exhibitions.

San Mateo County Historical Association and Museum

1700 West Hillsdale Boulevard
San Mateo, California 94402
(415) 574-6441

Monday–Thursday, 9:30 A.M.–4:30 P.M.; Sunday, 12:30–4:30 P.M.
Collection of fourteen quilts from people who made or brought quilts to San Mateo County. The majority is twentieth century, five date nineteenth century.
Study Services: By appointment. Reading room, accession cards/files, and photocopy facilities.

Bowers Museum

2002 North Main Street
Santa Ana, California 92706
(714) 972-1900

Tuesday–Saturday, 10:00 A.M.–5:00 P.M.; Sunday, 12:00–5:00 P.M.
Collection of forty-seven quilts mainly from eastern and midwestern states and brought to California. Techniques include piecework, appliqué, and white-on-white. About twenty-seven quilts date from the late 1800s; approximately twenty are from the early 1920s. Many are Log Cabin and crazy quilts.
NB: Bicentennial quilt, the California Quilt 1976, by nineteen quiltmakers.
Study Services: For scholars; entry arranged with museum registrar by advance notice. Work tables, accession cards/files, photocopy facilities, and microscope; reproduction postcard of the California Quilt, 1976.

Santa Cruz City Museum

1305 East Cliff Drive
Santa Cruz, California 95062
(408) 429-3773

Tuesday–Saturday, 10:00 A.M.–5:00 P.M.; Sunday, 12:00–5:00 P.M.
Five handsewn quilts (pieced and appliqué) may be seen by appointment with the registrar.

The Haggin Museum

1201 North Pershing Avenue
Stockton, California 95203-1699
(209) 462-4116

Tuesday–Sunday, 1:30–5:00 P.M.
Collection of sixty-three handsewn quilts: among them are forty-seven pieced, eighteen appliqué, twelve embroidered; seven incorporate flags, ribbons, and badges; ten crazy quilts; four Memory or Album quilts. Thirteen are California quilts; others from Kansas, Maine, New York, Maryland, Missouri, and Illinois. Museum has continuous exhibit of quilts.
NB: Hardman Medallion quilt made by Mrs. Edwin Hardman of New York, N.Y., c. 1860. Flags of All Nations quilt made by Elmira Frances Baldwin (West) of Stockton, CA., in 1857, and used as a fund-raiser during the Civil War.
Study Services: For specific research; contact director or curator of history. Reading room and photocopy facilities; photo prints, slides, and films.
Public Services: Exhibitions with tours, quilt case changes quarterly.

Tehama County Museum Foundation

275 C Street at 3rd Street
Tehama, California
(916) 384-2420

Mailing Address:
P.O. Box 275
Tehama, CA. 96090

Weekends, 1:00–4:00 P.M.
Eight handsewn quilts c. 1821 to 1940 may be seen by appointment with the curator.

California Department of Parks and Recreation

Office of Interpretive Services
1280 Terminal Street
West Sacramento, California 95691
(916) 322-8545

Weekdays, 8:00 A.M.–5:00 P.M.
A collection of twenty-eight California, Pioneer, and Old West quilts, and an undetermined number of quilt patterns and instructions. Eighty-five percent are embroidered quilts, sixty percent have decorative quilting, sixty percent appliqué, twenty-five percent piecework, ten percent trapunto, and five percent white-on-white. Thirty percent of the collection dates from the Victorian era, and fifteen percent from the Gold Rush era; eighty percent dates from the nineteenth century, fifteen percent is post-1900, and five percent is contemporary. Quilts are on continuous exhibition at many of the park units.
NB: Embroidered sailor's quilt with sailor's hat band and ribbons, 1886.
Study Services: Make written request specifying interest or project. Reading room, work tables, accession cards/files, and photocopy facilities.
Public Services: Programs vary with each park unit.

Sacramento Valley Museum Association

1491 E Street
Williams, California
(916) 473-2978

Mailing Address:
Route 1, Box 240
Williams, CA 95987-0240

November–March: Friday and Saturday, 10:00 A.M.–4:00 P.M.; Sunday, 1:00–4:00 P.M. April–October: call for days and hours of operation. Approximately twenty-five quilts, predominantly from the nineteenth century, some post-1900. There are pieced and appliqué quilts in fabrics of handwoven wool, cotton, velvet and satin. Quilts are on continuous exhibition.

NB: Boone Quilt; a family collection of quilt tops.
Study Services: Scheduled by advance permission. Reading room, work tables; photo prints and slides available by request.
Public Services: Quilt exhibits using the museum's collection and private collections.

Mendocino County Museum

400 East Commercial Street
Willits, California 95490
(707) 459-2736

Wednesday–Sunday, 10:00 A.M.–4:30 P.M.
Collection of thirty-nine local quilts made in Mendocino County from the nineteenth century to the present; taped interviews and oral histories from quiltmakers, with transcriptions. Among them are twelve pieced quilts, fourteen appliqué quilts, and three embroidered quilts.
NB: Bicentennial quilt.
Study Services: Arrange with curator. Reading room, work tables, accession cards/files, photocopy facilities, and books/journals; photo prints can be made.
Publications: Metzler, Sandra J., editor. *Behind the Stitches: A Portrait of Four Mendocino County Quiltmakers* (1984).

Siskiyou County Museum

910 South Main Street
Yreka, California 96097
(916) 842-3836

Tuesday–Saturday, 9:00 A.M.–5:00 P.M.
Collection of twenty-two regional and national quilts: eleven pieced, four appliqué, four crazy quilts with appliqué, embroidered, trapunto, and three pieced and appliqué quilts. Of those that have been identified one predates 1820, ten are 1821 to 1900, and two are post-1900.
NB: Four quilts made between 1800 and 1850.
Study Services: By appointment. Reading room, work tables, accession cards/files, and photocopy facilities; photo prints, and prints made from negatives.

COLORADO

There is a profusion of Centennial quilts, pioneer quilts, and crazy quilts.

Aurora History Center
1633 Florence Street
Aurora, Colorado 80010
(303) 360-8545

Tuesday–Friday, 9:00 A.M.–4:00 P.M.; Saturday, by appointment.
Eight quilts dating 1821 to the present may be seen by appointment.

Boulder Historical Society Museum
1206 Euclid Avenue
Boulder, Colorado 80302
(303) 449-3464

Hours not provided.
The Museum houses sixty-seven regional quilts, quilt tops, dolls, toys, and costumes. A whole-cloth German or Scandinavian quilt dates prior to 1820; the latest quilts are from the 1920s and 1930s. Patchwork, appliqué whole-cloth, crazy quilt with embroidery, and a Friendship quilt are included. A few quilts are on continuous exhibition.
Study Services: Call or write in advance for access to the stored collections. Archival material is located in the Carnegie Branch Library, Boulder, Colorado.
Public Services: Traveling trunk for schools.

Pioneers' Museum
215 South Tejon Street
Colorado Springs, Colorado 80903
(303) 578-6650

Monday–Saturday, 10:00 A.M.–5:00 P.M.; Sunday, 1:00–5:00 P.M. Office: Monday–Saturday, 8:00 A.M.–5:00 P.M.
The seventy-one quilts are primarily regional, about half appliqué; four are trapunto, one white-on-white. Of those that have been iden-
tified two quilts date prior to 1820, twenty are 1821 to 1900, and ten are twentieth century. Documentation includes thirty-seven personal narratives, diaries/journals; quotes from donors.
NB: Centennial quilts.
Study Services: Prior arrangement with curator or director. Reading room, work tables, accession cards/files, and photocopy facilities; photo reproductions.
Public Services: Exhibitions, guided tours.

The Colorado Historical Society
Broadway and 13th Avenue
Denver, Colorado 80203-2167
(303) 866-4691, Material Culture Department

Tuesday–Saturday, 10:00 A.M.–4:30 P.M.; Sunday, 12:00–4:30 P.M.
Seventy-four mainly regional quilts include those at state properties: Baca and Bloom Houses, in Trinidad, Colorado; Healy House, in Leadville, Colorado. Eighteen are from Colorado; others from California, Iowa, Michigan, Missouri, New York, Wisconsin, and Wyoming; one is German-American. Sixty-one are piecework, seven appliqué, two embroidered, and one printed whole-cloth. Forty-six are dated: one prior to 1820, forty from 1821 to 1900, four from 1901 to 1940, and one post-1940. Approximately five quilts are unfinished or fragmentary.
NB: Concentration in crazy quilts, Log Cabin, and other patchwork.
Study Services: Call curator of department for appointment. Reading room, work tables, accession cards/files, library, archives, photocopy facilities, microscopes, and books/journals; photo reproductions.

The Denver Art Museum
100 West 14th Avenue Parkway
Denver, Colorado 80204
(303) 575-2196

Tuesday, Thursday, Friday, Saturday, 9:00 A.M.–5:00 P.M.; Wednesday, 9:00 A.M.–8:00 P.M.; Sunday, 12:00–5:00 P.M.
Collection of 225, ninety-percent American

quilts. Twenty-five date prior to 1821, 125 from 1821–1900, fifty 1901–1940, twenty-five 1941 to present. Of these, twenty-five have been assigned specific dates. Collection shows broad range of techniques. Four quilts are Amish. Quilts are on continuous exhibition.
Study Services: Scholars; individual basis. Reading room, work tables, accession cards/files, slides/photographs, library, photocopy facilities, and seventy-five books/journals; photo prints and slides.
Public Services: Gallery tours.
Publications: DeGraw, Imelda G. *The Denver Art Museum Quilts and Coverlets* (1974). Dunham, Lydia Roberts. *The Denver Art Museum Quilt Collection* (1963).

Jefferson County Historical Society
Hiwan Homestead Museum
4208 South Timbervale Drive
Evergreen, Colorado
(303) 674-6262

Mailing Address:
P.O. Box 703
Evergreen, CO 80439

Tuesday–Sunday, 12:00–4:00 P.M.
In a total of twelve quilts three are satin and silk Friendship (crazy) quilts, and four are pieced scrap quilts (1920s to 1930s). The collection also contains 100 blocks identified as to pattern. Quilts are on continuous exhibition.

Georgetown Society, Inc.
305 Argentine Street
Georgetown, Colorado
(303) 569-2840

Mailing Address:
P.O. Box 667
Evergreen, CO 80444

Weekdays, 9:00 A.M.–4:00 P.M.; or by appointment.
Fewer than ten quilts, in worn condition; may be seen by appointment.

Grand Lake Area Historical Society
Pitkin and Lake Avenue
Grand Lake, Colorado
(303) 627-8562

Mailing Address:
P.O. Box 656
Grand Lake, CO 80447

June, July, August: 1:00–5:00 P.M.; and by appointment.
Fourteen nineteenth century handsewn quilts on continuous display; the majority is from Colorado. Five silk and velvet crazy quilts, two wool crazy quilts, three Log Cabins, three other patchwork quilts are part of the collection.
NB: Quilts of 1890s or before.
Public Services: Tours of historic restoration, Kauffman House.

City of Greeley Museums
919 7th Street
Greeley, Colorado 80631
(303) 353-6123, extension 414

Hours vary.
Three museums are under city jurisdiction. Sixty-five regional quilts represent work of the 1830s through 1940s: crazy quilts, appliqué, patchwork, five baby quilts, two white-on-white trapunto. Quilts are on continuous exhibition.
Study Services: Research request accepted by phone, by mail or in person. Reading room, work tables, accession cards/files, documentation of use and user, photocopy facilities.
Public Services: Exhibits, lectures, workshops, and demonstrations.

Loveland Museum and Gallery
503 Lincoln Avenue
Loveland, Colorado 80537
(303) 667-6070

Tuesday–Saturday, 9:00 A.M.–5:00 P.M.
Collection of twenty quilts contains one each from Ohio (brought to Colorado, 1889); St. Louis, Missouri; Indiana; and Kelim, Colorado. One made prior to 1820; the others evenly di-

vided between the nineteenth and twentieth centuries. Six are appliqué, six piecework, five embroidered, and three crazy quilts.
Study Services: Permission from director; accompanied by staff member. Accession cards/files.
Public Services: Occasional exhibits, quilting demonstrations.

Baca and Bloom Houses
Trinidad, Colorado
(303) 866-4697 or 866-4691

Mailing Address:
Colorado Historical Society
Broadway and 13th Avenue
Denver, Colorado 80203-2167

Weekdays, 8:00 A.M.–5:00 P.M.
Ten nineteenth century quilts from Colorado: six are piecework, four with decorative quilting, two also have bobbin lace edgings. Patterns include 1870s cotton Irish Chain, Bear Paw, Windmill, Flower Garden; 1880 and 1890 Victorian crazy quilts.
Study Services: Contact institution for appointment and access. Research facilities in Denver at Colorado Historical Society Headquarters.
Public Services: Crazy quilt presentations.

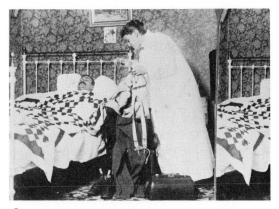
Stereopticon card, c. 1900. Courtesy of the Oral Traditions Project of Pennsylvania's Union County Historical Society.

CONNECTICUT

Local historical societies exhibit quilts significant in regional history.

Danbury Scott-Fanton Museum and Historical Society, Inc.
43 Main Street
Danbury, Connecticut 06810
(203) 743-5200

Office: Tuesday–Friday, 10:00 A.M.–5:00 P.M.; weekends, 2:00 - 5:00 P.M. Tours, Wednesday–Sunday, 2:00–5:00 P.M.
The collection of forty to fifty mostly hand-sewn quilts, half of which are regional, includes many examples of most quilting techniques. One or two quilts are on continuous exhibition.
NB: Quilts of local historical significance.
Study Services: Occasional tours, classes and workshops.

Darien Historical Society
45 Old King's Highway North
Darien, Connecticut 06820
(203) 655-9233

Tuesday–Friday, 9:00 A.M.–1:00 P.M.
Forty-two regional quilts include appliqué, trapunto, embroidered, and piecework. The majority is from the twentieth century.
NB: Bicentennial, historic blocks quilt, Connecticut Quilt.
Study Services: For scholars, by appointment. Very limited work space, accession cards/files, history of construction of 1976 Bicentennial quilt, photos and files of collection, photocopy facilities, approximately twenty-three volumes of journals on quilts/quiltmaking. Six years of *Quilters Newsletter*; also *Quilt World*. Photo prints and slides available.

Fairfield Historical Society

636 Old Post Road
Fairfield, Connecticut 06430
(203) 259-1598

Weekdays, 9:30 A.M.–4:30 P.M.; Sunday, 1:00–5:00 P.M.
Approximately sixty Fairfield, Connecticut area patchwork and whole-cloth, Log Cabin, and crazy quilts. Ten date prior to 1820, forty date from 1821 to 1900, and ten are from the twentieth century. Documentation includes four quilt patterns/instructions, ten personal narratives by quiltmakers, diaries/journals. Cataloging is in progress.
NB: White-on-white quilted fragments of bed-hangings, c. 1750, by Eunice Dehnie Burr of Fairfield.
Study Services: Apply to curator by letter or by telephone. Reading room, work tables, accession cards/files, in-house photographic services, photocopy facilities, microscope, and books/journals; photo prints and slides.
Public Services: Quiltmaking workshops.

Historical Society of Glastonbury

1944 Main Street
Glastonbury, Connecticut
(203) 633-6890

Mailing Address:
P.O. Box 46
Glastonbury, CT 06033

Monday, 10:00 A.M.–2:00 P.M.; Thursday, 1:00–5:00 P.M.; Sunday, 2:00–4:00 P.M.
There are twenty-one quilts. About five are from Connecticut. Seventeen are pieced, two silk Log Cabins, two hexagon (Grandmother's Flower Garden), three crazy quilts (one a table cover), one Alphabet, one Album, and one combination pieced/appliqué, one stuffed and corded. Signed quilts by Polly Asenath, Mrs. George Furman, Pearl Davis Burdick, Berthe Davis, Ann Reese. Three quilts date prior to 1820, fourteen from 1821 to 1900; and four 1901 to 1940.
NB: Tree Everlasting, c. 1820, pink roller printed fabric for center of tree.
Study Services: Call director for appointment.

Reading room, work tables, and accession cards/files.
Public Services: Workshops.

Goshen Historical Society

Old Middle Road
Goshen, Connecticut
(203) 491-2665

Mailing Address:
Rural Delivery #1
Goshen, CT 06756

Winter: Tuesday, 9:30 A.M.–12:00 P.M.; summer: Saturday, 2:00–4:00 P.M.; and by appointment.
Ten handsewn quilts include eight piecework, one stuffed, and one embroidered. Three are dated: one prior to 1820, and two from 1821 to 1900.
Study Services: By appointment. Accession cards/files. If necessary, quilts could be photographed.
Public Services: Programming.

The Antiquarian and Landmarks Society, Inc.

394 Main Street
Hartford, Connecticut 06103
(203) 247-8996

Tuesday, Thursday, and Sunday, 12:00–4:00 P.M.
The Society administers seven historic homes: The Butler-McCook Homestead, 396 Main Street, Hartford, CT (Tuesday, Thursday, and Sunday, 12:00–4:00 P.M.); The Eshem-Terry House, 211 High Street, Hartford, CT (Sunday, 12:00–4:00 P.M. July and August, Saturdays too); Amasa Day House, Moodus, CT (Tuesday and Sunday, 1:00–5:00 P.M.); The Hathaway House, Sutfield, CT (Wednesday, and Sunday 1:00–4:00 P.M.); The Joshua Hempstead, Nathanial Hempstead House, New London, CT (Tuesday and Sunday, 1:00–5:00 P.M.); The Nathan Hale Homestead, Coventry, CT (daily, 1:00–5:00 P.M.); The Buttolph-Williams House, Wethersfield, CT (September–October; Saturday and Sunday, 12:00–4:00 P.M.; closed Mon-

days). Handsewn quilts and coverlets are on continuous exhibition in the homes.

NB: Two blue resist quilts; calamanco; one whole-cloth, c. 1860; coverlet woven by Joanna Hale, sister of Nathan Hale.

Public Services: Nathan Hale Homestead offers colonial craft day demonstrations.

The Connecticut Historical Society
1 Elizabeth Street
Hartford, Connecticut 06105
(203) 236-5621

Monday–Saturday, 9:00 A.M.–5:00 P.M.; Sunday, 1:00–5:00 P.M.

Collection of approximately 120 quilts made in Connecticut from the eighteenth to twentieth centuries. Twenty date prior to 1820, eighty from 1821 to 1900, twenty from 1901 to 1940. Seventy-five are pieced, seventeen are printed whole cloth, twelve white-on-white, four (pieced) Friendship, three calamanco, one pieced quilt of copperplate printed fabric, one embroidered white-on-white quilt.

Study Services: By prior appointment with museum staff. Reading room, work tables, accession cards/files, photocopy facilites; photo prints, slides, transparencies can be ordered.

The Stowe-Day Foundation
77 Forest Street
Hartford, Connecticut 06105
(203) 522-9259

Daily, 8:30 A.M.–4:30 P.M.

Five patchwork quilts (1821 to 1900) may be seen by appointment.

Wadsworth Atheneum
600 Main Street
Hartford, Connecticut 06103
(203) 278-2670

Tuesday–Sunday, 11:00 A.M.–5:00 P.M.; first floor galleries, Tuesday–Friday, 4:00–7:00 P.M.

Collection of 220 American and French quilts includes about five dated prior to 1820, most

from 1821 to 1900. The collection cataloging is in progress.

NB: Canadian or American, 1785.

Study Services: For scholars, letter written at least one month in advance of visit. Reading room, work tables, accession cards/files, photocopy facilities, microscope, several research papers, and fifty books/journals; photo prints.

Litchfield Historical Society
Corner of South and East Streets
Litchfield, Connecticut
(203) 567-5862

Mailing Address:
P.O. Box 385
Litchfield, CT 06759-0385

Tuesday–Saturday, 10:00 A.M.–12:00 P.M. and 1:00–4:00 P.M. summer; winter by appointment.

Quilts number 205; approximately 150 from New England. One hundred date prior to 1820, 100 from 1821 to 1900, and five from 1901 to 1940. Techniques include embroidery, appliqué, trapunto, decorative quilting, white-on-white, and printed whole-cloth. Documentation: quilt patterns and instructions, ten personal narratives by quiltmakers, diaries/journals.

NB: Sarah Pierce School quilts.

Study Services: Call or write for appointment. Reading room, work tables, accession cards/files, photocopy facilities, and thirty-five books/journals; photo prints.

Middlesex County Historical Society
151 Main Street
Middletown, Connecticut 06457
(203) 346-0746

Monday and Tuesday, 1:00–4:00 P.M.; Sunday, 1:00–5:00 P.M.

Twenty-four handsewn quilts predominantly from Connecticut. The majority is from Middlesex County; two from Boston, Massachusetts; one whole-cloth from Rhode Island or Ohio. Quilts are largely from the nineteenth century. Techniques and patterns include one printed whole-cloth, c. 1820; two appliqué;

one appliqué and pieced; four embroidered crazy quilts, two with decorative quilting; fourteen pieced; three Sunburst; and two Album quilts.
Study Services: Contact director for appointment. Reading room, work tables, accession cards/files, and books/journals.
Public Services: Special tours and workshops.

New Canaan Historical Society
13 Oenoke Ridge
New Canaan, Connecticut 06840
(203) 966-1776

Tuesday–Saturday, 9:30 A.M.–12:30 P.M., and 2:00–4:30 P.M. Hours and days of operation vary for historic sites under Society's jurisdiction.
Approximately twenty handsewn quilts are stored and seldom viewed. They are cataloged as to donor, date, and type.
NB: Resist print from early nineteenth century.

New Haven Colony Historical Society
114 Whitney Avenue
New Haven, Connecticut 06510
(203) 562-4183

Tuesday–Friday, 10:00 A.M.–5:00 P.M.; weekends, 2:00–5:00 P.M.
In the collection of twenty quilts, ten were made or owned in the New Haven, Connecticut area; five others are from Connecticut; one from Massachusetts; four others from New England, probably Connecticut. Among them are one embroidered, four pieced, two appliqué, one corded, and two whole-cloth. Of those that have been dated one is prior to 1820, nine from 1821 to 1900.
NB: Quilt by Lydia Lord, Preston, Connecticut; and embroidered eighteenth century skirt fragment.
Study Services: Make appointment with museum curator. Reading room, work tables, accession cards/files, photocopy facilities, and books/journals; photo prints, and negatives.

Lyman Allyn Museum
625 Williams Street
New London, Connecticut 06320
(203) 443-2545

By appointment.
Fourteen predominantly patchwork quilts are from the nineteenth century.
NB: Signed quilts include those by Susanna Bitgood of Voluntown, Connecticut; Experience Avery Greer, snow ball pattern, c. 1830; Frances Newbury of Gales Ferry (who married Captain Jesse Comstock of Uncasville), c. 1850 with stenciled roses in each square on the quilt; and two Album quilts with approximately thirty-six signatures.

New London County Historical Society
11 Blinman Street
New London, Connecticut 06320
(203) 443-1209

Tuesday–Saturday, 1:00–4:00 P.M.
There are nineteen quilts. The majority is regional. Two children's quilts in cradles are continuously shown.
Study Services: Call for appointment. Reading room, work tables, accession cards/files, and photocopy facilities.

The Slater Memorial Museum
Norwich Art School, The Norwich Free Academy
108 Crescent Street
Norwich, Connecticut 06360
(203) 887-2505

Weekdays, 9:00 A.M.–4:00 P.M.; weekends, 1:00–4:00 P.M.; closed holidays.
Collection of twelve quilts, six dating from 1821 to 1900, and two from the twentieth century include Star of Texas or Star of Bethlehem patchwork c. 1860; silk Building Blocks or Baby Blocks, 1861; appliqué; 1851 crazy quilt with three-inch lace border; Log Cabin Courthouse Steps variation; Basket appliqué 1830 to 1850; nineteenth century cylinder print cotton, Chinoiserie design. Manuscript information is available for Bicentennial quilt.
NB: 1776 embroidered spread, crewel on

handwoven linen, floral design, style of Queen Anne.
Study Services: For scholars by advance appointment. Staff assistance.

Plainville Historic Center
29 Pierce Street
Plainville, Connecticut
(203) 747-6577

Mailing Address:
P.O. Box 464
Plainville, CT 06062

April–December: Wednesday and Saturday, 12:00–3:30 P.M.
Twenty-two quilts mainly from Connecticut, many made from copperplate printed fabric. The majority dates from 1821 to 1900 and includes crazy quilt with historic commemorative ribbons, "Harrison 1888"; early Ohio Star with signatures; quilt with 1,000 embroidered names from camp meeting for Methodist Church, 1936; crib size eight pointed star; copperplate printed whole-cloth, chenille, stuffed, 1850; handwoven black and white coverlet, linen and wool. Fourteen to eighteen are piecework. Quilts are on continuous exhibition.
NB: White-on-white coverlet by Dolly Botsford, born 1786.
Study Services: By appointment. Accession cards/files, photo reproductions, and books/journals.
Public Services: Major exhibit 1983.

Stamford Historical Society
1508 High Ridge Road
Stamford, Connecticut 06903
(203) 329-1183

Weekdays, 9:00 A.M.–5:00 P.M.; Saturday, 12:00–4:00 P.M.
Fifty mostly patchwork New England quilts: twenty-one are piecework, six appliqué, eight white-on-white, four printed whole-cloth, four woven, six embroidered, one trapunto. Ten are dated prior to 1820, thirty-one from 1821 to 1900, one from 1901 to 1940, and eight 1941 to present.

NB: Cotton trapunto coverlet, c. 1816; appliqué "story" quilt, 1854; appliqué summer bedcover, c. 1810.
Study Services: A written request preferred, appointments necessary. Reading room, work tables, accession cards/files, photocopy facilities, and books/journals; photo prints can be made.

Stratford Historical Society
367 Academy Hill
Stratford, Connecticut
(203) 378-0630

Mailing Address:
P.O. Box 382
Stratford, CT 06497

Tuesday–Thursday, 9:00 A.M. to 3:00 P.M.
Collection of thirty-seven pieced and appliqué regional quilts from local donors. Four date prior to 1821, thirty-two from 1821 to 1900, and one from 1901 to 1940.
Study Services: Make appointment thirty days in advance. No research facilities. Books/journals, slides are available.

Torrington Historical Society
192 Main Street
Torrington, Connecticut 06790
(203) 482-8260

Weekdays, 9:00 A.M.–4:00 P.M.; Saturday, 10:00 A.M.–3:00 P.M.
Collection of twenty-seven handsewn regional quilts from northwest Connecticut. Twenty-five date 1821 to 1900, two date 1901 to 1940. Twenty-six are piecework: three with appliqué, one with embroidery.
NB: Barn Raising; Basket of Tulips.
Study Services: By appointment. Reading room, work tables, accession cards/files, photocopy facilities, and books/journals.
Public Services: Periodic exhibits.

Mattatuck Museum

144 West Main Street
Waterbury, Connecticut 06702
(203) 753-0381

Tuesday–Saturday, 12:00–5:00 P.M.; Sunday, 2:00–5:00 P.M.

Sixteen quilts donated by Connecticut residents that date from 1821 to 1900 and a crazy quilt, c. 1885–1905; pieced silk Grand Army quilt, c. 1885; Cross and Crown or Goose Tracks; Double Irish Chain, and Eight-pointed Star c. 1870; Wild Rose appliqué.
NB: Grand Army quilt, c. 1885.
Study Services: Arrange for appointment. Reading room, work tables, accession cards/files, and photocopy facilities; photo prints, and slides.
Public Services: Art and history tours. Connecticut artists and local industry exhibits.

Noah Webster Foundation

227 South Main Street
West Hartford, Connecticut 06107
(203) 521-5362

Monday–Thursday, 10:00 A.M.–4:00 P.M.; Sunday, 1:00–4:00 P.M.

Collection of twelve to fifteen handsewn New England quilts, approximately twelve from the nineteenth century; twelve piecework, two appliqué. The quilt collection is in need of research, conservation, and documentation.
Study Services: Make appointment. Work tables, accession cards/files, and photocopy facilities.

Wethersfield Historical Society

150 Main Street
Wethersfield, Connecticut 06109
(203) 529-7656

Exhibits: weekdays, 1:00–4:00 P.M.; Saturday, 12:00–5:00 P.M. Office: weekdays, 9:00 A.M.–4:00 P.M.

Twenty regional quilts: fifteen piecework, three appliqué, one floral print with quilting, one trapunto. Of those that have been dated one is prior to 1820; ten 1821 to 1900.

NB: One signed and dated quilt appliquéd on both sides with two distinct designs.
Study Services: By appointment. Reading room, work tables, accession cards/files, and photocopy facilities; photographs, slides; photo prints can be made.

Wilton Heritage Museum

Wilton Historical Society
249 Danbury Road
Wilton, Connecticut 06897
(203) 762-7257

Tuesday–Thursday, 10:00 A.M.–4:00 P.M.; Sundays for special exhibitions and programs.

Thirty New England and New York State quilts primarily from the latter half of the nineteenth century includes a concentration of crazy quilts and traditional patterns such as Album, Flying Geese, Star of Bethlehem. Two or three date from the early nineteenth century, one using eighteenth century cotton. One or two quilts are on continuous exhibition.
Study Services: For scholars, written requests. Reading room, work tables, accession cards/files, modest reference library.
Public Services: Annual quilt programs, exhibitions, appraisals, and lectures.

"Jerry Bixler—Quilting Machine," 1914–15. From the collection of the Kentucky Historical Society.

DELAWARE

Home to one of the nation's premier decorative arts museums, the state's Dutch heritage is also reflected in several documented quilts in other institutions.

Delaware State Museum/Zwaanendael Museum

Bureau of Museums-Division of Historical and Cultural Affairs
102 South State Street
Dover, Delaware
(302) 736-5316

Mailing Address:
P.O. Box 1401
Dover, DE 19901

Tuesday–Saturday, 10:00 A.M.–4:30 P.M.; Sunday, 1:00–4:30 P.M.
The Museum owns thirty-eight Delaware/Amish quilts. One or two date prior to 1820, majority dates from 1821 to 1900; one is a Bicentennial quilt. Approximately thirty-eight narratives on the quilts. Two are white-on-white, thirteen appliqué, fourteen patchwork, seven crazy quilts, one embroidered, one a combination of techniques.
NB: All are documented.
Study Services: Contact curator of collections at above address. Reading room, work tables, accession cards/files, photocopy facilities, and books/journals; photo prints, prints made from negatives.

Folklore and Ethnic Art Center

University of Delaware
164 South College Avenue
Newark, Delaware 19716
(302) 451-2870

Hours not provided.
Approximately 150 pages of descriptive information on quilts acquired during "Delaware Quilt Registry" Day, fall 1984. Most of the quilts were not made in Delaware. Documentation includes two taped interviews and oral histories, and two research papers.
Study Services: For scholars, permission of the F.E.A.C. director and board of directors, Delaware Folklife Project, Inc. Work tables, photo reproductions, and slides; availability determined on ad hoc basis.

The Hagley Museum

Off 141, near the Tyler-McConnell Bridge
North of Wilmington, Delaware
(302) 658-2401

Mailing Address:
P.O. Box 3630
Wilmington, DE 19807

Offices: weekdays, 8:30 A.M.–4:30 P.M. Public hours not provided.
Collection of twenty-two handsewn quilts including one from Lebanon, Pennsylvania; one from Maryland; and twenty from the East Coast. Approximately ten are appliqué, twelve piecework. One dates prior to 1820, and twenty-one are from 1821 to 1900. Quilts were collected by Louise du Pont Crowninshield.
NB: 1842 signed Friendship quilt of Maryland origin.
Study Services: For scholars, write to the curator of collections. Reading room, work tables, accession cards/files, photocopy facilities, and microscope; photo prints, color slides, and prints made from negatives.
Public Services: Annual textile craft fair where quilters exhibit and sell.

The Henry Francis du Pont Winterthur Museum

Located on Route 52, Kennett Pike
Winterthur, Delaware 19735
(302) 656-8591

Tuesday–Saturday, 10:00 A.M.–4:00 P.M.; Sunday, Presidents' Day, Memorial Day, July 4, and Labor Day, 12:00–4:00 P.M. Closed other Mondays, Thanksgiving, December 24 and 25, and January 1.

Approximately 100 handsewn quilts nearly all collected from Mid-Atlantic and eastern states, include an estimated ten Marseilles quilts; twenty-one pieced; five with embroidery; twenty-five appliqué; thirty crazy quilts. Approximately forty were made prior to 1820, and sixty from 1821 to 1900. Ten are on continuous display in period rooms; also, sixty-one in Bedspread Storage may be seen by those taking a Special Subject-Needlework tour.

NB: American quilts, pre-1855. Hewson center, also whole Hewson top; Baltimore Quilt; three early Quaker silk quilts; 1793 appliqué; Palampores.

Study Services: Make an appointment with the textile curator. Library and rare books section open to the public weekdays, 8:30 A.M. to 4:30 P.M. Reading room, work tables, accession cards/files, photocopy facilities; photo prints, slides, transparencies, prints made from negatives.

Public Services: Tours by reservation through April 2, and June 6 through November 10. By appointment with textile curator, special subject tours of needlework given for groups of four by qualified guides. If all four guests agree tour can concentrate on quilts alone. Free clinic in conservation (by appointment) third Wednesday and fourth Thursday of each month except July and August.

Publications: Swan, Susan Burrows. *A Winterthur Guide to Needlework* (1976). Swan, Susan Burrows. *Plain and Fancy: American Women and Their Needlework, 1700–1850* (1977).

The Joseph Downs Manuscript and Microfilm Collection

The Henry Francis du Pont Winterthur
Museum Library
Winterthur, Delaware 19735
(302) 656-8591, extension 228

Weekdays, 8:30 A.M.–4:30 P.M.
Collection of unpublished documentation on quilts and/or quilting: personal narratives by quiltmakers; diaries and journals; one photocopy, and two original. Research papers: small undetermined number. Latimer papers include such items as an account of purchase of Marseilles quilt from Townsend Sharpless, Philadelphia, March, 1822; trade sheet, Smith Mfg. Co., New York, N.Y., May, 1885, listing variety of merchandise (including quilt) with prices; inventory of estate auction, Henry Wismer, Plumstead Township, Bucks County, PA., 1828, 1829, numerous listings of goods, including bed quilt. Account books, inventories, diaries, letters, invoices pertaining to quilts, quilting parties.

NB: A search of index would reveal a myriad of quilts among estate inventories.

Study Services: Open without appointment. Reading room, work tables, accession cards/files, termatrex retrieval system, extensive name card file, and photocopy facilities.

Transylvania, Louisiana. June 1940. A U. S. Department of Agriculture, Farm Security Administration Project. Grandmother quilting a Double Wedding Ring quilt. Photo by Marion Post Wolcott, negative number LC-USF34-54052-D. Courtesy of the Farm Security Administration Collection, Prints and Photographs Division, Library of Congress.

DISTRICT OF COLUMBIA

The nation's capital provides one of the highest concentrations of quilting resource material available in the country, along with inspiring examples of the quilter's art.

Daughters of the American Revolution Museum

1776 D Street, N.W.
Washington, D.C. 20006
(202) 879-3241

Weekdays, 8:30 A.M.–4:00 P.M.; and usually Sunday, 1:00–5:00 P.M. Period room tours: weekdays, 10:00 A.M.–3:00 P.M., Sunday, 1:00–5:00 P.M.

The Museum holds approximately 195 American quilts. The majority is from the eastern states. Two Quaker quilts. Strong representation of the Chesapeake Bay region. Fairly even balance of appliqué and piecework. A number have stuffed work. Printed and dyed wholecloth quilts. Research papers and early photographs; well-documented quiltmaker histories. *NB:* American quilts 1770–1890.
Study Services: By appointment. Reading room, work tables, accession cards/files, white gloves are distributed; extensive genealogical library on the premises, photocopy facilities, approximately forty volumes of books/journals, photo prints, slides; prints made from negatives.
Public Services: Frequent tours of quilt storage, classes in conjunction with Smithsonian Institution, lectures in connection with exhibitions, frequent exhibitions.
Publications: Garret, Elisabeth Donoghy. *The Arts of Independence* (1985). Allen, Gloria Seaman. *Old Line Traditions: Maryland Women and Their Quilts* (1985).

Index of American Design

National Gallery of Art
6th and Constitution Avenue, N.W.
Washington, D.C. 20008
(202) 842-6604

Weekdays, 10:00 A.M.–5:00 P.M.
Several hundred watercolor renderings of handsewn quilts, photographs and information sheets on the quilts. A general survey of quilts from all parts of the United States.
Study Services: Call for appointment. Reading room, accession cards/files, color microfiche of collection, books/journals available at the National Gallery of Art Library; photo prints, slides, transparencies may be rented.
Public Services: Tour of the index available.
Publications: Allyn, Nancy E. *The Index of American Design* (1984). *Index of American Design* (1950).

Library of Congress

10 First Street, S.E.
Washington, D.C. 20540
(202) 287-5523/5522 General Information
(202) 287-6400, Recorded Information

General Reading Rooms. Thomas Jefferson Building: Main Reading Room LJ100 (will be closed in December 1987 for at least one year); John Adams Building: Social Science Reading Room LA 5010: weekdays, 8:30 A.M.–9:30 P.M.; Saturday, 8:30 A.M.–5:00 P.M.; Sunday, 1:00–5:00 P.M. Special Reading Rooms. Thomas Jefferson Building: Archive of Folk Culture, Room LJ G152: weekdays, 8:30 A.M.–5:00 P.M. except federal holidays. James Madison Building: Motion Picture and Television Reading Room, Room LM 336 and Recorded Sound Reference Room LM 113: weekdays, 8:30 A.M.–5:00 P.M. except federal holidays; Prints and Photographs, Room LM 339: weekdays, 8:30 A.M.–5:00 P.M. except federal holidays.
Publications: A free general brochure is available upon request. Melville, Annette, compiler. *Special Collections in the Library of Congress: A Selective Guide* (1980). The nation's library has a vast assortment of quilt-related documentation. Approximately five hundred

books on quilts and quiltmaking and back issues of serials are available from the stacks by request at the Main or Social Science Reading Rooms. The Serials and Government Publications Division reading room, James Madison Building LM 133, has access to most recent quilt and quiltmaking serials, and articles.

THE AMERICAN FOLKLIFE CENTER
Thomas Jefferson Building, Room LJ G108
(202) 287-6590

Created in 1976 by an act of Congress, the Center assists in the development of field studies, general consultancies, exhibitions, conferences, workshops, and technical support services in nearly every state. Since 1978 the Library's Archive of Folk Culture (founded 1928) has been a part of the Center.
Public Services: Technical support through consultant visits, equipment loan program, research and reference assistance on folk cultural subjects through the resources and activities of the Archive of Folk Culture. Slides and photo prints may be duplicated from file negatives.
Publications: Descriptive brochure; postcards, notecards. *Folklife Center News,* a quarterly newsletter. Bartis, Peter T. *Folklife and Fieldwork* (1979). Eiler, Lyntha Scott, Terry Eiler, and Carl Fleischhauer. *Blue Ridge Harvest: A Region's Folklife in Photographs* (1981). Loomis, Ormond. *Cultural Conservation: The Protection of Cultural Heritage in the United States* (1983). Jabbour, Alan and James Hardin. *Folklife Annual* (1985; 1986). Bartis, Peter T. and Barbara C. Fertig. *Folklife Sourcebook* (1986).

THE ARCHIVE OF FOLK CULTURE
Thomas Jefferson Building, Room LJ G152
(202) 287-5510

Significant collections of folklore, folklife, oral history, and folk music. Quilt-related holdings include: fieldnotes, transcribed oral histories, sound recordings, slides, photographs, vertical files, and essays from six field projects conducted by the American Folklife Center in Chicago, South-Central Georgia, Blue Ridge Parkway (Virginia), Rhode Island, Montana, and the Pinelands (New Jersey). One example, the Blue Ridge Parkway Folklife Project, yielded sixty to seventy taped interviews with quiltmakers (fifty-five hours of listening time) and 1,600 quilt-related photographs/slides. Results of quilt collections surveys housed is in Archive.
Study Services: Advance arrangements are needed for special listening and duplication orders. Reading room, listening facilities, accession cards/files, computer search, microform readers, books/journals, photocopy facilities; slides and photo prints may be duplicated from file negatives.
Publications: Descriptive brochure. *A Guide to the Collections of Recorded Folk Music and Folklore in the Library of Congress* (1986); *An Inventory of the Bibliographies and Other Reference and Finding Aids Prepared by the Archive of Folk Culture* (1984); *Folk Recordings Selected from the Archive of Folk Culture* (1986) (LP catalog).

MOTION PICTURE, BROADCASTING, AND RECORDED SOUND DIVISION
James Madison Building, Room LM 336
(202) 287-1000
Recorded Sound Reference Center, James Madison Building, Room LM 113
(202) 287-7833

Largest collection of sound recordings, motion picture, television films, and videotapes in the United States. Many quilt and quiltmaking films and television programs are available. Card catalog lists holdings by titles.
Study Services: Viewing facilities provided for those conducting research leading toward a publicly available work such as a dissertation, publication, or film/television production. Reading room, accession cards/files, motion picture publicity stills, photocopy facilities.
Publications: Guidelines for Viewing Films and Videotapes and other brochures describing the division's collections and services are available upon request.

PRINTS AND PHOTOGRAPHS DIVISION
James Madison Building, Room LM 339
(202) 287-5836

The division has over twelve million items. Roughly nine million consist of photo prints and negatives of documentary interest. Photographs are cataloged as groups called "lots." Sixteen of these lots are devoted to quilting as a homecraft. Most of these photographs form part of the Farm Security Administration/Office of War Information collection covering the years 1935–1943.

Study Services: Reading room, indexes, accession cards/files, laser video disk and video disk computer index, microfilm readers, photocopy facilities; photo prints and slides.

Publications: Brochures describing the division's collections and services are available upon request.

National Museum of American History
Division of Textiles
Smithsonian Institution
Constitution Avenue between 12th and 14th Streets, N.W.
Washington, D.C. 20560
(202) 357-1889

Office: weekdays, 8:45 A.M.–5:15 P.M. Museum: daily, 10:00 A.M.–5:00 P.M.
There are approximately 275 quilts: among them seven Amish, two Quaker, five Afro-American. Provenances include Connecticut, District of Columbia, Georgia, Illinois, Indiana, Iowa, Kansas, Kentucky, Louisiana, Maryland, Maine, Massachusetts, Michigan, Mississippi, Missouri, New Hampshire, New Jersey, New York, North Carolina, Ohio, Pennsylvania, South Carolina, Tennessee, Vermont, Virginia, West Virginia, and Wisconsin. Techniques include piecework, appliqué, embroidered, stuffed or corded, decorative quilting, and printed whole-cloth. Approximately twenty date prior to 1820; 245 from 1821 to 1900; eight from 1901 to 1940; two are contemporary.

NB: American quilt, 1760. Harriet Powers Bible quilt.

Study Services: Call Division of Textiles for reservation or appointment. Reading room, photo and slide files, photocopy facilities, 120 volumes of books and journals; photo prints, slides, photo prints made from negatives in collection.

Public Services: Regularly scheduled slide lectures, and viewing of quilts in storage room.

National Trust for Historic Preservation
1785 Massachusetts Avenue, N.W.
Washington, D.C. 20036
(202) 673-4148

Weekdays, 9:00 A.M.–5:00 P.M.
The Trust headquarters oversees historic properties and their contents. The collection of twenty nineteenth century regional quilts primarily from the East Coast, chiefly, Baltimore, Maryland and Virginia, includes a Baltimore Album Quilt, a New Jersey Friendship quilt, and five quilts from Virginia. Among those identified two are appliqué, five pieced, and two are combinations of techniques.

NB: Woodlawn Plantation, a trust property in Mount Vernon, Virginia exhibits Baltimore Album, and New Jersey Friendship quilts.

Study Services: Contact the property director. Accession cards/files; photo prints.

Smithsonian Folklife Program Archives
Office of Folklife Programs
Smithsonian Institution
955 L'Enfant Plaza, Suite 2600
Washington, D.C. 20560
(202) 287-3424

Weekdays, 9:00 A.M.–5:00 P.M.
The Archive holds photographs, field notes, and audio recordings of quiltmakers from Tennessee, Oklahoma, Michigan and other regional communities in the southwest and south.

Study Services: By appointment. Listening and viewing rooms, photocopy facilities; prints made from negatives upon request.

Public Services: Annual Festival of American Folklife held the last week of June, first week of July, on the National Mall.

The Textile Museum Library
2320 S Street, N.W.
Washington, D.C. 20008
(202) 667-0441

Tuesday–Saturday, 10:00 A.M.–5:00 P.M.; Sunday, 1:00–5:00 P.M.
Although the Museum does not collect American or European textiles, the Library does own seventy-five volumes of published books/serials on all aspects of American quilts and quilt history.
Study Services: Library reading room, and photocopy facilities.

Fannie Lee Teals with her red, white, and blue Bicentennial quilt. American Folklife Center, South-Central Georgia Project, Tifton, Georgia, 1977. Photo by Beverly J. Robinson, negative number 6-17617, 29-A. Courtesy of the Archive of Folk Culture, Library of Congress.

FLORIDA

A tropical climate does not hinder an avid interest in quilts—Afro-American strip quilts to regional pieced quilts in traditional patterns.

Pioneer Florida Museum
Pioneer Museum Road
Dade City, Florida
(904) 567-0262

Mailing Address:
P.O. Box 335
Dade City, FL 34297-0335

Tuesday and Saturday, 1:00–5:00 P.M.
Approximately thirty-five quilts are on continuous display.
Study Services: Accession cards/files.

Jacksonville Museum of Arts and Sciences
1025 Gulf Life Drive
Jacksonville, Florida 32207
(904) 396-7062

Tuesday–Sunday, 9:00 A.M.–5:00 P.M.
Collection of twenty handsewn quilts including eleven that can be dated: six from 1821 to 1900, and five from 1901 to 1940. Others are: a c. 1860 appliqué from Pennsylvania; a c. 1860 Grandmother's Flower Garden from Indiana; three c. 1920–1930 pieced quilts from South Carolina. Five are crazy quilts, twelve pieced, two appliqué, and one embroidered Calendar quilt.
Study Services: Contact the curator or registrar. Accession cards/files, slides, photocopy facilities; slides and prints made from negatives.
Public Services: Classes can be arranged.

Historical Association of Southern Florida

101 West Flagler Street
Miami, Florida 33130
(305) 375-1492

Monday–Saturday, 10:00 A.M.–5:00 P.M.; Thursday, 10:00 A.M.– 9:00 P.M.; Sunday, 12:00–5:00 P.M.

Twelve local quilts (eleven pieced and one Yo-Yo) donated by Stella Tuttle Chapman. Three are dated: one from 1821 to 1900 and two from 1901 to 1940.

Study Services: Make formal request for curator to consider. Reading room, work tables, accession cards/files, photocopy facilities, books/journals; photo prints made from negatives.

Pensacola Historical Museum

405 South Adams Street
Pensacola, Florida 32501
(904) 433-1559

Monday–Saturday, 9:00 A.M.–4:30 P.M.
Eleven quilts from southern Florida donated by local citizens. Five are dated: three from 1821 to 1900 and two from 1901 to 1940.

Study Services: Letter to curator requesting appointment, giving sufficient lead time. Reading room, work tables, accession cards/files, photocopy facilities, and books/journals.

Lightner Museum

Museum–City Hall Complex
King Street
St. Augustine, Florida
(904) 824-2874

Mailing Address:
P.O. Box 334
St. Augustine, FL 32084

Daily, 8:30 A.M.–5:00 P.M.
Collection of roughly twenty quilts, six dated: three from the 1880s, three contemporary. Three Mosaic, six Log Cabin, four patchwork with embroidery, three twentieth century appliqué, one each: Northumberland Star, Tulip, Hill Top with variation, Lobster, and Texas Star.

NB: Patchwork quilt reputed to be "the Lincoln Quilt."

Study Services: Contact director. Reading room; accession cards/files, majority with partial photo views for identification on catalog cards; photocopy facilities; books/journals; one postcard; photo prints; and prints made from negatives.

Museum of Florida History

R. A. Gray Building
500 South Bronough
Tallahassee, Florida 32399-0250
(904) 488-1484

Weekdays, 9:30 A.M.–4:30 P.M.; Saturday, 10:30 A.M.–4:30 P.M.; Sunday, 12:00–4:30 P.M.; closed Christmas day.

A growing collection of twenty-five regional quilts has seventeen that date from 1821 to 1900; five from 1901 to 1940; three contemporary. The quilts are predominantly hand-sewn and pieced in a wide range of techniques. There are appliqué and embroidered ones as well. When it is completed, the Florida Quilt Heritage Project findings will be housed in the collection and will include a large number of quilt patterns, personal narratives by quiltmakers, and oral histories.

NB: 1938 citrus packing house quilt made by the packers; 1928 quilt made by a tourist group to Miami; 1851 Album quilt begun in Scotland and completed in 1892, Monticello, Florida.

Study Services: By written permission from the chief curator. Reading room, work tables, accession cards/files, archive/library, computerized access to collections, photocopy facilities, microscope; photo prints and slides.

Public Services: Annual quilt exhibition held in late October and early November with tours, classes, and workshops.

Tallahassee Junior Museum
3945 Museum Drive
Tallahassee, Florida 32304-9990
(904) 576-1636

Tuesday–Saturday, 9:00 A.M.–5:00 P.M.; Sunday,
12:30–5:00 P.M.
The twenty-three quilts in this collection include one Yo-yo, one appliqué, and twenty-one piecework. Sixteen are dated: eleven nineteenth century, five post-1900.
Study Services: By appointment; accession cards/files.

Bureau of Florida Folklife Programs
U.S. Highway 41 North
White Springs, Florida
(904) 397-2192

Mailing Address:
P.O. Box 265
White Springs, FL 32096

Weekdays, 8:00 A.M.–5:00 P.M.
Collection includes two contemporary Afro-American Strip quilts, two interviews, oral histories, seventeen photographs, and 120 slides.
Study Services: Staff must be advised of interest. Reading room, work tables, accession cards/files, Florida Folklife Archive; photo prints, slides, and prints made from negatives.
Publications: Pursuits and Pastimes: Florida Folklife in Work and Leisure (1983).

GEORGIA

The quilts exhibited run the gamut of techniques and styles within a regional tradition.

Atlanta Historical Society
3101 Andrews Drive, N.W.
Atlanta, Georgia 30305
(404) 261-1837

Monday–Saturday, 9:00 A.M.–5:30 P.M.; Sunday,
12:00–5:00 P.M.
Collection of seventy quilts. Sixty-four are dated: one made prior to 1820, fifty-three others from the nineteenth century, nine post-1900, and one contemporary. Thirty-six quilts are from southeastern states; three are Afro-American slave-made quilts; one each from Michigan and Texas. Techniques include piecework, appliqué, trapunto, piecework and appliqué combined, embroidery/patchwork, crazy quilts with embroidery, and piecework with decorative quilting.
NB: Focus on Georgia, 1850 to 1980. Album quilt: chintz appliqué from Charles Calcock Jones family, c. 1855, Liberty City, Georgia.
Study Services: Letter of request stating purpose of research. Reading room, work tables, accession cards/files, photocopy facilities, books/journals; photo prints can be made.
Public Services: When quilts are on exhibit: tours, classes, program on identifying quilts.
Publications: Southern Comfort: Quilts from the Atlanta Historical Society (1978).

The High Museum of Art
1280 Peachtree Street, N.E.
Atlanta, Georgia 30309
(404) 892-3600

Tuesday, 10:00 A.M.–5:00 P.M.; Wednesday,
10:00 A.M.–9:00 P.M.; Thursday–Saturday,
10:00 A.M.–5:00 P.M.; Sunday, 12:00–5:00 P.M.
Seven pieced and appliqué quilts: one c. 1820,

three 1821 to 1900, and one contemporary piece may be seen by advance appointment with registrar.

The Columbus Museum
1202 Front Avenue
Columbus, Georgia
(404) 322-0400

Mailing Address:
P.O. Box 1617
Columbus, GA 31902

Tuesday–Friday, 10:00 A.M.–5:00 P.M.; weekends, 1:00–5:00 P.M.
The Museum owns sixteen quilts, approximately 100 quilt patterns and instructions, four sixty-minute cassettes and transcriptions of interviews, oral histories. Two quilts are Afro-American, twelve local, one Amish, one Native American (Oklahoma); two are appliqué, fourteen piecework. Six are dated: one nineteenth century, three post-1900, two contemporary. Quilts are on continuous display.
NB: Regional patchwork, string quilts, appliqué. Several quilts from Columbus, Georgia, c. 1920.
Study Services: For scholars, request in writing on institutional letterhead. Work tables, accession cards/files, photocopy facilities, microscope, books/journals; photo prints, and prints made from negatives.
Public Services: Workshops, teacher staff development courses, and folk festival.

Westville Historical Handicrafts, Inc.
Lumpkin, Georgia
(912) 838-6310

Mailing Address:
P.O. Box 1850
Lumpkin, GA 31815

Monday–Saturday, 10:00 A.M.–5:00 P.M.; Sunday, 1:00–5:00 P.M.
There are sixteen nineteenth century hand-sewn quilts in piecework and appliqué from southwest Georgia. Quilts are on continuous exhibition.
Study Services: For scholars; written or telephoned request. Office work space, photocopy facilities, and books/journals.
Public Services: Educational workshops include tours of quilts.

Foxfire Fund, Inc.
Rabun Gap, Georgia
(404) 746-5318

Mailing Address:
P.O. Box B
Rabun Gap, GA 30568

By appointment.
There are ten southern Appalachian quilts (1901–1940), thirty to forty color slides of quilts, fifteen taped interviews (some transcribed) and a few quilt patterns and instructions. Principal source of the collection: Aunt Arie Carpenter.
NB: Two Friendship quilts.
Study Services: By appointment. Reading room, work tables, books/journals, and photocopy facilities; slide reproductions are available.
Publications: "A Quilt Is Something Human." In *The Foxfire Book* (1972). Edited by Eliot Wigginton. "Quilting, The Joy Of My Life." In *Foxfire 9* (1986). Edited by Eliot Wigginton.
Public Services: High school classes.

Juliette Gordon Low Girl Scout National Center
142 Bull Street
Savannah, Georgia 31405
(912) 233-4501

Monday, Tuesday, Thursday, Friday, and Saturday, 10:00 A.M.–4:00 P.M.; Sunday, 11:00 A.M.–4:30 P.M.; closed Wednesday, Sunday, December, and January.
Collection of approximately twenty-five nineteenth century quilts principally from Georgia; one dates prior to 1820. Twenty-three are piecework, one appliqué, one trapunto white-on-white eighteenth century quilt.
Study Services: Letter or telephone call to curator. Reading room, work tables, accession cards/files, photocopy facilities, and books/journals.
Public Services: Historical programs by request.

HAWAII

Hawaii gave its name to a unique style of quilting.

Bernice P. Bishop Museum
1525 Bernice Street
Honolulu, Hawaii
(808) 847-3511

Mailing Address:
P.O. Box 19000-A
Honolulu, HI 96817

Monday—Saturday, and first Sunday monthly, 9:00 A.M.—5:00 P.M.
The museum owns twenty-five quilts, 189 quilt patterns, and thirty quilt pillow patterns including one piecework, twenty-three appliqué in combination with piecework, and two trapunto. Nineteen are dated: eleven nineteenth century, six post-1900, two contemporary. Four are from New York, nineteen Hawaiian, one Hawaiian-style piecework. Quilts are on continuous display.
NB: Hawaiian quilting techniques are highlighted; also floral, and monarchy patterns. One Hannah Baker quilt (*Good Housekeeping* Great American Quilt Contest winner, Hawaii, March 1978).
Study Services: Make written request for appointment with curator. Reading room, accession cards/files, photocopy facilities, books/journals; photo prints, slides, photo prints from negatives may be ordered. Work tables; microscope usage can be arranged.
Public Services: Quilting classes and tours of exhibits are part of Education Programming.

Daughters of Hawaii
Queen Emma Summer Palace—Honolulu
(808) 595-3167
Hulihee Palace—Kailua-Kona
(808) 329-1877

Mailing Address:
2913 Pali Highway
Honolulu, HI 96817

Daily, 9:00 A.M.—4:00 P.M.
Collection of twenty predominantly nineteenth century, handsewn appliqué quilts. Eleven are Hawaiian family designs, flowers, and leaves; seven with Royal Hawaiian Flag motif; two with American Flag motifs.
Study Services: Are not available to public except by Board approval.
Public Services: Periodic exhibits and quilt-making classes.

Friends of 'Iolani Palace
King and Richards Streets
Honolulu, Hawaii
(808) 536-3552

Mailing Address:
P.O. Box 2259
Honolulu, HI 96804

Weekdays, 8:30 A.M.—4:30 P.M.
Eight nineteenth century Hawaiian quilts, two owned by Hawaiian monarchs. Access for scholars may be arranged through the acquisitions chairman.

Honolulu Academy of Arts
900 South Beretania Street
Honolulu, Hawaii 96822
(808) 538-3693

Tuesday—Saturday, 10:00 A.M.—4:30 P.M.
The Academy has fifty-four quilts; one research paper. Twenty-one are Hawaiian quilts, six from Pennsylvania, four from New Hampshire, three Amish, two from Wisconsin, two from New England, one from Maine, one from Michigan, one from Ohio, one from Kentucky, and one British quilt made in Hawaii. Twenty-nine are appliqué, twenty-three piecework, and two whole-cloth with quilting.

NB: Concentration of Hawaiian quilts and appliqué Luma Lau quilting. Hawaiian Flag quilt; and Hawaiian Adam and Eve quilt. Principal donor/source: Mrs. C.M. Cooke estate.
Study Services: For scholars, appointment by written request to textile curator. Reading room, accession cards/files, books/journals, and photocopy facilities; photo prints, and prints made from negatives.
Public Services: Docent-led tours and in-house lectures during quilt exhibitions.
Publications: Jones, Stella. *Hawaiian Quilts* (1930; rpt. 1973)

Mission Houses Museum
553 South King Street
Honolulu, Hawaii 96813
(808) 531-0481

Daily, 9:00 A.M.–4:00 P.M.
Collection of thirty-two handsewn quilts and six American piecework quilt tops: fourteen Hawaiian, eighteen American donated by the descendants of the American missionaries to Hawaii and Friends of the Mission Houses Museum. Fifteen are piecework, fifteen appliqué; one trapunto, one is stuffed.
Study Services: Reading room, accession cards/files, photocopy facilities; prints made from negatives.
Public Services: An annual quilt exhibit in June with tours of the exhibit.
Publications: Jones, Stella. *Hawaiian Quilts* (1930; rpt. 1973). Akana, Elizabeth A. *Hawaiian Quilting: A Fine Art* (1981).

Kaua'i Museum
4428 Rice Street
Lihue, Hawaii 96766
(808) 245-6931

Weekdays, 9:30 A.M.–4:30 P.M.
Twenty-two handsewn Hawaiian quilts: twenty appliqué, and two piecework. Half are nineteenth century, half post-1900. Quilts are on continuous exhibition.
Study Services: By appointment. Accession

cards/files; photo prints, and prints made from negatives.
Public Services: Quiltmaking classes, occasional exhibits.

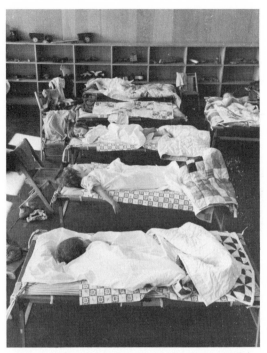

Woodville, California. March 1942. Nap time in the nursery school of the Farm Security Administration migratory farm workers' community. Photo by Russell Lee, negative number LC-USF33-13231-M5. Courtesy of the Farm Security Administration Collection, Prints and Photographs Division, Library of Congress.

IDAHO

Three World War I Red Cross Autograph fund raising quilts highlight collections in the state.

Idaho State Historical Society
610 N. Julia Davis Drive
Boise, Idaho 83702
(208) 334-2120

Monday–Saturday, 9:00 A.M.–5:00 P.M.; Sunday, 1:00–5:00 P.M.; closed New Year's Day, Thanksgiving, and Christmas.
The collection of approximately thirty quilts is currenty being cataloged.
Study Services: Call for an appointment. Work tables, accession cards/files, photocopy facilities.

Idaho State Historical Society Library and Archives
610 North Julia Davis Drive
Boise, Idaho 83702
(208) 334-3356

Weekdays, 9:00 A.M.–5:00 P.M. Closed holidays.
Unpublished papers and photographs on quilts and quiltmaking.
Study Services: By appointment.

Latah County Historical Society
110 South Adams Street
Moscow, Idaho 83843
(208) 882-1004

Wednesday–Saturday, 1:00–4:00 P.M.
In a collection of fifteen quilts seven are locally made (Palouse area, North Idaho); three Disciples of Christ Christian Church; two from eastern states. Ten are dated: three from the nineteenth century, and seven post-1900. Five are crazy quilts, four Autograph quilts, three pieced, one appliqué, one string quilt, one printed whole-cloth, tied. Quilts donated by Taylor-Lauder family.

NB: Three Autograph quilts made for Red Cross fund-raising in World War I; Seattle Regional winner Sears and Roebuck Century of Progress Quilt Contest, Chicago World's Fair, 1933.
Study Services: Call in advance for appointment with curator. Can arrange temporary space for serious researchers; reading room, accession cards/files, photocopy facilities, books/journals; and slides.
Public Services: Temporary exhibits for loan, lectures, workshops, programs for local clubs.
Publications: Siporin, Steve, editor, *We Came To Where We Were Supposed To Be* (1984). Rowley, Nancy J. "Red Cross Quilts for the Great War." *Uncoverings, 1982* (1983).

Upper Snake River Valley Historical Society
51 North Center
Rexburg, Idaho
(208) 356-9101

Mailing Address:
P.O. Box 244
Rexburg, ID 83440

Summer: Monday–Saturday, 10:00 A.M.–5:00 P.M.
Collection of eleven regional handsewn quilts: three from nineteenth century, majority from twentieth century; ten Mormon quilts, one contemporary. Nine are piecework, one appliqué, one printed.
NB: Centennial quilt.
Study Services: By appointment with director. Reading room, and photocopy facilities.

ILLINOIS

Far from any ocean, a quilt reputed to have been made by Lady Hamilton for Lord Nelson joins many examples of midwest quilts.

Arlington Heights Historical Society

500 North Vail Avenue
Arlington Heights, Illinois 60004
(313) 255-1225

Thursday–Sunday, 10:00 A.M.–4:00 P.M.
Approximately twenty Midwest quilts in collection. Fifteen nineteenth century, five post-1900. The quilts are on continuous exhibition.
Study Services: Call and request.

Aurora Historical Museum

305 Cedar Street
Aurora, Illinois 60506
(312) 897-9029

Wednesday, and weekends, 1:00–5:00 P.M.
The Museum holds twenty quilts, some made in the eastern states and brought west by pioneers, and others from the Midwest. The collection dates largely from 1840 to 1900.
Study Services: By written request. Reading room, work tables, accession cards/files, and local history research library.

Bishop Hill Heritage Museum

Bishop Hill, Illinois
(309) 927-3899

Mailing Address:
P.O. Box 1853
Bishop Hill, IL 61419

Daily, 9:00 A.M.–5:00 P.M.
Nine quilts of Swedish-American influence. Eight pieced and one crazy quilt may be seen by appointment.

McLean County Historical Society

201 East Grove Street
Bloomington, Illinois 61761
(309) 827-0428

Tuesday–Sunday, 1:00–5:00 P.M.
Collection includes approximately sixty-two quilts from McLean County, Illinois donated by McLean County residents. Thirty are dated: nineteen from the nineteenth century, nine post-1900, two contemporary. Fifty-one are piecework, seven appliqué, three trapunto, and one Yo-Yo. A limited number of quilts are on continuous display.
NB: 1853 Bloomington, embroidered and pieced; 1855 appliqué and trapunto wedding quilt.
Study Services: For scholars, make written request for appointment, limited available staff time. Reading room, work tables, accession cards/files, and photocopy facilities.
Public Services: When rotating exhibit is on display tours are conducted.

Champaign County Historical Museum

709 West University Avenue
Champaign, Illinois 61820
(217) 356-1010

Wednesday–Sunday, 1:00–4:00 P.M. Office: weekdays, 9:00 A.M.–4:00 P.M.
Collection of forty handsewn quilts from Champaign County and central Illinois. Thirty are from the nineteenth century, ten post-1900.
Study Services: Arrange appointment with staff. Reading room, accession cards/files, photocopy facilities, and books/journals.
Public Services: Quilts are displayed in special exhibits and individually in miscellaneous exhibits.

The Art Institute of Chicago

Department of Textiles
Michigan Avenue at Adams Street
Chicago, Illinois 60603
(312) 443-3696

Textile Study Room: by appointment, weekdays, 10:30 A.M.–4:15 P.M. Office: weekdays, 9:00 A.M.–5:00 P.M.

Until approximately 1988, major construction next to the department precludes any examination of the quilts because much of the collection has been moved to another location for the duration of construction. Visitors are still welcome to view the slide carousel. Collection of 100 quilts including child-sized quilts, parlor throw crazy quilts, one or two quilt tops. In addition, there are eight quilt blocks, a border fragment, and another Honeycomb pattern fragment from a bedcover. Eighty-two have approximate dates: six prior to 1820, sixty-five nineteenth century, five post-1900, and six contemporary. Emphasis is on building a collection which represents the broadest spectrum of pattern, technique, and geographical source.

NB: Four quilts made by Dr. Jeannette Dean Throckmorton; Album quilt made by Ella Maria Deacon.

Study Services: Make appointment one week to ten days in advance. Visitors may see maximum of three quilts per appointment, selected in advance by prior knowledge or from slide carousel of collection. If the choice is made from slide carousel, then a second appointment to view the quilts is necessary. Reading room, work tables, photocopy facilities, microscope by special arrangement; photo prints, slides, prints available from museum's negatives, books and pamphlets. The Ryerson and Burnham Libraries, which are part of The Art Institute of Chicago, have a more substantial collection of books on quilts.

Public Services: When there is a quilt exhibition museum education department provides tours, and sometimes the curator gives a guided walk-through of the exhibition. Members of the museum may request an appointment to bring in and discuss their textile objects with the curator. Conservation, identification, and exhibition questions may be discussed at that time.

Publications: Davison, Mildred. *American Quilts from The Art Institute of Chicago* (1966). Davison, Mildred. Coverlets (1973).

Chicago Historical Society

Clark Street at North Avenue
Chicago, Illinois 60614
(312) 642-4600

Monday–Saturday, 9:30 A.M.–4:30 P.M.; Sunday, 12:00–5:00 P.M.

Collection of eighty quilts: sixteen from Illinois, two from Ohio, two from New York, one attributed to Pennsylvania Dutch, others from Rhode Island, Connecticut, Michigan, Wisconsin. Among them are forty-four piecework, eighteen pieced crazy quilts, seven appliqué, two white-on-white. Of those that have been dated two were made prior to 1820, sixty-five from 1821 to 1900, eight post-1900.

NB: 1933 World's Fair quilt made by Bertha Stenge; Civil War commemorative top, Nuvda Lodge, Illinois.

Study Services: Call or write for appointment. Reading room, work tables, accession cards/files, photocopy facilities; prints, slides, and prints made from negatives.

The University Library–Special Collections

University of Illinois at Chicago
Chicago, Illinois
(312) 996-2742

Mailing Address:
P.O. Box 8198
Chicago, IL 60680

Weekdays, 8:30 A.M.–4:45 P.M.

Collection of correspondence and memoranda relating to Sears Roebuck, Inc. quilt contest at A Century of Progress International Exposition, Chicago, 1933–1934.

Study Services: Visitor must complete Reader Register form and comply with rules. Reading room, work tables, accession cards/files, campus photo lab, and photocopy facilities.

Vermilion County Museum Society

116 North Gilbert Street
Danville, Illinois 61832
(217) 442-2922

Tuesday–Saturday, 10:00 A.M.–5:00 P.M.; Sunday, 1:00–5:00 P.M.
Twenty-five handsewn quilts from Illinois: eleven from the nineteenth century, eight post-1900, six contemporary. Fifteen are pieced, six crazy quilts, three appliqué, and one pieced appliqué.
NB: Quilts from Vermilion County.
Study Services: Call director and make an appointment. Reading room, accession cards/files, and photocopy facilities.

Downers Grove Historical Museum

831 Maple Avenue
Downers Grove, Illinois 60515
(312) 963-1309

Wednesday, 1:00–4:00 P.M.; Sunday, 2:00–4:00 P.M.
The twenty-five quilts are from the Illinois region. Seventeen are dated: eight nineteenth century, seven post-1900, two contemporary. The majority is piecework; appliqué, embroidery, and decorative quilting techniques also are represented. Signature quilts, crazy quilts, and a commemorative quilt are in the collection.
NB: Historical quilt that depicts the story of Downers Grove.
Study Services: Make arrangements with the curator. Reading room, work tables, accession cards/files, and photocopy facilities.
Public Services: Annual quilt exhibition with tours.

Madison County Historical Museum

715 North Main Street
Edwardsville, Illinois 62025
(618) 656-7562

Wednesday, Thursday, and Friday, 9:00 A.M.–4:00 P.M.; Sunday, 1:00–4:00 P.M.
Collection of twenty-five handsewn Midwest quilts from Illinois, Ohio, and Tennessee. Twenty-one date from the nineteenth century, four post-1900. Eighteen are piecework, three embroidered, two appliqué, and two white-on-white, donated by Madison County residents. Quilts are on continuous exhibition.
NB: Tulip quilt, star quilt, Log Cabin quilt.
Study Services: By request and available staff time. Reading room, work tables, accession cards/files, photocopy facilities; photographs may be taken upon request.
Public Services: Several Museum-owned quilts on exhibit in cases in the lobby of Madison County Court House, Edwardsville, Illinois. Quilt exhibitions every two or three years.

Elmhurst Historical Museum

120 East Park Avenue
Elmhurst, Illinois 60126
(312) 833-1457

Tuesday and Thursday, 1:00–5:00 P.M.; Saturday, 10:00 A.M.–5:00 P.M.
Collection of sixteen quilts includes crazy quilt; stuffed quilt by Pearl Ringland; 1870 blue and white and 1880 Baby Blocks or Tumbling Blocks by Elizabeth Anne Challacombe; c. 1900, child-size Block quilt by Anna M. Challacombe; Courthouse Steps made of men's suiting by a tailor, Mr. Henrikson; c. 1908 baby quilt; 1900 Tulip design variation; Rocky Road to Kansas; blue and white striped quilt; Log Cabin quilt; knotted quilt; star design; Autograph tree with appliqué butterflies in lavender print alternate with green stitched names in the shape of trees, c. 1936. Autograph quilt in Sunburst design, made by members of Redeemer Lutheran Church, c. 1928. Crazy quilt with several sets of initials, c. 1885.
Study Services: Request appointment at least one week in advance to see quilts in storage. Reading room, accession cards/files, photocopy facilities, books/journals; photo prints, and slides of quilts that have been exhibited.
Public Services: Slide lectures related to quilt patterns.

Stephenson County Historical Society

1440 South Carroll Avenue
Freeport, Illinois 61032
(815) 232-8419

Friday, Saturday, and Sunday, 1:30–5:00 P.M.;
and by appointment.
The collection includes forty to fifty quilts
and coverlets. The majority is piecework; appliqué is also represented. The oldest is c.
1840.
NB: Autograph quilts made in local churches
and for celebrations.
Study Services: For scholars, by appointment.
Accession cards/files.
Public Services: Quilt exhibition every two or
three years.

Galena/Jo Daviess County History Museum

211 South Bench Street
Galena, Illinois 61036
(815) 777-9129

Daily, 9:00 A.M.–5:00 P.M.
A nineteenth century regional collection of
approximately fifteen patchwork quilts. Documentation includes fifty personal narratives by
quiltmakers; diaries and journals and fifty interviews and oral histories.
Study Services: By appointment. Work tables,
accession cards/files, photocopy facilities, microscope, and if ordered, photo reproductions
of quilts.
Public Services: Projects which result in an
exhibition.

Geneva Historical Society Museum

Geneva, Illinois
(312) 232-4951

Mailing Address:
P.O. Box 345
Geneva, Illinois 60134

Wednesday, Saturday, and Sunday, 2:00–4:30
P.M.
A collection of nineteen handsewn local Illinois quilts primarily from the nineteenth century. The collection is well-documented.

Seven are piecework, six appliqué, two crazy
quilts, two trapunto, one hand tufted, and one
white-on-white. Quilts are on continuous exhibition.
NB: 1849 quilt made by a group of Geneva
women; Bicentennial group quilt made in
1976.
Study Services: Under supervision of curator.
Reading room, work tables, accession cards/
files, microfilm reader, photocopy facilities,
and books/journals.
Public Services: Tours.

Highland Park Historical Society

326 Central Avenue
Highland Park, Illinois
(312) 432-7090

Mailing Address:
P.O. Box 56
Highland Park, IL 60035

Tuesday–Sunday, 2:00–5:00 P.M.
A collection of thirty-two regional quilts from
the nineteenth century.
NB: 1892 Cartwheel quilt with local signatures.

Marshall County Historical Society

314 Fifth Street
Lacon, Illinois 61540
(309) 246-2349

Weekdays, 8:00 A.M.–12:30 P.M.
Five quilts: three pieced, one embroidered,
and one Friendship (Names) quilt. Annual
quilt exhibition, and special viewing by prior
appointment with curator.

Illinois Pioneer Heritage Center, Inc.

315 West Main
Monticello, Illinois
(217) 762-4731

Mailing Address:
P.O. Box 12
Monticello, IL 61856

May–September: daily, 12:30–3:30 P.M. Closed October–April.
Ten handsewn Illinois quilts from the nineteenth century include piecework with fine quilting, and appliqué.
Study Services: By appointment. Work tables, and accession cards/files.
Public Services: Tours.

Naperville Heritage Society—Naper Settlement

201 West Porter
Naperville, Illinois 60540
(312) 420-6010

Office: daily, 8:30 A.M.–4:30 P.M. Open to the public: May 5–November 3: Wednesday, Saturday, and Sunday, 1:30–4:30 P.M. A collection of sixty-three quilts and research documentation: three date prior to 1820, forty-nine from 1821 to 1900, eleven post-1900. Approximately forty are from the Midwest, five from the East Coast. About twenty-eight are piecework, seventeen appliqué, six have combined techniques, nine have embroidery, two are printed whole-cloth, one white-on-white, one Bon-Bon. Quilts are on continuous display in room settings, and are rotated.
Study Services: Appointment should be made with curator of collections, two weeks in advance. Reading room, work tables, accession cards/files, photocopy facilities, books/journals.
Public Services: Daily tours, by appointment. Tours for groups of twenty or more are available year-round.

The University Museums

Illinois State University
Normal, Illinois 61761
(309) 438-8800

Office: weekdays, 8:00 A.M.–4:30 P.M.
Collection of eighteen quilts, half are dated: five nineteenth century, two post-1900, two contemporary. Three are from Illinois, one from Kentucky, one from Ohio. Twelve are piecework, four appliqué, two have appliqué and embroidery.
NB: Pieced cotton quilt commemorating 1901 Pan American Exposition.
Public Services: Tours are provided for quilt exhibitions; summer quilting workshop.

Historical Society of Oak Park and River Forest

217 Home Avenue
Oak Park, Illinois
(312) 848-6755

Mailing Address:
P.O. Box 771
Oak Park, IL 60303

Tuesday and Thursday, 1:00–5:00 P.M.; Friday and Sunday, 2:00–4:00 P.M.
Five nineteenth century regional quilts: four pieced, and one appliqué. May be seen by appointment with curator.

Lakeview Museum of Arts and Sciences

1125 West Lake Avenue
Peoria, Illinois 61614
(309) 686-7000

Tuesday–Saturday, 10:00 A.M.–5:00 P.M.; Wednesday nights 7:00–9:00 P.M.; Sunday, 12:00–5:00 P.M.
Five pieced quilts and ten coverlets may be seen by appointment with curator. Three date from 1821 to 1900.

Rockford Museum Center and Midway Village

6799 Guilford Road
Rockford, Illinois 61107
(815) 397-9112

Tuesday—Friday, 10:00 A.M.—4:00 P.M.; weekends, 12:00—4:00 P.M.
Collection of twenty-five Midwest quilts. Fifteen date from the nineteenth century, ten post-1900. Seventeen are piecework; four crazy quilts; two appliqué; one printed wholecloth, tied; one embroidered.
Study Services: Arrange with registrar and textile chairman; accession cards/files.
Public Services: Quilt exhibit from Museum collection and private collections for special events.

Illinois State Museum

Spring and Edwards Streets
Springfield, Illinois 62706
(217) 782-7125

Daily, 8:30 A.M.—5:00 P.M.; Sunday, 1:00—5:00 P.M.
The Museum has sixty-two quilts, sixty-one quilt patterns and instructions, and fourteen research papers. Fifty of the quilts are known to be from Illinois; two from Kentucky; four from Pennsylvania; one each from Indiana, Ohio, and Tennessee. Two were made prior to 1820, forty-seven are from 1821 to 1900, three post-1900, three contemporary. Two are Bicentennial quilts, one entitled "Spirit of America" was made by twelve-year-olds of Hillsboro Junior High School; the other was made by forty-one residents of Arenyville, Illinois. Types and techniques include pieced quilts, crazy quilts, Log Cabin; seven appliqué, two trapunto, one white-on-white.
NB: Crazy quilt, late nineteenth century, said to have a piece of Mrs. Lincoln's dress in it (assigned to the Governor's Mansion). Patchwork quilt top, c. 1864, Jo Daviess County, Illinois, each piece lined with template made of newspapers, letters, or copy exercises. Various dates are found on paper including 1859, 1863, and 1864. Maker was pioneer of Jo

Daviess County, husband, lieutenant in Black Hawk War.
Study Services: Call or write for appointment. Reading room, work tables, accession cards/files, photo prints, slides, prints made from negatives, books, and journals.

Lincoln Home National Historic Site

426 South Seventh Street
Springfield, Illinois 62701
(217) 492-4241

Daily, 8:00 A.M.—5:00 P.M.
Collection of twenty-five handsewn Midwest quilts, primarily nineteenth century, includes appliqué variation of Whig Rose pattern; unfinished Grandmother's Flower Garden or Honeycomb sewn on pieces of letters and other old paper; Grandmother's Bouquet, Nine Patch with diamonds pieced by Branine L. Freeland at eight years of age, cut by her grandmother Louisa J. Clayton; Star of Le Moyne; Log Cabin; Log Cabin variation; Wreath of Roses appliqué; nine squares arranged in Nine Patch pattern; diamond Nine Patch checkerboard; Lady Hamilton quilt; Basket; appliqué Pinwheel variation; star quilt pieced by Meahala Monk Clayton, Colchester, Illinois in 1876, and quilted in 1936 by Martha A. Freeland, Portland, Oregon; crazy quilt; pieced Sunburst Star. Site has a continuing exhibit of quilts.
NB: Quilt of satin and silk, reputed to have been made by Lady Hamilton for Lord Nelson.
Study Services: For scholars, write to superintendent. Books/journals on quilts/quiltmaking; photo reproductions of quilts can be arranged.
Public Services: Quilt demonstrations, special exhibits, slide lecture presentations.

McHenry County Historical Museum

6422 Main Street
Union, Illinois
(815) 923-2267

Mailing Address:
P.O. Box 434
Union, IL 60180

May–October: Wednesday and Sunday, 1:30–4:30 P.M. Office: weekdays, 9:00 A.M.–4:30 P.M. Thirty-two regional quilts include one prior to 1820, twenty-five from 1821 to 1900, five post-1900, one contemporary. About thirteen are piecework; six embroidered Signature quilts; eight crazy quilts; three made of printed cloth. Museum has a continuing exhibit of quilts.
Study Services: Reading room, work tables, accession cards/files, photocopy facilities, and books/journals. Qualified researchers may take photographs.

Textiles Department

University of Illinois
905 S. Goodwin
Urbana, Illinois 61801
(217) 333-0737 or 333-0518

Weekdays, 8:00 A.M.–12:00 P.M., and 1:00–5:00 P.M.
The collection has five quilts and eighty to one hundred coverlets which may be seen by appointment.

World Heritage Museum

University of Illinois
484 Lincoln Hall
702 South Wright Street
Urbana, Illinois 61801
(217) 333-2360

Weekdays, 9:00 A.M.–4:00 P.M.
Museum has twenty-three quilts: seven of these are Afro-American from Alabama, eleven from Indiana and Illinois. Of those that have been identified one has been dated prior to 1820, thirteen from 1821 to 1900, seven are contemporary. Collection includes six pieced

quilt tops, nine pieced and quilted, five hand-woven coverlets.
Study Services: Contact director for written permission. Reading room, work tables, accession cards/files, microscope; quilts may be photographed by special request.
Public Services: Textiles conservation workshops.

Lake County Museum

Lakewood Forest Preserve
Wauconda, Illinois 60084
(312) 526-7878

Weekdays, 8:30 A.M.–4:30 P.M.; weekends, 1:30–4:30 P.M.
Collection of fourteen handsewn pieced quilts in various patterns from Lake County, Illinois. Eleven date from the nineteenth century, one is post-1900. Two are embroidered, one appliqué. Principal sources of the collection are Viola Rockenbach, Mrs. Schlottman, and Mr. Stedman.
NB: Red Cross Signature quilt; Ladies Aide Signature quilt.
Study Services: Reading room, accession cards/files, books/journals, photocopy facilities; photo prints, slides, and prints made from negatives.

Iron quilting clamps used with large wooden frames displayed on applique blocks. Courtesy of Oral Traditions Project of Pennsylvania's Union County Historical Society.

INDIANA

The work of Hoosier quilters along with Afro-Americans, Germans, and English predominates.

Hillforest Historical Foundation, Inc.

213 5th Street
Aurora, Indiana
(812) 926-0087

Mailing Address:
P.O. Box 127
Aurora, IN 47001

Tuesday–Sunday, 1:00–5:00 P.M.
The collection of ten nineteenth century Midwest quilts is primarily from southern Indiana. Four are piecework, three crazy quilts with embroidery, two appliqué, one pieced trapunto. Quilts are displayed on the beds of historical 1850 home.
NB: Documented quilt of 1837, made by the woman who owned the mansion.
Study Services: Request access from executive secretary. Photo prints and slides are available.
Public Services: By specific request: tours of exhibitions, classes, workshops.

Monroe County Historical Museum

202 East Sixth Street
Bloomington, Indiana 47401
(812) 332-2517

Tuesday–Friday, 10:00 A.M.–4:00 P.M.; weekends, 10:00 A.M.–5:00 P.M.
The Museum has eleven quilts. The majority is nineteenth century; two are contemporary.
NB: 1840 quilt with quilted date and initials; 4,608 pieces in four Blazing Stars and appliquéd flower designs.
Study Services: Arrange with curator for supervised appointment. Work tables, accession cards/files, and books/journals.
Public Services: Annual quilt exhibit largely of quilts on loan supplemented by quilts from the collection.

William Hammond Mathers Museum

University of Indiana
601 East 8th Street
Bloomington, Indiana 47405
(812) 335-7224

Tuesday–Friday, 9:00 A.M.–4:30 P.M.; weekends, 1:00–4:30 P.M.
Of the Museum's twenty-five quilts ten are Afro-American from southeast coastal region (Gullah); twelve from Indiana; two Native American; one from Illinois. Eighteen are piecework, three appliqué, four embroidered crazy quilts. Seven date from the nineteenth century, and eighteen from the twentieth century.
NB: Small, well-documented southeast coast and Sea Island (Gullah) collection.
Study Services: By appointment with curator or staff. Work tables, accession cards/files, photocopy facilities; photo prints and slides.

Elkhart County Historical Society

Bristol, Indiana
(219) 848-4322

Mailing Address:
P.O. Box 434
Bristol, IN 46507

March 1–December 1: Saturday, 1:00–4:00 P.M.; Sunday, 1:00–5:00 P.M.; and by appointment.
Collection of thirty-two Pennsylvania Dutch and northern Indiana quilts, predominantly from the nineteenth century, one post-1900. Twenty-four are pieced, two appliqué and pieced, two embroidered and pieced, one trapunto, one appliqué and embroidered, two appliqué. Museum has a continuous exhibit of quilts.
NB: Wandering Foot or Turkey Tracks with trapunto quilting.
Study Services: By appointment. Reading room, work tables, accession cards/files, and photocopy facilities.
Public Services: Craft workshops.

Bartholomew County Historical Society

524 Third Street
Columbus, Indiana 47201
(812) 372-3541

Tuesday—Saturday, 10:00 A.M.—5:00 P.M.
Thirteen quilts are from south-central Indiana. Eight have dates attributed: two nineteenth century, four post-1900, two contemporary. Ten are piecework, one white quilt quilted with red thread, one printed whole-cloth with appliqué, one embroidered.
Study Services: Make appointment with curator of collections. Reading room, work tables, accession cards/files, books/journals.

Clinton County Museum

301 East Clinton Street
Frankfort, Indiana 46041
(317) 659-2030

April 1—December 31: weekends, 1:30—4:30 P.M.
Collection of twenty quilts made by persons of German or British Isles descent, either living in or with ties to Clinton County. One quilt was made prior to 1820; approximately fourteen are nineteenth century, five post-1900. Techniques include piecework, appliqué, embroidered, trapunto, white-on-white. Museum has a continuing exhibition of quilts.
NB: Baby quilt, Double Irish Chain, 1879. Church League quilt with embroidered names; 1884 Temperance League quilt with names in ink.
Study Services: By appointment with curator/registrar or museum committee member.

Elizabeth Smith airs her Block, Bow-tie, Flower Garden, and Yo-Yo quilts. American Folklife Center, Blue Ridge Parkway Project, Mount Airy, North Carolina, 1978. Fieldwork and photo by Geraldine Johnson, negative number 3-20492, 11A. Courtesy of the Archive of Folk Culture, Library of Congress.

The Children's Museum

3000 North Meridian Street
Indianapolis, Indiana
(317) 924-5431

Mailing Address:
P.O. Box 3000
Indianapolis, IN 46206

Tuesday—Saturday, 10:00 A.M.—5:00 P.M.; Sunday, 12:00—5:00 P.M.; Mondays, Memorial Day to Labor Day, 10:00 A.M.—5:00 P.M.; closed other Mondays.
Museum has approximately sixty Midwest quilts and some eastern examples, including twenty doll quilts. Forty can be dated: four prior to 1820, thirty-five from the duration of the nineteenth century, one post-1900. Provenances include Indiana Amish, other quilts from Indiana, Illinois, Ohio, and Michigan. Fifty are piecework, including the twenty doll quilts and one with an appliqué medallion; five appliqué; one whole cloth, Hudson River blue resist; one Yo-Yo; and one white-on-white trapunto.
NB: The strength of the collection is in Log Cabin and crazy quilts. Hudson Valley blue resist; white-on-white trapunto; signed and dated Indiana 1859 appliqué. Children's and doll quilts a specialty.
Study Services: Prior arrangement with curator, minimum of two weeks notice. Reading room in library, work tables, accession cards/files, photocopy facilities, microscope in conservation lab, books/journals, photo prints; prints made from negatives by special order.

Indiana State Museum and Historic Sites

202 North Alabama
Indianapolis, Indiana 46204
(317) 232-1637

Monday—Saturday, 9:00 A.M.—4:45 P.M.; Sunday, 12:00—4:45 P.M.
Approximately 230 quilts in a collection that includes four dated prior to 1820, 125 from 1821 to 1900, fifty post-1900, and twelve contemporary. Eighty-percent of the quilts were made in Indiana, two are Indiana Amish. Tech-

niques include appliqué, piecework, and white-on-white.

NB: Civil War period Abraham Lincoln political ribbon quilt in the form of American flag.

Study Services: Make appointment with curator of textiles and costumes. Work tables, accession cards/files; and prints made from available negatives.

Public Services: Occasional quilting workshops, exhibitions. The Museum is conducting a quilt documentation project for Indiana.

Indianapolis Museum of Art

1200 West 38th Street
Indianapolis, Indiana 46208
(317) 923-1331

Tuesday–Sunday, 11:00 A.M.–5:00 P.M.
Collection contains thirty-seven quilts, ten Webster quilt patterns and instructions. Seventeen can be attributed to Indiana, two are Amish quilts, one Hawaiian. Two were made prior to 1820, seventeen date from 1821 to 1900, sixteen from 1901 to 1940, two contemporary. Techniques include appliqué, piecework, embroidered, white-on-white, and wool whole-cloth.

NB: Pieced silk, embroidered with silk and cotton crazy quilt by Victorienne Parsons Mitchell, c. 1890; cotton pieced Hawaiian quilt c. 1890, appliqué on cotton; 1853 pieced and appliqué cotton quilt, embroidered with cotton and silk.

Study Services: Scholars, request appointment from curator of textiles. Reading room, work tables, accession cards/files, slides of majority of collection, photocopy facilities, microscope; slides and prints.

Public Services: Tours, special lectures, and symposiums for quilt exhibitions.

President Benjamin Harrison Memorial Home

1230 North Delaware Street
Indianapolis, Indiana 46202
(317) 631-1898

Monday–Saturday, 10:00 A.M.–4:00 P.M.; Sunday, 12:30–4:00 P.M.
Ten quilts from Indiana and California constitute a collection with a political emphasis. Six date from the nineteenth century. Quilts are continuously on exhibit.

NB: Five crazy quilts, especially a Signature crazy quilt signed by famous persons in 1889, with several presidents' signatures.

Study Services: Make appointment with curator. Work tables, accession cards/files, photocopy facilities; photo prints and slides.

Public Services: Programs on quilting as a craft, quilting conservation, and quilting demonstrations.

Tippecanoe County Historical Association

909 South Street
Lafayette, Indiana 47901
(317) 742-8411

Tuesday–Sunday, 1:00–5:00 P.M.
Collection of forty quilts, fifteen made in Tippecanoe or surrounding counties. One each from Maine, New York, Wisconsin, and Iowa. Twenty-eight are piecework, six appliqué, four Autograph/embroidered, two trapunto/stuffed. Crazy quilts are the most numerous. Thirty-four have dates attributed: one prior to 1820, twenty-five from 1821–1900, six from 1901–1940, two contemporary.

NB: Four c. 1890–1910 Autograph quilts made locally.

Study Services: Contact curator of collections, explain project, make appointment. Reading room, accession cards/files, photocopy facilities, and books/journals.

Public Services: Participant in an annual quilt show held at a community house in Lafayette, Indiana.

Marshall County Historical Society Museum

317 West Monroe Street
Plymouth, Indiana 46563
(219) 936-2306

Weekdays, 9:00 A.M.–5:00 P.M.; Sunday, 1:00–5:00 P.M.
Twelve piecework quilts are local heirlooms from Indiana. Six date from the nineteenth century, and six are post-1900.
Study Services: Give three to five days notice. Reading room, work tables, accession cards/files, and books/journals.

Vigo County Historical Society

1411 South Sixth Street
Terre Haute, Indiana 47802
(812) 235-9717

Sunday–Friday, 1:00–4:00 P.M.
Seventy-two regional quilts: one made prior to 1821, fifty-two from 1821 to 1900, seventeen from 1901 to 1940, two contemporary. Quilts are on continuous exhibition.
Study Services: Write or call for appointment. Reading room, work tables, and accession cards/files.
Public Services: Exhibitions, workshops, and programs within the community.

Durham, North Carolina. November 1939. Old quilts and burlap are used to keep tobacco moist and "in order" while waiting for auction sale. Photo by Marion Post Wolcott, negative number LC-USF34-52357-D. Courtesy of the Farm Security Administration Collection, Prints and Photographs Division, Library of Congress.

IOWA

Amana wool quilts, Norwegian-American quilts, a 1731 English chintz quilt, and Iowa pioneer quilts are preserved along with extensive documentation.

Amana Heritage Society

Amana, Iowa
(319) 622-3567

Mailing Address:
P.O. Box 81
Amana, IA 52203

Monday–Saturday, 10:00 A.M.–5:00 P.M.; Sunday, 12:00–5:00 P.M.; closed October 15–November 15.
Society has twelve quilts from the twentieth century, five quilt patterns and instructions.
NB: Amana wool quilts.
Study Services: For scholars, by appointment. Reading room, work tables, accession cards/files, computer system, photocopy facilities, microscope, photo prints.
Publications: "Quilting of the Amana Colonies." Art and Craft Series I (n.d.).

Cedar Falls Historical Society

303 Franklin Street
Cedar Falls, Iowa 50613
(319) 277-8817

Weekdays, 8:00 A.M.–5:00 P.M.; weekends, 2:00–4:00 P.M.
A collection of forty-two quilt-related items including a Shoo-fly design comforter by Verda McDonald. Other patterns and techniques represented are 1890 Log Cabin top; 1895 Friendship; crazy quilts, one dated 1900; 125-year-old appliqué variation of Pineapple design; doll quilt; Log Cabin by Martha Grant Vorce, c. 1865; dowery quilt from West Virginia, c. 1850; Four Patch with three different quilting designs; Goose Tracks, 125 years old;

pieced doll string quilt; Cedar Falls Bicentennial quilt; Broken Dishes or Birds in Air; 1909 Four Patch variation of the Nine Patch; Double Irish Chain variation; Churn Dash or Hole in the Barn Door; white-on-white baby quilt; Medallion quilt; quilted baby hat; sofa pillow covers; Hawaiian quilt blocks; Counterpanes: Log Cabin, Pinwheel, Greek Cross, Dresden Plate.
Study Services: Reading room, and accession cards/files.
Public Services: Quilt exhibitions.

Sanford Museum and Planetarium
117 East Willow Street
Cherokee, Iowa 51012
(712) 225-3922

Weekdays, 9:00 A.M.–5:00 P.M.; weekends, 12:00–5:00 P.M.
A collection of four contemporary quilts and more than 200 quilt block patterns national in scope. The collection was given by Virginia Herrick.
Study Services: Receive permission from director. Work tables, accession cards/files, library with twenty-five books/journals.
Public Services: Lectures, and tours for exhibitions.

Montauk
Clermont, Iowa 52135
(319) 423-5271

Memorial Day–October 31: daily, 12:00–5:00 P.M.; winter: by appointment.
Eleven regional pieced quilts which date from the 1850s to 1920s. The collection is part of original furnishings of this historic home at the time it was acquired from the Larrabee family. One quilt possibly Amish, Iowa made; one possibly Connecticut (point of origin of Larrabee family, c. 1850). One appliqué, eight pieced in different patterns, one printed whole-cloth.
NB: Crazy quilt with political ribbons from the 1880s and 1890s.
Study Services: Contact site manager. Reading room, work tables, and accession cards/files.

Johnson County Historical Society
310 Fifth Street
Coralville, Iowa
(319) 351-5738

Mailing Address:
P.O. Box 5081
Coralville, Iowa 52241

Hours not provided.
Collection of less than ten quilts.

Vesterheim, Norwegian-American Museum
502 West Water Street
Decorah, Iowa 52101
(319) 382-9681

May–October: daily, 9:00 A.M.–5:00 P.M.; November–April: daily, 10:00 A.M.–4:00 P.M.
Collection of fifty-two Norwegian-American quilts made between mid-nineteenth and mid-twentieth century. Twenty-seven are patchwork, thirteen crazy quilts, three embroidered, two appliqué, two white-on-white, two florals in wool pile, one woven coverlet quilted to backing. Two are genealogical quilts. Quilts are exhibited continuously as part of the Home in America exhibits.
Study Services: For scholars, contact curator, state nature of research. Reading room, accession cards/files, photo reproductions in catalog files, photocopy facilities; photographs may be taken by researcher.

Living History Farms
2600 Northwest 111th Street
Des Moines, Iowa 50322
(515) 278-5286

April–November: daily, 9:00 A.M.–5:00 P.M.; December–March: weekdays, 9:00 A.M.–5:00 P.M.
Collection of 212 quilts, tops, and comforters is one of the most extensive in this area of the Midwest and includes individual accounts about particular quilts. Twenty-six are dated from 1772–1930. Most were collected in Iowa, either made in or brought into Iowa and the Midwest. The collection was princi-

Sarah Willis Hayes (Mrs. Hugh
Hayes), appliqué quilt top from Gloucester County,
Virginia. The applique blue and white, and red and white
copper plates and the block printed chintzes date c.
1785; the blue print bands date later (about 1800). It is
thought that Mrs. Hayes appliqued the motifs (with a
reverse button-hole stitch) in the late eighteenth century
in Virginia and pieced together the bands after moving
to North Carolina in the early 1800s. Courtesy of the
Museum of Early Southern Decorative Arts.

Robbing Peter to Pay Paul or
Drunkard's Path, 1900. The quilt is from Stevensville,
Welland County, Ontario; the maker is unknown.
Accession number 970-251. Courtesy of the Royal
Ontario Museum, Toronto, Ontario.

Appliqué and reverse appliqué quilt
with pieced borders by Anna Catherine (Hummel)
Markey Garnhart (1773–1860) of Frederick, Frederick
County, Maryland, c. 1825. Courtesy of the Daughters of
the American Revolution Museum, Washington, D.C.
See page 214.

"The Graveyard Quilt" in a LeMoyne
or Lemon Star pattern by Elizabeth Roseberry Mitchell
of Lewis County, Kentucky in 1839. From the collection
of the Kentucky Historical Society.

Na Kihapai Nani Lua 'Ole O Edena A Me Elenale (The Beautiful Unequaled Gardens of Eden and Edenale), Hawaiian Islands, pre-1918, attributed to a male quilter. White ground with multicolored appliqués; plain weave; appliqué and quilted following pattern (luma lau) with shallow lump-hill texture (kulipu'u). Knotted fringe. Courtesy of the Honolulu Academy of Arts.

Quaker Friendship Quilt, from the
Phillips Family, Bucks County, signed and dated 1845.
Accession number 84.02.01. Courtesy of The Mercer
Museum of The Bucks County Historical Society.

Signature Quilt Number 1, 1982,
designed and cut by Charlotte Robinson with assistance
from Daphne Shuttleworth and Ruth Corning.
Silkscreened by Wenda F. Von Weise. Pieced by Bonnie
Persinger with assistance from Betty Guy, Gena
Simpson, and Lena Behme. Hand embroidered by Alice
Clagett, Barbara Rigdon, Cynthis Redick, and ten
members of the quilt research team. Hand quilted by
Bob Douglas. Courtesy of the Philip Morris Companies
Incorporated.

"Bird of Paradise" bride's quilt.
Maker unknown, from New York State, 1858–63.
Courtesy of the Museum of American Folk Art.

pally donated by Mary Barton of Ames, Iowa. Techniques represented are predominantly patchwork, appliqué, white-on-white, and trapunto. Exhibition of quilts at all times.
NB: 1772 Quilt.
Study Services: Make appointment at least two weeks in advance. Work tables, accession cards/files, photocopy facilities, and photo reproductions of quilts.
Public Services: Textile and quilting demonstrations on site, occasional adult education, off site exhibits, one or two per year. Slide lectures about quilts in the collection.

State Historical Society of Iowa
Capital Complex
Des Moines, Iowa 50319
(515) 281-3295

Daily, 8:00 A.M.–4:00 P.M.
Department has seventy-four quilts. Thirteen have dates attributed to them: eleven from 1821–1900, two from 1901–1940. The collection is currently being inventoried.
NB: Album quilts; Red Cross quilts.
Study Services: Scholars, request access from departmental collections committee; public access possible after relocation.

Iowa State Historical Department
402 Iowa Avenue
Iowa City, Iowa 52240
(319) 338-5471

Monday–Saturday, 8:00 A.M.–4:30 P.M.
Six Iowa quilts may be seen by appointment.

Kalona Historical Village
Kalona, Iowa 52247
(319) 656-3232

April 15–October 15: Monday–Saturday, 10:00 A.M.–4:00 P.M.
Collection of thirteen handsewn quilts primarily from nineteenth century Iowa. One Iowa Amish, three German, five from frontier Iowa, one Catholic, three Victorian. Five are piece-work, three appliqué, three decorative quilting, one piecework/appliqué, one embroidered. Quilts on exhibit at all times.

Grout Museum of History and Science
503 South Street
Waterloo, Iowa 50701
(319) 234-6357

Tuesday–Friday, 9:00 A.M.–4:30 P.M.
Approximately sixty-one quilts in a collection predominantly made by residents of Iowa, Illinois, Pennsylvania, and New York. Thirty-two have dates: two pre-1820, twenty-four from 1821 to 1900, and six from 1901 to 1940. Fifty are piecework, including more than thirteen crazy quilts; six are appliqué; two embroidered; two printed whole-cloth with quilting; one trapunto combined with other techniques. Quilts continuously on exhibit.
NB: Chintz quilt, dated 1731 from England, very fragile condition. North Carolina Lily with Grape Border, appliqué quilt with trapunto and verse in India ink, 1843, good condition. Civil War commemorative patchwork quilt with embroidered names, made by members of Women's Relief Corps of Cedar Falls in 1891.
Study Services: Write or call for appointment. Reading room, work tables, accession cards/files, and photocopy facilities.
Public Services: Tours of special quilt exhibits for groups of fifteen or more. Workshop and public programs in conjunction with quilt exhibits.

Alexandria, Louisiana, December 1940. A construction worker and one of his neighbor's children asleep under a block quilt. Photo by Marion Post Wolcott, negative number LC-USF34-56693-D. Courtesy of the Farm Security Administration Collection, Prints and Photographs Division, Library of Congress.

KANSAS

The nation's breadbasket is filled with examples of quilting from the nineteenth century to the present.

Dwight D. Eisenhower Library
Southeast Fourth Street
Abilene, Kansas 67410
(913) 263-4751

Daily, 9:00 A.M.–5:00 P.M.
The Library has twenty-eight quilts. Twenty are from Kansas. Approximately twenty date 1901 to 1940, six 1941 to present. Sixteen are pieced, four appliqué with embroidery, two trapunto, one candlewick, one is hand-knotted; the rest are not identified.
NB: Ida S. Eisenhower Collection. Quilts from former President Eisenhower's mother's handiwork. Handsewn Nine Block variation, velvet crazy quilts, Grandmother's Flower Garden.
Study Services: Write for appointment, state intent and topic. Reading room, work tables, accession cards/files, photocopy facilities, books/journals; prints may be ordered from Library's negatives.

Cherokee Strip Museum
South Summit Street
Arkansas City, Kansas
(316) 442-6750

Mailing Address:
R.D., Box 230
Arkansas City, KS 67005

Winter: Tuesday–Saturday, 1:00–5:00 P.M.; summer: 10:00 A.M.–5:00 P.M.
Collection of sixteen handsewn Midwest quilts, thirteen of which can be dated. Two are prior to 1820, five from 1821 to 1900, four from 1901 to 1940, one contemporary. In addition there is some unpublished documentation. Ten quilts are piecework, four appliqué, one Yo-Yo, one trapunto. Some have embroidery. Quilts are on exhibit at all times.

Study Services: Reading room, work tables, accession cards/files, and photocopy facilities.
Public Services: Tours and demonstrations.

Pioneer Museum
430 West 4th Street
Ashland, Kansas 67831
(316) 635-2227

Daily, 1:00–4:00 P.M.
Ten handsewn quilts by women of Clark County, Kansas form this collection. Four or five date from 1821–1900, four or five from 1901–1940, one is contemporary. Three are embroidered Friendship quilts, four piecework, one crazy quilt, one silk piecework, one combination of appliqué/piecework.
NB: Senior citizens centennial birthday quilt, 1984.
Study Services: General viewing of stored collection as one goes through Museum. Accession cards/files, prints made from negatives, and postcard.

Old Castle
Baker University
515 5th Street
Baldwin City, Kansas 66006
(913) 594-6809

Tuesday–Sunday, 2:00–4:00 P.M.
Of particular note in a collection of ten handsewn quilts: a Bicentennial quilt of Douglas County with fifteen picture blocks of buildings, sites, and symbols; Star pattern, c. 1900; New York Beauty owned by Baker University's first president, Dr. Werter Davis; patchwork squares made by three Quaker sisters at Shawnee Mission, Dove in the Window made by Ladies Sewing Circle of First Methodist Church; silk Tumbling Blocks, c. 1900; Star pattern, c. 1800; white-on-white made from hand-picked cotton by Heidi Ewing Rankin; a quiltmaker's diary or journal. All quilts are on exhibit.
Study Services: Accession cards/files.

Wyandotte County Museum

631 North 126th Street
Bonner Springs, Kansas 66012
(913) 721-1078

Tuesday–Saturday, 10:00 A.M.–5:00 P.M.
The Museum has twenty-four quilts, twenty-two made in Kansas or the Midwest. One is probably from Virginia; one was made in 1976 by kindergartners from Kansas City, Kansas. Eleven date between 1821 and 1900. Nine are pieced, seven appliqué, five crazy quilts.
Study Services: One week advance notice. Reading room, work tables, accession cards/files, photocopy facilities, books/journals; photographs may be taken as needed.
Public Services: Annual quilt exhibition in October which public may enter; also includes quilts from the collection.

Thomas County Historical Society and Museum

1525 West 4th Street
Colby, Kansas 67701
(913) 462-6972

Tuesday–Friday, 9:00 A.M.–5:00 P.M.; Sunday, 1:00–5:00 P.M.; closed holidays.
The Museum's forty-five to fifty quilts are primarily from a collection assembled by Joe and Nellie Kuska, formerly of Colby.
Study Services: For scholars, write or call staff to make appointment. Accession records and books from the Kulsa collection.

Boot Hill Museum, Inc.

Front Street
Dodge City, Kansas 67801
(316) 227-8188

Monday–Saturday, 9:00 A.M.–4:00 P.M.; Sunday, 1:00–4:00 P.M.
Four pieced and two appliqué quilts may be seen by appointment.

Lyon County Historical Museum

118 East 6th Street
Emporia, Kansas 66801
(316) 342-0933

Monday–Saturday, 9:00 A.M.–5:00 P.M.; Sunday, 2:00–5:00 P.M.
Twenty-six quilts from Kansas and Midwestern sources, especially Lyon County. Twenty-two are dated: ten, 1821–1900; seven, 1901–1940; and five, 1941–present. Documentation includes quilt patterns and instructions, Gilson Memorial Scrapbooks, clippings from area newspapers arranged by individuals. Twelve quilts are piecework, six crazy quilts, four embroidered, two appliqué, one is puffed, one white-on-white.
NB: Welsh wool quilt, 1870 Peony; 1890 printed crazy quilt.
Study Services: Contact registrar two weeks in advance. Reading room, work tables, and photocopy facilities.
Public Services: Girl Scouts quilting badge, junior high folk art program on quilting, quilt conservation program for adults, area quilters program.

Wilson County Historical Society Museum

420 North 7th Street
Fredonia, Kansas 66736
(316) 378-3965

Tuesday–Thursday, 1:30–4:30 P.M.; or by appointment.
The Museum owns nineteen quilts: ten hand-pieced and embroidered, eight pieced, one embroidered with names. Six were made by residents of Wilson County, six by various churches. Twelve are dated: seven, 1821–1900; six, 1901–1940; and two 1940 to the present. Quilts are on exhibit at all times.
NB: Handpieced Friendship quilt with names.
Study Services: Contact curator. Reading room, work tables, old magazines on quilts, books, and photocopy facilities.

Spencer Museum of Art

The University of Kansas
Lawrence, Kansas 66045
(913) 864-4710

Tuesday–Saturday, 8:30 A.M.–5:00 P.M.; Sunday, 12:00–5:00 P.M.
The collection includes 170 quilts primarily from the Midwest and hundreds of quilt patterns and instructions. Approximately sixty-percent are pieced, and forty-percent are appliqué, with occasional examples of trapunto, embroidery, and decorative quilting. Five pre-date 1820, approximately sixty-five are from 1821 to 1900, and 100 are from 1901 to 1940.
NB: Carrie Hall quilt block collection; Rose Kretsinger collection; c. eighteenth century British top.
Study Services: Make appointment with registrar. Reading room, work tables, accession cards/files, library in same building with books/journals, photocopy facilities; photo prints, slides, and some postcards; photo prints may be requested from museum's negatives.
Public Services: When related to an exhibition only: tours, films, workshops, and demonstrations.
Publications: Quilters Choice: Quilts from the Collection (1978).

Department of Clothing, Textiles, and Interior Design

Kansas State University
Justin Hall
Manhattan, Kansas 66506
(913) 532-6993

Weekdays, 8:00 A.M.–5:00 P.M.
There are thirteen quilts identified by technique: three crazy quilts, pieced and tied; two appliqué; eight pieced. Three or four date from the nineteenth century, the others after 1900.
Study Services: In-house faculty and students only. Work tables, accession cards/files, and microscope, special collection of costume and textile books in main library.

Public Services: Public tours cover entire collection.
Publications: Extension booklet on conservation.

Riley County Historical Museum

2309 Claflin Road
Manhattan, Kansas 66502
(913) 537-2210

Tuesday–Friday, 8:30 A.M.–5:00 P.M.; weekends, 2:00–5:00 P.M.
The Museum has a collection of fifty-three quilts, many from churches in Manhattan, and scrapbooks of patterns from 1920s and 1930s newspapers. Four are Name quilts, one embroidered with Kansas sunflowers and wildflowers, fourteen are crazy quilts, twenty-five piecework, five appliqué, one pieced with trapunto/stuffed areas, one machine quilted on plain background. Of those given dates twenty are from the nineteenth century, eight from after 1900, three are contemporary.
NB: One crazy quilt with a piece from Queen Victoria's bed hanging.
Study Services: Make appointment, must be staff assisted. Reading room, work tables, books/journals, and accession cards/files.

Kauffman Museum

Bethel College
North Newton, Kansas 67117
(316) 283-1612

Weekdays, 9:00 A.M.–5:00 P.M.
Ten handsewn Mennonite and central plains quilts are in this museum collection. There are seven patchwork, two crazy quilts, one Yo-Yo quilt. Two date from the nineteenth century, eight from post-1901. Mennonite families were the principal sources of the quilt collection.
NB: 1865 Crazy quilt, probably from Germany.
Study Services: Call or write for appointment. Reading room, work tables, accession cards/files, photocopy facilities, and at this time only two photo reproductions of quilts.

Kansas Museum of History

6425 Southwest 6th Street
Topeka, Kansas 66615
(913) 272-8681

Monday–Saturday, 9:00 A.M.–4:30 P.M.; Sunday,
1:00–4:30 P.M.; Offices: weekdays, 8:00 A.M.–
5:00 P.M.
Kansans owned or used the majority of these
110 quilts, many with interesting provenance
records. Approximately seventy-three are
pieced, twelve appliqué, two trapunto. Eighty-
five have been dated: four prior to 1821, fifty-
six from the nineteenth century, twenty-two
from after 1900, three are contemporary.
Study Services: Call or write curator of decorative arts for appointment. Reading room,
work tables, accession cards/files, books/jour-
nals, photocopy facilities, and microscope;
photo prints, prints can be ordered from negatives.

Kansas State Historical Society

Manuscript Department
120 West 10th Street
Topeka, Kansas 66612
(913) 296-3251

Hours not provided.
In cooperation with the Kansas Quilt Project
the society is conducting a search to learn
more about Kansas quilts, past and present.
The results will be organized as a permanent
collection.

Chisholm Trail Museum

502 North Washington
Wellington, Kansas 67152
(316) 326-3820

Hours not provided.
The Museum has twenty handsewn regional
quilts c. 1850 to 1940. Ten are pieced, five appliqué, three embroidered, two white-on-
white. Quilts are continuously exhibited.
Study Services: Scholars, access by request to
director. Work tables.

Joan O'Bryant Kansas Folklore Collection

Wichita Public Library
223 South Main Street
Wichita, Kansas 67202
(316) 262-0611

Monday–Thursday, 8:30 A.M.–9:00 P.M.; Friday
and Saturday, 8:30 A.M.–5:30 P.M.; Sunday,
1:00–5:00 P.M.
Ninety mounted quilt blocks covering the folk
history of Kansas, and 1,200 slide reproductions of quilts were collected by Joan
O'Bryant and her students from 1947 to 1964,
during the time she taught Folklore and English at Wichita State University. Quilt blocks
are always on exhibit.
Study Services: Call or write for appointment.
Work tables, accession cards/files, slide viewing equipment, 160 books/journals, photocopy
facilities, prints made from negatives, and
films.
Publication: Messineo, Leonard, Jr., editor. *The
Unburnished Mirror: An Interpretive Study of
Folklore and Content Description of the Joan
O'Bryant Collection* (1984).

Wichita-Sedgwick County Historical Society

204 South Main Street
Wichita, Kansas 67202
(316) 265-9314

Tuesday–Friday, 11:00 A.M.–4:00 P.M.; weekends, 1:00–5:00 P.M.
The Society has gathered seventy-nine mostly
handsewn and pieced quilts, several accompanied by documentation of Kansas origin.
Approximately half are appliquéd. Thirty have
decorative quilting. Three are embroidered,
one a Jewish quilt with embroidered scenes
from the Old Testament. One is a Yo-Yo quilt,
one printed whole-cloth. Fifty quilts date from
the nineteenth century, twenty-eight from
post-1900, one contemporary.
NB: Child's quilt from the late nineteenth century.
Study Services: For scholars, make appointment with curatorial staff member. Work table, accession cards/files, photocopy facilities,

and microscope; photo reproductions will be available in the future.
Public Services: Textile classes using the museum's quilt collection have been offered.

Cowley County Historical Museum
1011 Mansfield Street
Winfield, Kansas 67156

Weekends, 2:00–5:00 P.M.
Thirty handsewn quilts form a collection "typical of the region." Eighteen are piecework, six decorative or crazy quilts, five appliqué, one embroidered quilt. There are also six woven coverlets. Eight have dates ascribed to them: four from the nineteenth century, four from post-1900. Quilts continuously exhibited.
Study Services: Contact the president of the museum board for permission. Reading room, accession cards/files.
Public Services: Quilts are viewed in conjunction with tours of the museum.

Alvin, Wisconsin, May 1937. A quilting party. Photo by Russell Lee, negative number LC-USF34-10885-D. Courtesy of the Farm Security Administration Collection, Prints and Photographs Division, Library of Congress.

KENTUCKY

Since frontier days, the state has been at the heart of the American quilting tradition.

Weatherford-Hammond Mountain Collection and Southern Appalachian Archives
Special Collections
Hutchins Library
Berea College
Berea, Kentucky 40404
(606) 986-9341, extension 289 or 290

Weekdays, 9:00 A.M.–5:00 P.M. and during the academic year, September to May: Wednesday nights, 6:30–10:00 P.M.
A number of quilt related photographs in bound collections document the Appalachian region. In the official diaries of Hindman Settlement School founders Katherine Pettit and May Stone, quilts and quilting is mentioned. Settlement Institutions of Appalachia/Berea College Researcher Resources Project includes photographs and reel-to-reel tapes on quilts and quiltmaking in the following collections: Pine Mountain Settlement School, Red Bird Mission, John C. Campbell Folk School, Henderson Settlement School.
Study Services: During hours. Reading room, work tables, accession cards/files, books/journals, and photocopy facilities; research prints made from negatives upon request.

The Kentucky Library and Museum, Manuscript and Folklore, Folklife Archives Section
Western Kentucky University
Bowling Green, Kentucky 42101
(502) 745-2592

Library/Manuscript/Folklore sections: weekdays, 8:00 A.M.–4:30 P.M.; Saturday, 9:00 A.M.–4:30 P.M. Museum: Tuesday–Saturday, 9:30 A.M.–4:00 P.M.; Sunday, 1:00–4:30 P.M.

A collection of seventy-five quilts made or used in Kentucky, especially the western portion of the state or with western Kentucky associations, and fifty quilt patterns and instructions. The Folklife Archives has approximately 950 photo reproductions, about 260 slides of quilts, sixty reel-to-reel tapes; forty cassette tapes; manuscript section: sixty-five research papers; correspondence, research materials, galley proofs of *Kentucky Quilts and Their Makers,* by Mary W. Clarke. Thirty-six are pieced quilts, sixteen crazy quilts, twelve a combination of pieced and appliqué or pieced and stuffed, eight appliqué, three stuffed whole-cloth quilts. It is known that three were made prior to 1820, fifty-five are from the nineteenth century, six from post-1900, four contemporary.

NB: Henry Clay portrait quilt, c. 1860, made from polished cotton pieces, half embroidered with pastoral scenes surrounding a central needlework portrait. Calvery quilt, c. 1850, Tumbling Blocks pattern arranged to form a cross. Chester Dare quilt, c. 1882, crazy quilt with a central appliqué of the racehorse Chester Dare. Logan County, Kentucky quilt, c. 1810, whole-cloth, white stuffed quilt, from the Washington family who settled very early in Logan County and who are relatives of George Washington. In the Jackson Collection of old photos there is a tintype thought to be from Logan County, Kentucky, of a family seated in front of a quilt stretched out as a background.

Study Services: Contact registrar of the Kentucky Museum. Reading room, work tables, accession cards/files, folklife archives, books/journals, library reading room about 60 books and sixty issues of two quilt journals, photocopy facilities, and microscope; photo prints, slides, postcard.

Public Services: Annual quilt exhibition, tours of quilt exhibitions for special interest groups and scholars; periodic lectures and workshops. The folklore archives is compiling an index to the information on quilts as a computerized cross-reference tool.

Publications: Holstein, Jonathan and John Finley. *Kentucky Quilts, 1800–1900* (1982). Clarke, Mary Washington. *Kentucky Quilts and Their Makers* (1976).

Kentucky Historical Society
Corner of Lewis and Broadway
Frankfort, Kentucky
(502) 564-3016

Mailing Address:
P.O. Box H
Frankfort, KY 40602

Monday–Saturday, 9:00 A.M.–4:00 P.M.; Sunday, 1:00–4:00 P.M.
A collection of seventy-two Kentucky quilts, some Appalachian quilts and letters regarding quilts and quiltmaking. Forty are dated: two prior to 1820, thirty-two 1821 to 1900, and six post-1900. Forty-one are pieced, twenty appliqué, eighteen embroidered, nine have decorative quilting, five trapunto, two whole-cloth. The Graveyard Quilt alternates with others on exhibit.

NB: Graveyard Quilt; Orange Tree Quilt.
Study Services: For scholars, write to collections manager for appointment. Work tables, accession cards/files, books/journals, and photocopy facilities; photo prints, slides, prints may be requested from negatives, postcard of Graveyard Quilt.

Publications: Christopherson, Katy. *The Political and Campaign Quilt* (1984).

Homeplace-1850
Tennessee Valley Authority/Land Between the Lakes
Golden Pond, Kentucky 42231
(502) 924-5602

Monday–Wednesday, 9:00 A.M.–5:00 P.M.
Twelve quilts from the region are used as part of the living history program. The staff has pieced and quilted three new quilt tops in the past two years. Quilts continuously on exhibition.

Study Services: Telephone or write for appointment. Reading room, books/journals.

Public Services: Demonstrations of quiltmaking techniques and methods are a regular part of activities; there is a pattern exchange program.

Old Fort Harrod State Park
South College Street
Harrodsburg, Kentucky
(606) 734-3314

Mailing Address:
P.O. Box 156
Harrodsburg, KY 40330

Daily, 8:30 A.M.–5:00 P.M.; Museum: daily, 9:00 A.M.–5:30 P.M.
Six handmade Kentucky quilts.

The Filson Club
1310 South 3rd Street
Louisville, Kentucky 40208
(502) 582-3727

Weekdays, 9:00 A.M.–5:00 P.M.
Approximately fifty quilts made in Kentucky from the nineteenth century to pre-World War I are complemented by family letters from time of donation.
NB: Silk wedding quilt; documented Louisville, Kentucky quilts.
Study Services: Written request, explaining purpose explicitly. Work tables, accession cards/files, and books/journals.
Public Services: Specific programs on textiles, especially care and conservation for the private individual.

Appalachian Collection
Camden-Carroll Library
Morehead State University
Morehead, Kentucky 40351
(606) 783-2829

Monday–Thursday, 8:00 A.M.–10:00 P.M.; Friday, 8:00 A.M.–6:00 P.M.; Saturday, 9:00 A.M.–4:30 P.M.; Sunday, 2:00–10:00 P.M.
The Collection includes 1,030 quilt patterns, 135 quilt blocks, one taped oral history and slides of a quiltmaker.
Study Services: Make request to librarian.

Reading room, work tables, accession cards/files, quilt patterns, drawings, some quilt blocks, books/journals, and photocopy facilities.
Publications: Christopherson, Katy. "Kentucky's Own Carrie Hall, Linda Lowe." *Back Home in Kentucky* (1982).
Public Services: Exhibits to coincide with quilting symposium meetings on campus.

Owensboro Area Museum
2829 South Griffith Avenue
Owensboro, Kentucky 42301
(502) 683-0296

Weekdays, 8:00 A.M.–4:00 P.M.; weekends, 1:00–4:00 P.M.
A collection of twenty-five quilts, fourteen from the nineteenth century, and unpublished documentation on quilts and quilting.
NB: A quilt made from ball dresses/gowns which had been discarded by members of the Wickliffe and Beckham families. The quilt was made at Wickland in Bardstown, Kentucky not long after the Civil War ended. A written description of the history of the quilt was provided by a great-granddaughter of the maker.
Study Services: By appointment only. Reading room, work tables, accession cards/files, books, and microscope; in the process of photographing collection.

Greensboro, Greene County, Georgia. October 1941. Making a quilt from surplus commodity cotton. Photo by Jack Delano, negative number LC-USF34-21232-M3. Courtesy of the Farm Security Administration Collection, Prints and Photographs Division, Library of Congress.

LOUISIANA

Quilts of local provenance and regional influence are the core of most collections.

Louisiana Folklife Program
666 North Foster Drive
Baton Rouge, Louisiana
(504) 925-3930

Mailing Address:
P.O. Box 44247
Baton Rouge, LA 70804

Weekdays, 8:00 A.M.–4:30 P.M.
A collection of eight contemporary handsewn quilts made by Louisiana folk groups, six taped oral histories, and survey forms on Louisiana quiltmakers. Two Afro-American quilts, five anglo-made, one Cajun/Isleno. Seven are piecework quilts, one string/piecework. Quilts are on continuous display.
Study Services: For scholars, make appointment. Work tables, accession cards/files; photo reproductions of quilts upon request and approval.
Public Services: An ongoing survey of folklife in the state.

Rural Life Museum
Louisiana State University
Essen Lane at Interstate 10 on the
Burden Research Plantation
Baton Rouge, Louisiana
(504) 766-8241

Mailing Address:
6200 Burden Lane
Baton Rouge, LA 70808

Weekdays, 8:30 A.M.–4:00 P.M.
Ten quilts are on continuous exhibition.
Study Services: Reading room, accession cards/files, books/journals, and photocopy facilities; photo prints, slides, and prints made from negatives.

Oakland Plantation
Highway 119
Bermuda, Louisiana
(318) 352-5104

Mailing Address:
Route 2, Box 101
Natchez, LA 71457

By appointment.
Seven quilts.

The Shadows-on-the-Teche
117 East Main Street
New Iberia, Louisiana
(318) 369-6446

Mailing Address:
P.O. Box 254
New Iberia, LA 70561-0254

Weekdays, 9:00 A.M.–5:00 P.M.
Seven quilts may be seen by scholars by appointment.

Gallier House Museum
1118–1132 Royal Street
New Orleans, Louisiana 70116
(504) 523-6722

Monday–Saturday, 8:30 A.M.–5:00 P.M.
Most of the nine quilts in the collection are from the South. One may be slave-made. May be seen by appointment.

The Historic New Orleans Collection
533 Royal Street
New Orleans, Louisiana 70068
(504) 523-4662

Tuesday–Saturday, 10:00 A.M.–4:30 P.M.
Primarily works on paper: prints, photographs, manuscripts, books, sheet music, and emphemera, the collection includes fourteen quilt patterns c. 1935; approximately twelve photographs of quilts, quiltmakers; illustrations, c. 1920 to 1940.
Study Services: Apply at the museum for same-day use. Reading room, work tables, accession cards/files, books/journals, folklife/art subject files, fluorescent and other light scopes, pho-

tocopy facilities, and microscope-loupes; photo prints, slides, and prints made from negatives.

The Louisiana State Museum
751 rue Chartres (The Presbytère)
New Orleans, Louisiana
(504) 568-6968

Mailing Address:
P.O. Box 2458
New Orleans, LA 70176-2458

Tuesday–Sunday, 10:00 A.M.–6:00 P.M. Twelve quilts: eight have Louisiana provenance; three southern Afro-American; one from Danville, Kentucky and is associated with Zachary Taylor. Two are embroidered Toile de Jouy, two are parlor crazy quilts, one white-on-white. Two date prior to 1820, eight from the remainder of the nineteenth century, two post-1900. The Louisiana Historical Society was the principal source of the collection. *NB:* Presentation quilt for Cotton Centennial Exposition, New Orleans, 1884–1885; Presentation quilt owned by President Zachary Taylor, dated 1848.
Study Services: Make appointment with the curator of textiles. Reading room, work tables, accession cards/files, 50,000 volume reference library/archives, books/journals, and photocopy facilities; photo prints, slides; prints may be requested from negatives.
Public Services: Lectures, tours.

MAINE

Downeasterners have a long quilting tradition. Collections are varied, but concentrate in New England and northeastern quilts dating c. 1780 to the present.

Maine State Museum
State House Complex
Augusta, Maine
(207) 289-2301

Mailing Address:
State House Station 83
Augusta, ME 04333

Weekdays, 9:00 A.M.–5:00 P.M.; Saturday, 10:00 A.M.–4:00 P.M.; Sunday, 1:00–4:00 P.M. Approximately twenty-eight quilts form a collection that is Maine-made or related. Three or four quilts date prior to 1820, twenty others date from the nineteenth century, three post-1900, two contemporary. Eighteen are piecework/patchwork, four appliqué, four have decorative quilting (one white-on-white, three embroidered), one Yo-Yo or Bon-Bon quilt, one quilted whole-cloth.
Study Services: Contact Museum for permission, dependent upon staff availability. Reading room, work tables, accession cards/files, books/journals, and photocopy facilities; photo prints, prints may be ordered from Museum negatives.

Bethel Historical Society, Inc.

15 Broad Street
Bethel, Maine
(207) 824-2908

Mailing Address:
P.O. Box 12
Bethel, ME 04217

Weekdays, 8:00 A.M.–4:00 P.M.
A collection of eighteen handsewn piecework quilts from New England. Fifteen date from the nineteenth century, three are contemporary. The Society also holds unpublished research papers, and other research material. Quilts are exhibited continuously.
NB: A concentration of Friendship quilts of special note.
Study Services: Request permission from the director. Reading room, accession cards/files, and photocopy facilities; slides, prints may be ordered from negatives.
Public Services: Tours and demonstrations.

Pejepscot Historical Society

159 Maine Street
Brunswick, Maine 04011
(207) 729-6606

Three museums are under Society jurisdiction. Pejepscop Museum: weekdays, 1:00–4:30 P.M.; Wednesday, until 8:00 P.M. Joshua L. Chamberlain Civil War Museum: June 23–October 10: weekdays, 12:00–4:00 P.M.; Wednesday, until 8:00 P.M. Skolfield-Whitter House: by appointment only.
Nineteen quilts, seventeen made in the local area, include a Methodist Autograph Presentation quilt, and a Congregational Autograph Presentation quilt. Fourteen are piecework, four crazy quilts, one appliqué crazy quilt. Six can be dated in the nineteenth century, two are contemporary. Quilts are continuously on exhibition.
NB: Coffin cover.
Study Services: By appointment. Work table, accession cards/files, books/journals, and photocopy facilities.

Islesboro Historical Society

Islesboro, Maine
(207) 734-8800

Mailing Address:
Mrs. James E. Willis
CR 285
Islesboro, ME 04848

Summer: by appointment.
Society has a collection of eleven regional quilts, a National Educational Television film of their quilting group, and histories of sixty-five local quilts. Of the handsewn pieced and appliqué quilts in the collection four are nineteenth century, six date post-1900, and one is contemporary.
Study Services: Call or write for appointment. Reading room, work tables, accession cards/files, and book/journals. Photo prints made from negatives upon request.
Public Services: Weekly quilt lessons; annual quilt exhibition with demonstrations.

The Brick Store Museum

117 Main Street
Kennebunk, Maine
(207) 985-4802

Mailing Address:
P.O. Box 177
Kennebunk, ME 04043

Tuesday–Saturday, 10:00 A.M.–4:30 P.M.
A collection of forty quilts: thirty-seven from New England, one from Belgium, one from India. Thirty-five are piecework, two printed whole-cloth with quilting, one appliqué, one piecework and appliqué, one stuffed. One is dated prior to 1820, thirty-seven others from the nineteenth century, one is post 1900, one contemporary.
Study Services: For scholars, make appointment. Reading room, work tables, accession cards/files, books/journals, photocopy facilities; postcard.
Public Services: Workshops in conjunction with quilt exhibits.

Kennebunkport Historical Society

North Street
Kennebunkport, Maine 04046
(207) 967-2751

June 15–October 15: hours not provided.
Twelve predominantly regional quilts from local families supplemented with information
furnished by the donors. Four have patchwork
designs, two embroidered crazy quilts of silk
and velvet, one is 1844 white cotton candlewick, one silk piecework Pinwheel, one handloomed linsey-woolsey, one white-on-white.
NB: Hand embroidery on several quilts.
Study Services: For scholars by appointment.
Work tables, accession cards/files, and photocopy facilities.
Public Services: Quilt exhibitions.

Phillips Historical Society

Pleasant Street
Phillips, Maine 04966

August: Friday and Saturday or by appointment.
Six locally made quilts.

Shaker Museum

Sabbathday Lake
Poland Spring, Maine 04274
(207) 926-4597

Weekdays, 8:30 A.M.–4:30 P.M.
Handsewn regional quilts made by Shakers c.
1820.

Maine Historical Society

485 Congress Street
Portland, Maine 04101
(207) 774-1822

Tuesday, Wednesday, and Friday, 9:00 A.M.–
5:00 P.M.; Thursday, 9:00 A.M.–7:00 P.M.; second Saturday monthly, 9:00 A.M.–5:00 P.M.
The Society's collection of ten to twenty New
England quilts primarily from the late nineteenth century is currently being cataloged.
Study Services: Make arrangements with curator. Reading room, library and manuscript collections.

William A. Farnsworth Library and Art Museum

19 Elm Street
Rockland, Maine 04841
(207) 596-6457

Mailing Address:
P.O. Box 466
Rockland, ME 04841

Tuesday–Saturday, 10:00 A.M.–5:00 P.M.; Sunday, 12:00–5:00 P.M.; summer only: Monday,
10:00 A.M.–5:00 P.M.
Eight regional quilts may be seen by appointment.

York Institute Museum

371 Main Street
Saco, Maine 04072
(207) 282-3031

May 1–October 31: Thurday, 1:00–8:00 P.M.;
summer: Tuesday, Wednesday, and Friday,
1:00–4:00 P.M.; Saturday, 9:00 A.M.– 3:00 P.M.;
winter hours vary.
The Museum has fourteen local quilts: seven
patchwork, six crazy quilts, one white-on-
white.
NB: White-on-white with ruffle, c. 1780.
Study Services: Make appointment with curator, one week in advance. Reading room, work
tables, accession cards/files, books/journals,
microscope; some photographs, slides.
Public Services: Participant in statewide decorative arts survey for objects dating to state-
hood/federal period. Quilts from the
collection are on exhibit most of the time.
Quilt exhibits, tours, and workshops have
been offered.

Penobscot Marine Museum

Church Street
Searsport, Maine 04974
(207) 548-2529

Seven exhibit buildings, May 31–October 15:
Monday–Saturday, 9:00 A.M.–5:00 P.M.; library
and administrative buildings, year round:
weekdays, 9:00 A.M.–5:00 P.M.
Approximately ten to twelve quilts from sea-

faring families. Quilts are on exhibit at all times.

Study Services: Make inquiry at the curatorial office. Steven Phillips Memorial Library, books/journals, some photo prints; photo prints may be requested from negatives.

Public Services: The Museum has quilts on exhibit in some of the seafaring family homes, and gallery.

Lincoln County Cultural and Historical Association

Federal Street
Wiscasset, Maine
(207) 882-6817

Mailing Address:
P.O. Box 61
Wiscasset, ME 04578

September–November, and April–June: Tuesday–Thursday, 9:00 A.M.–3:30 P.M. July–August: Tuesday–Sunday, hours not provided. This collection includes twenty or more hand-sewn, nineteenth century quilts from Maine, many homespun coverlets, three or four crazy quilts, one signature Presentation quilt, one trapunto quilt given by residents of Lincoln County, Maine. Quilts are on exhibit at all times.

Study Services: Reading room, and accession cards/files.

Old York Historical Society

140 Lindsay Road
York, Maine
(207) 363-4974

Mailing Address:
P.O. Box 312
York, ME 03909

Weekdays, 9:00 A.M.–5:00 P.M.
A collection of seventy regional quilts: forty-five from Maine, twenty-five from New England. Twenty-five date prior to 1820, thirty-five are from the remainder of the nineteenth century, ten post-1900. Forty pieced quilts include Log Cabin and crazy quilts, fifteen are linsey-woolsey quilted coverlets, ten appliqué,

three white-on-white, two printed whole-cloth quilts.

NB: Quilts prior to 1820; late eighteenth century linsey-woolsey quilts.

Study Services: Call for appointment with curator. Reading room, work tables, accession cards/files, photocopy facilities; prints, slides made upon request.

Public Services: Quilting and related textile arts demonstrations; volunteer sewing circle makes reproduction quilts; special tours of textile collections.

The back of eight-pointed star silk quilt top, c. 1864, from Jo Davies County, Illinois, made in the English piecing style; templates made of newspapers, letters, or copy exercises still attached; various dates found on templates include 1859, 1863, and 1864. Maker was pioneer of Jo Davies County; husband was lieutenant in Black Hawk War. Courtesy of the Illinois State Museum, Springfield.

MARYLAND

Probably the most famous Maryland quilts are the exceptional Baltimore Albums.

Baltimore City Life Museums
Carroll Mansion Site
800 East Lombard Street
Baltimore, Maryland 21202
(301) 396-3523

Office: weekdays, hours not provided.
Baltimore City Life Museums own at least five quilts which are on continuous exhibit at the following sites: Peale Museum, Carroll Mansion, and 1840 House.

Peale Museum
225 Holliday Street
Baltimore, Maryland

Monday–Saturday, 10:00 A.M.–5:00 P.M.; Sunday, 12:00–5:00 P.M.

1840 House
50 South Albemarle Street
Baltimore, Maryland

Weekdays, by appointment for school groups; open to the public weekends, 10:00 A.M.–4:00 P.M.

The Baltimore Museum of Art
The Jean and Allan Berman Textile Gallery
Art Museum Drive
Baltimore, Maryland 21218
(301) 396-6266

Tuesday–Friday, 10:00 A.M.–4:00 P.M.; Thursday, 6:00–10:00 P.M.; weekends, 11:00 A.M.–6:00 P.M.; closed Monday, and major holidays.
The Museum has 234 quilts and the unpublished materials of early researcher Dr. William Dunton. Twenty-two quilts are from Baltimore, Maryland; thirteen are Amish; the rest have been collected from various north-eastern and midwestern states. Approximately twenty date prior to 1820, 196 from the nineteenth century, seventeen post-1900, one contemporary. Pieced quilts number about 134, fifty-eight appliqué, twenty-four crazy quilts, thirteen printed whole-cloth quilts, two trapunto or stuffed only, one stencilled, one crewelwork.
NB: Baltimore Album quilts, resists, and children's quilts.
Study Services: For scholars by appointment with curator. Reading room, accession cards/files in registrar's office, books/journals in library, photocopy facilities; photo prints, slides, transparencies for rent, prints may be ordered from negatives.
Public Services: Quilts are rotated with other textiles in the exhibition gallery. When quilts are on exhibit, tours and lectures are offered.
Publications: Katzenberg, Dena S. "The Great American Coverup: Counterpanes of the Eighteenth and Nineteenth Centuries." *Record* (1971). *Blue Traditions: Indigo Dyed Textiles and Related Cobalt Glazed Ceramics from the 17th Through 19th Century* (1973). *Less is More: 19th and Early 20th Century American Children's Quilts from the Collection of Linda and Irwin Berman* (1979). Katzenberg, Dena S. *Baltimore Album Quilts* (1981).

Lovely Lane Museum of the Baltimore Conference
United Methodist Historical Society
2200 St. Paul Street
Baltimore, Maryland 21218
(301) 889-4458

Weekdays, 10:00 A.M.–4:00 P.M.
The society has nine quilts and a taped oral history on quilts/quiltmaking. Eight quilts were made by or for Methodists in Maryland. Six are Album quilts, one crazy quilt, one embroidered quilt top, one trapunto. One dates prior to 1820, six nineteenth century, one post-1900, and one contemporary.
NB: Trapunto quilt made by Coggins in England, authenticated as seventeenth century, said to have come on the Mayflower.

Study Services: For scholars, make request, receive approval before visit. Reading room, work tables, and books/journals.
Public Services: Tours arranged for quilt groups.

The Maryland Historical Society
Enoch Pratt House
201 West Monument Street
Baltimore, Maryland 21201
(301) 685-3750

Tuesday–Friday, 11:00 A.M.–4:30 P.M.; Saturday, 9:00 A.M.– 4:30 P.M.; October–April: Sunday, 1:00–5:00 P.M..
The collection includes approximately 125 quilts, most with a Maryland provenance, catalog information and photographs of the quilts in the collection.
NB: Pheasants and Feather quilt; The Maryland Governor's quilt; The Lafayette quilt.
Study Services: For scholars, make appointment. The society has a library, charges a small fee for usage; reading room, accession cards/files, books/journals, and photocopy facilities; photo prints, slides, prints may be ordered from negatives.
Public Services: Quiltmaking demonstration, quilt workshops have been offered.

Star-Spangled Banner Flag House/1812 Museum
844 East Pratt Street
Baltimore, Maryland 21202
(301) 837-1793

Monday–Saturday, 10:00 A.M.–4:00 P.M.; Sunday, 1:00–4:00 P.M.
A collection of fifteen quilts varying in style and workmanship and made prior to 1840, ten quilt patterns, woven coverlets and histories. One embroidered quilt. Three quilts are on continuous exhibit and rotated by season.
Study Services: For scholars by prior appointment. Work tables, accession cards/files, books/journals, and photocopy facilities.
Public Services: Occasional exhibitions.

Baltimore County Historical Society
9811 Van Buren Lane
Cockeysville, Maryland
(301) 666-1876

Mailing Address:
P.O. Box 81
Cockeysville, MD 21030

Saturday, 10:00 A.M.–3:00 P.M.
Twenty-eight handsewn Maryland quilts form a collection that is piecework and appliqué. One dates prior to 1820, twenty-five others are from the nineteenth century, two are contemporary.
Public Services: The stored collections are shown by appointment.

History House Museum of the Alleghany County Historical Society
218 Washington Street
Cumberland, Maryland 21502
(301) 777-8678

May–October: Tuesday–Sunday, 1:30–4:00 P.M.
The Museum has fourteen quilts. Of note are four pieced, three embroidered, one trapunto, one appliqué, one Amish. Quilts are exhibited continuously.
Study Services: By appointment. Reading room, work tables, and accession cards/files.
Public Services: Tours.

Montgomery County Historical Society
103 West Montgomery Avenue
Rockville, Maryland 20850
(301) 762-1492

Tuesday–Saturday, 12:00–4:00 P.M.; first Sunday, 2:00–5:00 P.M.
Twenty piecework, appliqué, and embroidered quilts are currently being documented. One Quaker quilt, others are from Montgomery County, Maryland. Quilts are exhibited at all times.
NB: Two quilts of special regional significance.
Study Services: Scholars, submit written inquiry. Supervised access to records, books/journals, and photocopy facility.

Public Services: Conservation materials are for sale in museum shop: acid free boxes and tissue.
Publications: Heirloom Quilting Designs From The Woodbourne Quilt (1985).

Carroll County Farm Museum
500 South Center Street
Westminster, Maryland 21157
(301) 848-7775

April 1–October 31: scheduled group tours available from 10:00 A.M.–4:00 P.M. May 1–October 31: weekends, 12:00–5:00 P.M. July and August: Tuesday–Sunday, 10:00 A.M.–4:00 P.M.
Twenty to twenty-five pieced and handsewn local Maryland quilts from the nineteenth to the twentieth centuries are supplemented by unpublished documentation on quilts/quilt-making. The quilts are presently being reinventoried. Quilts are on continuous exhibition.
Study Services: By appointment. Reading room, work tables, and accession cards/files.

MASSACHUSETTS

Early colonial period quilts made in Massachusetts and New England are in abundance at museums across the state.

Dyer Memorial Library
Centre Avenue
Abington, Massachusetts
(617) 878-8480

Mailing Address:
P.O. Box 2245
Abington, MA 02351

Monday, Tuesday, Thursday, Friday, 1:00–5:00 P.M.; and by appointment.
Seven handsewn quilts.

Arlington Historical Society
7 Jason Street
Arlington, Massachusetts 02174
(617) 648-4300

April–November: Tuesday–Saturday, 2:00–5:00 P.M.; other times by appointment.
The Society has fifteen New England piecework and trapunto quilts given by local families. Of those ascribed dates two are prior to 1820, nine from the duration of the nineteenth century, and one post-1900.
NB: Welfare quilt, 1932, donor's signatures embroidered on the quilt.

Beverly Historical Society and Museum
117 Cabot Street
Beverly, Massachusetts 01915
(617) 922-1186

Wednesday–Saturday, 10:00 A.M.–4:00 P.M.; Sunday, 1:00–4:00 P.M.
Eighteen New England quilts with local histories. Quilts are exhibited in room settings.
Study Services: By written request. Reading room, work tables, accession cards/files, and photocopy facilities.

Bank of Boston

100 Federal Street
Boston, Massachusetts 02110
(617) 434-2200, general information
(617) 654-6314, art curator

Office hours: weekdays, 8:00 A.M.–5:30 P.M.
The Bank owns approximately twenty quilts, both contemporary and antique. Some commissioned and some found in Vermont antique shops. Two cradle quilts, one Log Cabin.
NB: One-hundred year old baby quilt.
Study Services: Collection is available for viewing by special prior arrangements; slides and photographs may be arranged.

Museum of Fine Arts, Boston

Department of Textiles
465 Huntington Avenue
Boston, Massachusetts 02115
(617) 267-9300

Weekdays, 9:00 A.M.–5:00 P.M.
The Museum's holdings include forty-eight handsewn quilts: thirty-two date before 1820, sixteen from the nineteenth century. Six are French, sixteen English, twenty-six are American (one is from Pennsylvania, one from Virginia, one from Georgia, one from Kentucky, seven from New England). Twenty-two have decorative quilting, twelve embroidered, eight patchwork, six appliqué. The principal source of the collection, Elizabeth Day McCormick.
NB: Appliqué quilt made by Harriet Powers, 1895–98; c. 1850–1900 appliqué and embroidered with scenes of Lynn, Massachusetts by Celestine Bacheller. The collection has a concentration in American eighteenth century quilts with decorative quilting on solid color grounds.
Study Services: Make appointment. Reading room, work tables, accession cards/files, photocopy facilities, and books/journals; photo prints, slides, and prints made from negatives, slide sets of twenty or forty slides, entitled "Harriet Powers: Afro-American Quilt 1895–1898" are available for purchase.
Publications: A Pattern Book (n.d.). Based on the appliqué quilt by Mrs. Harriet Powers.

Fairbanks Family in America, Inc.

511 East Street
Dedham, Massachusetts 02026
(617) 326-1170

Tuesday–Sunday, 9:00 A.M.–12:00 P.M., and 1:00–5:00 P.M. Closed during winter months. Between twenty and thirty quilts, woven bedspreads, and embroidered blankets have been collected from members of the Fairbanks family. Many of them were made by members of the family, and are documented. The majority date from the nineteenth century. The Fairbanks Homestead is a historic house and the contents have been donated by the descendants of Jonathan Fairbanks who built the house in 1636. Seven quilts are exhibited on beds in the old house.
Study Services: Make written request for appointment, allowing adequate time to make arrangements.

Historic Deerfield, Inc.

Deerfield, Massachusetts
(413) 774-5581

Mailing Address:
P.O. Box 32K
Deerfield, MA 01342

Daily, 9:30 A.M.–4:30 P.M.; Sunday, 11:00 A.M.–4:30 P.M.; closed, Christmas and New Year's. The collection has approximately 100 quilts from England and New England, primarily of the seventeenth and eighteenth century, as well as ten nineteenth century quilts. Techniques represented: piecework, appliqué, embroidered, stuffed or corded quilting, decorative quilting, white-on-white, printed whole-cloth. In addition there are unpublished research papers and family documentation on quilts available. Quilts are continuously exhibited.
NB: Stencilled, resist, and several whole-cloth calamanco quilts, stuffed work. A large number of early colonial quilts from the region.
Study Services: Make appointment with a member of the curatorial department. Reading room, accession cards/files, books/journals,

and photocopy facilities; slides, photo prints may be ordered from negatives.
Public Services: Exhibitions and workshops.

Memorial Hall Museum

Pocumtuck Valley Memorial Association
Memorial Street
Deerfield, Massachusetts 01342
(413) 774-7476

May 1–October 31: weekdays, 10:00 A.M.–4:30 P.M.; weekends, 12:30–4:30 P.M.
The museum has forty or more quilts from Massachusetts, primarily Franklin County. Four quilts predate 1820, thirty to thirty-five date later in the nineteenth century, two post-1900. Approximately thirty-five are piecework, three appliqué, one white-on-white, one printed whole-cloth, one whole-cloth, one stencilled. Quilts are on exhibit at all times.
Study Services: Make appointment with curator. Reading room, accession cards/files, library with books/journals, and photocopy facilities; photo prints, slides, photo prints may be ordered from negatives.
Public Services: Workshops and classes.

Fall River Historical Society

451 Rock Street
Fall River, Massachusetts 02720
(617) 679-1071

Tuesday–Friday, 9:00 A.M.–4:30 P.M.; closed, January and February.
There are twelve regional quilts primarily made in the nineteenth century: ten piecework, one trapunto, one embroidered. Some of the patterns represented include: Postage Stamp, Log Cabin, Hexagon, and Basket. Quilts are on continuous exhibition.
NB: Quilt backed with local flour bags.
Study Services: Work tables and accession cards/files.

Fitchburg Historical Society

50 Grove Street
Fitchburg, Massachusetts 01420
(617) 345-1157

Hours not provided.
Ten quilts, may be seen by appointment made two weeks in advance.

Cape Ann Historical Association

27 Pleasant Street
Gloucester, Massachusetts 01930
(617) 283-0455

Tuesday–Saturday, 10:00 A.M.–5:00 P.M.; Closed, February.
The Association has forty-four quilts the majority local and some from other parts of the region. Four predate 1820, thirty-four date from the nineteenth century, six date after 1900. Thirty-eight are piecework, three have decorative quilting, two are printed whole-cloth with quilting, one appliqué.
NB: Pieced Pyramid quilt made by Mrs. Elizabeth Plumer while on a voyage to China with her husband Captain David Plumer, c. 1765-1780.
Study Services: Contact curator for appointment. Reading room, work tables, accession cards/files, and photocopy facilities; photographs can be requested from Association negatives.

Porter-Phelps-Huntington Foundation, Inc.

130 River Drive
Hadley, Massachusetts 01035
(413) 584-4699

Saturday–Wednesday, 1:00–4:30 P.M.
Five piecework and one Yo-Yo quilt made by members of the family may be seen by appointment.

Lexington Historical Society

Lexington, Massachusetts
(617) 861-0928

Mailing Address:
P.O. Box 514
Lexington, MA 02173

April 19–October 31: Monday–Saturday, 10:00 A.M.–5:00 P.M.; Sunday, 1:00–5:00 P.M.
The Society has collected twenty-seven New England quilts, probably all from Lexington, Massachusetts. Two predate 1820, four can be assigned dates between 1821 and 1900. About twenty-two are patchwork, two have decorative quilting, one is appliqué.
NB: Friendship/Bridal quilt, Sampler quilt.
Study Services: For scholars, phone for appointment. Work table, and limited accession cards/files.

Museum of Our National Heritage

33 Marrett Road
Lexington, Massachusetts
(617) 861-6559

Mailing Address:
P.O. Box 519
Lexington, MA 02173

Monday–Saturday, 10:00 A.M.–5:00 P.M.; Sunday, 12:00–5:00 P.M.
Of the twenty-two quilts in this collection, seven were made by Fraternal groups, ten are New England region quilts, one each is from New York, Maryland, Ohio, Illinois, Pennsylvania. Twenty-one are piecework, one appliqué, and one has embroidery. One quilt predates 1820, sixteen date from the nineteenth century, five date later than 1900.
NB: Quilts displaying fraternal symbols.
Study Services: Contact registrar or curator. Reading room, work tables, accession cards/files, books/journals, and photocopy facilities; photo prints, slides, photo prints may be requested from negatives.
Public Services: Tours of quilt exhibitions.

New England Quilt Museum

256 Market Street
Lowell, Massachusetts 01852
(617) 452-4207

Tuesday–Saturday, 10:00 A.M.–4:00 P.M.; Sunday, 12:00–5:00 P.M.
Museum has ten antique and contemporary quilts, a library of 400 quilt reference books, and patterns. Quilts may be loaned to other institutions. Programs such as lectures, workshops, and classes are planned.

Isaac Royall House

15 George Street
Medford, Massachusetts 02155
(617) 396-9032

Tuesday–Thursday, and weekends, 2:00–5:00 P.M.
This collection has approximately twenty handsewn piecework, appliqué, and white-on-white quilts from New England, all made prior to 1820. In addition, two or three personal narratives by quiltmakers, either diaries or journals.
NB: Whole-cloth quilt.
Study Services: By appointment. Limited accession cards/files.
Public Services: Exhibitions.

Nantucket Historical Association

2 Union Street
Nantucket, Massachusetts
(617) 228-1894

Mailing Address:
P.O. Box 1016
Nantucket, MA 02554

Weekdays, 8:00 A.M.–4:00 P.M.
The Association has approximately fifty handsewn quilts, probably from New England. Techniques represented include: piecework, appliqué, Yo-Yo or Bon-Bon, embroidery, trapunto or stuffed quilting, decorative quilting, and printed whole-cloth with quilting. About ten-percent of the quilt collection predates 1820, eighty-five percent dates from the nine-

teenth century, and five-percent dates later than 1900.

NB: Quilt said to have been made by Lucretia Mott, born on Nantucket.

Study Services: Inquire concerning access to the stored collection (allowed under special circumstances). Reading room, accession cards/files, and photocopy facilities.

The Jackson Homestead
527 Washington Street
Newton, Massachusetts 02158
(617) 552-7238

Weekdays, 8:30 A.M.–4:00 P.M.
The Homestead owns a collection of fifty-seven quilts: about fifty-two are from New England, three definitely from Massachusetts, one from Vermont, one from Maine. Nine date from the nineteenth century. The quilts are primarily pieced: Log Cabin quilts, crazy quilts, and Baby Block patterns predominate. Six have embroidery, three are appliqué, one white-on-white quilt, and one printed whole-cloth with quilting. Quilts are continuously exhibited.

Study Services: Telephone or write to make appointment with curator. Work tables, minimal accession cards/files, books/journals, and photocopy facilities.

Public Services: Tours of exhibitions.

Museum of American Textile History
800 Massachusetts Avenue
North Andover, Massachusetts 01845
(617) 686-0191

Tuesday–Friday, 9:00 A.M.–5:00 P.M.; weekends, 1:00–5:00 P.M.
This unusual collection has two small groups of quilt blocks and thousands of textile samples.

Study Services: Call or write for an appointment. Reading room, work tables, accession cards/files, photocopy facilities, and microscope.

Northampton Historical Society
46 Bridge Street
Northampton, Massachusetts 01060
(413) 584-6011

Wednesday and weekends, 2:00–4:30 P.M. Offices: Tuesday–Friday, 9:00 A.M.–5:00 P.M.
The collection contains seventy-two hand-sewn quilts from Northampton, Massachusetts. Two predate 1820, sixty-five are nineteenth century, three post-1900, two contemporary. The greater part of the collection is piecework, some have embroidery, one or two are trapunto quilts, one is handpainted and quilted. A few quilts are on exhibit on the beds of historic houses.

Study Services: Call or write for appointment. Work tables, accession cards/files, photocopy facilities, and microscope.

Petersham Historical Society
North Main Street
Petersham, Massachusetts 01366
(617) 724-3380

Hours not provided.
Five handsewn pieced quilts c. 1821–1900.

Berkshire County Historical Society
780 Holmes Road
Pittsfield, Massachusetts 01201
(413) 442-1793

Weekdays, 9:00 A.M.–5:00 P.M.
The Society has approximately thirty quilts from New England, seven from Berkshire County, Massachusetts; one from Brooklyn, New York. The collection is predominantly piecework, three quilts are white-on-white, two trapunto. It is known that one quilt dates prior to 1820, twenty-five from the nineteenth century, one post-1900.

NB: Mystic Maze quilt.

Study Services: Call for appointment and explain purpose of research. Reading room, work tables, accession cards/files, library with books/journals, and photocopy facilities; slides, photo prints may be ordered from negatives.

Public Services: The society organizes tours to other museums' quilt collections; lectures, and workshops.

Helen McCarthy Memorial Museum of the Rowe Historical Society, Inc.
Zoar Road
Rowe, Massachusetts 01367
(413) 339-4716

July–September: weekends, 2:00–4:30 P.M.; and by appointment.
Twenty-six handsewn quilts from Rowe, Massachusetts and the small New England towns in the immediate area. Piecework quilts predominate: there are five crazy quilts, one with embroidery; three Signature piecework, two Log Cabin, one Bicentennial quilt with all techniques, one appliqué. Ten quilts are dated: eight nineteenth century, one after 1900, one contemporary. Quilts are continuously exhibited.
NB: Bicentennial quilt, one crazy quilt, three quilts with signatures of local people.
Study Services: Call (413) 339-4729 or 339-5598 for appointment. Reading room.

Essex Institute
132 Essex Street
Salem, Massachusetts 01970
(617) 744-3390

Weekdays, 9:00 A.M.–5:00 P.M.; winter: Tuesday–Friday, 9:00 A.M.–5:00 P.M.
Seventy-eight quilts, the greater number from Essex County, Massachusetts, form the Institute's collection. Approximately fifty-four are piecework, eight printed whole-cloth, five have decorative quilting, four trapunto, two appliqué, two embroidered. Thirty-six have been dated: fourteen pre-1820, nineteen quilts after 1820, two after 1900, one contemporary.
Study Services: Call for appointment. Reading room, work tables, accession cards/files, books/journals, and photocopy facilities; there are negatives for a small portion of the collection and prints may be ordered.

Ropes Mansion
318 Essex Street
Salem, Massachusetts 01970
(617) 744-0718

Hours not provided.
Five quilts.

Old Sturbridge Village
Sturbridge, Massachusetts 01566
(617) 347-3362

Museum: April–October: daily, 9:00 A.M.–5:00 P.M.; November–March: Tuesday–Sunday, 10:00 A.M.–4:00 P.M. Closed, New Year's day and Christmas. Offices: weekdays, 8:30 A.M.–5:00 P.M.
Old Sturbridge Village has approximately 150 quilts: twenty-two from Massachusetts, four from Connecticut, three from Maine, three from New Hampshire, three from Rhode Island, one from Vermont. About sixty-nine are pieced, thirty-four are decoratively quilted, fifteen are white-on-white, fourteen appliqué, eight tufted, two trapunto, one is stencilled. Roughly forty-one date prior to 1820, and sixty-five from 1821 to 1900. There are four to six quilt patterns available. The principal source of the collection, Wilbur family of Swansea, Massachusetts, and gifts from other families. Quilts are exhibited at all times.
NB: Concentration of New England pre-1850 quilts, and pieced white wool. Silver medal winner of an 1841 state exhibition.
Study Services: Make appointment with senior curator. Research library with fifty books/journals on quilting, open weekdays, 8:30 A.M.–5:00 P.M.; photo prints, slides, photo prints may be ordered from negatives.
Public Services: Not on a regular basis, although senior curator lectures extensively on quilts and quilt making.

Old Colony Historical Society

66 Church Green
Taunton, Massachusetts 02780
(617) 822-1622

Tuesday–Saturday, 10:00 A.M.–4:00 P.M.
Thirteen locally made quilts from Massachusetts form a collection of six piecework and some Friendship quilts, five silk crazy quilts, one crewel, one calico print quilt. One dates prior to 1820, ten are nineteenth century, two post-1900. The Society has unpublished pattern and recipe books for local calico printworks. Quilts are exhibited continuously.
NB: The "Duxbury" quilt, with fabrics by Giles Duxbury, c. 1850; eighteenth century crewel quilt.
Study Services: By appointment. Reading room, work tables, accession cards/files, library, and photocopy facilities.
Public Services: Tours, lectures, workshops, seminars.

Wenham Museum

132 Main Street
Wenham, Massachusetts 01984
(617) 468-2377

Weekdays, 11:00 A.M.–4:00 P.M.; Saturday, 1:00–4:00 P.M.; Sunday, 2:00–5:00 P.M.
The seventy quilts in the collection were made or given by local people from the north shore area of Boston. Of particular note are eighteen patchwork, ten Cross Patch, seven Log Cabin, five star quilts, four crazy quilts, four State House Steps, two are eighteenth century linsey-woolsey, two quilted calamanco quilts from the 1750s, two Friendship, two Irish Chain, one an 1830 crewel, one 1824 satin quilt, one Drunkard's Trail. Five predate 1820, approximately forty date from the nineteenth century, and thirty date after 1900. In addition, the Museum has unpublished portfolios of patchwork patterns and unfinished patchwork squares, c. 1850. One, two or more quilts are on exhibit at all times.
NB: Regional quilts from Essex County, north of Boston: 1724 bed rug, seventeenth century calamanco, linsey-woolsey quilt, eighteenth century silk quilt, and a crewel quilt.
Study Services: Quilt storage area can be shown to visitors. Reading room, accession cards/files, and books/journals.
Public Services: Exhibits.

Edwin Smith Historical Museum in the Westfield Athenaeum

6 Elm Street
Westfield, Massachusetts 01085
(413) 568-7833

September 16–June 14: Monday–Wednesday, Friday and Saturday, 1:00–5:00 P.M. June 15–September 15: Monday–Wednesday, and Friday, 1:00–5:00 P.M.; closed holidays.
Fifteen quilts, one quilt top, and one quilt frame from New England are contained in the collection. The quilts date from 1850 to the present. They are predominantly patchwork. The principal sources of the collection include Katharine Parsons Dell, Beatrice Fowler Denslow, Mrs. Theodore Harding, Jeffrey Kingsbury, Harold Loomis, Ms. L. Ruth Mills, and Mrs. B.J. Truslow.
NB: One red and white piecework with names written on patches, made to raise money by the Women's Society of Christian Service in the Methodist Church. Patchwork Album quilt with twenty-five names and two verses written in ink. Patchwork quilt in Texas Star pattern made in 1850 by Mahitable Curtiss (Mrs. Edmund Spring) at the age of 14; 1860 handmade and dyed wool coverlet by the same maker.
Study Services: By appointment. Reading room, work tables, other facilities, books/journals, and photocopy facilities.

Atheneum Society of Wilbraham
450 Main Street
Wilbraham, Massachusetts

Mailing Address:
P.O. Box 294
Wilbraham, MA 01095

Hours not provided.
Five crazy quilts (c. 1821–1900) and one bi-centennial quilt.

The quilting bee in Meadows of Dan Baptist Church in Meadows of Dan, Virginia, next to the parkway, is a regular gathering of local women who work on "special" quilts either for specific gifts or for sale. American Folklife Center, Blue Ridge Parkway Project, 1978. Fieldwork by Geraldine Johnson, photo by Terry Eiler, negative number 11-20423, 16. Courtesy of the Archive of Folk Culture, Library of Congress.

MICHIGAN

Good resources for quilt study as well as over 1,000 quilts from 1750 to the present can be found.

Lenawee County Historical Museum
110 East Church Street
Adrian, Michigan
(517) 265-6071

Mailing Address:
P.O. Box 511
Adrian, MI 49221

Tuesday–Saturday, 1:00–5:00 P.M.
This is a collection of fifty-three handsewn quilts from Lenawee County, Michigan and one from Virginia. Twenty-five are dated: nineteen from the nineteenth century, five after 1900, one contemporary. Quilts are on exhibit at all times.
Study Services: By advance appointment. Reading room, work tables, and accession cards/files.

Jesse Besser Museum
491 Johnson Street
Alpena, Michigan 49707
(517) 356-2202

Weekdays, 9:00 A.M.–5:00 P.M.; weekends, 1:00–5:00 P.M.
The Museum has approximately twenty-five quilts from Michigan, Pennsylvania, Ohio, Indiana, and Illinois. About ten date from the nineteenth century, ten from post-1900, one is contemporary.
Study Services: For serious researchers, make appointment. Reading room, accession cards/files with staff assistance, books/journals, and photocopy facilities; slides of some quilts.
Public Services: Tours of exhibitions and occasional quilting classes.

Paulson House Museum

Forest Lake Road
Au Train, Michigan
(906) 892-8293

Mailing Address:
Star Route Box 275
Au Train, MI 49806

May 15–October 15: daily, 8:00 A.M.–7:00 P.M. Quilts donated by family are exhibited as part of furnishings in period rooms in the house.

Dearborn Historical Museum

915 Brady Street
Dearborn, Michigan 48124
(313) 565-3000

Museum: November 1–May 1; Monday–Saturday, 1:00–5:00 P.M.; May 1–October 31; Monday–Saturday, 9:00 A.M.–5:00 P.M.; Office hours: daily, 8:30 A.M.–5:30 P.M.
The Museum has 125 quilts, sixty-six were made in Michigan or were brought to the state by pioneers, and fifty-nine are from the upper Midwest. Seventy-six are pieced, sixteen crazy quilts and throws, eleven star quilts, five appliqué and pieced, five embroidered, five Log Cabin and its variations, four appliqué, two stuffed, one whole-cloth. There are also some unfinished quilts. One or two date before 1820, about ninety are from the nineteenth century, thirty date after 1900, two are contemporary. There are also approximately twenty transcriptions of oral histories, some 1979–1980 research papers about the collection, and several scrapbooks.
NB: White-on-white stuffed quilt, pre-Civil War; appliqué pre-Civil War quilt; children's Bicentennial embroidered patchwork tied quilt; more than twenty crazy quilt throws, quilts, and other pieces.
Study Services: By appointment. Reading room, work tables, books/journals, and photocopy facilities; slides available for reproduction.
Public Services: Local displays, and community slide lectures.

The Edison Institute

Greenfield Village-Henry Ford Museum
20900 Oakwood Boulevard
Dearborn, Michigan
(313) 271-1620

Mailing Address:
P.O. Box 1970
Dearborn, MI 48121

Monday–Sunday, 9:00 A.M.–5:00 P.M.
The Museum has 200 quilts that are national in scope and range in date from 1750 to 1970. In addition, there are twenty-five stencils and templates. Approximately thirty are documented Midwest pieced quilts. About forty are whole-cloth, 120 pieced, twenty pieced and appliqué, twenty appliqué, five trapunto. It is estimated that thirty quilts predate 1820, 125 quilts date from the remainder of the nineteenth century, thirty-five quilts date after 1900, and five are contemporary.
NB: The greatest part of the collection is 1870 to 1910 pieced quilts; ten quilts made by Susan McCord between 1875 to 1910, in McCordsville, Indiana.
Study Services: Make arrangements in advance, staff time is limited. Reading room, accession cards/files, twenty books/journals, and photocopy facilities; photo prints, slides, photo prints may be ordered from negatives.
Public Services: Occasional lectures.

Detroit Historical Museum

5401 Woodward Avenue
Detroit, Michigan 48202
(313) 833-1805

Wednesday–Sunday, 9:30 A.M.–5:00 P.M.
In this collection of 175 quilts, fifty have Michigan associations and eight have direct Detroit provenances: four with religious associations, one from the Hungarian-American community in Detroit, and one sports-oriented Detroit Tigers quilt. About 113 are pieced, fourteen are a combination of pieced, appliqué, or embroidered, twelve are appliqué, six are embroidered, two are printed cotton, one white-on-white quilt. Two quilts predate 1820, 160 are nineteenth century,

twelve date after 1900, one is contemporary.
There are thirty-five quilt patterns.
NB: White-on-white c. 1825-50; broderie
perse, Tree of Life, c. 1830.

The Detroit Institute of Arts
5200 Woodward Avenue
Detroit, Michigan 48202
(313) 833-7900

Tuesday–Sunday, 9:30 A.M.–5:30 P.M.
Eight early quilts including an eighteenth century white-on-white with borders of handmade silk fringe.

Computerized Folklore Archive
University of Detroit
Briggs Building
4001 West McNichols Road
Detroit, Michigan 48221
(313) 927-1081

By appointment.
Approximately twenty quilt-related photo-
graphs from the Peabody Archive in Nashville,
Tennessee.
Study Services: By appointment with Professor
James T. Callow, Director. Slides available at
cost.

Folklore Archives
Purdy Library, Room 448
Wayne State University
Detroit, Michigan 48202
(313) 577-4053

Weekdays, 10:00 A.M.–5:00 P.M.
Document collection contains thirty-four
color slides, eleven taped oral histories, five
transcriptions, and three quilt patterns.
Study Services: Inquire in person, by mail or
by phone. Reading room, work tables, accession cards/files, and audio equipment; photo
prints, slides, photo prints may be ordered
from negatives.

Michigan State University Museum
Michigan Folk Arts Archive
Michigan State University
East Lansing, Michigan 48824
(517) 355-2370

Weekdays, 9:00 A.M.–5:00 P.M.; weekends,
1:00–5:00 P.M.
The Museum maintains an archive of approximately 2,000 questionnaires with photographs, quilt patterns, taped interviews and
transcriptions, research papers and other materials. These were collected by the Michigan
Quilt Inventory of the Michigan State University, which gathered information on quilters
and quilts made or used in Michigan. The
quilts are predominantly from the Midwest.
Study Services: Make appointment. Work tables, accession cards/files, computer, books/
journals, the university library collections, and
photocopy facilities; photo prints, slides,
prints can be ordered from negatives, and
films.
Public Services: Textile conservation workshops, lectures, and film showings.
Publications: Publication on Michigan quilting anticipated by 1987.

Gerald R. Ford Museum
303 Pearl Street, NW
Grand Rapids, Michigan 49504
(616) 456-2675

Monday–Saturday, 9:00 A.M.–4:45 P.M.; Sunday,
12:00–4:45 P.M.
The Museum's holdings include fifty-two contemporary quilts presented to Gerald R. Ford
and the United States during the 1976 Bicentennial, forty or more personal narratives by
quiltmakers, and news articles. Of note are
seven quilts by Boy Scouts and Girl Scouts,
eighteen made by schools, eleven by individuals, four from nursing homes, three from
churches, three were made by professional
quilters. Two are white-on-white, the rest of
varied techniques and patterns. Continuous
exhibit of Bicentennial quilts.
NB: Concentration of Bicentennial themes.
Study Services: Make written request. Work ta-

bles, accession cards/files, and photocopy facilities; photo prints, slides, prints may be ordered from negatives.
Public Services: Tours.

Grand Rapids Public Museum
54 Jefferson Avenue SE
Grand Rapids, Michigan 49503
(616) 456-3977

Monday–Saturday, 10:00 A.M.–5:00 P.M.; Sunday, 1:00–5:00 P.M. Closed national holidays. This collection of eighty to 100 quilts was given by families living in Grand Rapids or western Michigan. Donor's ancestors (in cases of the older quilts) may have brought the quilts with them from New York, Ohio and other states. It is estimated that fifty or more are piecework quilts, twelve or more crazy quilts, two white-on-white, two trapunto or stuffed, one printed whole-cloth. One quilt predates 1820, the majority date from the nineteenth century and after 1900, two are contemporary. One is a 1976 Bicentennial quilt produced by children. Quilts are on continuous exhibition.
Study Services: For scholars, write to arrange appointment. Work tables, accession cards/files, books/journals, photocopy facilities, and microscope; prints may be ordered from negatives.

Ella Sharp Museum
3225 Fourth Street
Jackson, Michigan 49203
(517) 787-2320

Weekdays, 8:30 A.M.–5:00 P.M.; weekends, 1:30–5:00 P.M.
The Museum has seventy-two quilts. Fifty are from the Midwest and Great Lakes, twenty-two from New York State and the Northeast. Among them are thirty-one pieced, twenty-one crazy quilts, thirteen embroidered, eight Log Cabin, six appliqué, five white-on-white, three stuffed. Sixty-eight quilts date from the nineteenth century and four date later than 1900.

NB: Concentration of crazy quilts, Log Cabin, and other piecework.
Study Services: Scholars, make appoinment with registrar. Reading room, work tables, accession cards/files, and fifteen books/journals.
Public Services: Tours and classes.
Publications: Manning, Susan, compiler. *Quilts and Coverlets in the Collection of the Ella Sharp Museum* (1973).

Michigan Historical Museum
208 North Capitol Avenue
Lansing, Michigan 48918
(517) 373-1979

Weekdays, 9:30 A.M.–4:30 P.M.; Saturday, 12:00–4:30 P.M.
Seventy of this collection of 100 quilts are cataloged, and there are five scrapbooks of patterns and notes. Nearly the entire collection was made in Michigan. Fifteen probably came from the Upper Penninsula, others were made in New York State. There are about thirty-seven pieced, fifteen tied, eight crazy quilts, seven appliqué, seven quilts with decorative quilting, and two trapunto. Fifty-one are dated: one predates 1820; thirty-three 1821–1900, fifteen post-1900, and two contemporary.
NB: Representative collection of Michigan quilts, especially from the nineteenth century; glazed linsey-woolsey and white-on-white trapunto, both with decorative quilting.
Study Services: Make an appointment. Work tables, accession cards/files, photocopy facilities, and microscope; slides, prints may be ordered from negatives.
Public Services: Lectures, and workshops offered during exhibits.
Publications: Quilts and Coverlets. Checklist to exhibit "The Art of Needle and Loom" 1984.

Mason County Historical Society and White Pine Village-Rose Hawley Museum

115 West Loomis Street
Ludington, Michigan 49431
(616) 843-2001

Year-round: weekdays, 9:30 A.M.–4:30 P.M.; in addition, July and August: Saturday, 9:30 A.M.–4:30 P.M.
Fifty or more quilts are being cataloged. Work should be completed in 1987.
Study Services: Examine quilts in storage only in staff presence. Reading room, work tables, accession cards/files in progress, books/journals, and photocopy facilities.
Public Services: Quilt exhibit and workshops planned for 1987.

Marshall Historical Society

Marshall, Michigan
(616) 781-8909 or 781-8544

Mailing Address:
P.O. Box 68
Marshall, MI 49068

May–October: daily, 1:00–5:00 P.M.
Six to eight nineteenth century quilts and Jacquard woven coverlets are on continuous exhibition.

Menominee County Historical Museum

906 11th Avenue
Menominee, Michigan

Mailing Address:
P.O. Box 151
Menominee, MI 49858

May 30–Labor day: daily, 10:00 A.M.–5:00 P.M.; Sunday, 1:00–5:00 P.M.
Five quilts are owned and exhibited by the Museum along with occasional exhibitions of quilts from local owners.

Muskegon County Museum

430 West Clay Avenue
Muskegon, Michigan 49440
(616) 722-0278

Weekdays, 9:30 A.M.–4:30 P.M.; weekends, 12:30–4:30 P.M.
Sixteen handsewn regional quilts primarily from Nebraska, are mainly embroidered and patchwork. Five date from the nineteenth century. Donors are principally from Muskegon.
NB: Album quilt with the names of early Muskegon business men.
Study Services: By arrangement with the collections curator. Reading room, accession cards/files, archives, books/journals, and microscope.

Troy Museum and Historic Village

60 West Wattles Road
Troy, Michigan 48098
(313) 524-3570

Tuesday–Saturday, 9:00 A.M.–5:30 P.M.
Thirty predominantly regional quilts, twenty-eight from the Midwest, one Appalachian quilt, one from Ireland are contained in the collection. Twenty-six piecework, three appliqué, one embroidered quilt. Seven nineteenth century quilts, six date post-1900, two contemporary.
NB: Signature/Autograph quilt with embroidered names of residents of Big Beaver, Michigan.
Study Services: Make arrangements with curator. Reading room, work tables, and books/journals.

Ypsilanti Historical Museum

220 North Huron Street
Ypsilanti, Michigan 48197
(313) 482-4990

Weekdays, 9:00 A.M.–12:00 P.M.
The collection includes seventeen handsewn quilts donated by local people. One quilt is from Michigan residents with Scottish background. Additional types and patterns are: one trapunto, one Log Cabin, one Fan, one Cluster-of-Stars, one Double Irish Chain, and one

star. Five are known to be from the nineteenth century, and one dates after 1900.
Quilts are continuously exhibited.
Study Services: For scholars, make appointment. Reading room, work tables, accession
cards/files, books/journals, and photocopy facilities.
Public Services: Public programming for the
quilt collection is offered.

Hinesville (vicinity), Georgia, April 1941. A woman quilting in a
smoke house. Photo by Jack Delano, negative number LC-
USF34-43775-D. Courtesy of the Farm Security Administration
Collection, Prints and Photographs Division, Library of Congress.

MINNESOTA

*A painted cambric quilt, wool quilts,
early pioneer quilts, and Friendship
quilts are some of the interesting examples in seventeen institutions.*

Isanti County Historical Society
Cambridge, Minnesota
(612) 396-3957

Mailing Address:
P.O. Box 525
Cambridge, MN 55008

Tuesday, 9:00–4:30 P.M.
Six handsewn patchwork quilts from the nineteenth century have been donated by local
women and may be seen by appointment.

Glensheen
3300 London Road
Duluth, Minnesota 55804
(218) 724-8864

Office: weekends, 8:30 A.M.–4:30 P.M.
Collection of eighteen handsewn quilts all of
which date from 1900 to 1940 includes two
Appalachian, seven piecework, four with decorative quilting, four appliqué, two white-on-
white, one printed whole-cloth with quilting.
The quilts were collected and/or made by
Clara Congdon and/or her daughters.
Study Services: For scholars, make written request to director, stating purpose. Work tables, and photocopy facilities; black and white
photo prints, color slides, photo prints may be
ordered from negatives.

St. Louis County Historical Society

506 West Michigan Street
Duluth, Minnesota 55802
(218) 722-8911

Weekdays, 9:00 A.M.–5:00 P.M.
Twenty quilts, the majority from Minnesota, have been given primarily by relatives of the quiltmakers. Predominatly patchwork, the collection has one white-on-white quilt with a lace border, three with triangular patterns, two silk and velvet Log Cabin made c. 1900, a quilt made of suit material from the F.A. Patrick woolen mills of Duluth, and a c. 1895 piecework quilt with embroidery. The quilts date from c. 1775 to 1937.
NB: An appliqué flower quilt with the following inscription: "Mrs. Lucey Andrews pieced and quilted this quilt in her 73rd year of age, 1853, born in the year, 1780."
Study Services: Request permission from society director. Reading room, work tables, accession cards/files, books, and photocopy facilities; some slides.
Public Services: Occasionally provide public programming for quilt collection.

Otter Tail County Historical Society Museum

1110 West Lincoln Avenue
Fergus Falls, Minnesota 56537
(218) 736-6038

Weekdays, 9:00 A.M.–5:00 P.M.
Forty-four Minnesota quilts and two taped and transcribed oral histories form the bulk of this collection. There is one Virginia quilt made by slaves. Thirty piecework, eight have embroidery, three appliqué, and three are wholecloth. Thirteen are nineteenth century quilts, twenty-nine date after 1900, two are contemporary. Some quilts are always on exhibit.
NB: Completely handsewn Friendship Bicentennial quilt by fifth and sixth graders.
Study Services: Make appointment. Reading room, work tables, accession cards/files, books/journals, and photocopy facilities; slides.
Public Services: Quilt exhibits in addition to selected quilts on permanent exhibit. Quilting class for children held in conjunction with local group. Sunday afternoon demonstrations by local quilting group have been offered.

Koochiching County Historical Society

Smokey Bear Park International Falls,
Minnesota
(218) 283-4316
Mailing Address:
P.O. Box 1147
International Falls, MN 56649

Summer: Monday–Saturday, 10:00 A.M.–4:00 P.M. Winter, offices only: Monday and Tuesday, 8:30 A.M.–4:00 P.M.
Six well-documented quilts from the twentieth century on continuous exhibition.

Western Hennepin County Pioneers Association, Inc.

1953 West Wayzata Boulevard
Long Lake, Minnesota
(612) 473-6557
Mailing Address:
P.O. 433
Long Lake, MN 55356

Sunday, 2:00–5:00 P.M.; summer: weekends, 2:00–5:00 P.M., or by special appointment. Thirty-one handsewn quilts in a collection in which thirty were brought by settlers or made in Minnesota, and one is a quilt with religious provenance. In addition, the collection includes eight to ten quilt patterns, many quilt blocks, two Marseilles spreads, one coverlet from 1857. Sixteen are pieced, six are crazy quilts, three are embroidered, two are appliqué, two are Victorian silk quilts, one is a silk child's quilt. Twenty-two date from the nineteenth century, eight date after 1900, and one is contemporary. Quilts are exhibited continuously.
Study Services: Write or phone for appointment. Reading room, book and manuals, and nearby photocopy facilities.
Public Services: History tours and lectures; presentations at schools.

Blue Earth County Historical Society Museum

606 South Broad Street
Mankato, Minnesota 56001
(507) 345-4154

Tuesday–Sunday, 1:00–5:00 P.M.
Three of these fifteen quilts were made in Illinois and brought to Minnesota; twelve are originally from Minnesota. Six are patchwork, five crazy quilts, three appliqué, one is a Yo-Yo quilt. Of those that have been dated: five are nineteenth century, three date after 1900, one is contemporary.
Study Services: Make appointment with staff to do quilt research. Accession cards/files, and photocopy facilities.
Public Services: Local quilt group holds meetings at Museum. Quilt collection exhibited at that time.

Sibley House Museum

55 D Street
Mendota, Minnesota 55150
(612) 452-1596

Tuesday–Saturday, 10:00 A.M.–5:00 P.M.; Monday and holidays, 12:00–5:00 P.M.
The collection includes twenty-five to thirty handsewn pieced, appliqué, embroidered, and crazy quilts.
NB: Appliqué and trapunto Adam and Eve quilt c. 1900 and a painted cambric quilt.

Hennepin County Historical Society Museum

2303 Third Avenue South
Minneapolis, Minnesota 55404
(612) 870-1329

Tuesday–Friday, 9:00 A.M.–4:30 P.M.; Sunday, 1:00–5:00 P.M.; research library, Tuesday–Friday, 9:00 A.M.–4:30 P.M.
These 103 quilts are from Minnesota, the Midwest, and New England. Approximately fifty-nine are pieced (twenty-seven crazy quilts, fourteen Log Cabin), twelve appliqué, twelve have highly decorative stitching and/or stuffed work, four embroidered. Thirty-six are silk and velvet, and thirteen are wool quilts. The greater part of the collection dates from the 1830s to 1920s. Fifty-six are nineteenth century, fifteen date after 1900, and four are contemporary.
NB: Many historic quilts used by local settlers. Appliqué quilt portraying maker's house, family, and farm animals, with palm trees and starry sky, from Iowa, 1880s; Mariner's Compass quilt with decorative quilting; profusely embroidered crazy quilt containing record of donor's many pets, mementos of her family, and embroidered verses, from St. Paul, Minnesota, 1893; chintz appliqué wedding quilt with huge central wreath surrounded by fifteen smaller wreaths and medallions, with a swag border, 1872.
Study Services: All quilts are documented on 3x5 inch color prints. After examining the prints, researchers may request to see specific items. Viewing will be arranged with twenty-four hour notice. Reading room, work tables, accession cards/files, 3x5 color prints (overall view and detail) of each quilt, and photocopy facilities; photo prints, slides, prints may be ordered from negatives, researchers may photograph or sketch quilts, for private use. Special permission, fee, and a credit line are required for publication use.

The Minneapolis Institute of Art

2400 Third Avenue South
Minneapolis, Minnesota 55404
(612) 870-3047

Tuesday–Sunday, 10:00 A.M.–5:00 P.M.
The Institute's collection includes eleven quilts, nine from the Midwest; two Baltimore Album/Friendship quilts, c. 1840s; notes on one quilt by the maker; and video documentation on a quilt by Jan Myers commissioned for the collection. Five are piecework, three pieced crazy quilts with embroidery, three appliqué. Eight are nineteenth century, two date after 1900, one is contemporary.
NB: Baltimore Album quilt and 1900 crazy or Friendship quilt from Minneapolis.
Study Services: Call or write for appointment. Work tables, accession cards/files, photocopy

facilities, and microscope; photo prints, slides, postcard, videotape, photo prints may be ordered from negatives.

Public Services: Public lectures and seminars on occasion.

Pipestone County Museum
113 South Hiawatha Street
Pipestone, Minnesota
(507) 825-2563

Mailing Address:
P.O. Box 114
Pipestone, MN 56164

Daily, 10:00 A.M.–5:00 P.M.
The collection includes nineteen handsewn quilts; four tops, pieced but not quilted; two doll quilts; three piecework pillows. Sixteen quilts are piecework, two appliqué, one embroidered. Three are nineteenth century, one post-1900, one contemporary. The majority of the quilts probably date from 1901 to 1940. Winifred Bartlett is the principal donor. Quilts are exhibited continuously.

NB: Concentration in patchwork quilts.

Study Services: Make appointment with the director or assistant director. Reading room, work tables, accession cards/files, microfilm reader/printer, and photocopy facilities; photo prints, prints may be ordered from negatives.

Publications: A Harvest of Quilts. Winona County Historical Society catalog of historical quilts in southern Minnesota; lists two quilts from the collection.

Fillmore County Historical Society/Center
Fillmore County Courthouse (basement)
Preston, Minnesota
(507) 765-2368

Mailing Address:
P.O. Box 373
Preston, MN 55965

Weekdays, 11:30 A.M.–4:30 P.M.; weekends by appointment only.
Of the sixteen quilts, all but five were made by old county families. Fourteen are piecework, two appliqué and embroidered; one has decorative quilting, one embroidered/pieced quilt. Eleven are nineteenth century, five contemporary. Quilts are rotated in a continuous exhibition.

Study Services: By appointment. Accession cards/files, and photocopy facilities.

Gibbs Farm Museum
2097 West Larpenteur Avenue
St. Paul, Minnesota 55113
(612) 646-8629

April–December: Tuesday–Friday, 10:00 A.M.–4:00 P.M.; Sunday, 12:00–4:00 P.M. June, July, and August also open Saturday, 12:00–4:00 P.M.
Seventy-five quilts form a collection from Minnesota and the Midwest, two from New York/eastern United States; one from French Canada. Sixty-seven are piecework, five appliqué, and three whole-cloth. Thirty-nine are nineteenth century, thirty-three date after 1900, three contemporary.

NB: Concentration of pieced quilts, crazy quilts, and Log Cabin patterns. Crazy quilt robe, dated 1949; an elaborately embroidered crazy quilt with two pillow shams; a homespun quilt that is from the mid-nineteenth century and entirely handmade, dyed and quilted; and a crazy quilt that belonged to Agnes Rondeau, a Chicago actress of the late nineteenth century, made from scraps of each of her stage costumes.

Study Services: Call to make appointments for viewing quilts. Work tables, and accession cards/files; photo prints of about 15 percent of the quilts.

Public Services: Annual month-long exhibition with speakers and programs.

Goldstein Gallery

University of Minnesota
1985 Buford Avenue
St. Paul, Minnesota 55108
(612) 376-1488

Weekdays, 9:00 A.M.–5:00 P.M.
The Gallery has fifteen quilts including one from Kansas, eight research papers, and two transcriptions of taped interviews. Fourteen quilts are pieced, two appliqué, five are embroidered, three have decorative quilting, one trapunto. Four date from the nineteenth century, ten are later than 1900, and one is dated 1979.
NB: Concentration in crazy quilts.
Study Services: For scholars, make appointment. Reading room, work tables, accession cards/files, and photocopy facilities.

Minnesota Historical Society

Museum Collections
1500 Mississippi Street
St. Paul, Minnesota 55101
(612) 296-0147

Weekdays, 8:30 A.M.–5:00 P.M.
More than 100 of the 195 quilts in the collection have Minnesota associations. There are three North Star Quilters taped interviews, and research done on about fifty quilts from the collection for an exhibit in 1979. Fifty percent of the quilts are patchwork, twenty-five percent are crazy quilts, and twelve percent are appliqué. Of those assigned dates: four are pre-1820, 117 nineteenth century, twenty-one after 1900, and three contemporary.
NB: First prize winner 1859 Minnesota State Fair; an 1840s appliqué chintz quilt; 1886 St. Paul Winter Carnival quilt; and a quilt made in 1982 called "Minnesota Postcard" by a local fiber artist.
Study Services: Write for proper request form. If approved, appointment will be made. Reading room, work tables, accession cards/files, books/journals, in addition, 1880s to 1940s farm publications with patterns and hints, photocopy facilities; duplicates of black and white identification photos in museum photo file can be ordered. Slides, black and white prints made from negatives, and color 2x3 transparencies that can be rented and used for publications.

Spring Valley Community Historical Society, Inc.

112 South Washington
Spring Valley, Minnesota

Mailing Address:
909 South Broadway
Spring Valley, MN 55975

June–October: Sunday, 2:00–4:00 P.M.
A collection of twenty traditional quilts by local women. An unusual 1892 silk quilt top is well-documented with a transcribed oral history. A few quilts are on exhibit at all times.

Washington County Historical Society

602 North Main Street
Stillwater, Minnesota
(612) 439-5956

Mailing Address:
P.O. Box 167
Stillwater, MN 55082

Tuesday, Thursday, and weekends, 2:00–5:00 P.M.
The Society has twenty-six quilts including crazy quilts, Log Cabin, and Postage Stamp quilts. One predates 1820, fourteen are nineteenth century, ten date later than 1900, and one is contemporary. Quilts are continuously exhibited.
NB: Bicentennial quilt by members of local Catholic churches.
Study Services: Write to curator for appointment. Reading room, work tables, and accession cards/files.
Public Services: Exhibitions and workshops.

Winona County Historical Society
160 Johnson Street
Winona, Minnesota 55987
(507) 454-2723

Weekdays, 10:00 A.M.–5:00 P.M.; weekends,
1:00–5:00 P.M.
The Society has collected fifty quilts, most
made in the Winona area. Approximately
thirty-five are patchwork, seven crazy quilts,
five embroidered, and one ribbon quilt. Fifteen are nineteenth century, five date after
1900, and five are contemporary. Principal
sources of the collection include Mrs. E.L.
King, and area residents.
NB: Bunnell Family quilt; prize winning crazy
quilt.
Study Services: Write for appointment. Reading room, work tables, and accession cards/
files; slides, photo prints can be ordered from
negatives.
Public Services: Exhibitions, classes, and workshops offered through area quilt guild. Annual
nine day quilt exhibit in September.
Publications: A Harvest of Quilts.

"The 'Brothers' Assisted in the Quilting," wood engraving,
subsequently handcolored from *Harper's Weekly,* April 21, 1883.
One of the artists was W. L. Sheppard. Courtesy of the Historic
New Orleans Collection, 533 Royal Street, Acc. No. 1979.122.

MISSISSIPPI

*Collections highlight Afro-American
quilts made before and after the Civil
War.*

Marshall County Historical Museum
220 East College Avenue
Holly Springs, Mississippi
(601) 252-4437

Mailing Address:
P.O. Box 806
Holly Springs, MS 38635

Weekdays, 9:00 A.M.–11:00 P.M., and 2:00–
4:00 P.M.; closed Thursday afternoons, national
holidays, December and January.
The Museum has fourteen handsewn quilts
from Marshall County, Mississippi. Nine are
piecework, three appliqué, one printed whole-
cloth, and one is a coverlet with embroidery
and beadwork. Continuous exhibit of all the
quilts in the collection.
NB: Printed whole-cloth quilt made from
sacks painted with flags of the allies in World
War I. The man who made the designs for the
sacks was in the Navy during World War I.
Study Services: Upon request. Reading room,
and work tables; photo prints, slides, photo
prints may be ordered from negatives.
Public Services: Guided tours; annual county
quilt show each April.

Mississippi State Historical Museum

Mississippi Department of Archives and History
100 South State Street
Jackson, Mississippi
(601) 354-6222

Mailing Address:
P.O. Box 571
Jackson, MS 39205-0571

Weekdays, 8:00 A.M.–5:00 P.M.; Saturday, 9:30 A.M.–4:30 P.M.; Sunday, 12:30–4:30 P.M.
This collection contains 123 nineteenth and twentieth century Mississippi-made quilts. Twenty-nine are Afro-American dating from the twentieth century. Ninety-two are pieced, twenty-four appliqué, three embroidered, two Yo-Yo, one stuffed and corded, and one is a homespun whole-cloth quilt.
NB: Concentration of strip quilts which incorporate sacking (flour, grain, etc.); two slave-made quilts; c. 1810 appliqué Princess Feather and Eagle quilt.
Study Services: Contact curator of collections for appointment. Accession cards/files, books/journals, and photocopy facilities; slides, and prints made from negatives.
Public Services: Tours of temporary exhibits; textile identification and conservation workshops.
Publications: Made by Hand: Mississippi Folk Art (1980).

Department of Archives and Special Collections

J. D. Williams Library
University of Mississippi
University, Mississippi 38677
(601) 232-7408

Weekdays, 8:30 A.M.–5:00 P.M.; Saturdays, 10:00 A.M.–4:00 P.M.
The William R. Ferris, Jr. Collection includes several hundred photographs of quilts and quiltmakers, mostly of Pecolia Warner of Mississippi, and several hours of recorded interviews on one-fourth inch tape for a film.
Study Services: Walk-in, access to the collection by permission of the archivist. Reading room, accession cards/files, books/journals in library, photocopy facilities, five to ten days advance notice required to listen to the recordings; slides copied by permission with a minimum of two weeks notice.

The University Museums

The University of Mississippi
University, Mississippi 38677
(601) 232-7073

Tuesday–Saturday, 10:00 A.M.–4:00 P.M.; Sunday, 1:00–4:00 P.M.
There are approximately thirty quilts principally from Mississippi. Twenty-five are Afro-American. Primarily piecework with some appliqué and embroidery. Some date prior to 1900 (no quilt is earlier than 1870) but the majority is contemporary. Two crazy quilts, Presentation quilt with painted panel, and one 1900 Star and Square quilt. Donated by William Ferris.
NB: Several quilts by Pecolia Warner, Minnie Watson, and Amanda Gordon; 1970s Sunburst quilt by Sadie Mae Blackburn.
Study Services: Supervised access to serious scholars. Write or call director or collections manager, at least one week in advance. Work tables, accession cards/files, videotapes, photocopy facilities, and microscope; duplication of photo prints and slides available on file.
Public Services: During special exhibitions guided tours may be arranged for groups.

MISSOURI

Hundreds of patchwork, appliqué, and embroidered quilts can be seen at sixteen museums.

Powers Museum
1621 West Oak at
Highway 71 Bypass
Carthage, Missouri
(417) 358-2667

Mailing Address:
P.O. Box 593
Carthage, MO 64836

New building under construction. Anticipated opening fall of 1987. Call for hours. Collection includes twelve handsewn quilts, predominantly Missouri-made. Six are piecework, six appliqué; two tops, one comforter, a group of patches, one pattern with instructions, Esther O'Neil quilt kit fliers, one white-on-white quilted petticoat c. 1870–1890, and a trapunto personal accessory bag. Two are nineteenth century, eight post-1900, two contemporary. The quilts were collected by Marian L. Powers Winchester of Carthage, Missouri. Continuous exhibit of quilts is planned.
NB: 1850 Dutch Rose quilt; c. 1915 Poppy made by Marie Webster; 1922 Dolly Varden quilt by Esther O'Neil.
Study Services: Make written request. Reading room, work tables, accession cards/files, books/journals, and photocopy facilities will be arranged; photo prints, slides, and prints available from Museum's negatives.
Public Services: Slide programs currently available.

Historic Costume and Textile Collection
University of Missouri
137 Stanley Hall
Columbia, Missouri 65211
(314) 882-6410

Weekdays, 8:00 A.M.–5:00 P.M.
Six nineteenth century piecework quilts and one quilt thesis may be seen by appointment with curator.

Cass County Historical Society
400 East Mechanic Street
Harrisonville, Missouri 64701
(816) 884-5352

Weekdays, 9:00 A.M.–3:00 P.M.
Collection of fifteen handsewn nineteenth century quilts from the Ozark area includes thirteen piecework and two appliqué. Society has continuous exhibit of quilts.
NB: Quilts in use during pioneer days.
Study Services: Make appointment with secretary.

Deutschheim
State Historic Site
109 West 2nd Street
Hermann, Missouri 65041
(314) 486-2200

Tuesday–Saturday, 8:00 A.M.–4:00 P.M.
Five handsewn German-American quilts may be seen by advance appointment.

Hickory County Historical Society
Hermitage, Missouri 65668
(417) 745-6452

May–October: 1:00–4:00 P.M.; and by appointment.
Society has about fourteen handsewn quilts: seven pieced, two appliqué, two crazy quilts, and one pieced Friendship quilt gives the history of the Elkton Baptist Church. Of those assigned dates one is pre-1820, seven are nineteenth century, and four post-1900. Society maintains continuous exhibit of quilts.
NB: 1847 pieced quilt by twelve year old girl; handwoven red, white, and blue quilt made to

commemorate the United States Centennial; crazy quilt made from World War I uniforms.
Study Services: Reading room.

Cole County Historical Society

B. Gratz Brown House
109 Madison Street
Jefferson City, Missouri 65101
(314) 635-1850

Weekdays, 9:30 A.M.–3:30 P.M.
Collection of fifteen quilts includes twelve nineteenth century, two post-1900, one Cole County Sesquicentennial quilt (1976), and unpublished quilt/quilting documentation. Ten are piecework, four embroidered, and one white-on-white.
Study Services: Make appointment with curator. Reading room, work tables, accession cards/files, and photocopy facilities.
Public Services: Museum tours of periodic quilt exhibitions.

Missouri State Museum

Missouri State Capitol
Room B-2
Jefferson City, Missouri 65101
(314) 751-2854

Daily, 8:00 A.M.–5:00 P.M.
Nine quilts.

The Kansas City Museum

3218 Gladstone Boulevard
Kansas City, Missouri 64123
(816) 483-8300

Tuesday–Saturday, 9:30 A.M.–4:30 P.M.; Sunday, 12:00–4:30 P.M.
Eighty-five regional quilts primarily predate 1920. Techniques include pieced, embroidered, crazy quilts, stuffed work (one with corded initials, and one an appliqué flower quilt), one whole-cloth quilt. Seventy-two are dated: one prior to 1820, fifty-six are nineteenth century, fourteen post 1900, one contemporary. One or two quilts on exhibit at all times.
NB: Concentration of crazy quilts and Log Cabin patterns. Medal winning Lone Star dated 1852 and exhibited in 1853 New York Crystal Palace Exposition.
Study Services: For those with scholarly intent, make appointment with curator at least two weeks in advance. Office hours for researchers, Tuesday–Friday, 8:00 A.M.–5:30 P.M. Reading room, work tables, accession cards/files, books/journals, photocopy facilities, and microscope; slides, prints made from negatives, and notecards.
Public Services: Periodic seminars, public programs, and tours of exhibit.

Centralia Historical Society

319 East Sneed Street
Moberly, Missouri 65240
(314) 682-5711

Sunday–Wednesday, 2:00–4:00 P.M.
Twenty-five piecework, appliqué, and embroidered quilts are from local families in and around Centralia, Missouri; one Appalachian quilt; and one from Kentucky. Eleven are nineteenth century and fourteen are twentieth century. Society maintains continuous exhibit of quilts.
NB: The second oldest quilt in Missouri, 1839; and four unusual crazy quilts.
Study Services: Make formal request for approval by Board of Directors. Work tables, accession cards/files, books/journals, and photocopy facilities.
Public Services: Sponsor annual quilt exhibit for the community.

St. Joseph Museum

11th and Charles Streets
St. Joseph, Missouri 64501
(816) 232-8471

Monday–Saturday, 8:00 A.M.–5:00 P.M.; Sunday, 2:00–5:00 P.M.
There are twenty piecework, appliqué, and embroidered quilts in a collection of which fifty percent have been dated.
Study Services: Make appointment. Reading room, work tables, accession cards/files, and photocopy facilities; slides.

Concordia Historical Institute

801 DeMun Avenue
St. Louis, Missouri 63105
(314) 721-5934

Weekdays, 8:00 A.M.–5:00 P.M.
Seven quilts.

Missouri Historical Society

Jefferson Memorial Building
Forest Park
St. Louis, Missouri 63112
(314) 361-1424

Tuesday–Sunday, 9:30 A.M.–4:45 P.M.
Society has more than 100 quilts, the majority with a Missouri provenance. Seventy-five are patchwork quilts, twelve appliqué, three decorative and white-on-white quilting, two are embroidered, one printed whole-cloth, and one Yo-Yo. Five to ten quilts predate 1820, sixty-five are nineteenth century, twenty quilts date post-1900, five are contemporary.
NB: Regional patchwork, crazy quilts, and appliqué quilts.
Study Services: Make appointment with curator stating research topic. Reading room, accession cards/files, books/journals, and photocopy facilities; some slides.
Public Services: Tours available through education department when quilt exhibition is open. However, tours are most suitable for school audiences.

The St. Louis Art Museum

Forest Park
St. Louis, Missouri 63110
(314) 721-0067

Weekdays, 8:30 A.M.–5:00 P.M.
Museum has thirty-five quilts: six from Missouri, others from Massachusetts, Pennsylvania (two are Amish); Baltimore, Maryland; New England, Kentucky, and Illinois. Techniques represented include piecework, appliqué, candlewicking and stuffed work, white-on-white, embroidered, and a printed quilt (not whole-cloth, but a large section). Seven quilts predate 1820, twenty-two are nineteenth century, four date post-1900, two are contemporary.

Quiltmakers of half the quilts in the collection are known.
NB: Hewson quilt, Baltimore Album quilt.
Study Services: Contact curator in advance to discuss research. Library reading room, work tables, accession cards/files, books/journals, photocopy facilities, and microscope; slides.
Public Services: The loan of a twenty-five slide set, "Quilts and Coverlets," is available to residents of Illinois and Missouri. Orders should be addressed to the Resource Center of the museum.

Sappington House Foundation

1015 South Sappington Road
St. Louis, Missouri 63126
(314) 966-4700, extension 271

Tuesday–Friday, 11:00 A.M.–3:00 P.M.; Saturday, 12:00–3:00 P.M.
Collection includes thirteen handsewn quilts: six piecework, four appliqué, and four embroidered quilts made before 1920. Patterns include Colonial Strip quilt, Oak Leaf eagle and flower basket designs in corners, a variation of the star pattern, Cake Stand/Flower Basket or Flower Pot, Triangles, or Thousand Pyramids, (also called Old Homestead), Whig Rose, President's Wreath (similar to Martha Washington Wreath), crib quilt with a tulip design, Sawtooth, and crazy quilts with embroidery. Foundation holds continuous exhibit of quilts.
Study Services: By special arrangement only. Reading room, and books/journals; photo prints.
Public Services: Quilt exhibits. Handout with descriptive listing of quilts available.

Ste. Genevieve Historical Museum

Merchant and DuBourg Streets
Ste. Genevieve, Missouri 63670
(314) 883-3461

Daily, 8:30 A.M.–4:00 P.M.
Seven quilts.

Museum of Ozarks' History
603 East Calhoun Street
Springfield, Missouri 65802
(417) 869-1976

Tuesday–Saturday, 11:30 A.M.–4:30 P.M.
Collection of twelve regional quilts of local interest from the Midwest and Missouri: six pieced and embroidered, two crazy quilts, two appliqué, two trapunto. Nine are nineteenth century, three date post-1900.
NB: 1853 pieced quilt in excellent condition.
Study Services: Make appointment with director. Reading room, work tables, and accession cards/files.
Public Services: Annual month-long quilt and needlework exhibit.

Hammond (vicinity), Louisiana. April 1939. Berry picker's child peers from behind a fan quilt hung to separate one family's quarters from another. Photo by Russell Lee, negative number LC-USF34-32881-D. Courtesy of the Farm Security Administration Collection, Prints and Photographs Division, Library of Congress.

MONTANA

Museums in the Big Sky Country have collected western U.S. quilts. An Autograph quilt dates from 1834.

Western Heritage Center
2822 Montana Avenue
Billings, Montana 59101
(406) 256-6809

Tuesday–Saturday, 10:00 A.M.–5:00 P.M.; Sunday, 1:00–5:00 P.M.
Fifteen to twenty Northern Great Plains regional quilts from the late nineteenth century to World War I include a few crazy quilts and Log Cabin quilts.
Study Services: By prior arrangement. Reading room, work tables, accession cards/files, and photocopy facilities.
Public Services: Large annual contemporary exhibition of quilts from Montana, Wyoming and other states.

Museum of the Rockies
Montana State University
Bozeman, Montana 59717
(406) 994-2251

Monday–Saturday, 9:00 A.M.–4:30 P.M.; Sunday, 1:00–4:30 P.M.
Approximately sixty-five quilts, tops, fragments of quilts, quilt blocks, and coverlets are from the region. Others were made in Iowa or other states and brought to Montana by migration families. The majority dates from 1860 to 1940. About half of the quiltmakers are known. There are crazy quilts which contain ribbons from the 1889 period of Montana statehood and a number of Signature quilts. Quilts are on continuous exhibition.
NB: Sarah Tracy's diary, crazy quilt, dress with the same fabric used in the quilt, and a photograph of her wearing the dress. Unpublished material and quilt by Lucy Nave Tinsley who came to Montana from Missouri in 1864.

Study Services: By appointment. Reading room, work tables, accession cards/files, books/journals, photocopy facilities, microscope, and photographic/studio lab; photo prints, and slides.
Public Services: Community outreach lectures; quilt exhibitions offered every other year.

Fort Missoula Historical Museum
Building 322
Fort Missoula, Montana 59801
(406) 728-3476

Winter: Tuesday–Sunday, 12:00–5:00 P.M. Summer: Tuesday– Sunday, 10:00 A.M.–5:00 P.M.
Twenty to twenty-five quilts from Kansas, Nebraska, and Montana date primarily from 1910 to 1940. There are also a number of coverlets.
Study Services: Contact curator for appointment. Library reading room, work tables, accession cards/files, books/journals, photocopy facilities, slide viewer; slides.
Public Services: Tours of exhibitions, classes, and workshops during quilt exhibitions.

Cascade County Historical Society
1400 1st Avenue North
Great Falls, Montana 59401
(406) 452-3462

Tuesday–Friday, 10:00 A.M.–5:00 P.M.; weekends, 1:00–4:00 P.M.
Ten regional quilts from Montana that date from 1901 to 1940 include five piecework crazy quilts, four appliqué, and one embroidered Name quilt.
NB: Name quilt and Oak Leaf quilt with fan quilting.
Study Services: Make appointment with the director/curator. Reading room, work tables, and accession cards/files.

Ravalli County Museum
Old Courthouse
205 Bedford
Hamilton, Montana 59840
(406) 363-3338

Winter: Monday, Wednesday, and Friday, 1:00–4:00 P.M.; Sunday, 2:30–5:00 P.M. Summer: weekdays, 10:00 A.M.–4:00 P.M.; Sunday, 2:30–5:00 P.M.
Ten to fifteen regional quilts and approximately 100 American needlework patterns and instructions date mainly from 1821 to 1900. A few are from the 1930s. The earliest is an 1834 Autograph quilt with signatures in India ink. Other patterns include Flying Geese, Yo-Yo, Tumbling Blocks, and a Sioux/Lone Star quilt.
NB: Farnsworth silk crazy quilt made from the linings of Stetson hats and political ribbons.
Study Services: By appointment. Research reading room, work tables, accession cards/files, books/journals, photocopy facilities, and local newspapers from 1891 to the present.
Public Services: Occasional quilt exhibitions.

Montana Historical Society
225 North Roberts Street
Helena, Montana 59620-9990
(406) 444-3714

Winter: Monday–Saturday, 8:00 A.M.–5:00 P.M.; Summer: daily, 9:00 A.M.–6:00 P.M.
This collection of thirty-two quilts has twenty-eight from Montana or western United States, two from Minnesota, one from Kentucky, and one from Pennsylvania. Sixteen are piecework, eight crazy quilts, four embroidered, three appliqué, and one trapunto. Seventeen are nineteenth century, fifteen quilts are post-1900. Individual histories of specific quilts are available.
NB: Quilts with political and social motifs (Red Cross, WCTU).
Study Services: Advance notice required. Work tables, accession cards/files, books, and access to other libraries, photocopy facilities, and microscope; prints made from Society's negatives for educational purposes.

Marias Museum of History and Art

12th Avenue and 1st Street North
Shelby, Montana
(406) 434-7127

Mailing Address:
P.O. Box 378
Shelby, MT 59474

October–May: Wednesday, 12:00–4:00 P.M.;
September–June: Monday–Saturday, 1:00–
5:00 P.M.; and 7:00–9:00 P.M.
Eight to ten quilts.

Mondak Heritage Center

120 Third Avenue, S.E.
Sidney, Montana
(406) 482-3500

Mailing Address:
P.O. Box 50
Sidney, MT 59270

Daily, 1:00–5:00 P.M.
Fourteen Montana-made quilts, all but one
handsewn, include ten pieced, two appliqué,
and two embroidered crazy quilts. Of those
that have been ascribed dates one is a nineteenth century quilt, eight date between 1901
to 1940, two are contemporary. Center has
continuous quilt exhibit.
NB: Embroidered crazy quilt made in 1885.
Study Services: Make appointment with executive director or art director. Reading room,
work tables, accession cards/files, books in art
library, microfilm reader, and photocopy facilities.
Public Services: Tours and an annual competi-
tive quilt show open to public participation.

NEBRASKA

*Midwestern quilts of all types
abound—pioneer, Czech, German,
and Scandinavian piecework.*

Plainsman Museum

210 16th Street
Aurora, Nebraska 68818
(402) 694-6531

April 1–October 31: daily, 9:00 A.M.–5:00 P.M.;
November 1–March 31: daily, 1:00–5:00 P.M.
Scope of the collection of eighteen quilts is
regional and national, including eleven piecework, five embroidered, and two appliqué. Of
those dated: four are nineteenth century, nine
post-1900, two are contemporary. Personal
narratives by quiltmakers, diaries/journals are
cataloged. Quilt patterns include Friendship,
Log Cabin, Postage Stamp, and patriotic designs. Principal donors are residents and former residents of Hamilton County, Nebraska.
Quilts are on continuous exhibition.
NB: Red Cross, Bicentennial, Sunburst-pieced
and quilted on Lock-stitch machine in 1863.
Study Services: Make request several days in
advance to see quilts in storage. Work tables,
accession cards/files, and photocopy facilities;
photo prints, slides, and photo prints made
from Museum negatives available.
Public Services: Biennial quilt exhibit of pri-
vately-owned local quilts and Museum's collection.

Gage County Historical Museum

P.O. Box 793
Beatrice, Nebraska 68310
(402) 228-1679

Hours not provided.
Collection of approximately ten to fifteen
quilts.

Homestead National Monument

Beatrice, Nebraska
(402) 223-3514

Mailing Address:
Route 3, Box 47
Beatrice, NE 68310

Daily, 8:30 A.M.–5:30 P.M. except, Memorial Day–Labor Day: daily, 8:00 A.M.–8:00 P.M. Seven handsewn nineteenth century quilts from the Midwest may be seen by appointment.

Merrick County Historical Museum

211 E Street
Central City, Nebraska
(308) 946-5316

Mailing Address:
c/o Stanley Bice
1415 15th Street
Central City, NE 68826

Open by appointment.
Eight handsewn quilts may be seen by appointment.

Washington County Historical Museum

14th and Monroe Streets
Ft. Calhoun, Nebraska
(402) 468-5740

Mailing Address:
P.O. Box 178
Ft. Calhoun, NE 68023

Wednesday, Friday, and weekends, 1:30–4:30 P.M.
In the collection of nineteen quilts, eighteen have been dated: one prior to 1820, six others from the nineteenth century, eleven post-1900, and one contemporary. Quilts on exhibition at all times.
Study Services: Make request. Reading room, work tables, and accession cards/files; photo prints, and prints made from negatives.
Public Services: Tours.

Stuhr Museum of the Prairie Pioneer

3133 West Highway 34
Grand Island, Nebraska 68801
(308) 384-1380

October 1–April 30: Monday–Saturday, 9:00 A.M.–5:00 P.M.; Sunday, 1:00–5:00 P.M. May 1– September 30: daily, 9:00 A.M.– 6:00 P.M.; closed Thanksgiving, Christmas, and New Year's Day.
The Museum has a collection of 121 regional, German, and some Scandinavian quilts. About 101 pieced quilts include crazy quilts, Log Cabin patterns, and other designs. Twelve are appliqué, five Signature quilts, two embroidered, one Yo-Yo. Ninety-six are dated: two pre-1820, sixty nineteenth century, thirty-two post-1900, and two contemporary.
NB: Flag Insignia Civil War Signature quilt, Fiftieth Anniversary quilt with signatures of first Grand Island settlers.
Study Services: Write for appointment. Accession cards/files, books/journals, and photocopy facilities.

Hastings Museum

J. M. McDonald Planetarium
1330 North Burlington Avenue
Hastings, Nebraska 68901
(402) 461-2399

Monday–Saturday, 9:00 A.M.–5:00 P.M.; Sunday, 1:00–5:00 P.M.
Collection of thirty-six quilts includes twenty-one piecework, nine appliqué, four embroidered, two stuffed. Twenty were made in the nineteenth century. Quilts are always exhibited.
Study Services: For scholars, make request in advance. Work tables, accession cards/files.

Dawson County Historical Society

805 North Taft
Lexington, Nebraska
(308) 324-5340

Mailing Address:
P.O. Box 369
Lexington, NE 68850

Monday–Saturday, 8:00 A.M.–5:00 P.M.
Collection contains approximately twenty-seven quilts: seven Friendship, three Log Cabin, one Yo-Yo, one appliqué, one embroidered bed spread and six woven coverlets. Sixteen are nineteenth century, nine date after 1900, two are contemporary. Quilts exhibited at all times.
Study Services: Make request. Reading room, work tables, accession cards/files, library/archives, and photocopy facilities; prints made from Society's negatives; photographs of quilts upon request.
Public Services: Tours of museum facilities.

The State Museum of History

1500 R Street
Lincoln, Nebraska
(402) 471-3270

Mailing Address:
P.O. Box 82554
Lincoln, NE 68501

Monday–Saturday, 8:00 A.M.–5:00 P.M.; Sunday and holidays, 1:30–5:00 P.M.; closed New Year's, Thanksgiving, and Christmas.
Formerly called the Nebraska State Historical Museum, the collection includes approximately twenty quilts.

Sheldon Memorial Art Gallery

University of Nebraska
12th and R Streets
Lincoln, Nebraska 68588-0300
(402) 472-2461

Thursday–Saturday, 12:00–5:00 P.M. Sunday, 2:00–9:00 P.M.
Collection of six quilts.
Publications: Quilts from Nebraska Collections (1974).

Joslyn Art Museum

2200 Dodge Street
Omaha, Nebraska 68102
(402) 342-3300

Tuesday–Saturday, 10:00 A.M.–5:00 P.M.; Sunday, 1:00–5:00 P.M.
Collection of thirty-three quilts: approximately twenty-nine are from the Midwest, one southern, one from New England, one from Connecticut, one from Pennsylvania. Techniques and patterns: pieced quilts, crazy quilts, Chimney Sweep, Log Cabin, Octagonal Star, Tulip, Hanging Diamond, Rose, Friendship, Carpenter's Wheel, Peony, Star of Bethlehem, Meadow Lily, Birds in the Air, Heart and Hand, Double Monkey Wrench, Lemon Star/Star of Lemoyn, and Leaf Border. Materials include cotton, silk, taffeta, and wool. About half are dated: two pre-1820, fifteen pre-1900, and one contemporary.
NB: Leaf Border quilt which won first place in 1948 New York State Fair.
Study Services: Make appointment with registrar. Accession cards/files, books/journals, and photocopy facilities; photo prints can be ordered.

Wilber Czech Museum

102 West 3rd
Wilber, Nebraska
(402) 821-2183 or 821-2485

Mailing Address:
P.O. Box 652
Wilber, NE 68465

May–December: daily, 1:00–4:00 P.M.
Fourteen Czechoslovakian piecework, appliqué, and embroidered quilts are from the region. One quilt predates 1820, one is nineteenth century, six are post-1900, and six are contemporary. Quilts are on continuous exhibition.
Public Services: Tours and open house.

NEVADA

Thirty-eight quilts (four made in the state) can be seen in two museums.

Churchill County Museum and Archive
1050 South Main Street
Fallon, Nevada 89406
(702) 423-3677

Winter: Monday, Tuesday, Wednesday, Friday, and Saturday, 10:00 A.M.–4:00 P.M.; Sunday, 12:00–4:00 P.M. Summer: Monday, Tuesday, Wednesday, Thursday, and Saturday, 9:00 A.M.–5:00 P.M.; Sunday, 12:00–5:00 P.M.
Museum has twenty-four handsewn American quilts: four from Nevada, three from Iowa, one each from Oregon, Kansas, and Michigan. Collection includes patchwork, crazy quilts, appliqué, Friendship, and one embroidered quilt. Twelve made in the nineteenth century, and twelve date 1901 to 1940. Quilts are on continuous exhibition.
NB: North Carolina Lily quilt, Heavenly Steps quilt, Boxed T quilt, and Courthouse Square quilt.
Study Services: Make written request specifying date of intended visit, allowing two weeks. Work tables, accession cards/files, photocopy facilities, and microscope; photo prints, slides, prints made from negatives.

Nevada Historical Society
1650 North Virginia Street
Reno, Nevada 89701
(702) 789-0190

Wednesday–Sunday, 10:00 A.M.–5:00 P.M. Office: weekdays, 8:00 A.M.–5:00 P.M.; weekends, 10:00 A.M.–5:00 P.M.
Collection of fourteen quilts and eight quilt tops. Most were brought from Illinois to Nevada. Quilts date from c. 1840 to 1940. There are seventeen historic photographs and other materials generated from *Quilts in Nevada* exhibition (January 1984). Some patterns represented: Grandmother's Flower Garden, Log Cabin Barn Raising variation, machine quilted whole-cloth crib quilt, Tulip appliqué, crazy quilt, crazy style pillow shams, Nine Patch with embroidered signatures, Jacob's Ladder variation and Sunflower. Top patterns: Honeycomb, Wild Goose Chase, Pinwheel, Frog in a Pond, Variable Star, contained crazy quilt, Spider Web string-type, and Mosaic. Materials include: cotton, satin, silk, taffetas, velvet, and one piece of wool.
NB: Sunflower quilt, c. 1860, stolen in raid during the Civil War; doll quilt, Puss-in-the-Corner, c. 1860 (Puss-in-the-Corner was a popular children's game of the period); 1890 crazy quilt, and Maltese Cross quilt, c. 1840.
Study Services: Must have valid research or collections management interests. Reading room, work tables, accession cards/files, library photographic and manuscript collection, books/journals, and photocopy facilities; slides and photo prints can be ordered.
Public Services: Exhibitions, lectures, and films.

Warner (vicinity), Oklahoma. June 1939. An American flag quilt covers tenant farmer's bed. Photo by Russell Lee, negative number LC-USF34-33472-D. Courtesy of the Farm Security Administration Collection, Prints and Photographs Division, Library of Congress.

NEW HAMPSHIRE

Four institutions exhibit regional New Hampshire and New England quilts.

New Hampshire Historical Society

30 Park Street
Concord, New Hampshire 03301
(603) 225-3381

Monday–Saturday, 9:00 A.M.–4:30 P.M.;
Wednesday, to 8:00 P.M.
Fifty-five quilts were made and/or used in New Hampshire. In addition, Society has 198 quilt patterns and instructions. Techniques include piecework, plain (linen and/or wool), appliqué, white-on-white, and embroidered. More than half are dated: six pre-1820, twenty-one others are nineteenth century, one post-1900.
Study Services: Write for appointment. Reading room, work tables, accession cards/files, books/journals, and photocopy facilities; photo prints, slides, and photo prints may be ordered.
Public Services: Occasional quiltmaking workshops.

New Hampshire Antiquarian Society

Maine Street, Hopkinton Village
Hopkinton, New Hampshire
(603) 746-4292

Mailing Address:
R.R. 3, Box 132
Hopkinton Village, NH 03229

Monday and Wednesday, 1:00–5:00 P.M.
Seven quilts from New Hampshire may be seen by appointment.

Lady's stomacher, Holland, early eighteenth century. Embroidered and stuffed on white linen ground. Courtesy of the Alice Schott Bequest, catalog number 78, the American Quilt Research Center, Los Angeles County Museum of Art.

The Currier Gallery of Art

192 Orange Street
Manchester, New Hampshire 03104
(603) 669-6144

Office: weekdays, 9:00 A.M.–5:00 P.M.
A collection of nine quilts.

Strawberry Banke

454 Court Street
Portsmouth, New Hampshire
(603) 433-1100

Mailing Address:
P.O. Box 300
Portsmouth, NH 03801

Offices: weekdays, 9:00 A.M.–5:00 P.M.
Approximately fifty regional quilts from New England. The quilts are uncataloged and unretrievable pending renovation of storage area.
Study Services: Make advance appointment with collections department. Reading room, work tables, accession cards/files, and photocopy facilities; prints made from negatives upon request.

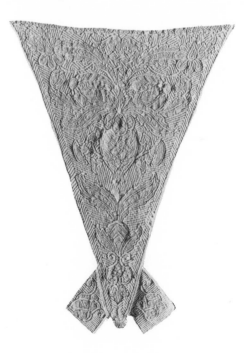

NEW JERSEY

Quilts are exhibited in all sections of the state: early New Jersey-made quilts as well as Quaker, Dutch-American and others from the Delaware Valley.

Allaire Village
Allaire State Park
Route 524
Allaire, New Jersey
(201) 938-2253

Mailing Address:
Post Office
Farmingdale, NJ 07727

May 1–Labor Day: 10:00 A.M.–5:00 P.M.
Collection of twenty quilts.

Warren County Historical and Genealogical Society
313 Mansfield Street
Belvidere, New Jersey
(201) 475-2512

Mailing Address:
P.O. Box 313
Belvidere, NJ 07823

Thursday, 9:30 A.M.–2:00 P.M.; Sunday, 2:00–4:00 P.M.; or by appointment.
Ten handsewn quilts are from northern New Jersey and include five crazy quilts with decorative embroidery, three embroidered Album quilts, two piecework, and one appliqué. Of those dated, seven were made in the nineteenth century, and three date after 1900. Quilts on exhibit at all times.
NB: Crazy quilt.
Study Services: Visit the museum during regular hours or make appointment. Reading room, work tables, and accession cards/files; photo prints, and slides by arrangement.
Public Services: Annual quilt exhibit each November.

Burlington County Historical Society
457 High Street
Burlington, New Jersey 08016
(609) 386-4773

Tours: Monday–Thursday, 1:00–4:00 P.M.; Sunday, 2:00–4:00 P.M.
Forty-five regional pieced and/or appliqué quilts are continuously on exhibition.
NB: Burtis Album quilt, Deacon Star of Bethlehem, and Eastwood appliqué quilt.
Study Services: A new textile storage area is being built and will be accessible in 1987. Reading room, books/journals, and photocopy facilities.
Public Services: Tours.

Camden County Historical Society
Park Boulevard and Euclid Avenue
Camden, New Jersey 08013
(609) 964-3333

Monday–Thursday, 9:30 A.M.–4:30 P.M.; Sunday, 2:00–4:40 P.M.
Twenty-two quilts from the Delaware Valley include four from southern New Jersey, and eight to ten quilts from the Philadelphia area. Eighteen are pieced quilts, two appliqué, one white-on-white, one pieced and embroidered. Eighteen are nineteenth century, three date post-1900, one is contemporary.
Study Services: Arrange with curator. Reading room, work tables, accession cards/files, and photocopy facilities; photo prints, slides; prints can be made from negatives in compliance with Society photographic policy.

Cape May County Historical & Genealogical Society
Cape May Court House
Route 9, Rural Delivery 1
Cape May, New Jersey 08210
(609) 465-3535

Hours not provided.
Collection of ten quilts.

Barclay Farmstead

Barclay Lane
Cherry Hill, New Jersey
(609) 795-6225

Mailing Address:
820 Mercer Street
Cherry Hill, NJ 08002

Tuesday–Friday, 9:00 A.M.–4:00 P.M.
In the collection of twelve quilts half are from
south New Jersey. There are also five quilt
patterns/instructions, and photographs. Eleven
quilts are piecework and one is appliqué; collection dates from the nineteenth and first
four decades of the twentieth century.
Study Services: By appointment. Work tables,
accession cards/files, and books/journals;
photo prints, slides, and prints made from
negatives by request.
Public Services: Seasonal workshops, continuing quilting bee.

Chester Historical Society

Chester, New Jersey
(201) 879-7740 or 879-5750

Mailing Address:
P.O. Box 376
Chester, NJ 07930

By appointment only.
Four quilts and five quilt tops are from northwest New Jersey.

Clinton Historical Museum Village

56 Main Street
Clinton, New Jersey
(201) 735-4101

Mailing Address:
P.O. Box 5005
Clinton, NJ 08809-5005

April 1–October 31: daily, 1:00–5:00 P.M.
Approximately 30 quilts in collection; five can
be dated. Quilts always on exhibition.
Study Services: For scholars, by appointment.

Reading room, work tables, accession cards/
files, and photocopy facilities.
Public Services: Guided tours which include
quilts on exhibition.

Monmouth County Historical Association

70 Court Street
Freehold, New Jersey 07728
(201) 462-1466

Tuesday–Saturday, 10:00 A.M.–4:00 P.M.; Sunday, 1:00–4:00 P.M.
Collection of fifty regional quilts from Monmouth County and New Jersey, including
thirty-five piecework quilts, five appliqué, and
one trapunto. Five quilts predate 1820, thirty-
five predate 1900, and five are post-1900.
Study Services: Make appointment with curator. Reading room, work tables, accession
cards/files, books/journals, and photocopy facilities; photo prints, slides, prints made from
negatives upon request.
Public Services: Programs in conjunction with
quilt exhibits.

Museum of Early Trades and Crafts

Main Street at Green Village Road
Madison, New Jersey 07940
(201) 377-2982

Monday–Saturday, 8:30 A.M.–5:00 P.M.; Sunday,
2:00–5:00 P.M.
Collection of eight quilts.

Morris County Historical Society

68 Morris Avenue
Morristown, New Jersey
(201) 267-3465

Mailing Address:
P.O. Box 170
Morristown, NJ 07960

Thursday, 11:00 A.M.–3:00 P.M.; Sunday, 1:30–
4:00 P.M.
Society has eleven Northeastern regional
quilts, mostly from New Jersey, Pennsylvania,
New York, and Massachusetts. Eight are piecework, some with decorative quilting, three are
crazy quilts. All quilts are pieced with a con-

centration on crazy quilts and Log Cabin quilts. Three date from the nineteenth century. Principal source of the collection is Alice Kollar of the house donor family.

NB: One quilt dated 1847 with campaign ribbons from 1840 election.

Study Services: Call for appointment. Reading room, work tables, accession cards/files, and photocopy facilities; slides, and prints made from negatives.

Morris Museum
6 Normandy Heights Road
Morristown, New Jersey 07960
(201) 538-0454

Tuesday–Saturday, 10:00 A.M.–5:00 P.M.; Sunday, 1:00–5:00 P.M.

There are thirty-four quilts, approximately twenty-nine from New Jersey and Pennsylvania. Patterns and techniques include appliqué, crazy quilts, embroidered, piecework, Log Cabin, trapunto, and Amish Diamond. Five predate 1820, twenty-five are nineteenth century, three are post-1900, and one is contemporary.

NB: 1820 to 1850 Star of Bethlehem quilt.

Study Services: By appointment. Reading room, work tables, accession cards/files, books/journals, and photocopy facilities; photo prints, slides, and prints made from negatives upon request.

Public Services: Programs that complement quilt exhibits.

Publications: New Jersey Quilters: A Timeless Tradition (1983).

Morristown National Historical Park
Washington Place
Morristown, New Jersey 07960
(201) 539-2016

Daily 9:00 A.M.–5:00 P.M.
Collection of seven quilts.

The New Jersey Historical Society
230 Broadway Street
Newark, New Jersey 07104
(201) 483-3939

Monday–Saturday, 12:00–4:00 P.M.

Approximately forty handsewn regional quilts are predominantly from New Jersey; a few are foreign. Nine are estimated to predate 1820, twenty-five are nineteenth century. A broad range of techniques represented.

NB: Quaker Friendship Album quilt, Burlington and Camden counties, 1850; Signature quilt, Ladies Aid Society of Mount Pleasant Baptist Church, Newark, 1880; Newark observance of United States Centennial quilt, 1876; Friendship Album quilt; Bible class of 3rd Presbyterian Church, Newark, 1855; trapunto wine and grape design, c. 1810; Friendship Album quilt, Pointville Methodist/Episcopal Church, Burlington County, 1889.

Study Services: Contact curator, state purpose. Quilts are not readily accessible. Reading room, work tables, accession cards/files, books/journals, and photocopy facilities.

The Newark Museum
49 Washington Street
Newark, New Jersey 07101
(201) 733-6600

Tuesday–Sunday, 12:00–5:00 P.M.

In the collection of 135 quilts, eighty-three are from the United States: thirty from New Jersey, including Newark; ten from New York State; others from Pennsylvania, Massachusetts, Vermont, Connecticut, and Delaware. There are examples from other regions: the South, New England, Mid-Atlantic, the Midwest. An estimated eighty-four quilts are piecework, thirty-four appliqué, eighteen stuffed and/or corded, five whole cloth, three white-on-white. Dates range from the early eighteenth century to the 1940's; fourteen quilts date prior to 1820, 105 from the nineteenth century, eleven post-1900, and five post-1941.

NB: A number of New Jersey made/owned quilts, and almost all donated to the Museum from direct descendents of the quiltmakers. Centennial quilt commemorates Philadelphia Centennial Exposition of 1876. Appliqué, stuffed work and embroidered quilt, made in East Orange, New Jersey, c. 1860-65, by Emeline Dean Jones. Voorhees quilt, made between 1830 and 1831 by Jane Voorhees, white-on-white stuffed work.

Study Services: For the public only by special arrangement; for scholars with specific interest, by appointment, contact curator. Reading room, limited access to accession cards/files, until completion of new storage/study, books/journals, photocopy facilities; photo prints, some slides, color 4x5 transparencies, and photo prints to order from negatives.

Public Services: During exhibitions, broad range of educational tours for different age groups. Quilting workshops offered in adult arts workshop department.

Publications: Curtis, Phillip. *American Quilts in the Newark Museum Collection* (1973). White, Margaret Evelyn. *Quilts and Counterpanes* (1948).

Passaic County Historical Society
Lambert Castle
Valley Road
Paterson, New Jersey 07503
(201) 881-2761

Hours not provided.
Collection of thirteen quilts.

Pennsauken Historical Society
Burrough-Dover House
Burrough-Dover Lane
Pennsauken, New Jersey
(609) 662-0873 or 662-9175

Mailing Address:
P.O. Box 56
Pennsauken, NJ 08110

Hours vary, and by appointment.
Collection contains twenty-two handsewn quilts, eighteen from Southen New Jersey. Eighteen are pieced quilts, four appliqué. Three are lined with homespun, one Victorian crazy quilt is embroidered and tied, one silk quilt top is English piecing, and one is pieced and appliqué on wool. Twenty are dated: ten nineteenth century, six after 1900, and four after 1940. Rotating quilt exhibitions at all times.

Study Services: By appointment. Work tables, accession cards/files, and other facilities by arrangement.

Public Services: Annual quilt exhibit in which the majority of the collection is on view.

Drake House Museum
602 West Front Street
Plainfield, New Jersey 07060
(201) 755-5831

Saturday, 2:00–4:00 P.M.; or by appointment.
Collection of six nineteenth century quilts.

Historical Society of Princeton
Bainbridge House
158 Nassau Street
Princeton, New Jersey 08542
(609) 921-6748

Not provided.
Collection of six nineteenth century quilts.

Thomas Clarke House
500 Mercer Street
Princeton, New Jersey 08540
(609) 921-0074

Wednesday–Friday, 9:00 A.M.–12:00 P.M., 1:00–5:00 P.M. Saturday, 10:00 A.M.–12:00 P.M., 1:00–5:00 P.M., Sunday, 1:00–5:00 P.M.
Collection of six quilts on long term loan from area residents.

Bergen County Historical Society

1209 Main Street
River Edge, New Jersey
(201) 487-1739

Mailing Address:
P.O. Box 55
River Edge, NJ 07661

Wednesday–Saturday, 10:00 A.M.–12:00 P.M.;
Sunday, 2:00– 5:00 P.M.; closed New Year's
and Christmas.
Collection contains thirty-three quilts; one is
from Denmark. Techniques include piecework, appliqué, and trapunto. Eighteen are
dated: one pre-1820, thirteen nineteenth century, two post-1900, and one contemporary.
NB: Betsy Haring quilt, 1859.
Study Services: Request in writing. Hackensack
Public Library has reading room, some photographs and books, and photocopy facilities;
slides.
*Publications: The Tree of Life: Selections of
Bergen County Folk Art* (1983).

Salem County Historical Society

79-83 Market Street
Salem, New Jersey 08079
(609) 935-5004

Tuesday–Friday, 12:00–4:00 P.M.
Twelve handsewn quilts from the New Jersey
and Mid-Atlantic region include one Quaker
quilt and notes from donor families, citizens
of Fenwick Colony. Two definitely date from
the nineteenth century. Patterns include star
and Log Cabin. Quilts are on continuous exhibition.
NB: Friendship quilt with 1842 signature;
crazy quilt containing 1870-75, and political
mementos.
Study Services: By appointment. Reading
room, work tables, accession cards/files, and
photocopy facilities; some photo prints and
slides, prints made from file negatives by request.
Public Services: Lectures series with speakers
from Winterthur Museum, Winterthur, Delaware.

Museum of the Atlantic County

Historical Society
907 Shore Road
Somers Point, New Jersey
(609) 641-2405 or 927-5218

Mailing Address:
P.O. Box 301
Somers Point, NJ 08201

Thursday–Saturday, 10:00 A.M.–4:00 P.M.
Museum has nineteen quilts; five date from
the nineteenth century, one is contemporary.
One or two quilts always on exhibition.
NB: 1843 Signature/Autograph wedding quilt
presented to the groom, from Abington, Pennsylvania. Unit Triangle quilt 1870, made of lining scraps from a hat factory.
Study Services: Contact curator for permission. Reading room, accession cards/files,
books/journals, and photocopy facilities.

New Jersey State Museum

205 West State Street
Trenton, New Jersey 08625-0530
(609) 292-6300

Tuesday–Saturday, 9:00 A.M.–4:45 P.M.; Sunday,
1:00–5:00 P.M.
Twenty-one quilts from New Jersey/Delaware
Valley region and documentation on particular
quilts/quiltmakers comprise the collection. Fifteen are nineteenth century, one after 1900,
and five are contemporary.
Study Services: For scholars, write for appointment two to four weeks in advance. Accession
cards/files, and books/journals; photo prints,
slides; photo prints may be ordered from Museum negatives.
Public Services: Special programs during exhibitions.

Old Barracks Museum

Barrack Street
Trenton, New Jersey 08608
(609) 396-1776

Monday–Saturday, 10:00 A.M.–5:00 P.M.; Sunday, 1:00–5:00 P.M.; closed major holidays. There are six handmade quilts: two memory quilts (from New Jersey and Pennsylvania), one campaign quilt, one white trapunto, one white and green geometric floral, one child's patchwork.

Dey Mansion

199 Totowa Road
Wayne, New Jersey 07470
(201) 696-1776

Tuesday, Wednesday, and Friday: 1:00–4:00 P.M.; Saturday, 10:00 A.M.–12:00 P.M., and 1:00–4:00 P.M.; Sunday, 10:00 A.M.– 4:00 P.M. Five nineteenth century quilts may be seen by appointment.

Van Riper-Hopper House/Wayne Museum

533 Berdan Avenue
Wayne, New Jersey 07470
(201) 694-7192

Friday–Tuesday, 1:00–5:00 P.M.; special groups by appointment. Closed New Year's and Christmas.
Museum has twelve handsewn quilts. Four are early Dutch-American quilts. Six date from the nineteenth century. Quilts always on exhibit.
Study Services: Make appointment with curator. Reading room, work tables, and microscope.
Public Services: House tours, quilts on display in period rooms.

Gloucester County Historical Society

58 North Broad Street
Woodbury, New Jersey 08096
(609) 845-4771

Wednesday and Friday, 1:00–4:00 P.M.
In the collection of approximately twenty-five quilts, the majority dates from the nineteenth century. A few quilts are exhibited on beds at all times.
Study Services: Call or write for appointment a week in advance, quilts in storage may be seen if staff is available.
Public Services: Quilts usually featured at annual open house.

Crystal Cruise of Vesta, Virginia piecing a Flower Garden quilt. American Folklife Center, Blue Ridge Parkway, 1978. Fieldwork and photo by Geraldine Johnson, negative number 4-20343, 11. Courtesy of the Archive of Folk Culture, Library of Congress.

NEW MEXICO

Cowboys' quilted bedrolls along with colonial patchwork and southwestern regional quilts are on view.

High Plains Historical Foundation
411 Main Street c/o Lyceum Theater
Clovis, New Mexico 88101
(505) 763-6361

Weekdays, 4:00–9:00 P.M.
Foundation's collection of twenty-six hand-sewn regional quilts includes ten piecework, seven trapunto, three appliqué, two with decorative quilting, two printed quilts, and two suggins (quilted bed roll used by cowboys). Three are nineteenth century quilts, eight post-1900, fifteen post-1941.
Study Services: Contact president for appointment. Slides and prints made from negatives.

Deming Luna Mimbres Museum of the Luna County Historical Society, Inc.
301 South Silver Street
Deming, New Mexico
(505) 546-2382

Mailing Address:
P.O. Box 1617
Deming, NM 88031

Monday–Saturday, 9:00 A.M.–4:00 P.M.; Sunday, 1:30–4:00 P.M.; closed Thanksgiving, Christmas, and New Year's Day.
The collection contains ten quilts, another six on loan to museum, and eight woven coverlets. Ninety-five percent are from Deming, New Mexico residents. Most have names; all have descriptions, donors, and approximate years ascribed. Techniques represented are piecework and appliqué. Quilts with dates include two pre-1820, ten nineteenth century, three post-1900, and one contemporary. Exhibits of quilts are continuous.
NB: Whig Rose, made in the eighteenth century, Tree of Life made in the early 1900s.

Study Services: By appointment. Accession cards/files, and collection on computer.
Publications: Gilmore Quilt Room is pictured in the general Museum brochure.

Museum of International Folk Art
Museum of New Mexico
706 Camino Lejo
Santa Fe, New Mexico
(505) 827-8350

Mailing Address:
P.O. Box 2087
Santa Fe, NM 87504-2087

Tuesday–Sunday, 10:00 A.M.–5:00 P.M.
Museum has fifty-five quilts of which twenty-five are from New Mexico (Anglo, Afro-American, Hispanic New Mexican, and Navajo); also one Amish quilt, two Afro-American quilts, one Hawaiian quilt. The remainder of the collection is from the Midwest and East Coast. The range of techniques is very broad. Documentation includes nineteen taped interviews/oral histories of quiltmakers, ten transcriptions of the tapes, and research-in-progress on New Mexican quiltmaking.
Study Services: Write well in advance and explain needs. Library reading room, work tables, accession cards/files, books/journals, photocopy facilities, and microscope.
Public Services: Exhibitions, programs, lectures, and tours.

The History Division
Museum of New Mexico
706 Camino Lejo
Santa Fe, New Mexico
(505) 827-8350

Mailing Address:
P.O. Box 2087
Santa Fe, NM 87504-2087

By appointment.
Collection of twenty quilts made between 1850 and 1940; the majority are from the Midwest.

Silver City Museum
312 West Broadway Street
Silver City, New Mexico 88062
(505) 538-5921

Tuesday–Friday, 9:00 A.M.–4:30 P.M.; weekends, 1:00–4:00 P.M.
Collection of sixteen piecework quilts; seven were made or brought by early southwest New Mexico settlers, nine were made in New Mexico. Six date from the nineteenth century.
Study Services: Contact director to arrange appointment. Accession cards/files, and photocopy facilities.

The Singer Manufacturing Company, color lithograph and printed tradecard, "The Improved Family Singer Sewing Machine," copyright 1884. Courtesy of the Historic New Orleans Collection, 533 Royal Street, Acc. No. 1958.31.73.

NEW YORK

Although New York City is a center for quilts and quilt study, quilt resources can be found all across the Empire State.

Albany Institute of History and Art
125 Washington Avenue
Albany, New York 12208
(518) 463-4478

Tuesday–Saturday, 10:00 A.M.–4:45 P.M.; Sunday, 2:00–5:00 P.M.
The Institute has twenty-eight quilts from the upper Hudson-Mohawk region of New York State. Fifteen are piecework, six printed whole-cloth with quilting, three white-on-white, two embroidered, and two stuffed. Ten quilts predate 1820, seventeen are nineteenth century, one is contemporary.
Study Services: Make appointment at least two weeks in advance. Reading room, work tables, accession cards/files, books/journals, and photocopy facilities.
Publications: Groft, Tammis K. *The Folk Spirit of Albany* (1978).

Schuyler Mansion State Historic Site
32 Catherine Street
Albany, New York 12202
(518) 474-3953

Hours not provided.
A collection of five quilts; two trapunto, two appliqué, and one pieced.

The Erpf Catskill Cultural Center
Route 28
Arkville, New York 12406
(914) 586-3326

Weekdays, 9:00 A.M.–5:00 P.M.
A collection of documentation on quilting includes eight transcribed taped oral histories of quiltmakers; photo prints, slides, books/journals, prints of quilts and quiltmakers made from negatives.

Roberson Center for the Arts and Sciences
30 Front Street
Binghamton, New York 13905
(607) 772-0660

Tuesday–Saturday, 10:00 A.M.–8:00 P.M. Summer: hours may vary.
Collection includes less than fifty quilts.

South East Museum
67-69 Main Street
Brewster, New York
(914) 279-7500

Mailing Address:
P.O. Box 88
Brewster, NY 10509

Wednesday, 12:00–4:00 P.M.; weekends, 2:00–4:00 P.M.
Of this collection of twenty-one quilts one is a Connecticut Yankee quilt, and three are from New York State. Among them are eight pieced, four pieced and appliqué, three appliqué, five crazy quilts. Of those dated eight are from the nineteenth century, five date after 1900. Quilts are on continuous exhibition.
NB: Autograph quilt made in 1869; two crazy quilts made in the Brewster area.
Study Services: For scholars, make appointment. Accession cards/files.

The Brooklyn Museum
200 Eastern Parkway
Brooklyn, New York 11238
(718) 638-5000

Monday, Wednesday, Thursday, and Friday, 10:00 A.M.–5:00 P.M.; Saturday, 10:00 A.M.–6:00 P.M.; Sunday, 1:00–6:00 P.M.; Offices: weekdays, 9:00 A.M.–5:00 P.M.
A collection of approximately 150 quilts from the United States, Great Britain, and Europe.
Study Services: By appointment. Reading room, work tables, accession cards/files, books/journals, photocopy facilities, and microscope for printed material; photo prints, slides, prints made from negatives; postcards, and notepaper.
Public Services: Gallery tours when quilts are on view.

Buffalo and Erie County Historical Society
25 Nottingham Court
Buffalo, New York 14216
(716) 873-9644 or 874-0670

By appointment.
A rapidly expanding collection of forty-three regional quilts. Twenty-seven pieced, four appliqué (six are crazy quilts), five embroidered, and one white-on-white. There is some unpublished documentation on quilts/quilting. Twenty-seven are dated: twenty-three from the nineteenth century, four are post-1900.
NB: Pan-American Exposition quilt; Friendship quilt.
Study Services: Requests in writing are reviewed. Reading room, work tables, accession cards/files, photocopy facilities; photo prints made from negatives, slides.
Public Services: In planning stages.

Cheektowaga Historical Association
3329 Broadway
Cheektowaga, New York 14227
(716) 684-6544

Tuesday, 9:00 A.M.–12:00 P.M.; Sunday, 2:00–4:00 P.M.; and by appointment.
Eighteen handsewn regional quilts have been collected from within a six square mile area.

Documentation includes eighteen quilt patterns and instructions, and taped interviews with quiltmakers. Concentration in patchwork quilts; five silk-and-velvet crazy quilts, three appliqué. Nine are nineteenth century, six made after 1900, three are contemporary. Association has continuous exhibit of quilts.
NB: Bicentennial quilt.
Study Services: For scholars, make appointment with curator. Work tables, accession cards/files, and books/journals.
Public Services: One quilt class each year, and one quilt workshop with a neighboring historical society.

Putnam County Historical Society
63 Chestnut Street
Cold Spring, New York 10516
(914) 265-4010

Wednesday, 9:30 A.M.–4:00 P.M.; Sunday, 2:00–5:00 P.M.
The majority of this collection of twelve handsewn quilts was made locally. Among them are seven piecework, three appliqué, one stuffed. Those dated are four nineteenth century, three post-1900, one contemporary.
NB: Several quilts with embroidered names made by groups as fund-raisers.
Study Services: Access to the stored collections on Wednesdays only. Work tables, accession cards/files, books/journals, and photocopy facilities.

The New York State Historical Association and the Farmers' Museum
Lake Road
Cooperstown, New York
(607) 547-8533

Mailing Address:
P.O. Box 800
Cooperstown, NY 13326

May–December: daily, 9:00 A.M.–5:00 P.M.; closed January–April.
Thirty-one of the 129 quilts in the collection are from New York State and the surrounding region, approximately ninety-eight are from the Northeast. Among them are fifty-nine

pieced, sixteen embroidered, fifteen appliqué, seven trapunto, six printed whole-cloth with quilting, two white-on-white, and one candlewick. Approximately 102 are dated: nineteen pre-1820, eighty-two pre-1900 quilts, one contemporary.
Study Services: Members and scholars may make appointments to study the collections. Reading room, work tables, accession cards/files, books/journals, photocopy facilities, and microscope; photo prints, slides, photo prints may be requested.
Public Services: Summer seminar workshops on quilts.

Cortland County Historical Society
25 Homer Avenue
Cortland, New York 13045
(607) 756-6071

Tuesday–Saturday, 1:00–4:00 P.M.
The Society's thirty-six quilts were made or used in Cortland County, New York. Eight are pieced, seven embroidered crazy quilts, five Album, two appliqué, two printed whole-cloth with quilting. Twenty-three are dated: one pre-1820, seventeen nineteenth century, four post-1900, one contemporary.
NB: 1976 Bicentennial quilt.
Study Services: Scholars, make appointment. Reading room, work tables, accession cards/files, books/journals, and photocopy facilities.
Public Services: Special programs offered for quilt exhibits.

Poplar Springs Quilters, Surry County, North Carolina, putting a quilt in the frame. American Folklife Center, Blue Ridge Parkway Project, 1978. Fieldwork by Geraldine Johnson, photo by Lyntha Eiler, negative number 8-20493, 18. Courtesy of the Archive of Folk Culture, Library of Congress.

Bronck Museum

Greene County Historical Society
Route 9 West
Coxsackie, New York
(518) 731-8862

Mailing Address:
c/o S.A. Kriele, Curator
Bronck Museum
45 Lafayette Avenue
Coxsackie, NY 12051

July–August only: Tuesday–Saturday, 10:00
A.M.–4:30 P.M.
The Museum has twenty or more quilts native
to the Hudson Valley and Greene County,
New York. Approximately fifteen are piecework, five appliqué, four machine quilted or
tied piecework, one whole-cloth, one white-
on-white trapunto pillowsham, and one Bicentennial quilt in long-term storage. Three are
known nineteenth century quilts, one is later.
Exhibit of quilts is continuous.
NB: Whole-cloth linsey woolsey quilt, c. 1770.
Study Services: For scholars, call or write the
curator. Reading room, and accession cards/
files; photo prints, and prints may be requested from Museum's negatives.
Public Services: Quilting groups or other interested groups may arrange access to entire
collection by writing or calling curator.

Delaware County Historical Association

Delhi, New York
(607) 746-3849

Mailing Address:
R.D. 2, Box 201-C
Delhi, NY 13753

Tuesday–Friday, 10:00 A.M.–4:30 P.M.; weekends, 1:00–4:30 P.M.; or by appointment.
The fifty quilts from Delaware County, New
York in this collection include forty-five piecework, two appliqué, two embroidered, one
white-on-white. Two quilts predate 1820,
seven are nineteenth century, six are early
twentieth century, six are contemporary.
NB: 1780 Linen piecework quilt; 1976 Delaware County, New York Bicentennial quilt.

Study Services: For scholars, make appointment. Accession cards/files, and photocopy facilities.

Millard Fillmore House Museum

24 Shearer Avenue
East Aurora, New York
(716) 652-1203 or 652-1252

Mailing Address:
281 Parkdale Avenue
East Aurora, NY 14052

June–October: Wednesday and weekends,
2:00–4:00 P.M.
The quilt collection comprises fifteen handsewn piecework and appliqué quilts, and one
1810 white-on-white quilt from the western
New York region. In addition, there is unpublished documentation on quilts and quilting in
museum files.
NB: Crazy quilt that went across the country
in a covered wagon.
Study Services: For scholars, make appointment. Reading room, work tables, accession
cards/files, and photocopy facilities; photo
prints.
Public Services: Quilt exhibits, exhibitions of
members' quilts.

East Hampton Historical Society

101 Main Street
East Hampton, New York 11937
(516) 324-6850

Weekdays, 9:00 A.M.–5:00 P.M.
Society has a collection of approximately seventy-five quilts from eastern Long Island.
Study Services: Write to curator. Accession
cards/files and photocopy facilities; the majority of the collection has been photographed;
sections of the quilts were photographed
prior to storage.
Public Services: Periodic exhibits.

"Home Sweet Home" Museum

14 James Lane
East Hampton, New York 11937
(516) 324-0713

June–October: daily, 10:00 A.M.–4:00 P.M.; October–June: by appointment.
Fifteen handsewn quilts form a collection primarily from New York State and Long Island in particular. Among them are two crazy quilts, one satin, one velvet; two triangle patterns, one locally-made trapunto bride's quilt; one Flying Geese quilt, and one Basket pattern quilt. Four have been dated between 1830 and 1840. The quilts were collected by Mr. and Mrs. Gustave Buck between 1907 and 1927. Quilts are on continuous exhibition.
Study Services: Make arrangements three or four days in advance. Accession cards/files; photo reproductions of quilts can be arranged.
Public Services: Quilts are shown during general house tours.

Chemung County Historical Society

415 East Water Street
Elmira, New York 14901
(607) 734-4167

Weekdays, 9:00 A.M.–5:00 P.M.
Sixty in this collection of seventy quilts are from southern New York, primarily Chemung County; ten are from northern Pennsylvania. There are also twenty coverlets from southern New York State. The collection is strong in piecework and crazy quilts, appliqué, embroidered, and decorative quilting. A small percentage date prior to 1820, thirty-percent from the nineteenth century, nineteen-percent date after 1900, and ten-percent are contemporary. A few quilts are always on exhibition.
Study Services: Make appointment at least one week in advance. Visitors must be accompanied by a staff member. Reading room, work tables, accession cards/files, thirty books/journals, and photocopy facilities.
Public Services: Workshops on quiltmaking, tour of exhibition, and slide show for groups.

Bowne House Historical Society

37-01 Bowne Street
Flushing, New York 11354
(718) 359-0528

Tuesday and weekends, 2:30–4:30 P.M.
The collection of thirteen local historic quilts includes two that are contemporary appliqué quilts and thirty-five completed squares. Honeycomb, Chimney Sweep, and Caesar's Crown are among the patterns. Three quilts have decorative quilting, two are trapunto, one Log Cabin, one embroidered crazy quilt, and one patchwork crib quilt. Four quilts can be dated with certainty: one predates 1820, one is nineteenth century, two are contemporary.
Study Services: For scholars, write for appointment. Work tables, accession cards/files, and use of office space for reading.

Historical Museum of the D. R. Barker Library

7 Day Street
Fredonia, New York 14063
(716) 672-2114

Tuesday, Thursday, Friday, and Saturday, 2:30–4:30 P.M.; Thursday evenings, 7:00–9:00 P.M.
Fourteen regional quilts made in western New York State form the Museum's collection. They are pieced cotton and silk crazy quilts; embroidered and appliqué, pieced, pieced and embroidered, two embroidered, one white-on-white quilted counterpane. Of those dated: one is pre-1820, seven nineteenth century, one post-1900, two contemporary.
Study Services: For scholars, write to the curator for appointment. Work tables, accession cards/files, and photocopy facilities.
Public Services: Programs for special exhibits and for groups interested in quilts.

Geneva Historical Society
543 South Main Street
Geneva, New York 14456
(315) 789-5151

Tuesday–Saturday, 1:30–4:30 P.M. Society maintains Rose Hill Mansion: May 1–October 30: Monday–Saturday, 10:00 A.M.–4:00 P.M.; Sunday, 1:00–5:00 P.M.
Within a collection of forty-eight quilts twenty-eight are piecework, fourteen appliqué, five or more embroidered, four trapunto, one Yo-Yo or Bon-Bon, one printed cloth quilt. Of those that have been identified: fourteen date from the nineteenth century, two or more date after 1900.
Study Services: Make appointment. Reading room, work tables, accession cards/files, books/journals, and photocopy facilities.
Public Services: Temporary exhibitions and children's workshops.

Horseheads Cultural Center and Historical Society
Corner of Grand Central Avenue and Broad Street
Horseheads, New York 14845
(607) 739-1526

Hours not provided.
Collection of seven quilts.

Huntington Historical Society
209 Main Street
Huntington, New York 11743
(516) 427-7045

Tuesday–Friday, and Sunday, 1:00–4:00 P.M., except holidays; Office: weekdays, 9:00 A.M.–4:30 P.M.
The sixty-eight Long Island quilts in this collection are complemented by thirty-five drawings of quilt patterns and eight patterns. The strength of the collection is in patchwork and appliqué, Oakleaf and Log Cabin quilt designs, and crazy quilts. There are forty-eight piecework quilts, eight appliqué, seven whole-cloth with quilting, four crazy quilts, one white-on-white, and one embroidered. Forty-one are dated: one prior to 1820, thirty nineteenth

century, eight post-1900, two contemporary. Part of the collection on exhibit at all times.
NB: Presentation and Friendship quilts.
Study Services: Make appointment with director. Reading room, work tables, accession cards/files, library, photocopy facilities; photo prints, and slides; prints from the museum negatives may be ordered.
Public Services: Classes and workshops as part of craft program; periodic exhibitions.

DeWitt Historical Society of Tompkins County
116 North Cayuga Street
Ithaca, New York 14850
(607) 273-8284

Tuesday–Friday, 12:30–5:00 P.M.; Saturday, 10:00 A.M.–3:00 P.M.
The Society has ninety-five quilts. Seventy-five were made in Tompkins County, ten are from the Finger Lakes region of New York State, and ten are of unknown provenance. In addition, the society has collected personal narratives by quiltmakers. Approximately seventy quilts are piecework and/or piecework combined with other techniques, twenty quilts with decorative embroidery, fifteen pieced and appliqué, two tied, two white-on-white, and one with painted decoration. A few of the quilts date from before 1820, nearly half are from the nineteenth century, some date after 1900, a few are contemporary.
NB: Large collection from Frear family, approximately thirty-five quilts; Slaterville Friendship quilt; and Tompkins County Bicentennial quilt.
Study Services: For scholars, call or write director or curator for appointment. Reading room, accession cards/files, slides and photographs, and photocopy facilities; photo prints, slides. Prints from Society negatives may be ordered.
Public Services: Slide-lecture "The Frear Family Quilts," available for loan to organizations.

Herbert F. Johnson Museum of Art

Cornell University
Ithaca, New York 14850
(607) 255-6464

Tuesday–Sunday, 10:00 A.M.–5:00 P.M.
Ten quilts may be seen by appointment. Seven Album quilts, one Amish, and one contemporary example. Two from Baltimore, Maryland; New York, Massachusetts, and Pennsylvania.

John Jay Homestead State Historic Site

Route 22
Katonah, New York
(914) 232-5651

Mailing Address:
P.O. Box 148
Katonah, NY 10536

Hours not provided.
Collection of eight quilts. One is a signed Friendship quilt from the nineteenth century.

Senate House State Historic Site

312 Fair Street
Kingston, New York 12401
(914) 338-2786

Hours not provided.
The collection of twenty-two quilts includes fourteen pieced, four appliqué, two printed whole-cloth with quilting, one trapunto, one white-on-white. One is known to predate 1820 and one is a nineteenth century quilt.
Study Services: For scholars by appointment. Reading room, work tables, and accession cards/files; photos, in some cases prints can be made from negatives.

Herkimer Home State Historic Site

Route 169
Little Falls, New York
(315) 823-0398

Mailing Address:
R.D. 12, Box 631
Little Falls, NY 13365

Hours not provided.
The site owns eleven quilts. Nine are pieced and two are whole-cloth with quilting. Two predate 1820.
Study Services: For scholars, make appointment. Accession cards/files; photo prints and prints made from negatives for some of the quilts.
Public Services: Historic house museum tour; periodic quilting demonstrations and workshops offered.

Genesee County Village and Museum

Flint Hill Road
Mumford, New York
(716) 538-6822 or 538-2887

Mailing Address:
P.O. Box 1819
Rochester, NY 14603

May 11–October 20: daily, 10:00 A.M.–5:00 P.M.; spring and fall weekdays, 10:00 A.M.–4:00 P.M.
The museum stores sixty quilts that range from chintz Log Cabin to pieced crazy quilts. They are not easily accessible.

Fort Delaware

Museum of Colonial History
Narrowsburg, New York 12764
(914) 252-6660

July–August: daily, 10:00 A.M.–5:30 P.M.
Ten handsewn quilts from the region include five appliqué quilts, two trapunto, two piecework, and one printed whole-cloth quilt. Two quilts predate 1820, six are nineteenth century, and two date after 1900. Quilts always on exhibit.
Public Services: Workshops and demonstrations.

Historical Society of Rockland County

20 Zukor Road
New City, New York 10956
(914) 634-9629

Weekdays, 9:30 A.M.–4:00 P.M.; Sunday, 2:00–5:00 P.M.
Comprised of eighteen quilts from the Hudson River Valley the quilts in the collection were made by Dutch, English, and European settlers. The collection's concentration is piecework Album quilts, crazy quilts, and an Eight-Point Star quilt. There are also two appliqué quilts. Twelve are dated: eight are nineteenth century, two post-1900, and two contemporary.
NB: 1854 Thompson-Gurnee family Album quilt, Emery family.
Study Services: By appointment. Reading room, work tables, accession cards/files, and photocopy facilities; photo prints may be made from museum negatives.
Public Services: Exhibits, lectures, and workshops at various times.

Huguenot Historical Society of New Paltz

17 Broadhead Avenue
New Paltz, New York
(914) 255-1660

Mailing Address:
P.O. Box 339
New Paltz, NY 12561

Tuesday–Saturday, 9:00 A.M.–4:30 P.M.
Approximately fifty-two regional quilts and two doll quilts have been collected primarily from the area. Thirty-seven are piecework, nine appliqué, three white-on-white, one Yo-Yo, one printed whole-cloth with quilting, and one commemorative quilt from 1898. Patterns include Fan, Quilt Wheel, crazy quilt, Friendship appliqué, Flying Geese, appliqué star, leaf, and flower design; blindwork, Oak Leaf, Rose Wreath, Medallion, block-within-blocks, Eight-Pointed Star; quilt commemorating the Spanish American War by Charles DuBois Low, Navigator Compass, Friendship, Oak Leaf and Reel. Many are signed quilts. Seventeen are assigned dates: fourteen from the nineteenth century, two after 1900, one contemporary. Quilts are always on exhibit.
Study Services: Call or write for appointment. Work tables, and accession cards/files.
Public Services: Guided tours of display areas.

American Telephone and Telegraph Company (AT&T)

550 Madison Avenue
New York, New York 10022
(212) 605-5500, ask for art administrator

Office hours: weekends, 8:30 A.M.–4:00 P.M.
Nineteen American quilts include six Amish (four of these are Pennsylvania Amish), two Pennsylvania Mennonite quilts, one from New York State, one from New Hampshire. Patterns represented are Tree of Life, Double Irish Chain, Princess Feather, Medallion Star, Prairie Flower, Mariner's Compass, Baby Blocks, Star with Nine Patch, Log Cabin, Broken Dishes, Fan, Around the World, Flower Basket, Cactus Basket, Patch Block Flowers and Pinwheel. The quilts date c. 1860 to 1940.
Study Services: By written request to the art administrator.

The Chase Manhattan Bank

Art Program
410 Park Avenue
New York, New York 10022
(212) 223-6130

Weekdays, 9:00 A.M.–5:00 P.M.
The collection of seventy-eight quilts includes twelve Amish-made, three Native American (two contemporary and one from the 1930s), two Afro-American, and four Pakistani quilted cloths with embroidery. The majority of the collection was made in the late 1800s. Twenty-eight of the quiltmakers have been identified. Fourteen of the quilts are thought to have been made in Pennsylvania, with at least three from Lancaster County; three each from Massachusetts and Ohio, two from New York State, and one quilt each from Maine, Kentucky, Indiana, Tennessee, Virginia, and Georgia. Most are pieced quilts made of cotton. There are several appliqué, and at least

one quilted whole-cloth. The most numerous patterns are variations on star and Log Cabin. Two quilts date prior to 1820, forty-eight are nineteenth century, twenty-one are post-1900, and seven are contemporary. Quilts are exhibited in banking offices in domestic and international locations.

Study Services: Individuals must make requests. Researchers must be assisted by staff. Books/journals, photocopy facilities, and computer system print-outs; many quilts in the collection have photo prints, slides, and color transparencies.

Public Services: Special tours for museum and arts-related groups.

Publications: Annual acquisitions report states information on quilts purchased during the year; occasional photo reproductions.

The Metropolitan Museum of Art
American Decorative Arts Department
Fifth Avenue at 82nd Street
New York, New York 10028
(212) 879-5500

Tuesday–Sunday, 9:30 A.M.–5:15 P.M.
This collection of forty-five handsewn quilts is complemented by reference file material on individual ones. Six of the forty-five are Amish. Twenty-eight are primarily piecework, sixteen mainly appliqué, many of mixed techniques, one printed and quilted whole-cloth. Two quilts date prior to 1820, forty-two nineteenth century, one contemporary quilt. Continuous display of quilts.

Study Services: Call or write for appointment with textile curator. Reading room, work tables, books/journals, and accession cards/files; photo prints, and slides.

Publications: Bordes, Marilynn Johnson. *Twelve Great Quilts from the American Wing* (1974).

Museum of American Folk Art
444 Park Avenue South
New York, New York 10016
(212) 481-3080

Administrative offices: weekdays, 9:30 A.M.–5:30 P.M.

The offices will be at this address for the next two or three years and during this time exhibitions will be in various corporate galleries and traveling exhibitions. The Museum will re-open at a newly constructed building at 53 West 53rd Street, New York, New York 10019. The expanding collection (currently 190 quilts) also holds a pattern for Bird of Paradise quilt and templates for Amish quilts. Approximately 175 are pieced, 117 are Amish, fifteen are appliqué, fifteen are crazy quilts, one printed and quilted whole-cloth. Three can be dated prior to 1820, fifty-six are nineteenth century, 123 date between 1901 and 1940, and eight are contemporary. Principal sources of the collection are David Pottinger, William and Dede Wigton (Amish quilts); crazy quilts from Margaret Cavigga.

NB: Amish quilts; Bird of Paradise quilt, Baltimore Album quilt, Commemorative Patriotic quilt.

Study Services: For scholars, make appointment with curatorial department. Reading room, work tables, accession cards/files (usage by appointment only), over 100 books/journals, and photocopy facilities; photo prints, slides, and prints made from negatives.

Public Services: Museum quilt exhibitions; quilting bees, lectures, workshops, demonstrations, quilt contests, and festivals.

Publications: Pottinger, David. *Quilts from the Indiana Amish* (1983).

Museum of the City of New York
Fifth Avenue at 103rd Street
New York, New York 10029
(212) 534-1672

Tuesday–Saturday, 10:00 A.M.–5:00 P.M.; Sunday, 1:00–5:00 P.M. Closed New Year's, Thanksgiving, and Christmas.
Approximately forty-two quilts are from New

York City: seventeen patchwork, six printed whole-cloth, five appliqué, one stuffed, and one embroidered quilt. Seventeen quilts predate 1820, twenty-two are nineteenth century, and three are contemporary.
Study Services: For scholars, make appointment.

The New York Historical Society
170 Central Park West
New York, New York 10024
(212) 873-3400

Tuesday–Friday, 11:00 A.M.–5:00 P.M.; Saturday, 10:00 A.M.–5:00 P.M.; Sunday, 1:00–5:00 P.M.
The Society has thirty-five quilts, primarily of New York origin. They were collected chiefly by Elie Nadelman. Fifteen are known to predate c. 1820, and twenty date from the nineteenth century.
Study Services: For scholars, make appointment with registrar. Reading room, work tables, accession cards/files, books/journals, photocopy facilities, and microscope; prints made from negatives.

Philip Morris Companies, Inc.
120 Park Avenue
New York, New York 10017
(212) 880-4104

Weekdays, 9:00 A.M.–4:30 P.M.
The company owns thirty quilts, nineteen from The Artist and the Quilt Exhibition. One each from Maine; Baltimore, Maryland; Beatrice, Nebraska; Gordon, Texas; New England/Canadian border; and Buck's County, Pennsylvania. One is Amish; also Navajo quilts. Of those identified three are piecework, two are appliqué, two embroidered, one stuffed and quilted, one with decorative quilting, and one printed and quilted whole-cloth. Nine date from the nineteenth century, two from after 1900, and nineteen are contemporary. Quilts on exhibit at all times.
Study Services: Slides and prints made from negatives.
Publications: Robinson, Charlotte, editor. *The Artist and the Quilt* (1983).

Chenango County Historical Society
45 Rexford Street
Norwich, New York 13815
(607) 334-9227

Summer: Wednesday and weekends, 2:00–5:00 P.M.; winter: Wednesday, 2:00–5:00 P.M.
The Society has fifty pieced quilts from Chenango County and central New York. Research is currently being done on the collection. Continuous exhibit of quilts is offered.
NB: Signature quilts, Victorian crazy quilts.
Study Services: By appointment. Reading room, work tables, accession cards/files, and photocopy facilities.
Public Services: Tours, but no specific quilt tours.

Madison County Historical Society
435 Main Street
Oneida, New York
(315) 363-4136

Mailing Address:
P.O. Box 415
Oneida, NY 13421

Weekdays, 9:00 A.M.–5:00 P.M.
Twenty-six quilts are complemented by photographic and written documentation of approximately 400 quilts and quilted items from Madison County and the surrounding area. Part of the collection includes five appliqué, five crazy quilts, four Pinwheel pattern, one printed and quilted whole-cloth, one Friendship quilt signed by quilters, and one Revenue quilt made by the Baptist Church and signed by 564 residents. All but one are dated: seventeen quilts from the nineteenth century, and eight from the twentieth century.
NB: Crazy quilt; Revenue quilt; and Hawaiian appliqué quilt.
Study Services: By appointment. Reading room, work tables, accession cards/files, photographic and written documentation on 400 quilts and quilted items in Madison County, and photocopy facilities; slides, and photo prints may be ordered from Society's negatives.

Oysterponds Historical Society Museum
Village Lane
Orient, New York 11957
(516) 323-2480

July and August: Tuesday, Thursday, and weekends, 2:00–5:00 P.M.; June and September: weekends only.

Collection of approximately forty-five quilts from eastern Long Island includes a number of variants of Log Cabin, Wild Goose, star quilts, and others. Thirty-five are piecework, five are crazy quilts with embroidery and/or painted medallions, two appliqué, two printed whole-cloth, one white-on-white trapunto or raised quilting. All of the quilts in the collection have been dated. Approximately four predate 1820, thirty-seven are nineteenth century, four date after 1900. Quilts are always on exhibition.

NB: Crazy quilt with Fan motif and painted medallion, c. 1886; blue resist quilt, eighteenth century; gray, red, and pink Nine Patch variant.

Study Services: For scholars, make appointment with managing director or officer of board. Reading room, work tables, and accession cards/files.

Public Services: Local quilting groups meet regularly at Museum; quilt exhibit open during regular Museum hours but study groups may be arranged by appointment.

Tioga County Historical Society Museum
110-112 Front Street
Oswego, New York 13827
(607) 687-2460

Tuesday–Friday, 10:00 A.M.–12:00 P.M.; Tuesday–Sunday, 1:30–4:30 P.M.; Wednesday, 7:00–9:00 P.M.

The Museum has thirty quilts made or used in Tioga County, New York, the surrounding area, and one taped oral history from a quiltmaker. Twenty-nine are piecework, one is white-on-white with quilting. Twenty-six are dated: one pre-1820, twenty-three nineteenth century, and two post-1900. Quilts are on exhibit at all times.

NB: Friendship quilt, Honeycomb quilt, Vine and Rose quilt, Morning Glory quilt, and others.

Study Services: For scholars, contact museum staff. Reading room, work tables, and accession cards/files.

Raynham Hall Museum
20 West Main Street
Oyster Bay, New York 11771
(516) 922-6808

Tuesday–Sunday, 1:00–5:00 P.M.

Twelve regional quilts from Oyster Bay and Long Island comprise this collection that includes eight piecework, two wool, one appliqué, one corded quilt. Two predate 1820, and ten are nineteenth century. Quilts are always on exhibition.

NB: Autograph quilt: Theodore Roosevelt, Andrew Carnegie, and many other signatures.

Study Services: Make appointment with director. Reading room, work tables, accession cards/files, small library with books/journals, and photocopy facilities.

Public Services: Occasional quilt workshops for adults and children.

Kent-Delord House Museum
17 Cumberland Avenue
Plattsburgh, New York 12901
(518) 561-1035

Tuesday–Saturday, 9:00 A.M.–5:00 P.M.

Collection is approximately twelve quilts. More information will be available January 1987 upon completion of cataloging process.

Study Services: By appointment with director. Work tables, accession cards/files, photocopy facilities.

Potsdam Public Museum

Civic Center
Potsdam, New York 13676
(315) 265-6910

Tuesday—Saturday, 2:00—5:00 P.M.
Fifty-eight quilts gathered from the Museum's region include twenty-six piecework and twenty-one other quilts with decorative quilting and piecework, eight appliqué, one crazy quilt, and three embroidered. Twenty-eight are dated: one pre-1820, twenty-four are nineteenth century, two post-1900, one contemporary.
NB: Signature quilt.
Study Services: For scholars, make appointment. Reading room, work tables, accession cards/files, and books/journals; photo prints, and slides.
Public Services: Periodic exhibits, demonstrations, and lectures.

The Landmark Society of Western New York

130 Spring Street
Rochester, New York 14608
(716) 546-7028

Operates two historic sites. Stone-Tolan House Museum (2370 Eastern Avenue): Wednesday—Friday, 10:00 A.M.—4:00 P.M.; weekends, 1:00—4:00 P.M. The Campbell-Whittlesey House (123 South Fitzhugh Street): Tuesday—Friday, 10:00 A.M.—4:00 P.M.; Sunday, 1:00—4:00 P.M. There are seventeen nineteenth century quilts. Of particular note are a Mariner's Compass piecework quilt, 1832; four patchwork; three silk Log Cabin, a baby quilt or lap robe; two crazy quilt lap robes; white cotton trapunto Tree of Life quilt c. 1813; star pattern quilt; and one white-on-white with intricate stitched designs. The quilts are exhibited in two historic house museums.
Study Services: Access to quilts in storage is by appointment only. Work tables, accession cards/files, and photocopy facilities.

The Margaret Woodbury Strong Museum

1 Manhattan Square
Rochester, New York 14607
(716) 263-2700

Tuesday—Saturday, 10:00 A.M.—5:00 P.M.; Sunday, 1:00—5:00 P.M.
Of seventy-three quilts thirteen are from New York State, one is from New Brunswick, Canada; one is from Massachusetts, one is from Indiana, one from Pennsylvania, and one Amish-made quilt is from Ohio. Thirty-five are pieced (two are Autograph quilts), ten crazy quilts, nine appliqué, six whole-cloth, five pieced and appliqué, (including one Autograph cyano print quilt), two trapunto, two Yo-Yo, and several tops. Two quilts predate 1820, fifty-eight nineteenth century, twelve date after 1900, and one is contemporary.
Study Services: For scholars, make appointment. Some photo prints, slides, and prints made from negatives.
Public Services: Periodic quilt workshops offered.

Rochester Historical Society

485 East Avenue
Rochester, New York 14607
(716) 271-2705

Weekdays, 10:00 A.M.—4:00 P.M.; closed New Year's, Easter, July 4, Thanksgiving, and Christmas.
More than ten quilts are in this collection which is in the process of being documented and cataloged.
Study Services: For scholars, make appointment. Reading room, work tables, accession cards/files, and library.

Rochester Museum and Science Center

657 East Avenue
Rochester, New York
(716) 271-4320

Mailing Address:
P.O. Box 1480
Rochester, NY 14603

Monday–Saturday, 9:00 A.M.–5:00 P.M.; Sunday, 1:00–5:00 P.M.
In a collection of 139 quilts thirty are from western New York State, four from eastern New York, two from the New England states, two from the Mid-Atlantic states, and one from the South. Eighty-four are piecework, twenty-five crazy quilts, twenty Log Cabin, eleven a combination of piecework and appliqué, four stuffed, four whole-cloth, and one is white-on-white with quilting. There are also thirty-two quilt tops and twenty-five quilted chair throws and table covers. Five quilts predate 1820, 125 are nineteenth century quilts, eight date later than 1900, and one is contemporary.
NB: Commemorative quilts and Friendship quilts.
Study Services: Make written request, for committee review. Reading room, work tables, accession cards/files, books/journals, and photocopy facilities; some slides, prints may be requested from negatives.
Public Services: Regular quiltmaking classes in museum's adult education school, supplemented by learning from quilts in the collection.

Nassau County Museum Collections

95 Middle Neck Road
Sands Point, New York 11050
(516) 883-1610

Saturday–Wednesday, 9:00 A.M.–4:45 P.M.
Seventy-four quilts form a collection emphasizing quilts from Long Island. In addition there are fifteen or more early and mid-nineteenth century quilt frames. More than thirty quilts are from Long Island, New York; approximately fifteen are from the Mid-Atlantic and New England. About fifty are piecework,

eight have decorative quilting, seven are appliqué, three printed whole-cloth with quilting, three white-on-white, two trapunto, one Yo-Yo. Four predate 1820, forty-five date from the nineteenth century, and twenty-five quilts are later than 1900.
NB: Two quilts dated late eighteenth century and several histories.
Study Services: For scholars; write to collections supervisor for appointment. Work tables, accession cards/files, books/journals, photocopy facilities, and microscope.

Schenectady County Historical Society

32 Washington Avenue
Schenectady, New York 12305
(518) 374-0263

Weekdays, 1:00–5:00 P.M.
The Society has fifteen quilts. Seven are pieced, five appliqué, two trapunto, one is printed whole-cloth with quilting. Thirteen are nineteenth century, and two are post-1900. Quilts are exhibited continuously.
NB: Friendship quilt made by a young woman from Schenectady.
Study Services: Genealogy library open to the public. Scholars, make appointment for access to the stored collections. Reading room, work tables, accession cards/files, and photocopy facilities.
Public Services: Tours, slide shows.

Schenectady Museum and Planetarium

Nott Terrace Heights
Schenectady, New York 12308
(518) 382-7890

Tuesday–Friday, 10:00 A.M.–4:30 P.M.; weekends, 12:00–5:00 P.M. Closed: New Year's, July 4, Easter, Thanksgiving, and Christmas.
The collection is forty-eight handsewn quilts: thirty are pieced, ten appliqué, five crazy quilts, two white-on-white, and one linsey-woolsey. One predates 1820, forty-two are nineteenth century quilts, three date later than 1900, and two are contemporary.
NB: Schenectady Bicentennial quilt.
Public Services: Occasional quilt exhibits.

The Matterhorn Quilt by Myrtle M.
Fortner of Llano, California, 1934. Accession number
1967.89. Courtesy of The Denver Art Museum.

Amish Center Diamond quilt made
in Lancaster County, Pennsylvania, c. 1910; quiltmaker
unknown. The fabric is pieced wool, hand-quilted.
Accession number 1981.4.1. Courtesy of the Museum of
American Folk Art.

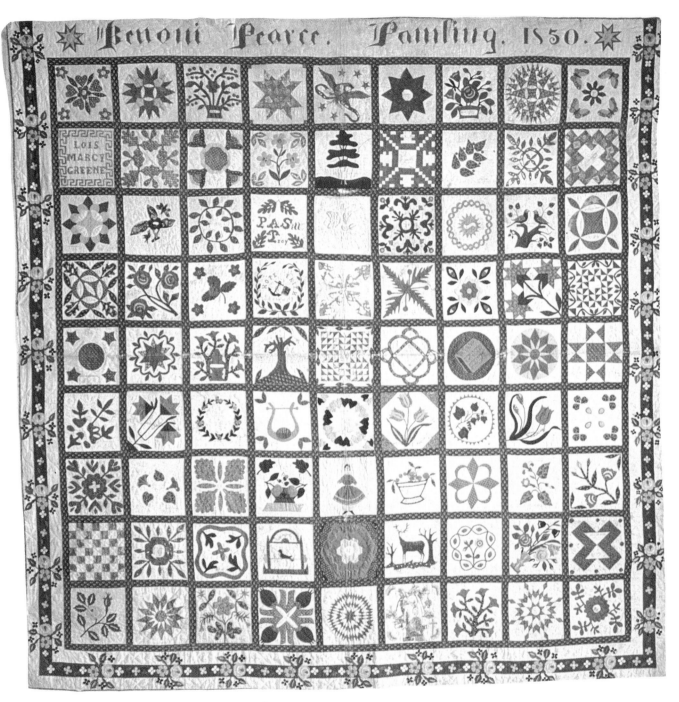

Pieced work and appliqué quilt by
friends and relatives of Benoni Pearce of Pawling, New
York. Presented to him on his engagement. Dated 1850.
Courtesy of the National Museum of American History,
Smithsonian Institution.

Stuffed chintz applique quilt in
cotton, silk, and taffeta by Martha Jane Singleton Hatter
(Mrs. Richard Hatter) 1815–96 of Selma, Alabama,
made c. 1861. Family history and a local newspaper of
1862 reveal that it was auctioned to raise money for an
Alabama Gunboat for the Confederacy. The museum
purchased the quilt with partial funds from the Quilt
Conservancy. Courtesy of the Birmingham Museum of
Art.

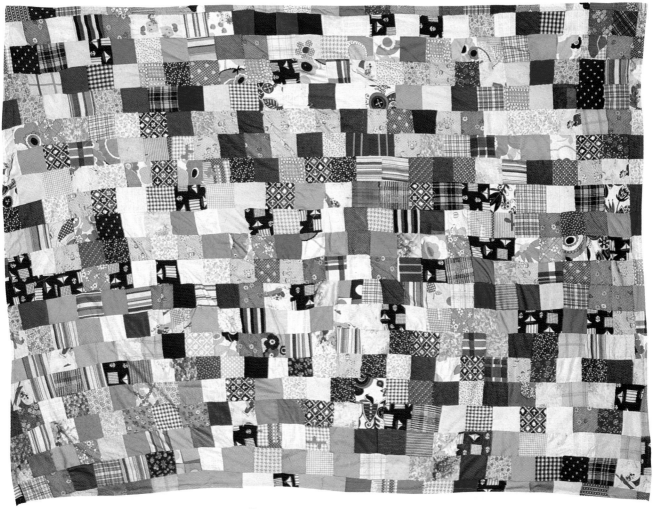

Patchwork quilt hand stitched by
Cub Scout Pack #867 of Franconia, Virginia, 1976.
Courtesy of the Gerald R. Ford Museum, National
Archives and Records Administration.

Appliqué "Princess Feather" quilt.
Made of homespun cotton by slaves, c. 1830 to 1850.
According to family history, this quilt was made by
slaves on the Cogburn Plantation near Montgomery,
Alabama. It was brought to Mississippi shortly before the
Civil War. Accession number 83.1. Collection of State
Historical Museum/Mississippi Department of Archives
and History.

Wagon Wheel Quilt, from Cape
Girardeau County, c. 1900. Courtesy of the collection of
the American Quilt Museum.

Celestine Bacheller (1850-1900).
From Wyoma, Massachusetts. Contained crazy quilt.
Pieced, appliqué, and embroidered silk and velvet.
Accession number 63.655. Courtesy of the Museum of
Fine Arts, Boston.

Stone Fort Museum
North Main Street
Schoharie, New York
(518) 295-7192

Mailing Address:
P.O. Box 69
Schoharie, NY 12157

Memorial Day–Labor Day: daily, 10:00 A.M.–
5:00 P.M. May 1– October 31: Tuesday, 12:00–
5:00 P.M.; Saturday, 10:00 A.M.– 5:00 P.M.
A collection of twenty-two quilts, eight are
from Schoharie County, New York. Nineteen
are piecework, two crazy quilts, ten have embroidery, three appliqué. Four are known to
be nineteenth century quilts.
NB: Eight locally made Signature quilts with
embroidery.
Study Services: Make appointment one week
in advance. Reading room, work tables, accession cards/files, books/journals, and photocopy
facilities.

Seneca Falls Historical Society
55 Cayuga Street
Seneca Falls, New York 13148
(315) 568-8412

Weekdays, 9:00 A.M.–5:00 P.M.
In addition to thirty finished quilts this collection given by Seneca County residents, there
are twenty unfinished quilts. Four are appliqué, four are embroidered crazy quilts, two
whole-cloth, the remainder piecework. Of
those dated nine are nineteenth century, and
one post-1900. Quilts are on continuous exhibition with seasonal rotation in one bedroom.
NB: International Flag quilt, and one quilt
made from military and political ribbons.
Study Services: Make appointment with director. Reading room, work tables, accession
cards/files in-progress, and photocopy facilities.

Smithtown Historical Society
North Country Road (behind the Smithtown
Library)
Smithtown, New York
(516) 265-6768

Mailing Address:
P.O. Box 69
Smithtown, NY 11787

Weekdays, 8:00 A.M.–4:00 P.M.
Thirty-two quilts are in the Society's collection. Of these, twenty-seven are piecework,
three printed whole-cloth, and two white-on-
white. One quilt fragment dates prior to 1820,
and twelve are nineteenth century.
NB: Hallock quilt; and Obadiah quilt.
Study Services: Make request to director.
Accession files, books/journals, and photocopy
facilities.
Public Services: Quilts have been presented at
meetings of local quilting associations.

Southampton Colonial Society
17 Meeting House Lane
Southampton, New York
(516) 283-2494

Mailing Address:
P.O. Box 303
Southampton, NY 11968

Mid-June–Mid-September: Tuesday–Sunday,
11:00 A.M.–5:00 P.M.
The Society has forty to forty-five quilts of
various techniques that primarily date from
the nineteenth century; several are later than
1900. Quilts are continuously on exhibition.
NB: Centennial quilt, 1876, made by a man.
Study Services: For scholars, make appointment. Reading room, and books/journals.

Staten Island Historical Society

Richmondtown Restoration
441 Clarke Street
Staten Island, New York 10306
(718) 351-1617

Wednesday–Friday, 10:00 A.M.–5:00 P.M.;
weekends, 1:00–5:00 P.M.
One-hundred sixty quilts from Staten Island and environs form the collection. It is estimated there are 100 piecework, eighteen crazy quilts, twelve Log Cabin variations, ten appliqué, five pieced Album, and five printed whole-cloth. Quilts made or used in Staten Island number about 100. Another fifty are from northeastern states, primarily New York State and New Jersey. Less than ten were made before 1820, 100 or more are nineteenth century, approximately thirty date after 1900, and less than ten are contemporary.
NB: Best known are three pieced and appliqué quilts c. 1935 by Mary Totten.
Study Services: For scholars, make appointment with curator. Reading room, work tables, accession cards/files, twenty books/journals, and photocopy facilities.
Public Services: Occasional changing exhibition; interpretive staff demonstrate quiltmaking in historic houses using mid to late nineteenth century techniques.

The Museums

State University of New York at Stony Brook
1208 Route 25A
Stony Brook, New York 11790
(516) 751-0066

Tuesday–Saturday, 10:00 A.M.–5:00 P.M.; Sunday, 12:00–5:00 P.M.
The collection includes forty-eight quilts. Thirty-nine are piecework, seven appliqué, and two printed whole-cloth with quilting. Of those that have been dated: four predate 1820, thirty-five are nineteenth century, three date after 1900, and four are contemporary.
NB: Local Album quilt, 1859, from Port Jefferson, New York.

Study Services: By appointment. Reading room, work tables, accession cards/files, books/journals, photocopy facilities, and microscope; photo prints, slides, prints made from negatives, and several note cards.

Historical Society of Walden and Wallkill Valley

37 North Montgomery Street
Walden, New York
(914) 778-5862

Mailing Address:
P.O. Box 48
Walden, NY 12586

By appointment.
Approximately ten quilts on continuous exhibition.

New York State Office of Parks, Recreation and Historic Preservation

Bureau of Historic Sites
Peebles Island
Waterford, New York 12188
(518) 237-8090

Office: weekdays, 8:30 A.M.–4:30 P.M. Not open to the public.
The Bureau of Historic Sites administers 34 state owned historic properties. Sixty-one quilts from New York State are stored at various sites. Thirty-nine are pieced quilts, nine appliqué, nine whole-cloth, three trapunto, and one white-on-white.
Study Services: Most of the sites store their own collections. Limited staffing makes it necessary to restrict access of these collections to scholars only. It is strongly suggested that scholars contact the curatorial staff at Peebles. They can give an overview of the quilts at all the sites. Some of the sites have very limited work space and it may be necessary to arrange transportation of quilts to Peebles for viewing. Work tables, accession cards/files, photography if needed, photocopy facilities, and microscope; photo prints, and prints made from negatives.

Jefferson County Historical Society

228 Washington Street
Watertown, New York 13601
(315) 782-3491

Tuesday–Saturday, 10:00 A.M.–5:00 P.M.; Office:
Monday–Saturday, 9:00 A.M.–5:00 P.M.
Forty-six regional quilts from Jefferson
County, New York, display various techniques
and patterns. Twenty-nine are piecework,
seven crazy quilts, four stuffed white-on-
white, two appliqué, two printed whole-cloth
with quilting, one embroidered, and one is
white-on-white. Thirteen are dated: two pre-
1820, nine nineteenth century, one post-1900,
and contemporary.
NB: Early nineteenth century quilt made of a
copperplate print, probably French; a quilt of
early resist/dye print; white stuffed quilt; and
several appliqué quilts.
Study Services: Request appointment one
week ahead. Reading room, accession cards/
files, nearby photocopy facilities.
Public Services: When quilts are exhibited
tours are provided.

Wilson Historical Society Museum

4559 Chestnut Road
Wilson, New York 14172
(716) 751-9886 or 751-9827

Hours not provided.
Five or more quilts.

The Hudson River Museum

Trevor Park-on-Hudson
511 Warburton Avenue
Yonkers, New York 10701
(914) 963-4550

Wednesday–Saturday, 10:00 A.M.–5:00 P.M.;
Sunday, 1:00–5:00 P.M.
Six American quilts, one dated 1887, may be
seen by scholars by appointment.

NORTH CAROLINA

*Chintz broderie perse quilts, Mora-
vian quilts, and myriad other examples of patchwork and appliqué are
exhibited.*

Appalachian Cultural Center

University Hall
Appalachian State University
Boone, North Carolina 28608
(704) 262-3117

Tuesday–Sunday, 9:00 A.M.–5:00 P.M.
More than five pieced utilitarian Appalachian
mountain quilts that date from 1901 to 1940,
and unpublished research papers. Quilts are
on continuous exhibition.
Study Services: By appointment. Reading room
in library, work tables, accession cards/files,
books/journals, photocopy facilities, microscope, and large collection of craft revival textiles; photo prints, slides, and prints made
from negatives upon request.
Public Services: Special quilt exhibitions.

Hezekiah Alexander Home Site and History Museum

3500 Shamrock Drive
Charlotte, North Carolina 28215
(704) 568-1774

Tuesday–Friday, 10:00 A.M.–5:00 P.M.; weekdays, 2:00–5:00 P.M. Closed holidays.
More than seventy quilts and many coverlets
form this collection of regional and national
work dating from prior to 1820 to contemporary. A wide range of techniques are represented. There are a large number of crazy
quilts and Medallion quilts.
NB: Novelty quilt from 1902.
Study Services: For scholars, by appointment.
Reading room in library, work tables, accession cards/files, books/journals, collection on

slides, photocopy facilities; photo prints, slides, and prints made from negatives.
Public Services: Special exhibitions, public programs.

The Frank Clyde Brown Papers
Manuscript Department
William R. Perkins Library
Duke University
Durham, North Carolina 27706
(919) 684-3372

Weekdays, 8:00 A.M.–5:00 P.M.; Saturday, 9:00 A.M.–12:30 P.M. Closed official holidays.
Three folders that each contain ten to fifteen fabric quilt squares and more paper patterns that date from the 1920s.
Study Services: Walk-in registration. Reading room, work tables, accession cards/files, books/journals, and photocopy facilities; photo reproduction possible.

Greensboro Historical Museum
130 Summit Avenue
Greensboro, North Carolina 27401
(919) 373-2043

Tuesday–Saturday, 10:00 A.M.–5:00 P.M.; Sunday, 1:00–5:00 P.M.
Of the sixty quilts in the collection fifty are from the Piedmont area of North Carolina; ten are from the southeastern region. Techniques and patterns include piecework or pressed pieced quilts, appliqué, geometric and floral pattern variations. Approximately forty-five quilts are nineteenth century, ten date after 1900, and five are contemporary.
NB: Tobacco Leaf quilt; chintz Medallion quilt, 1830 to 1840; pieced Log Cabin quilt.
Study Services: Write or call for appointment, indicating research topic. Reading room, work tables, accession cards/files, books/journals, and photocopy facilities; slides, photo prints may be ordered from negatives. (Not all of the collection has been photographed.)
Public Services: Special programs created for exhibitions.

High Point Historical Society, Inc.
1805 East Lexington Avenue
High Point, North Carolina 27262
(919) 885-6859

Tuesday–Saturday, 10:00 A.M.–5:00 P.M.; Sunday, 1:00–5:00 P.M.
The collection has twenty-three quilts, principally patchwork, two from High Point, North Carolina; one is from Massachusetts. Nineteen are patchwork, three crazy quilts with embroidery, and one is appliqué. Of those dated nine are nineteenth century, and four post-1900.
Study Services: Make appointment with curator. Reading room, work tables, accession cards/files, and photocopy facilities.
Public Services: Tours; demonstrations during special events; scheduled quilting bees, community college holds quilting classes here.

Orange County Historical Museum, Inc.
201 North Churton Street
Hillsborough, North Carolina
(919) 732-8648

Mailing Address:
P.O. Box 871
Hillsborough, NC 27278

Tuesday–Sunday, 1:30–4:30 P.M.
Six nineteenth century quilts from Orange County on exhibition most of the year.

North Carolina Museum of History
109 East Jones Street
Raleigh, North Carolina 27611
(919) 733-3894

Tuesday–Saturday, 9:00 A.M.–5:00 P.M.; Sunday, 1:00–6:00 P.M.
The Museum has ninety-nine quilts. Eighty-three are of North Carolina origin, two are Afro-American, two from Virginia, one from Ohio, and one from Washington, D.C. In addition the Museum is the repository for information collected by the North Carolina Quilt Project: slides and histories of quilts and quilt-makers. This information will serve people interested in quiltmaking, women's studies,

folklore, textiles, and North Carolina history. Of the quilts in the collection seventy-nine are pieced, twenty-five appliqué, twelve pieced and appliqué, two trapunto, and two white-on-white quilts. Four predate 1820, sixty-six are nineteenth century, twenty-two are later than 1900, seven are contemporary.
Study Services: Call or write for appointment with collections staff. Accession cards/files, and books/journals.
Public Services: The Museum is a sponsor of the statewide North Carolina Quilt Project and will eventually house the results. A selected number of quilts from the North Carolina Quilt Project will be exhibited at the Museum in 1988. An illustrated book about quilts and quiltmaking in North Carolina will be published.
Publications: Artistry in Quilts (1974).

New Hanover County Museum
814 Market Street
Wilmington, North Carolina 28401
(919) 763-0852

Tuesday–Saturday, 9:00 A.M.–5:00 P.M.; Sunday, 2:00–5:00 P.M.
The Museum has eighteen quilts from the Cape Fear region and three Afro-American quilts. Sixteen are pieced, four have decorative quilting, three embroidered, two appliqué, and one stuffed and quilted. Eight are quilt tops. Nine are nineteenth century, seven date after 1900, two are contemporary.
Study Services: Write or call curator for appointment. Work tables, accession cards/files, and photocopy facilities; photo prints, slides, photo prints may be ordered from negatives.
Public Services: Temporary quilt exhibits, and quilting class held in cooperation with local technical institute.

Museum of Early Southern Decorative Arts
924 South Main Street
Winston-Salem, North Carolina 27108
(919) 722-6148

Daily, 10:30 A.M.–5:00 P.M.
A group of fifty-six handsewn southern quilts includes twenty-four quilts from North Carolina, seven from South Carolina, seven from Georgia, five from Maryland, two from Virginia, one from Tennessee, and one from Kentucky. Quilt patterns and instructions, unpublished personal narratives by quiltmakers, and research papers are available. Twenty-seven quilts are pieced, seventeen appliqué, seven are Friendship quilts, four stuffed and corded, one white-on-white quilt. Twenty-nine predate 1820, twenty-four are nineteenth century, and three are later than 1900. Quilts are continuously exhibited.
NB: Concentration of late eighteenth century through 1880 quilts. Eighteenth century appliqué chintz quilts.
Study Services: By appointment. Reading room, work tables, accession cards/files, books/journals, microfilm, and photocopy facilities; photo prints, slides, photo prints may be ordered from negatives.
Public Services: Classes on quiltmaking, workshops on conservation of quilts and other textiles; consultation on dating of quilts.

Old Salem, Inc.
600 South Main Street
Winston-Salem, North Carolina
(919) 723-3688

Mailing Address:
Drawer F, Salem Station
Winston-Salem, NC 27108

Monday–Saturday, 9:30 A.M.–4:30 P.M.; Sunday, 1:30–4:30 P.M. Closed Thanksgiving, Christmas eve, and Christmas day.
Thirty handsewn quilts from North Carolina made by Moravian women or young women attending early community's boarding school comprise this collection. Sixteen are pieced, four candlewick, three appliqué, three white-

on-white, three have decorative quilting, one is embroidered. Three predate 1820, and twenty-seven are nineteenth century quilts.
Study Services: Make appointment with the curator of collections. Reading room, accession cards/files, books/journals, and photocopy facilities; photography may be arranged.

White-on-white cradle quilt designed by John Robert Degge and quilted by his wife, Mary Frances Degge, c. 1851–1853, made in Petersburg, Illinois. Courtesy of the Illinois State Museum.

NORTH DAKOTA

Signature quilts, pioneer quilts, and even a quilt belonging to the first governor may be seen.

State Historical Society of North Dakota
North Dakota Heritage Center
Bismarck, North Dakota 58505
(701) 224-2666

Monday–Thursday, 8:00 A.M.–5:00 P.M.; Friday, 8:00 A.M.–8:00 P.M.; Saturday, 9:00 A.M.–5:00 P.M.; Sunday, 11:00 A.M.–5:00 P.M.
A collection of seventeen quilts: thirteen are from North Dakota, one from Kentucky, one from Ireland, one from Norway, one from Quebec, Canada. Ten are piecework, five embroidered, one with decorative quilting, and one appliqué. Ten are dated: five nineteenth century, one post-1900, four are contemporary.
NB: A quilt which belonged to John Miller, first governor of North Dakota; and quilt made by Anna Plummer, first settler's child born on town site of Bismarck, North Dakota, July 14, 1873.
Study Services: Make appointment. Reading room, work tables, accession cards/files, books/journals, and photocopy facilities; photo prints, and prints may be ordered from negatives.

Cooperative Extension Services
North Dakota State University
216 Family Life Center
Fargo, North Dakota
(701) 237-7255

Mailing Address:
P.O. Box 5016
Fargo, ND 58105

Weekdays, 8:00 A.M.–5:00 P.M.
One quilt, six quilt patterns and instructions, eighty unpublished personal narratives by quiltmakers, and eighty transcripts form the

collection. In 1975 slides of the oldest quilt in each county were made into a slide lecture circulated nationally and throughout the state. The set of sixty-five slides is entitled "Old Quilts in North Dakota." Another slide set features New Hampshire quilts and is called "Antique Quilts."

Study Services: By appointment. Slides can be viewed and script can be read on site, books/journals, slide set/script is available on loan; slides, and prints made from slides at cost.

Public Services: Slide sets may be borrowed for two weeks; make request to Media Library, Morrill Hall, Box 5655, North Dakota State University, Fargo, North Dakota 58105.

Lake Region Pioneer Daughters Museum
Cavalry Square
Fort Totten, North Dakota
(701) 662-3514

Mailing Address:
Ms. Joan Galleger
Route 5, Lakewood
Devils Lake, ND 58301

Memorial Day–Labor Day: daily, 1:00–5:00 P.M.; theater days, 1:00–8:00 P.M.
Twenty-five handsewn quilts focus on the Scandanavian-German heritage of the Lake Region of North Central North Dakota. Eleven piecework, ten handwoven or knitted, two appliqué, two embroidered, one Bon-Bon (Yo-Yo) quilt, one with decorative quilting. Two predate 1820, twenty are nineteenth century, three are later than 1900. Quilts given by members of pioneer families who homesteaded this area from 1882 to 1900. Quilts are on continuous exhibition.

NB: Red Star quilt made by Teni Moore, late 1800s; pieced quilt made by daughter of Chief Wonatah; three crazy quilts, one made for Red Cross in 1917 with a crewel appliqué of billy goat in center blocks.

Study Services: Contact office at Cavalry Square, or president of Lake Region Pioneer Daughters. Reading room, work tables, accession cards/files, historical setting with camp-

ing, picnic tables, and rest areas; prints (of some of the collection) may be ordered.

Public Services: School children's tours, open at special hours for bus tours with guides.

Grand Forks County Historical Society
2405 Belmont Road
Grand Forks, North Dakota 58201
(701) 775-2216

Thursday–Tuesday, 1:00–5:00 P.M.
The Society has twenty handsewn regional quilts with a concentration in Signature quilts and crazy quilts. About half date from the nineteenth century. Quilts are on exhibit at all times.

NB: Linsey-woolsey quilt; and Emerado Church Signature quilt.

Study Services: Contact director/curator for appointment. Reading room, work tables, accession cards/files, catalog cards, and photocopy facilities planned.

Public Services: General tours.

Traill County Historical Society
218 West Caledonia
Hillsboro, North Dakota
(701) 436-5571

Mailing Address:
P.O. Box 273
Hillsboro, ND 58045

June 1–August 15: Saturday, Sunday, Tuesday, and Wednesday, 2:00–5:00 P.M.
Twelve handsewn quilts were made by quilt-makers of Norwegian/German extraction. Piecework, appliqué, embroidered, decorative quilting, and white-on-white quilting techniques are represented. Seven are nineteenth century, four post-1900, one is contemporary. Quilts are on exhibit continuously.

Study Services: Contact curator for appointment. Reading room, work tables, accession cards/files, photocopies not at museum but can be arranged; photo prints could be made if requested.

OHIO

Mennonite and Amish quilt country; collections of quilts of every kind including a 1786 quilt, a John Hewson 1811 embroidered quilt, an eighteenth century saye quilt, and one made from cigar bands!

Belmont County Historical Museum
512 North Chestnut Street
Barnesville, Ohio
(614) 425-2926

Mailing Address:
P.O. Box 434
Barnesville, OH 43713

Thursday, 1:00–4:00 P.M.; Sunday, 1:00–4:00 P.M.
A number of crazy quilts are on exhibition in a domestic setting.

Hale Farm and Village
2686 Oak Hill Road
Bath, Ohio 44210
(216) 666-3711

Mailing Address:
P.O. Box 256
Bath, OH 44210

Tuesday–Sunday, 10:00 A.M.–5:00 P.M.
Twenty-one nineteenth century handsewn quilts are mainly from the Western Reserve of Ohio. Seventeen are piecework, three appliqué, one trapunto.
Study Services: Call curator of collections for admittance. Accession cards/files, and books/journals.
Public Services: Special textile weekends, and exhibits of collection.

Historic Lyme Village Association
5487 State Route 113 East
Bellevue, Ohio
(419) 483-4949 or 483-6052

Mailing Address:
P.O. Box 342
Bellevue, OH 44811

June–August: Tuesday–Sunday, 1:00–5:00 P.M.; May and September: weekends.
Twelve handsewn quilts include nine that are piecework, one crazy quilt in velvets and satins with embroidered names, one white-on-white, and one embroidered. Three are nineteenth century, eight date later than 1900, one is contemporary. Quilts are on continuous exhibition.
Study Services: By appointment. Photocopy facilities; some photo prints, and slides.

Mennonite Historical Library
Bluffton College
Bluffton, Ohio 45817
(419) 358-8015

Academic year: Monday–Thursday, 8:00 A.M.–10:00 P.M.; Friday, 8:00 A.M.–5:00 P.M.; Saturday, 1:00–5:00 P.M.; Sunday, 2:00–10:00 P.M.
June–August: weekdays, 8:00 A.M.–5:00 P.M.
A number of books on quilts with special interest in Mennonite and Amish quilts.

Burton Century Village
Geauga County Historical Society
Burton, Ohio
(216) 543-2341

Mailing Address:
Helen Burns
17770 Chillicothe Road
Chagrin Falls, OH 44022

Tuesday–Sunday, call for hours.
The collection includes thirty-five regional quilts showing a wide range of techniques. Of those that have been dated two predate 1820, approximately twenty-five are nineteenth century, five are later than 1900. The collection is now in the process of being cataloged. A few quilts are on continuous exhibition.

NB: 1745 Handwoven linen and cotton indigo-dyed quilt.
Study Services: By appointment.

McKinley Museum of History, Science and Industry

749 Hazlett Avenue, NW
Canton, Ohio
(216) 455-7043

Mailing Address:
P.O. Box 483
Canton, OH 44701

September–May: Monday–Saturday, 9:00 A.M.–5:00 P.M., Sunday, 11:00 A.M.–5:00 P.M. June–Labor Day: daily, 9:00 A.M.–7:00 P.M.
Sixty-two quilts in a collection from Stark County residents. Thirty are pieced, fifteen crazy quilts, nine appliqué, three are comforters, three Signature quilts, and two embroidered. Fifty-three are nineteenth century, and nine date later than 1900.
NB: Flower Baskets quilt.
Study Services: Scholars, call in advance for appointment. Reading room, work tables, and accession cards/files.

Mercer County Historical Museum

130 East Market Street
Celina, Ohio 45822
(419) 586-6065

Wednesday, Thursday, and Friday, 8:30 A.M.–4:00 P.M.; Sunday, 1:00–4:00 P.M.
Eleven handsewn nineteenth century quilts made or used by Mercer County Germans and one southern quilt form the collection. The Museum also has a dozen quilt patterns and instructions, many unpublished personal narratives by quiltmakers, many oral history tapes and transcriptions, and other archival materials. The following quilt designs are represented: Four Patch, Yo-Yo, Double X, Ohio Star or Variable Star, Weathervane, Baby Blocks or Tumbling Blocks, Tree of Life, Double Irish Chain, Album or Chimney Sweep or Christian Cross, Cat's Cradle, crazy quilt, and Jacob's Ladder. Quilts are continuously on display.

NB: Yo-Yo quilt that belonged to former President Jimmy Carter's grandmother.
Study Services: Write to director. Reading room, work tables, accession cards/files, books and articles, display, photocopy facilities, and magnifying glass; photo prints, prints may by requested from negatives.
Public Services: Workshops and lectures.
Publications: Annual brochure with scheduled events.

Ross County Historical Museum

45 West 5th Street
Chillicothe, Ohio 45601
(614) 772-1936

April–October: Tuesday–Sunday, 1:00–5:00 P.M. Closed, November–March.
The Museum has forty handsewn regional quilts representing trapunto, English piecing, and appliqué. One is made of antique chintz. Quilts date from 1808 to 1890. Five quilts predate 1820, and thirty-five others are nineteenth century. Quilts are on continuous exhibition.
Study Services: Make appointment. Accession cards/files, and books/journals; some photo prints.
Public Services: Tours.

Cincinnati Art Museum

Art Museum Drive
Cincinnati, Ohio 45202
(513) 721-5204

Tuesday–Saturday, 10:00 A.M.–5:00 P.M.; Sunday, 1:00–5:00 P.M.
The collection consists of fifty handsewn quilts. Twenty-two are pieced, eleven crazy quilts, seven Log Cabin, two white-on-white, and one is whole-cloth with quilting. Seven predate 1820, forty-two are nineteenth century, and one is contemporary.
NB: Blue and white resist; John Hewson embroidered quilt, 1811; white-on-white quilt embroidered 1856, quilted by a slave.
Study Services: Call or write curator for appointment. Reading room, work tables, accession cards/files, thirty-six books/journals,

photocopy facilities, and possibly microscope; black-and-white prints, slides, and prints may be ordered from negatives.
Publications: Shine, Carolyn R. *Quilts from Cincinnati Collections* (1985).

Western Reserve Historical Society
10825 East Boulevard
Cleveland, Ohio 44106
(216) 721-5722

Tuesday–Friday, 12:00–5:00 P.M.; weekends, 12:00–5:00 P.M.
The Society's holdings include 260 predominantly nineteenth century Ohio quilts, a few quilt patterns and instructions, and accompanying documentation. The majority is piecework/appliqué, approximately forty-five are crazy quilts with embroidery, four are white-on-white, three trapunto, two printed whole-cloth with quilting, two Bon-Bon, and one saye quilt. Two quilts predate 1820, approximately 185 are nineteenth century, and seventy-five later than 1900. Selected examples are on continuous exhibition in period rooms.
NB: One eighteenth century saye quilt; eighteenth century batik quilt.
Study Services: Make appointment, access restricted. Reading room in adjacent library building, and accession cards/files under supervision; photo prints, slides, and prints made from negatives.
Public Services: Programs offered for special exhibitions.

Ohio Historical Society
1985 Velma Avenue
(Interstate 71 and 17th Avenue)
Columbus, Ohio 43211
(614) 466-1500

Monday–Saturday, 10:00 A.M.–5:00 P.M.; Sunday and holidays, 10:00 A.M.–5:00 P.M.
About one quarter of these 225 Midwestern quilts are from Ohio, including seventeen quilts from the Zoar community. A little more than half of the collection is piecework. There are approximately fifty-six appliqué quilts and two or three whole-cloth with quilting; and

one is white-on-white. About ten quilts date prior to 1820, roughly 130 date from the nineteenth century, sixty-seven date after 1900, and another ten are contemporary. The collection is currently being cataloged. Principal source of the collection, Mary K. Borkowski.
NB: Phoebe Cook quilt; Hatfield-McCoy Victory quilt.
Study Services: Make appointment with collections department. Accession cards/files.
Public Services: During exhibitions: tours, classes, and workshops.

Montgomery County Historical Society
7 North Main Street
Dayton, Ohio 45402
(513) 228-6271

Tuesday–Friday, 8:30 A.M.–4:30 P.M.; Saturday, 12:00–4:00 P.M.
Twenty-five quilts are from Montgomery County, Ohio: twenty-two piecework, two appliqué, and one printed whole-cloth with quilting. Eight can be dated nineteenth century.
Study Services: Write for access, stating reason for research. Work tables, accession cards/files, and photocopy facilities; slides, prints may be ordered from negatives.
Public Services: Exhibitions.

Hancock County Historical Museum
422 West Sandusky Street
Findlay, Ohio 45840
(419) 423-4433

Friday–Sunday, 1:00–4:00 P.M.
Thirty-three handsewn quilts, and several dozen woven coverlets have been collected from Hancock County, Ohio: twenty are piecework, nine appliqué, two embroidered, one whole-cloth with quilting, one trapunto. There are two piecework squares dated 1849. Concentration in floral appliqué and block piecework. Most quilts are signed and dated. Ten are nineteenth century, twenty-one date after 1900, two are contemporary. Quilts are on continuous exhibition.

NB: Centennial fabric quilt, Log Cabin design silk and velvet quilt.
Study Services: By appointment. Reading room, work tables, accession cards/files, and books/journals; photo reproductions of quilts are planned.
Public Services: Tours.

Lakewood Historical Society
14710 Lake Avenue
Lakewood, Ohio 44107
(216) 221-7343

Sunday and Wednesday, 2:00–5:00 P.M.; office: weekdays, 9:00 A.M.–1:00 P.M.
Collection of thirty-six quilts includes twenty-one pieced and six appliqué, as well as six crazy quilts, one embroidered, and one cigar band quilt. Half have been ascribed dates: two predate 1820, fourteen are nineteenth century, and two date after 1900. Quilts are continuously exhibited.
Study Services: Make appointment with staff. Reading room, and accession cards/files.

Warren County Historical Society
105 South Broadway Street
Lebanon, Ohio
(513) 932-1817

Mailing Address:
P.O. Box 223
Lebanon, OH 45036

Tuesday–Saturday, 9:00 A.M.–4:00 P.M.; Sunday, 12:00–4:00 P.M. Glendower (105 Cincinnati Avenue): Sunday, 12:00–4:00 P.M.
The Society has collected sixty-seven quilts and woven coverlets from southwestern Ohio. Forty-five are pieced, thirteen crazy quilts, five appliqué, three appliqué and pieced, one pieced trapunto quilt. Sixty are nineteenth century, seven date later than 1900.
Study Services: Request permission and assistance of director or assistant director. Reading room, work tables, accession cards/files, ten books/journals, microfilm readers, and photocopy facilities.
Public Services: Annual quilt exhibit and seminar, plus quilt appraisals by outside experts.

The Allen County Historical Society
620 West Market Street
Lima, Ohio 45801
(419) 222-9426

Monday–Saturday, 8:00 A.M.–5:00 P.M.; Sunday, 1:30–5:00 P.M.
In the collection of seventy-six quilts, most were made or owned by persons living in Allen County, Ohio; others are from the Midwestern states. Several scrapbooks of quilt pieces and newspaper clippings dealing with quilts are also in the collection. Roughly forty-three are piecework, fifteen embroidered, and eleven appliqué. Thirty-eight have dates ascribed: two quilts predate 1820, twenty-seven are nineteenth century, nine post-1900.
Study Services: Make appointment with the assistant curator of collections. Reading room, work tables, accession cards/files, books/journals, photocopy facilities, and microscope; photo prints, slides, prints may be ordered from negatives.
Public Services: Occasional lectures and temporary exhibitions.

The Massillon Museum
212 Lincoln Way, East
Massillon, Ohio 44646
(216) 833-4061

Tuesday–Saturday, 9:30 A.M.–5:00 P.M.; Sunday, 2:00–5:00 P.M.
The Museum has assembled twenty-nine quilts, most made by women of this area and three Amish quilts. Fourteen are piecework, the majority with embroidery; ten appliqué, three embroidered, one printed whole-cloth with quilting, and one decorative quilting. Two predate 1820, twenty are nineteenth century, three date after 1900, and four are contemporary.
NB: Album quilt.
Study Services: Make appointment. Work tables, accession cards/files, and photocopy facilities; some prints made from negatives.
Public Services: Exhibitions (some quilt

shows, sometimes quilts displayed as part of other shows), quilting classes offered two or three times a year, and occasional workshops.

Medina County Historical Society
206 North Elmwood Street
Medina, Ohio
(216) 722-1341

Mailing Address:
P.O. Box 306
Medina, OH 44258

Tuesday and Thursday, 9:00 A.M.–5:00 P.M.; and by appointment.
In the collection of fourteen handsewn quilts, thirteen were made in or brought to Medina County, and one is from Pompey, New York. There are twenty quilt patterns/instructions. Concentration in pieced Log Cabin, Victorian crazy quilts, and home-spun. Eleven quilts are piecework, three are Victorian fancy work (embroidery), one is homespun and dyed whole-cloth with quilting, one is a Signature quilt by the Ladies Aid Society, and one embroidered block c. 1940s. One quilt predates 1820, ten are nineteenth century, two date after 1900, and one is contemporary. Quilts are on continuous exhibition.
Study Services: Contact museum curator. Reading room, and accession cards/files.
Public Services: Tours.

Milan Historical Museum
10 Edison Drive
Milan, Ohio
(419) 499-2968

Mailing Address:
P.O. Box 491
Milan, OH 44846

April, May, September, October: Tuesday–Sunday, 1:00–5:00 P.M. June–August: Tuesday–Sunday; 10:00 A.M.–5:00 P.M.
Twenty quilts form a collection of ten piecework, two white-on-white quilts (one a baby quilt), one appliqué, one silk Log Cabin quilt c. 1866, one crazy quilt c. 1895, one trapunto, two quilts with decorative quilting, one em-

broidered W.C.T.U. comforter, one candlewick, one partially quilted, and one on a frame.
NB: Tied campaign quilt for James Blaine's nomination for president in 1876; W.C.T.U. Album quilt.

Follett House Museum
404 Wayne Street
Sandusky, Ohio
(419) 627-9608

Mailing Address:
c/o Sandusky Library
Sandusky, OH 44870

Tuesday, Thursday, and Sunday, 1:00–4:00 P.M. Library: Monday–Saturday, 9:00 A.M.–5:00 P.M.
The Museum has twenty-five quilts: seven doll quilts, six appliqué and pieced quilts from 1845 to 1890, four pieced, embroidered crazy quilts in silks and velvets; three Signature blocks, one 1850 trapunto and embroidered Baltimore Album quilt, one wool patchwork quilt. Twenty-one are nineteenth century, two date later than 1900, and two are contemporary. Quilts are always on display.
NB: 1850 Baltimore Album quilt with appliqué, embroidered, and stuffed.
Study Services: For scholars. Work tables, accession cards/files, and books/journals; photo prints made from negatives.
Public Services: Quilt collection included in tours.
Publications: Quilts and Carousels: Folk Art in the Firelands (1983).

Clinton County Historical Society
149 East Locust
Wilmington, Ohio
(513) 382-4684

Mailing Address:
P.O. Box 529
Wilmington, OH 45177

Tuesday–Friday, 1:00–4:30 P.M.
A collection of twenty-two quilts from local donors in assorted techniques and patterns. Two date from the nineteenth century.
Study Services: Make request to curator for

appointment. Reading room, work tables, accession cards/files, books/journals, and photocopy facilities.

Wayne County Historical Society
546 East Bowman Street
Wooster, Ohio 44691
(216) 264-8856

Tuesday–Sunday, 2:00–4:30 P.M.; closed Mondays and holidays.
Society has nineteen quilts given by various residents of Wayne County. One is a Signature quilt made in the 1930s. Quilts are on continuous exhibition.
Study Services: Available to scholars. Reading room, accession cards/files, and books/journals.

The Greene County Historical Society
74 West Church Street
Xenia, Ohio 45385
(513) 372-4606

Tuesday–Friday, 9:00 A.M.–12:00 P.M., and 1:00–3:30 P.M.
Eight quilts from Ohio. A few are on continuous exhibition.

The Mahoning Valley Historical Society
The Arms Museum
648 Wick Avenue
Youngstown, Ohio 44502-1289
(216) 743-2589

Tuesday–Friday, 1:00–4:00 P.M.; weekends, 1:30–5:00 P.M.
The Museum has twenty-three quilts, sixteen from Ohio, one from New York, and one from Pennsylvania. Twenty-three are pieced, six are also appliqué and embroidered, three embroidered Signature quilts, and one printed wholecloth with homespun linen backing. Of those that have dates: one quilt is dated 1786, eleven are nineteenth century, four date after 1900, three are contemporary.
NB: 1786 quilt; Mary Logan Hall 1884 patchwork quilt.
Study Services: For scholars, make appointment. Reading room, accession cards/files, books/journals, and photocopy facilities; photo prints may be requested from negatives.
Public Services: Periodic exhibits.

Zoar Village State Memorial
Ohio Historical Society
Main Street
Zoar, Ohio
(216) 874-3011
Mailing Address:
P.O. Box 404
Zoar, OH 44697

Hours not provided. May–October: Wednesday–Sunday; the rest of the year, weekdays.
Fifteen handsewn quilts were made by quiltmakers of German descent; thirteen were made by members of the Zoar Society before 1898; two were made by former members of the Zoar Society after that date. Eleven are pieced and tied wool comforters, two are traditional pieced, one crazy quilt, one reverse appliqué. Continuous exhibition of quilts in room settings.
NB: Known more for coverlets than quilts.
Study Services: For scholars, write or call one week before visit; accession cards/files.
Public Services: Quilt exhibit every other year; the next will be in 1987, open to the public, old and new quilts are judged.

San Angelo, Texas, March 1940. Cowboys asleep in cattle show barns at the San Angelo stock show. Photo by Russell Lee, negative number LC-USF34-35505-D. Courtesy of the Farm Security Administration Collection, Prints and Photographs Division, Library of Congress.

OKLAHOMA

State history quilts, Albums, and a quilt made from county fair ribbons are displayed.

Lincoln County Historical Society

717 Manvel Avenue
Chandler, Oklahoma
(405) 258-2425

Mailing Address:
P.O. Box 458
Chandler, OK 74834

Tuesday–Saturday, 1:00–5:00 P.M.; Sunday, 2:00–5:00 P.M.
Society has collected twenty handsewn quilts all made by Lincoln County people. One is a Friendship quilt made by a church Ladies Aid Society, one is a Jewish Tree of Life quilt of 1885; and one is a county fair ribbon quilt. There are three star, three crazy quilts, three other patchwork, two Friendship, two Log Cabin, one Yo-Yo, one Tumbling Blocks, and one Double Wedding Ring. Of those dated: five are nineteenth century, four date later than 1900, one is contemporary. The collection stems from donations by Gwen Jones, and the quiltmakers' descendants. The majority of the quilts is on continuous exhibition.
NB: 1944 Silk Yo-Yo made from German parachute.
Study Services: For scholars. Work tables, accession cards/files, and microfilm reader.

Granny's Quilt House

East McKinny
Cheyenne, Oklahoma 73628
(405) 497-2771

Weekdays, 9:00 A.M.–5:00 P.M.
Two-hundred handsewn contemporary quilts, and thousands of quilt patterns/instructions. Continuous exhibit of quilts; photo prints made from negatives.

Old Greer County Museum and Hall of Fame, Inc.

222 West Jefferson Street
Mangum, Oklahoma 73554
(405) 782-2851

Tuesday–Friday, 8:30 A.M.–12:00 P.M., and 1:00–4:00 P.M.
A collection of twenty handsewn quilts in various techniques. Two are nineteenth century, and eighteen were made prior to 1907. Quilts are on exhibit at all times.
NB: Old Caesar's Crown quilt.
Study Services: For scholars. Reading room, work tables, and accession cards/files.
Publications: Brochures.

Norman/Cleveland County Historical Museum

508 North Peters Street
Norman, Oklahoma
(405) 321-0156

Mailing Address:
P.O. Box 260
Norman, OK 73070

Weekdays, 1:00–5:00 P.M.; Sunday, 2:00–5:00 P.M.
The Museum holds twelve handsewn local Oklahoma quilts and documentation on specific pieces in the collection. Of those that have dates: five quilts date from the nineteenth century; seven are later than 1900. Quilts are on continuous exhibition.
Study Services: Apply to museum director. Reading room, work tables, accession cards/files, and books/journals.
Public Services: Tours, workshops, and conservation programs.

Stovall Museum of Science and History

University of Oklahoma
1335 Asp Avenue
Norman, Oklahoma 73019
(405) 325-4711

Weekdays, 8:00 A.M.–5:00 P.M.
Collection consists of twelve quilts: one of Scottish origin, ten piecework, two appliqué and embroidered Autograph quilts. There is a concentration of crazy quilts. One is a nineteenth century, one dates after 1900: the others are probably contemporary.
Study Services: Make written request to curator, director, or collections manager. Work tables, accession cards/files, photocopy facilities, and microscope.
Public Services: All textiles are available to university classes or for loan to other institutions for exhibit or research.

State Museum

Oklahoma Historical Society
2100 North Lincoln Boulevard
Oklahoma City, Oklahoma
(405) 521-2491

Mailing Address:
Wiley Post Historical Building
State Capitol Complex
Oklahoma City, OK 73105

Monday–Saturday, 9:00 A.M.–5:00 P.M.
Forty or more quilts are pieced, embroidered and trapunto. The quilts date from the nineteenth century to the present. Two or three quilts are on continuous exhibition.
NB: Oklahoma Album quilt, Townsend Plan quilt, and Oklahoma historical quilt.
Study Services: Make written request in advance of visit, give specific interest and credentials. Limited work space, accession cards/files, books/journals, photocopy facilities, and microscope; slides, and catalogs.

Pioneer Woman Museum

701 Monument Road
Ponca City, Oklahoma 74604
(405) 765-6108

Wednesday–Saturday, 9:00 A.M.–5:00 P.M.; Sunday, 1:00–5:00 P.M.
Nine quilts from Oklahoma, Kansas, and Ohio on continuous exhibition.

Pioneer Museum and Art Center

2009 Williams Avenue
Woodward, Oklahoma
(405) 256-6136

Mailing Address:
P.O. Box 1167
Woodward, OK 73802

Tuesday–Saturday, 10:00 A.M.–5:00 P.M.; Sunday, 1:00–4:00 P.M.
Eight quilts on continuous exhibition.

Kern County, California. February 1936. Oklahoma grandmother proudly displays her Dresden Plate quilt. Photo by Dorothea Lange, negative number LC-USF34-1780-C. Courtesy of the Farm Security Administration Collection, Prints and Photographs Division, Library of Congress.

OREGON

Quilts that comforted travelers along the harsh Oregon Trail, Aurora Colony quilts, and Autograph quilts are some of the treasures in public collections.

Clatsop County Historical Society

1618 Exchange Street
Astoria, Oregon 97103
(503) 325-2203

Weekdays, 9:00 A.M.–5:00 P.M.
The Society owns twelve Oregon quilts that date from the nineteenth and first half of the twentieth century.
Study Services: Make appointment. Reading room, work tables, accession cards/files, and photocopy facilities.

Ox Barn Museum

Museum of the Aurora Colony
15038 2nd Street
Aurora, Oregon
(503) 678-5754

Mailing Address:
P.O. Box 202
Aurora, OR 97002

Wednesday–Sunday, 9:00 A.M.–5:00 P.M.
Collection of fifty quilts made by women of Aurora Colony from 1856 to 1910. Forty are piecework, eight stuffed or corded, and two are appliqué. Patterns include Fans, Baskets, and Double X (among others). Some quilts are made of homespun. Forty are nineteenth century, and ten date after 1900. Quilts are on continuous exhibition.
NB: The Colony Bird quilt.
Study Services: Make written request, giving credentials. Reading room, work tables, and accession cards/files; note cards.
Public Services: Some quilts are always exhibited and there is an annual quilt exhibition.

Horner Museum

Oregon State University
Corvallis, Oregon 97331
(503) 754-2951

Tuesday–Friday, 10:00 A.M.–5:00 P.M.; Saturday, 12:00–4:00 P.M.; Sunday, 2:00–5:00 P.M.
The Museum's collection includes approximately sixty-eight quilts: fifteen from Oregon, twenty from the East Coast, ten from the Midwest, five from the West, two Appalachian West Virginia quilts, one Afro-American, and one Canadian quilt. Fifty are pieced, fifteen appliqué, ten embroidered, and one printed whole-cloth with quilting. Six predate 1820, fifty are nineteenth century, ten date after 1900, two are contemporary. Susan Cockroll was the principal source of the collection.
NB: Union quilt, with appliquéd eagle and stars.
Study Services: Write or call for appointment and state area of interest. Accession cards/files, books/journals, and photocopy facilities.
Public Services: Tours and workshops are offered for special temporary exhibits.

Lane County Historical Museum

740 West 13th Street
Eugene, Oregon 97402
(503) 687-4239

Tuesday–Friday, 10:00 A.M.–4:00 P.M.; Saturday, 12:00–4:00 P.M.; office: weekdays, 8:30 A.M.–5:00 P.M.
Sixty quilts made or used by residents of Lane County, Oregon, some with origins East of Oregon, are supplemented by quilt patterns and instructions. Thirty-five are piecework, thirteen crazy quilts, three appliqué, one pieced and appliqué, one trapunto, one white-on-white. Of those with dates: nineteen are nineteenth century, fifteen post-1900, one is contemporary. Principal sources include the Whiteaker collection, and Edna Harris Gray collection.
NB: Quilts as early as 1820s brought across plains to Lane County.
Study Services: For scholars, make written request, explaining need, goal of research, and

dissemination plans. Reading room, accession cards/files, books/journals, and photocopy facilities; photo prints, and slides.

Randall V. Mills Archives of Northwest Folklore
English Department
University of Oregon
Eugene, Oregon 97403
(503) 686-3925

Weekdays, 8:30–10:30 A.M. and 12:30–2:30 P.M.
A collection of unpublished materials on quilts and quiltmaking, twenty-five to fifty quilt patterns and instructions; four taped interviews; thirty-nine research papers; and one film: *Kathleen Ware: Quiltmaker.*
Study Services: Patron requests collection from archivist. Reading room, work tables, accession cards/files; cameras, and tape recorders; photocopy facilities; photo prints, and slides.

Southern Oregon Historical Society
206 North Fifth Street
Jacksonville, Oregon
(503) 899-1847

Mailing Address:
P.O. Box 480
Jacksonville, OR 97504

Tuesday–Saturday, 10:00 A.M.–5:00 P.M.
The society has assembled 260 quilts, 125 from Oregon. Of those that have been ascribed dates: 150 are nineteenth century, ten date after 1900, fifteen are contemporary. Quilts are always on exhibition.
Study Services: Available to scholars. Reading room, books/journals, and photocopy facilities.

Klamath County Museum
1451 Main Street
Klamath Falls, Oregon 97601
(503) 882-2501, extension 208

Tuesday–Saturday, 11:00 A.M.–5:00 P.M.
Twenty-five quilts form a collection including a Hawaiian quilt, a Bow Tie quilt used in Missouri and Texas, two brought from Pennsylvania and one comforter top from Vermont. Some of the patterns include Ripple or Zig Zag, and Double Wedding Ring. Of those that have been dated: five are nineteenth century, and one is post-1900.
Study Services: Make appointment. Reading room and photocopy facilities.

Yamhill County Historical Museum
6th and Market Streets
Lafayette, Oregon

Mailing Address:
P.O. Box 484
Lafayette, OR 97127

Weekends, 1:00–4:00 P.M.
Collection of forty-nine quilts contains eighteen Oregon Pioneer quilts, twelve post-1900 quilts, and five Autograph church and community fund-raising quilts. Twenty-six are pieced, eleven crazy quilts, eight embroidered, and four appliqué. Of those with dates: twenty-eight are nineteenth century, twelve later than 1900. Quilts are on continuous exhibition.
NB: Oregon Pioneer quilts; two World War I Red Cross quilts.
Study Services: For scholars. Work tables, accession cards/files, and books/journals; some photo prints, prints may be ordered from negatives.

Schminck Memorial Museum
128 South E Street
Lakeview, Oregon 97630
(503) 947-3134

February–November: Tuesday–Saturday, 1:00–5:00 P.M. Closed holidays.
There are thirty-two quilts and three tops primarily from Oregon. Sixteen are pieced, nine

appliqué, five crazy quilts, five of combined techniques. Pansy, Balsam Apple, Flowers sampler, Wreath of Roses, Rose of Sharon, Poke Stalk, Prickly Pear, and Drooping Lily are some appliqué patterns represented. Pieced quilt patterns include Rose Star, Double Wedding Ring, Tree of Life, Dove in the Window, Ocean Wave, Modern Nine Patch, Flying Star, Album, Double Irish Chain, Blazing Star, and Broken Star. Pieced and appliqué quilt patterns are Dresden Plate, Flower Basket, Mexican Lily, Grandmother's Flower Garden, and Grandmother's Fan. Roughly fourteen are nineteenth century quilts, twenty-two later than 1900, and one is contemporary. Principal donor/source: Lula Schminck and Elizabeth Currier Foster. There is a continuous exhibit of quilts.
Study Services: By advance appointment. Accession cards/files.

Molalla Area Historical Society
South Molalla Avenue
Molalla, Oregon
(503) 829-8637

Mailing Address:
Christine Cline
15555 South Herman Road
Molalla, OR 97038

By appointment.
The Society has eighteen handsewn quilts and an unpublished personal narrative by a quiltmaker; letters, notes, and other material. Eleven quilts are from Oregon, one from Indiana, one from Oklahoma, and one is from France. Five are pieced, four appliqué, three pieced and embroidered (one is tied), two are pieced quilt tops, one is pieced and tied, one is a pieced and tied quilt with embroidery, and one is appliqué with embroidery. Eight are nineteenth century, ten date later than 1900.
NB: The Oregon Rose quilt, Robbins family gift from neighbors.
Study Services: Make appointment. Reading room, work tables, and accession cards/files;

some photo prints; photo prints may be ordered from negatives.
Public Services: Annual Mother's Day exhibition.

Hoover-Minthorn House Museum
115 South River Street
Newberg, Oregon 97132
(503) 538-6629

Wednesday—Sunday, 1:00–4:00 P.M.
Seven quilts on continuous exhibition.

Lincoln County Historical Society
545 Southwest 9th Street
Newport, Oregon 97365
(503) 265-7509

Tuesday—Saturday, 11:00 A.M.–4:00 P.M.
Of these twenty-three quilts from Oregon, twenty-one are patchwork and crazy quilts, one an appliqué contemporary quilt, another a contemporary quilt with birds and embroidery. Nineteen are nineteenth century, two later than 1900, two are contemporary.
Study Services: Make appointment. Reading room, work tables, accession cards/files, and photocopy facilities.

Coos County Historical Museum
Simpson Park
North Bend, Oregon 97420
(503) 756-6320

Tuesday—Saturday, 10:00 A.M.–4:00 P.M.
Twenty-eight quilts form a collection including thirteen pieced and seven embroidered. Of those dated: twelve are nineteenth century, and five are post-1900.
Study Services: Make appointment with director. Reading room, accession cards/files, and photocopy facilities.

McLoughlin House National Historic Site

713 Center Street
Oregon City, Oregon 97045
(503) 656-5146

Tuesday–Saturday, 10:00 A.M.–4:00 P.M.; Sunday, 1:00–4:00 P.M.
A collection of eleven quilts: seven are pieced, three woven, and one is whole-cloth with quilting. One quilt predates 1820 and ten are nineteenth century (three are blue and white woven pieces). Quilts are on exhibit at all times.
NB: 1790 quilt of handmade linen dyed with indigo and filled with black (natural, undyed) wool.
Study Services: Make application to board of directors. Some photo reproductions of quilts.

Oregon Historical Society

1230 Southwest Park Avenue
Portland, Oregon 97205
(503) 222-1741

Monday–Saturday, 10:00 A.M.–4:45 P.M.
The Society holds about 100 handsewn quilts, quilt tops, doll and dollhouse quilts, blocks, and research papers. Approximately eighty-three are piecework, twenty-three appliqué, two embroidered, one trapunto. Two predate 1820, eighty-eight are nineteenth century, fourteen later than 1900, two are contemporary.
NB: Quilt made by Abigail Scott Duniway; Murder quilt made by the community in reaction to a lover's triangle trial; collection of eighteen quilts by one woman; quilt made by mother of General Sherman.
Study Services: Make appointment. Reading room, books/journals, and photocopy facilities; slides and photo prints may be ordered from negatives; postcards, and posters.
Public Services: Lectures with slide programs.

Washington County Museum

17677 Northwest Springville Road
Portland, Oregon 97229
(503) 645-6606

Monday–Saturday, 9:00 A.M.–4:30 P.M.
Twenty-seven quilts include twenty-one pieced, four appliqué, one tied, one with decorative quilting. Eleven are nineteenth century, eleven later than 1900, five are contemporary.
Study Services: Make request. Reading room, work tables, indexing systems for public, and photocopy facilities; volunteer staff photographer could photograph collection.
Public Services: Exhibitions.

Crook County Historical Museum

Bowman Museum
246 North Main Street
Prineville, Oregon 97754
(503) 447-3715

March–December: Wednesday–Saturday, 12:00–5:00 P.M.; and by appointment.
The Museum has ten post-1900 quilts.
Study Services: Write or call for appointment.

Tillamook County Pioneer Museum

2106 2nd Street
Tillamook, Oregon 97141
(503) 842-4553

Monday–Saturday, 8:30 A.M.–5:00 P.M.; Sunday, 12:00–5:00 P.M.; closed Mondays, October 1–May 1.
Seventeen quilts form a collection dating between 1825 and 1923. Quilts are continuously exhibited.
NB: Many of the quiltmakers and dates of completion are known.
Study Services: For scholars. Reading room, work tables, accession cards/files, and photocopy facilities.
Public Services: Two cases of quilt exhibits that are rotated every three or four months.

PENNSYLVANIA

A long quilting history is well documented in many institutions. Regional examples of Pennsylvania-German, Quaker, Amish, and Mennonite quilts are of particular note.

Old Economy Village
14th and Church Streets
Ambridge, Pennsylvania 15003
(412) 266-4500

Tuesday–Saturday, 9:00 A.M.–4:00 P.M.; Sunday, 12:00–4:00 P.M.
This collection includes about thirty-five handsewn nineteenth century quilts from western Pennsylvania and catalogs from previous quilt exhibitions. Twenty-nine are patchwork, three appliqué, two whole-cloth with quilting, one embroidered, one trapunto white-on-white with sham. Exhibits of quilts in summer and coverlets in winter are in room contexts.
Study Services: For scholars, make appointment. Work tables, accession cards/files, and photocopy facilities.
Public Services: Quilts and coverlets exhibited in room settings contribute to learning about the history of the Harmony Society.

Centre County Library and Historical Museum
203 North Allegheny Street
Bellefonte, Pennsylvania 16823
(814) 355-1516

Museum: weekdays, 9:00 A.M.–5:00 P.M. Library located across the street: Monday–Thursday, 9:00 A.M.–9:00 P.M.; Friday and Saturday, 9:00 A.M.–5:00 P.M.
There are fifteen local quilts, quilt tops and fragments donated by area families. Some patterns are Robbing Peter to Pay Paul, Peonies or Cactus Rose, Turkey Foot (1860–1870), Eternal Triangle (1870), Nine Patch variation,

appliqué floral and wreath pattern, Wild Goose Chase or Odd Fellows quilt top, and an autograph quilt from the twentieth century. The bulk of the collection dates from the 1850s to the 1880s. Most of the makers and their families are documented. The film *Quilts in Women's Lives* is also in the collection. Many quilts are on continuous exhibition.
NB: Silk and satin crazy quilt, embroidered in each patch, dated 1885–1888, made by Margaret Evans Strohm.
Study Services: By written request at least one week in advance. Reading room, work tables, accession cards/files, photocopy facilities, magnifying glasses, books/journals in the main library, extensive genealogical library, microfilm readers, and film/video projectors.
Public Services: Occasionally.
Publications: Lasansky, Jeannette. *In the Heart of Pennsylvania: 19th and 20th Century Quiltmaking Traditions* (1985).

Annie S. Kemerer Museum
427 North New Street
Bethlehem, Pennsylvania 16823
(215) 868-6868

Weekdays, 9:00 A.M.–12:00 P.M., and 1:00–4:00 P.M.; Saturday, 10:00 A.M.–4:00 P.M.
Twenty-two regional quilts form a body of work by Pennsylvania Germans from the Lehigh Valley. Nine are piecework, seven embroidered, three appliqué, two white-on-white, one strip quilt. Ten are nineteenth century quilts. Principal source: family of Annie S. Kemerer. Quilts are on exhibit at all times.
NB: 1825 white cotton quilt quartered with leaf designs, made by Caroline Heil.
Study Services: Make written request to director. Accession cards/files.
Public Services: House tour that includes room with quilts.

Cumberland County Historical Society

21 North Pitt Street
Carlisle, Pennsylvania 17013
(717) 249-7610

Monday, 7:00–9:00 P.M.; Tuesday–Friday,
1:00–4:00 P.M.
The Society's thirteen handsewn quilts from
Pennsylvania are associated with Cumberland
County families. Seven are piecework and six
are appliqué. Of particular note are a c. 1840
flowered chintz quilt, an 1846 large pieced
star quilt made for the minister by the Dills-
burg Monaghan Presbyterian Church, four
1851 to 1898 Friendship quilts (one made by
the German Reformed Congregation in 1858),
c. 1890s pieced star, c. 1860s Feathered Star
variation with sawtooth border, c. 1870s Basket, 1930s Irish Chain, 1976 Bicentennial appliqué with scenes of Cumberland County
made by the YWCA. Eleven are nineteenth
century quilts, one is post-1900, and one is
contemporary.
NB: C. 1840s flowered chintz quilt in strips
that alternate with solid white fabric.
Study Services: For scholars, make appointment with executive director. Reading room,
work tables, accession cards/files, and photocopy facilities.

The Mercer Museum

Pine Street
Doylestown, Pennsylvania 18901
(215) 345-0210

Monday–Saturday, 10:00 A.M.–5:00 P.M.; Sunday, 1:00–5:00 P.M.
This collection contains twenty-four Pennsylvania quilts: six are Quaker, one Amish, eleven
are from Bucks County, one is from the Lancaster area, and one is from Montgomery
County. There are many Nine-Patch, nineteen
pieced, two pieced and appliqué, two embroidered, and one printed whole-cloth with
quilting. Of those dated: one quilt predates
1820, fifteen are nineteenth century, and two
date later than 1900.
NB: Signed and dated Quaker Friendship

quilts, and one copperplate-printed fabric
quilt.
Study Services: For scholars, make written or
telephoned request for appointment at least
two weeks in advance. Reading room, work
tables, accession cards/files, twenty-five books/
journals, photocopy facilities, and microscope;
study photo prints and study slides, prints
may be ordered from negatives.
Public Services: Temporary exhibits and textile care workshops.

Rodale Press, Inc.

33 East Minor Street
Emmaus, Pennsylvania 18049
(215) 967-5171

Offices: weekdays, 8:00 A.M.–5:00 P.M.
The majority of this forty-five quilt collection
is contemporary; however several date from
the nineteenth century. Various patterns and
techniques. Concentration of crib size quilts.
NB: One-hundred year old Amish quilt, provenance unknown. Many contemporary quilts by
Mary Hartman, of Narvon, Pennsylvania.
Study Services: By appointment with director
of interior coordination, or assistant. Photo
duplication upon special request.

Westmoreland Museum of Art

221 North Main Street
Greensburg, Pennsylvania 15601
(412) 837-1500

Tuesday and Saturday, 10:00 A.M.–5:00 P.M.;
Sunday, 1:00–5:00 P.M.
Collection includes thirty piecework, appli-
qué, and white-on-white Pennsylvania quilts.
Ten date from the nineteenth century.
Study Services: For scholars, by appointment.
Reading room, work tables, accession cards/
files, photocopy facilities, books/journals;
photo prints and slides available.
Public Services: Quilt exhibition every two
years and workshop.

Dauphin County Historical Society

219 South Front Street
Harrisburg, Pennsylvania 17104
(717) 233-3462

Weekdays, 9:00 A.M.–5:00 P.M.; tours, 1:00–4:00 P.M.
Twenty-five Pennsylvania German quilts focus on the southern and central portions of the state. Nine are piecework, five appliqué, two embroidered, two trapunto, one white-on-white. A few quilts at a time are exhibited on beds on a rotating schedule.
Study Services: Call or write for an appointment and state interest. Reading room, work tables, accession cards/files, and photocopy facilities; pictures may be taken; but there are none on file.
Public Services: Occasional lectures on textiles using collection materials.

State Museum of Pennsylvania

3rd and North Streets
Harrisburg, Pennsylvania
(717) 787-4978

Mailing Address:
P.O. Box 1026
Harrisburg, PA 17108-1026

Tuesday–Saturday, 9:00 A.M.–5:00 P.M.; Sunday, 12:00–5:00 P.M.
The Museum has 180 quilts, all hand quilted, some machine pieced. Most have Pennsylvania histories, some well documented; three are Amish quilts. The majority is pieced, twenty-one appliqué, ten appliqué and pieced, thirteen cradle or doll quilts, six white-on-white (including three dresser covers), four stuffed, and three embroidered. In addition there are pieced pillow covers, quilted petticoats and quilted bonnets. Of those dated three are pre-1820, fifteen are nineteenth century, two are post-1900, and three are contemporary.
Study Services: For groups by special prearrangement; for scholars, make appointment with curator. Reading room, work tables, accession cards/files, photocopy facilities, and microscope; slides, and photo prints may be ordered from negatives.

Haverford Township Historical Society

Nitre Hall, Karakung Drive
Havertown, Pennsylvania
(215) 353-1213

Mailing Address:
P.O. Box 825
Havertown, PA 19083

May–October: Sunday, 1:00–4:00 P.M.
The Society has fourteen quilts, several cardboard quilting patterns, several unfinished quilt tops of diamonds and hexagons sewn onto paper backing, a Log Cabin top, and two unpublished research papers. Six quilts are piecework, three appliqué, three crazy quilts both embroidered and pieced, one is decorative quilting on a solid color ground, one is a Bicentennial quilt with a combination of techniques. Of those dated four are nineteenth century, one is contemporary.
Study Services: Make appointment. Reading room, work tables, accession cards/files, and books/journals.
Public Services: Workshops on patchwork and appliqué quiltmaking offered.

Hershey Museum of American Life

West end of Hersheypark Arena
Hershey, Pennsylvania
(717) 534-3439

Mailing Address:
P.O. Box 170
Hershey, PA 17033

Daily, 10:00 A.M.–5:00 P.M.; Memorial Day–Labor Day: daily, 10:00 A.M.–6:00 P.M.
Thirty-six quilts have been collected from central Pennsylvania, especially Lancaster County. Some were made by Pennsylvania Germans. Piecework, appliqué, trapunto, and white-on-white quilting are represented. Approximately twenty are nineteenth century quilts, and about ten date after 1900. Principal source: George Danner, late nineteenth century collector in Lancaster County, Pennsylvania.
NB: Several documented Lancaster County, Pennsylvania quilts.

Study Services: For scholars, write or call curator of collections. Work tables, accession cards/files, and photocopy facilities.
Public Services: Classes in quiltmaking, quilting demonstrations, other programs by request.

Pennsylvania Farm Museum
2451 Kissel Hill Road
Lancaster, Pennsylvania 17601
(717) 569-0401

Tuesday–Saturday, 9:00 A.M.–5:00 P.M.; Sunday, 1:00–5:00 P.M.
The collection contains thirty to fifty Pennsylvania quilts from the nineteenth century, and two or three Pennsylvania Amish quilts. About half are piecework and half appliqué, but there are two or three white-on-white quilts.
Study Services: Write director. Accession cards/files and books/journals.
Public Services: Quilt craft classes and limited tours by reservation.

Lebanon County Historical Society
924 Cumberland Street
Lebanon, Pennsylvania 17042
(717) 272-1473

Monday, Wednesday, Friday, and Sunday, 1:00–4:00 P.M.; Monday, 7:00–9:00 P.M.
Twenty-eight handsewn quilts, typically Pennsylvania German from Lebanon County in particular, five embroidered quilts, and some newer quilts comprise the collection. About eighteen are patchwork, five embroidered, two appliqué, one white-on-white. Twenty-two are nineteenth century, three are post-1900, and three are contemporary. Quilts are on exhibit at all times.
Study Services: Make appointment. Work tables, and accession cards/files; photo reproductions could be available if necessary.
Public Services: Occasional exhibitions.

Pennsylvania Dutch Folk Culture Center
Lenhartsville, Pennsylvania 19534
(215) 562-4803

April, May, September, and October: Saturday, 10:00 A.M.–5:00 P.M.; Sunday, 1:00–5:00 P.M.
June–August: weekdays, 10:00 A.M.–5:00 P.M.; Sunday, 1:00–5:00 P.M.
Six quilts, many patches, and unfinished quilt tops.

The Packwood House Museum
10 Market Street
Lewisburg, Pennsylvania
(717) 524-0323

Mailing Address:
15 North Water Street
Lewisburg, PA 17837

Tuesday–Saturday, 10:00 A.M.–5:00 P.M.; Saturday, 1:00–5:00 P.M.; Sunday, 2:00–5:00 P.M.
The Museum houses twenty-two handsewn regional Pennsylvania quilts made by German, Quaker, and other quiltmakers. They are pieced and appliqué in a wide assortment of patterns such as Log Cabin, Four Patch, Nine Patch, Double and Irish Chain. One of the principal donors was Mrs. John T. Fetherston. Quilts are on continuous exhibition.
NB: Quaker silk quilt from Williamsport area.
Study Services: Make appointment. Reading room, work tables, accession cards/files, and photocopy facilities.

Union County Historical Society Courthouse
South Second Street
Lewisburg, Pennsylvania
(717) 524-4461, extension 56

Mailing Address:
Oral Traditions Project
P.O. Box 154
Laurelton, PA 17835

Weekdays, 8:30 A.M.–4:30 P.M., appointment advised.
The collection consists of six handsewn Pennsylvania German and Scotch-Irish quilts, twenty-five to thirty-five oral history tapes and

transcriptions, approximately 6,000 slides, roughly 225 photo prints and transparencies, and about fifteen stereopticon cards of quilt images.

Study Services: Call for appointment one to two weeks in advance of visit. Work tables, accession cards/files, slide viewers, and photocopy facilities; slides and photo prints made from negatives; catalogs from multi-media shows.

Public Services: Three day symposia, one in 1985, one planned for 1987 with nationally known authorities; major exhibits in 1985 and another major series planned for 1987.

Publications: Lasansky, Jeannette. *In the Heart of Pennsylvania: 19th and 20th Century Quiltmaking Traditions* (1985).

The American Quilt Museum
Market and New Haven Streets
Marietta, Pennsylvania

Mailing Address:
P.O. Box 65
Marietta, PA 17547-0065

Hours not provided. The museum will open in December 1987.

More than ten quilts representing a wide variety of techniques and patterns will form the collection.

Study Services: By appointment. Library reading room, work tables, accession cards/files; slides.

Public Services: Loan exhibitions, lectures, films, seminars, quilting instruction, and a newsletter for members are planned.

Schwenkfelder Library
One Seminary Street
Pennsburg, Pennsylvania 18073
(215) 679-3103

Weekdays, 9:00 A.M.–4:00 P.M.
Six nineteenth century patchwork quilts.

Germantown Historical Society
5214 Germantown Avenue
Philadelphia, Pennsylvania 19144
(215) 844-0514

Tuesday and Thursday, 10:00 A.M.–4:00 P.M.; Sunday, 1:00–5:00 P.M.
The Society's collection of eighty-six quilts come mainly from the Germantown region. Five were made by Pennsylvania Germans; a few are from elsewhere in Pennsylvania and Baltimore, Maryland. Of note is a tin object identified as a quilting (stamping) pattern in a feathers motif. Fifty-four are pieced quilts, fourteen crazy quilts, ten appliqué, four are white-on-white, three are pieced and appliqué, and one is a Yo-Yo quilt. Of those dated: three are prior to 1820, nineteen are nineteenth century, and one quilt dates after 1900. Quilts are continuously on exhibit.

Study Services: Scholars call for appointment; photographs by written request. Work tables, accession cards/files, and photocopy facilities.

Public Services: Lectures, and school tours.

The Goldie Paley Design Center
Philadelphia College of Textiles and Science
4200 Henry Avenue
Philadelphia, Pennsylvania 19144
(215) 951-2860

Tuesday–Saturday, 10:00 A.M.–4:00 P.M.
The collection includes twenty-three quilts from Pennsylvania and quilt instructions. About fourteen are piecework, seven crazy quilts, one Yo-Yo, one printed (block print) whole-cloth with quilting, and one appliqué. One quilt predates 1820, thirteen are nineteenth century, and nine date later than 1900.

NB: Quilts of fabric by John Hewson, 1775 to 1815, first block printer in Philadelphia.

Study Services: Membership required. Reading room, work tables, accession cards/files, books/journals, and microscope.

Public Services: Tours, and workshops.

Philadelphia Museum of Art

Parkway at 26th Street
Philadelphia, Pennsylvania
(215) 787-5404

Mailing Address:
P.O. Box 7646
Philadelphia, PA 19101-7646

Tuesday–Friday, 9:00 A.M.–5:00 P.M., by previous appointment.
The Museum's holdings include sixty handsewn quilts. Forty-three are American quilts from Maine; North Carolina; New Hampshire; Baltimore and Cambridge, Maryland. Eleven quilts are from Pennsylvania and include Pennsylvania German, Amish, and Mennonite. There are four English quilts and one French quilt. Thirty-six are patchwork, eleven appliqué, four crazy quilts, four printed plain cloth quilts, three white-on-white counterpanes with stuffed work, one whole-cloth with quilting, and one plain quilt with center square. Of those dated seven predate 1820, twenty-eight are nineteenth century, one is contemporary. Principal sources: Horace Wells Sellers, bequest of Lydia Thompson Morris.
NB: Quilt made by Sophonisba Peale, daughter of Charles Wilson Peale, and one quilt made by Elizabeth Coates Paschall.
Study Services: Make appointment. Reading room, work tables, accession cards/files, museum library with books and periodicals, photocopy facilities, and microscope; slides and prints may be ordered from negatives.
Publications: Garvan, Beatrice B. *The Pennsylvania German Collection: Handbooks in American Art, No. 2* (1982). *Philadelphia, Three Centuries of American Art* (1976).

The Center for the History of American Needlework Located at Carlow College

3333 Fifth Avenue
Pittsburgh, Pennsylvania 15213
(412) 578-6016

Hours not provided.
A collection of five quilts and approximately 300 quilt squares. There is a library with books on quilting.

Historical Society of Berks County

940 Centre Avenue
Reading, Pennsylvania 19601
(215) 375-4375

Tuesday–Saturday, 9:00 A.M.–4:00 P.M. Library: Tuesday, Wednesday, Friday, and Saturday, 9:00 A.M.–2:00 P.M.
Of twenty-six handsewn quilts by local makers twenty-four are patchwork and two are appliqué. Twenty-one date from the nineteenth century, two date post-1900, and three are contemporary.
Study Services: Arrange for appointment in advance. Reading room, work tables, accession cards/files, books/journals, and photocopy facilities; photo prints made from negatives.

Mennonite Historians of Eastern Pennsylvania

Peter Wentz Farmstead Mennonite Heritage Center
24 South Main Street
Souderton, Pennsylvania 18964
(215) 723-1700 or 287-8888

April–November: Wednesday–Saturday, 10:00 A.M.–4:00 P.M.
Thirteen Pennsylvania German/Mennonite quilts are from southeastern Pennsylvania. Ten are piecework quilts, two embroidered, and one piecework and appliqué. Four date from the nineteenth century, eight date after 1900, and one is contemporary. Regularly changing exhibits usually include quilts.
NB: Friendship quilt with many autographs; and Sunburst quilt.
Study Services: By appointment with curator. Reading room, work tables, accession cards/files with staff assistance, and a library with books on textiles; photographs can be taken upon request.
Public Services: Tours for groups upon request.

Greene County Historical Society

Rural Delivery 2, Old Route 21
Waynesburg, Pennsylvania
(412) 627-3204

Mailing Address:
P.O. Box 127
Waynesburg, PA 15370

Tuesday–Sunday, 12:30–4:00 P.M.
Sixty handsewn piecework, appliqué, and embroidered quilts are from western Pennsylvania. Of those quilts that are dated five are nineteenth century, ten date after 1900, ten are contemporary. Quilts are continuously exhibited.
Study Services: Ask at office. Reading room, work tables, accession cards/files, library with several display rooms, and photocopy facilities.
Public Services: Tours, planning quilt exhibitions in which the public is invited to participate.

Chester County Historical Society

225 North High Street
West Chester, Pennsylvania 19380
(215) 692-4800

Tuesday–Saturday, 10:00 A.M.–4:00 P.M.;
Wednesday, 1:00–8:00 P.M.
Of the 187 quilts in this collection all are attributed to Chester County. One hundred-fifteen are pieced, forty-seven pieced and autographed, twenty-one appliqué, and four appliqué and embroidered.
Study Services: Write or phone for appointment. Work tables, accession cards/files, books/journals, and photocopy facilities; photographs may be taken by researcher.
Public Services: Programs only when quilts are on public view.

Wyoming Historical and Geological Society

49 South Franklin Street
Wilkes-Barre, Pennsylvania 18701
(717) 823-6244

Hours not provided.
Thirty-five quilts from northeastern Pennsylvania and central New York. One quilt each is from Wyoming Valley, Susquehanna County, and Berwick, Pennsylvania. One was made by the Ladies Aid Society of Lehman Methodist Church in Lehman, Pennsylvania. Two Dutch quilts are from Orange County, New York. Twenty-eight are piecework and two are appliquéd. Sixteen are nineteenth century, two later than 1900, and one is contemporary.
Study Services: For scholars, give written notice at least one week in advance. Reading room, accession cards/files, and photocopy facilities.
Public Programs: On occasion.

Lycoming County Historical Society and Museum

858 West 4th Street
Williamsport, Pennsylvania 17701
(717) 326-3326

Tuesday–Saturday, 9:30 A.M.–4:00 P.M.; Sunday, 1:30–4:00 P.M.; closed holidays.
A collection of approximately fifty local quilts. Pieced and appliqué, crazy quilts, and a number of Friendship quilts. Two are Quaker. Mostly nineteenth and early twentieth century.
NB: Cotton Quaker Friendship quilt with names in ink from Delaware County.
Study Services: By appointment.
Public Services: Occasional exhibitions.

Historical Society of York County

250 East Market Street
York, Pennsylvania 17403
(717) 848-1587

Monday–Saturday, 9:00 A.M.–5:00 P.M.; Sunday, 1:00–5:00 P.M. No Sunday hours, January–March.
Eighty quilts are from the York County area.

Of those, six were made prior to 1820; forty 1821–1900, twelve 1901–1940, and two are contemporary. There are fifty-four pieced quilts, ten crazy quilts, ten appliqué, two trapunto, two printed whole-cloth, and two white-on-white.

Study Services: Access by written request for appointment. Reading room, work tables, accession cards/files, books/journals, and photocopy facilities; some black-and-white photographs, and color slides; some photo prints from negatives available.

Coffee County, Alabama, April 1939. Typical farmhouse spring house cleaning; homemade quilts and bedding in sun. Photo by Marion Post Wolcott, negative number LC-USF34-51424. Courtesy of the Farm Security Administration Collection, Prints and Photographs Division, Library of Congress.

RHODE ISLAND

Rhode Island can boast 117 quilts shown in five collections.

Western Rhode Island Civic Historical Society
Paine House
1 Station Street
Coventry, Rhode Island

Mailing Address:
William Sedgley
Central Pike
North Scituate, RI 02857

Saturday, 1:00–4:00 P.M.
Many undocumented quilts.

Pettaquamscott Historical Society
1348 Kingstown Road
Kingston, Rhode Island
(401) 783-1328

Mailing Address:
P.O. Box 59
Kingston, RI 02881

May–October: Tuesday, Thursday, and Saturday, 1:00–4:00 P.M.
Eight regional quilts may be seen by scholars by appointment.

Historic Textile and Costume Collection
University of Rhode Island
306 Quinn Hall
Kingston, Rhode Island 02881-0809
(401) 792-2299 or 792-2275

Academic year only.
In a collection of eighty quilts from New England, fifty are complete. The majority is patchwork. Some are appliqué and crazy quilts. They primarily date from the nineteenth century.
Study Services: Make appointment (during the academic year). Work tables, accession cards/files, university library, and microscope.

Public Services: The collection is used in special teaching and in selective exhibitions. It is open to the public by individual appointment during the academic year.

Museum of Art
Rhode Island School of Design
Providence, Rhode Island 02903
(401) 331-3511, extension 334

Hours not provided.
Approximately five quilts may be seen by appointment.

Rhode Island Historical Society
John Brown House
52 Power Street
Providence, Rhode Island
(401) 331-8575

Mailing Address:
Headquarters
110 Benevolent Street
Providence, RI 02906

Tuesday–Saturday, 11:00 A.M.–4:00 P.M.; Sunday, 1:00–4:00 P.M.
In addition to twenty-one Rhode Island-made quilts, quilts from Connecticut, Maine, and England, the Society has some documentation and three quilted petticoats (two on loan). Five are pieced; five are crazy quilts. Of the five with decorative quilting, two were made from petticoats. Four are appliqué, three trapunto or stuffed, and two printed whole-cloth. About seven predate 1820, fifteen are nineteenth century, and two date after 1900.
NB: Mary Judkins Signature quilt, c. 1855, and quilted petticoats.
Study Services: Work tables, accession cards/files, library with genealogy and reading room materials, and microscope; some slides, photo prints may be ordered from negatives.
Public Services: Occasional tours of storage, volunteer training, lectures during exhibitions.

SOUTH CAROLINA

From the Carolina Low Country to the mountains in the west, a quilt tour of South Carolina affords many fine and varied regional collections plus good study resources.

Aiken County Historical Museum
433 Newberry Street, S.W.
Aiken, South Carolina 29801
(803) 649-4658

Tuesday–Friday, 9:30 A.M.–4:30 P.M.; and first Sunday of the month, 2:00–5:00 P.M.
Scholars may see seven local quilts by appointment.

The Charleston Museum
360 Meeting Street
Charleston, South Carolina 29403
(803) 722-2996

Daily, 9:00 A.M.–5:00 P.M.
A small percentage of these 100 quilts from South Carolina were made by Afro-Americans. Sixty-four are pieced (twenty-three were paper pieced), twenty-three are appliqué, seven trapunto or corded, two white-on-white, two embroidered, one Yo-Yo, and one printed whole-cloth. Of those dated nine quilts predate 1820, fifty are nineteenth century, six date after 1900, three are contemporary.
NB: Chintz appliqué; and paper pieced quilts.
Study Services: For scholars, write or call for appointment. Reading room, accession cards/files, books/journals, library/archives, and photocopy facilities; some photo prints, and slides.
Public Services: Public programming is offered on a limited basis through the Education Department and by special request. Occasional exhibits.
Publications: Bullard, Lacy Folmar and Betty Jo Shiell. *Chintz Quilts—Unfading Glory* (1983).

Old Slave Mart Museum

6 Chalmers Street
Charleston, South Carolina
(803) 722-0079

Mailing Address:
P.O. Box 446
Sullivan's Island, SC 29482

Monday–Saturday, 10:00 A.M.–4:30 P.M.
Eight Afro-American quilts on continuous exhibition, and unpublished documentation.

Fort Hill-John C. Calhoun Mansion

Clemson University
Clemson, South Carolina 29631
(803) 656-2475

Monday–Saturday, 10:00 A.M.–12:00 P.M., and
1:00–5:30 P.M.; Sunday, 2:00–6:00 P.M.
Thirteen handsewn nineteenth century quilts include twelve made in the Piedmont area of South Carolina and one from Fairfax County, Virginia. Seven are white-on-white, and six have decorative quilting.
NB: Quilts that date back to plantation life in the antebellum South. These quilts are historically significant because they belonged to the John C. Calhoun family and were made from cotton and wool that was grown on the plantation.
Study Services: Inquire of the tour guide; slides; postcard, and booklet.

McKissick Museum

University of South Carolina
Columbia, South Carolina 29208
(803) 777-7251

Weekdays, 9:00 A.M.–5:00 P.M.; Saturday, 10:00 A.M.–5:00 P.M.; Sunday, 1:00–5:00 P.M.
The thirty-two southeastern quilts are primarily from South Carolina. Six are twentieth century Afro-American quilts. One is from Alamance County, North Carolina; one from Georgia; the remainder are attributed to South Carolina. Thirty are piecework quilts, one a Rose of Sharon appliqué, and one a solid whole-cloth with quilting. Of those dated five

are nineteenth century, fifteen post-1900, five are contemporary quilts.
Study Services: Make appointment with the curator of history. Work tables, accession cards/files, thirty books and journals, and photocopy facilities; photo prints, and slides.
Public Services: Exhibitions, tours, and quilting demonstrations.

South Carolina Folk Art Archive

McKissick Museum
University of South Carolina
Columbia, South Carolina 29208
(803) 777-7251

Weekdays, 9:00 A.M.–4:00 P.M.
A collection of 2,800 data forms and questionnaires about quilts made or owned in South Carolina: 2,200 forms on quilts of South Carolina origin, 250 forms about quilts by Afro-American makers, 300 forms about quilts by German-American makers, and 600 forms on quilts of out of state origin. The questionnaires noted: 1,400 piecework quilts; 1,000 appliqué quilts, 100 white-on-white quilts including trapunto and candlewick; 400 crazy quilts; 100 Yo-Yo and other novelty designs (biscuits, puffs, and stuffed triangles); 100 English template pieced quilts.
Study Services: Make appointment. Reading room, work tables, accession cards/files, books/journals, and photocopy facilities; photo prints, slides; restrictions apply to prints made from negatives.
Public Services: Tours of exhibitions; extensive outreach programs include slide lectures.
Publications: Horton, Laurel. "Quiltmaking Tradition in South Carolina." *Uncoverings 1984.* Sally Garoutte, editor. Horton, Laurel. "South Carolina Quilts and the Civil War." *Uncoverings 1985.* Sally Garoutte, editor. Horton, Laurel and Lynn Robertson Myers, editors. *Social Fabric: South Carolina's Traditional Quilts* (1985). Horton, Laurel. "Down Home and Uptown: A Patchwork of Carolina Textiles." *Carolina Folk: The Cradle of a Southern Tradition* (1985). George Terry and Lynn Robertson Myers, editors.

South Carolina State Museum

2221 Devine Street, Suite 302
Columbia, South Carolina
(803) 758-8197

Mailing Address:
P.O. Box 11296
Columbia, SC 29211

The Museum will not officially open until July, 1988.
The collection includes seventy-five South Carolina quilts of many techniques, and fifteen patterns/instructions. Two quilts predate 1820, forty-five are nineteenth century, twenty date after 1900, eight are contemporary. Continuous exhibitions of quilts are planned.
Study Services: By written request, with ten days advance notice, if possible. Reading room, work tables, accession cards/files, books/journals, photocopy facilities, and microscope; photo prints, slides, and prints made from negatives.
Public Programs: planned.

Lexington County Museum

230 Fox Street
Lexington, South Carolina
(803) 359-8369

Mailing Address:
P.O. Box 637
Lexington, SC 29072

Tuesday–Saturday, 10:00 A.M.–4:00 P.M.; Sunday, 1:00–4:00 P.M.
The Museum has sixty-two quilts from central South Carolina, mainly from Lexington County. Some were made by Lutheran Germans who settled in the 1750s. Fifty-nine are piecework quilts and three are appliqué. Forty-six are nineteenth century, thirteen post-1900, three are contemporary. Exhibits of quilts are continuous.
Study Services: For scholars, write for appointment. Accession cards/files; photo prints, slides. Prints may be made from negatives in collection of the McKissick Museum at the University of South Carolina.

York County Historical Commission

Headquarters: Historic Brattonsville
Route 1
McConnells, South Carolina 29726
(803) 684-2327

Tuesday–Thursday, and Sunday. Hours not provided.
Collection of fourteen nineteenth century pieced and appliqué quilts primarily from the northern section of South Carolina and made by quiltmakers of Scotch-Irish and English origin. Quilts are on exhibit at all times.
NB: Chintz quilts.
Study Services: Make appointment.
Public Services: Quilt exhibits and quilts exhibited as part of the historic site tours.

Spartanburg County Regional Museum

501 Otis Boulevard
Spartanburg, South Carolina 29302
(803) 596-3501

Tuesday–Saturday, 10:00 A.M.–12:00 P.M., and 3:00–5:00 P.M.; Labor Day–May: Sundays, 3:00–5:00 P.M.
Of the seventeen quilts at the Museum, five are from Spartanburg County. There are three quilt tops; two quilts are hand pieced but machine quilted. Fourteen are piecework, three are appliqué. Twelve date from the nineteenth century. Principal sources of the collection are Mrs. Thomas B. Butler, and Mr. and Mrs. Fred Epting.
Public Services: Periodic exhibits.

Fairfield County Museum

231 South Congress Street
Winnsboro, South Carolina 29180
(803) 635-9811

Monday, Wednesday, and Friday, 10:30 A.M.–12:30 P.M., and 1:30–4:30 P.M.; second and fourth Sunday, 2:00–4:00 P.M.
A collection of thirteen South Carolina quilts made prior to 1900. One is embroidered and machine quilted. Five are chintz appliqué, four are piecework, three are Victorian crazy

quilts, one is an embroidered name quilt. Quilts continuously on exhibit.

Study Services: Make appointment. Reading room, work tables, and photocopy facilities.

Joseph Silbernagel family, Beiseker, Alberta, c. 1910–11; note the crazy quilt backdrop. The father was born in Russia and emigrated to North Dakota c. 1900. In 1908 they moved northwest of Beiseker. Negative number NA-4079-44. Courtesy of the collection of the Glenbow Museum, Calgary, Alberta, Canada.

SOUTH DAKOTA

Native American quilts highlight the rich heritage of the Plains Indians.

Smith-Zimmermann State Museum
South Dakota State College
Madison, South Dakota 57042-1799
(605) 256-5308

Tuesday–Saturday, 8:00 A.M.–5:00 P.M.
The Museum has fourteen handsewn quilts from southeast South Dakota. Thirteen date from 1880 to 1900, and one quilt from 1932. Eleven are piecework quilts (three are Signature quilts), two are appliqué, and one crazy quilt.

Study Services: Make appointment with curator. Work tables, and accession cards/files; photo prints made from negatives.

Public Services: Periodic exhibitions.

Robinson State Museum
Memorial Building
500 East Capitol
Pierre, South Dakota 57501
(605) 773-3797

Weekdays, 8:00 A.M.–5:00 P.M.; Saturday, 10:00 A.M.–5:00 P.M.; Sunday, 1:00–5:00 P.M.
The twenty-four quilts in this collection include three by Sioux Indians (two star quilts), four from South Dakota, two from Iowa, one from Connecticut. Fourteen are piecework, six are crazy quilts, two are appliqué, one is a turkey red embroidered, and one quilt has mixed techniques. Seven are nineteenth century, fifteen date after 1900, two are contemporary.

NB: 1890 State Constitutional Convention quilt signed by delegates.

Study Services: Make appointment. Work tables, accession cards/files, and photocopy facilities; photographs will be taken upon request.

The Heritage Center

Red Cloud Indian School
Pine Ridge, South Dakota
(605) 867-5888

Mailing Address:
Box 100
Pine Ridge, SD 57770

Weekdays, 8:00 A.M.–5:00 P.M.
The center has twenty-three Oglala Lakota handsewn quilts with a concentration of contemporary Sioux Indian Star quilts by local artisans.
Study Services: For scholars, make appointment. Reading room, and work tables.

Siouxland Heritage Museums

Old Courthouse Museum
200 West 6th Street
Sioux Falls, South Dakota 57102
(605) 335-4210

Monday–Saturday, 9:00 A.M.–5:00 P.M.; Sunday, 2:00–5:00 P.M.
The collection contains thirty-eight quilts. Thirty are from the northern plains region and two were made by American Indians. Twenty-two are pieced quilts, seven have decorative quilting, five are mixed techniques, and four are appliqué. Of those dated one quilt predates 1820, fourteen are nineteenth century, fifteen date later than 1900, and two are contemporary.
Study Services: Write to curator for appointment. Reading room, work tables, accession cards/files, books/journals, and photocopy facilities.
Public Services: Special tours offered during exhibits.

W. H. Over State Museum

North Campus
University of South Dakota
Vermillion, South Dakota
(605) 677-5228

Mailing Address:
University of South Dakota
414 East Clark
Vermillion, SD 57069

Closed temporarily while building is under construction.
Scholars may make an appointment to see six handsewn quilts.

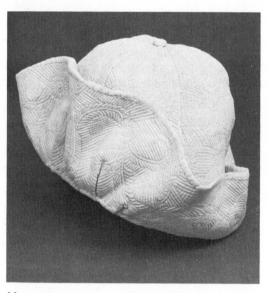

Man's nightcap, England, c. 1720. Quilted white linen. Courtesy of Costume Council Fund, catalog number 318A, the American Quilt Research Center, Los Angeles County Museum of Art.

TENNESSEE

Appalachian patchwork is plentiful, but Afro-American quilts and Hmong piecework can also be seen.

McMinn County Living Heritage Museum

Tennessee Wesleyan College
Old College Building
Athens, Tennessee
(615) 745-0329

Mailing Address:
P.O. Box 889
Athens, TN 37303

Tuesday–Friday, 10:00 A.M.–5:00 P.M.; weekends, 2:00–5:00 P.M.
The collection contains twelve quilts made primarily in Tennessee and documentation on six quilts. Six are pieced, three crazy quilts, one white-on-white c. 1870, one appliqué c. 1880, and one Friendship quilt with embroidered names from the late 1800s. Of those dated four are nineteenth century, one dates later than 1900, and one is contemporary. Quilts on continuous exhibition.
NB: Two quilts included in traveling exhibit sponsored by the Hunter Museum of Art in Chattanooga, Tennessee.
Study Services: For scholars, make appointment. Reading room, work tables, accession cards/files, and books/journals; some slides, and photo prints made from negatives.
Public Services: February and March are quilt exhibit months, with special lectures and workshops offered.

Rocky Mount Historical Association

Bluff City, Tennessee
(615) 538-7396

Mailing Address:
Route 2, Box 70
Bluff City, TN 37686

March 1–December 21: Monday–Saturday, 10:00 A.M.–5:00 P.M.; Sunday, 2:00–6:00 P.M. January 5–March 1: weekdays, 10:00 A.M.–5:00 P.M.; Closed: Thanksgiving and December 21–January 5.
The collection includes thirty-three quilts. Ten are from Tennessee, ten from Virginia, and one from Florida. Thirty are piecework, two embroidered, and one appliqué. Eleven are dated: one pre-1820, eight nineteenth century, one post-1900, and one contemporary. Quilts on continuous exhibition.
Study Services: For scholars, make request to director and curator of collections, one of whom must be present during visit. Reading room, work tables, accession cards/files, books/journals, and photocopy facilities; slides.
Public Services: Lecture series for local quilting groups.

Houston Antique Museum

201 High Street
Chattanooga, Tennessee 37403
(615) 267-7176

Tuesday–Saturday, 10:00 A.M.–4:30 P.M.; Sunday, 2:00–4:30 P.M.
Five quilts may be seen by appointment with curator.

Clarksville-Montgomery County Historical Museum

200 South Second Street
Clarksville, Tennessee
(615) 645-2507

Mailing Address:
P.O. Box 383
Clarksville, TN 37041

Tuesday–Saturday, 10:00 A.M.–4:00 P.M.; Sunday, 1:00–4:00 P.M.
Of ten handsewn quilts there are eight patchwork and appliqué quilts made in Montgomery County, one 1825 German wool, cotton, and linen Pineapple quilt throw; and one 1880 patchwork and appliqué Clarksville, Tennessee quilt. Photographs of quilts and quiltmakers are also part of the museum holdings. Eight quilts are patchwork, two appliqué. Eight are nineteenth century and two are later than 1900. Quilts on exhibit at all times.
NB: 1880 Episcopal Churchwomen patchwork and appliqué quilt, and German Pineapple throw quilt, 1825.
Study Services: Apply to director for approval, arrange to be accompanied by staff member. Reading room, work tables, accession cards/files, books/journals, research papers, library, microfilm reader, and photocopy facilities; photo print collection; and prints may be requested from negatives; videotapes.
Public Services: Tours, workshops, and weekly demonstrations.

Red Clay Historic Park

Cleveland, Tennessee
(615) 472-2627

Mailing Address:
Route 6, Box 306
Cleveland, TN 37311

Daily, 8:00 A.M.–4:30 P.M.
There are twenty-five quilts. All except one is from the southern Appalachian area, with a concentration in sampler quilts. Twenty-two are pieced pattern quilts; three are appliqué and embroidered. Three date from the nineteenth century, and twenty-two are contem-

porary. Quilts are exhibited in the context of daily life of the nineteenth century Cherokee.
NB: One quilt top that is pieced, appliqué, and embroidered.
Study Services: Write or call manager before visiting. Reading room, work tables, and photocopy facilities.

Great Smoky Mountains National Park

Gatlinburg, Tennessee 37738
(615) 436-5615

Weekdays, 8:00 A.M.–4:30 P.M.
Ten quilts from the Appalachian region; nine are piecework and one is embroidered. Two are nineteenth century, seven date after 1900, one is contemporary.
Study Services: Make appointment with curator.

Archives of Appalachia

The Sherrod Library
East Tennessee State University
Johnson City, Tennessee 37614-0002
(615) 929-4338/929-5339

Weekdays, 8:00 A.M.–4:30 P.M.; weekends by appointment.
Unpublished material about quilts, audio tapes, video tapes, slide/tape presentation, and materials in vertical files, clippings, and pamphlets.
Study Services: Walk-in basis. Reading room, work tables, accession cards/files, books/journals, computerized print-out of collections; photocopy facilities.

Carroll Reece Museum

East Tennessee State University
Gilbreath Drive
Johnson City, Tennessee
(615) 929-4392

Mailing Address:
P.O. Box 22,300A
Johnson City, TN 37614-0002

Weekdays, 9:00 A.M.–4:00 P.M.; weekends,
1:00–5:00 P.M.
Eight American quilts my be seen by appointment with director.

Center for Southern Folklore Archives

1216 Peabody Avenue
Memphis, Tennessee
(901) 726-4205

Mailing Address:
P.O. Box 40105
Memphis, TN 38174

Weekdays, 9:00 A.M.–5:00 P.M.
A collection of approximately seventy-five regional Anglo and Afro-American quilts, information on contemporary quiltmakers in Arkansas, Mississippi, and Tennessee; quilt blocks; several dozen Hmong piecework examples; photographs, sound recordings, and transcriptions. The bulk of the collection is work done in the 1960s and 1970s by Pecolia Warner, from Mississippi. There are also ten baby quilts from the 1930s Park Commission Community Center of Tennessee. The majority is piecework but includes a few appliqué. Quilts are on continuous exhibition.
NB: American flag quilt by Pecolia Warner.
Study Services: By appointment. Reading room, accession cards/files (cards with photographs of each quilt), books/journals, photocopy facilities; slides, postcards, film *Four Women Artists* (Pecolia Warner is one of the subjects), 16mm, also available in all video formats for purchase or rental.
Public Services: Occasional quilt exhibitions, lectures, workshops, and festivals.
Publications: Ramsey, Bets, and Merikay Waldvogel. *Quilts of Tennessee* (1986).

Memphis Brooks Museum of Art

Overton Park
Memphis, Tennessee 38112
(901) 722-3525

Weekdays, 9:00 A.M.–5:00 P.M.
The permanent collection contains twenty-one quilts; thirty-four others are on loan to the museum. Thirteen are piecework, four pieced and appliqué, three appliqué, and one is a Yo-Yo quilt. Six in the collection date from the nineteenth century, thirteen are later than 1900, and two are contemporary. Of those on loan, six date from the nineteenth century, twenty-five are post-1900, three are contemporary.
Study Services: Call curator's or registrar's office for appointment. Reading room, work tables, accession cards/files, and books/journals; slides.

Memphis Pink Palace Museum

3050 Central Avenue
Memphis, Tennessee 38111
(901) 454-5600

Tuesday–Sunday, 10:00 A.M.–5:00 P.M.
The collection maintains thirteen handsewn regional quilts: eleven from Tennessee and the Mid-South region, and two from the eastern United States. Five are piecework, three appliqué, three crazy quilts, two are decorative quilting on solid color whole cloth. Two quilts predate 1820, ten are nineteenth century, and one dates after 1900. Quilts are on exhibit at all times.
NB: Paperbacked silk patchwork quilt.
Study Services: For scholars, make appointment. Reading room, work tables, accession cards/files, and books/journals.
Public Services: Guided tours through permanent exhibits.

Davy Crockett Tavern Museum

Morningside Drive
Morristown, Tennessee 37814
(615) 581-8585

Monday–Saturday, 9:00 A.M.–5:00 P.M.; Sunday, 1:00–6:00 P.M.
Five quilts on continuous exhibition, and three oral histories.

Oaklands Historic House Museum

900 North Maney Avenue
Murfreesboro, Tennessee
(615) 893-0022

Mailing Address:
P.O. Box 432
Murfreesboro, TN 37133

Tuesday–Saturday, 10:00 A.M.–4:00 P.M.; Sunday, 1:00–4:00 P.M.
Six Tennessee-made quilts on continuous exhibition.

Cumberland Museum

800 Ridley Avenue
Nashville, Tennessee 37203
(615) 259-6099

Hours not provided.
Less than ten quilts in the collection.

Museum of Tobacco Art and History

800 Harrison Street
Nashville, Tennessee 37203
(615) 242-9218

Monday–Saturday, 10:00 A.M.–4:00 P.M.; Sunday, 12:00–4:00 P.M.
Two nineteenth century quilts on continuous exhibition; three research papers; one unpublished letter.

The Tennessee State Museum

505 Deaderick Street
Nashville, Tennessee 37219-5196
(615) 741-2692

Monday–Saturday, 10:00 A.M.–5:00 P.M.; Sunday, 1:00–5:00 P.M.
The Museum has eighty-four quilts from Tennessee; one was slave-made. Piecework, appliqué, embroidered, trapunto, and white-on-white quilting techniques are represented. Of those identified four predate 1820, sixty are nineteenth century, eight date later than 1900, and seven are contemporary. Quilts are continuously on exhibition.
NB: Earliest dated Tennessee quilt; documented slave-made quilt.
Study Services: For scholars, make appointment with curator. Reading room, work tables, accession cards/files, books/journals, photocopy facilities, and microscope; slides.
Public Services: Occasional lectures; Museum sometimes hosts workshops organized by quiltmakers.

Museum of Appalachia

Norris, Tennessee
(615) 494-7680

Mailing Address:
P.O. Box 359
Norris, TN 37828

Open during daylight hours year-round. Summer: daily, 8:00 A.M.–8:00 P.M. Winter: daily, 9:00 A.M.–5:00 P.M. Closed Christmas.
Approximately thirty-five to forty quilts are in storage and not accessible. Within the next three years there will be a new building with exhibition space for the quilt collection.
Publications: Irwin, John Rice. *A People and Their Quilts* (1983).

Rocky Mount Historical Association

Overmountain Museum
Piney Flats, Tennessee
(615) 538-7396

Mailing Address:
Route 2, Box 70
Piney Flats, TN 37686

Monday–Saturday, 10:00 A.M.–5:00 P.M.; Sunday, 2:00–6:00 P.M.
A collection of forty-five to fifty quilts.

Sam Davis Memorial Home

Sam Davis Road
Smyrna, Tennessee 37167
(615) 459-2341

Weekdays, 10:00 A.M.–5:00 P.M.; Sunday, 1:00–4:00 P.M.
Fifteen handsewn nineteenth century quilts from central Tennessee are complemented by one quilt pattern and unpublished documentation. Eight quilts are piecework, four pieced and embroidered, and three appliqué. Quilts are exhibited at all times.
NB: Mayapple quilt and Sassafras and Rose quilt.
Study Services: Apply to the regent for appointment. Work tables, and accession cards/files; photo cataloging of quilts now in progress.

Turlock, California. May 1942. PTA President (left) and Red Cross representative admire quilts the Parent-Teachers Association has made for the Red Cross. Photo by Russell Lee, negative number LC-USF34-72693-D. Courtesy of the Farm Security Administration Collection, Prints and Photographs Division, Library of Congress.

TEXAS

Where but Texas would you expect to see a ranch brands quilt or a cowboys' reunion Autograph quilt?

Museum of the Big Bend

Sul Ross State University
Alpine, Texas
(915) 837-8143

Mailing Address:
Box C-210
Alpine, TX 79830

Tuesday–Saturday, 9:00 A.M.–5:00 P.M.; Sunday, 1:00–5:00 P.M.
The Museum's collection includes four quilts and six quilt tops from Texas, fifty quilt patterns and instructions, and one taped oral history. Eight are patchwork quilts and two are crazy quilts with appliqué and embroidery. Eight date from the 1880s to the 1890s, and two date after 1900. Principal source of the collection: Mrs. A. Smith.
NB: Two c. 1890s regional crazy quilts.
Study Services: Make appointment with curator. Work tables, accession cards/files, books/journals, photocopy facilities, and microscope; photo prints, and slides.
Public Services: Lectures for groups available by appointment. Temporary exhibits of quilts.

Texas Folklife Resources

1902B West 35th Street
Austin, Texas
(512) 482-9217

Mailing Address:
P.O. Box 49824
Austin, TX 78765

Weekdays, 8:00 A.M.–5:00 P.M.
An undetermined number of interviews with quiltmakers, slides, and photographs.
Study Services: Contact the Texas Folklife Resources for access to archives. Slides, and prints made from negatives.

Texas Memorial Museum

University of Texas
2400 Trinity
Austin, Texas 78705
(512) 471-3551 or 471-1604 (message)

Weekdays, 9:00 A.M.–5:00 P.M.; weekends, 1:00–5:00 P.M.
There are thirty-one quilts and eleven quilt squares from the Germantown area of New York and quilt squares from Texas. Fifteen quilts were made or used in Texas, six are from Illinois, two from Wyoming, one from New Jersey, one is Appalachian, and one Italian-American. Twenty-one are pieced quilts, six feature embroidery, five appliqué, three crazy quilts, two pieced and appliqué, two trapunto, and one is a quilted calimanco coverlet. Twenty-eight are dated: two prior to 1820, eighteen nineteenth century, six post-1900, and two contemporary.
NB: Earliest quilt dates to 1814; quilt with colorful Texas history; and quilt that dates to 1818.
Study Services: Contact collection manager's office, describe project, obtain permission to view appropriate quilts, and set up appointment with office. Work tables, books/journals, materials in conservation lab available by special arrangement and under strict supervision, photocopy facilities, and microscope by special arrangement; photo prints and slides made from negatives, and transparencies; and exhibit catalog.
Public Services: Docent-led tours, children's classes, and lecture series for special exhibits.
Publications: From Our Hands: A Sequicentennial Celebration of Texas Quilts (1986).

Sam Rayburn House Museum

Bonham, Texas
(214) 583-5558

Mailing Address:
Route 3, Box 308
Bonham, TX 75418

Weekdays, 8:00 A.M.–5:00 P.M.; Saturday, 1:00–5:00 P.M.; Sunday, 2:00–5:00 P.M.
Seven Tennessee or Texas-made quilts may be seen by appointment.

Panhandle-Plains Historical Museum

West Texas State University
2401 4th Avenue
Canyon, Texas
(806) 655-7191

Mailing Address:
P.O. Box 967
West Texas Station
Canyon, TX 79016

Monday–Saturday, 9:00 A.M.–5:00 P.M.; Sunday, 2:00–6:00 P.M.
Ninety quilts (forty-two are documented) form a collection supplemented by an ongoing oral history project with regional quilters assisted by the High Plains Quilters Guild. Some quilts were quilted by slaves, thirteen are Texas quilts, three are from Tennessee, one from California, one from Nebraska, one from Indiana, one from Virginia, one from Mississippi. Seventy-two quilts are piecework, seventeen appliqué, some are appliqué on piecework. Fifteen quilts have embroidery on piecework. Three are printed whole-cloth tied, with old quilts inside for batting. Two are trapunto, one white-on-white, one printed whole-cloth with quilting. One predates 1820; the greater part of the collection dates from 1860 to 1940.
NB: XIT Ranch Cowboy Reunion Autograph quilt, and reverse appliqué c. 1809.
Study Services: Submit serious research requests to curator of textiles. Reading room, work tables, accession cards/files, books/jour-

nals, photocopy facilities, and microscope; photo prints, and slides.
Public Services: Tours of exhibits and outreach programs.

Crosby County Pioneer Memorial
Crosbyton, Texas
(806) 675-2331

Mailing Address:
P.O. Box 386
Crosbyton, TX 79322

Tuesday–Saturday, 9:00 A.M.–12:00 P.M., and 2:00–5:00 P.M.
A collection of twenty-three handsewn southern quilts and one transcribed oral history tape. Fifteen quilts are piecework, five appliqué, and three are white-on-white. About eight are nineteenth century, eleven date after 1900, and four are contemporary. Exhibits of quilts are continuous.
Study Services: For scholars, make appointment. Reading room, work tables, books/journals, and accession cards/files.

Dallas County Heritage Society
Old City Park
1717 Gano Street
Dallas, Texas 75215
(214) 421-5141

Tuesday–Friday, 10:00 A.M.–4:30 P.M. ; weekends, 1:30–4:30 P.M. Office: weekdays, 8:30 A.M.–5:00 P.M.
The Society has fifty quilts that are Texas-made or donated by Texas pioneer families. Thirty-five are nineteenth century, and fifteen date after 1900. Quilts are on exhibit at all times.
Study Services: For scholars, make appointment. Work tables, and accession cards/files.

Dallas Historical Society
Hall of State
Grand Avenue at Nimitz
Fair Park
Dallas, Texas
(214) 421-5136

Mailing Address:
P.O. Box 26038
Dallas, TX 75226

Monday–Saturday, 9:00 A.M.–5:00 P.M.; Sunday, 1:00–5:00 P.M.
Approximately thirty-five southern quilts are in the Society's collection; ten are from Texas. Twelve are piecework, ten crazy quilts, three appliqué, two are Yo-Yo, and one is stencilled. Two predate 1820, twenty-five are nineteenth century, six date after 1900, and two are contemporary.
NB: 1845 stencilled quilt.
Study Services: For scholars, submit project for approval, then make appointment. Reading room, and photocopy facilities; photo prints, and slides.

Wise County Heritage Museum
1602 South Trinity
Decatur, Texas
(817) 627-5586

Mailing Address:
P.O. Box 427
Decatur, TX 76234

Weekdays, 9:00 A.M.–5:00 P.M.; Sunday, 1:00–5:00 P.M.
Collection of fifteen to twenty quilts from Wise County, Texas. Three quilts can be dated from the nineteenth century, and four date after 1900. Quilts always on exhibition.
Public Services: Tours of exhibits.

Fort Davis National Historic Site

Fort Davis, Texas
(915) 426-3225

Mailing Address:
P.O. Box 1456
Fort Davis, TX 79734

Winter: daily, 8:00 A.M.–5:00 P.M.; summer: daily, 8:00 A.M.–6:00 P.M.
Thirteen quilts are owned by the Fort Davis Site, some probably from Texas. Ten are piecework quilts, one appliqué, one combined piecework and appliqué, and one is a piecework/embroidery crazy quilt top. Ten are nineteenth century, and three post-1900.
Study Services: Request permission from superintendent. Reading room, work tables, accession cards/files, and photocopy facilities.

Neill Museum

7th and Court
Fort Davis, Texas
(915) 426-3969

Mailing Address:
P.O. Box 801
Ft. Davis, TX 79734

Hours not provided.
The Museum has eleven handsewn quilts and one personal narrative by a quiltmaker. Two are crazy quilts, one dated 1880 and the other 1890. One is a Cake Stand quilt of 1880, others are 1880 Ocean Waves, 1885 Drunkards Path, 1885 Wheel of Fortune, 1915 Around the World, 1930 Fence Rail, 1930 Martha Washington's Flower Garden, 1960 American Glory reproduction, and an Octagonal Star or Dutch Rose quilt. Quilts are continuously exhibited.
Study Services: Make appointment. Accession cards/files and books.

Annie Riggs Memorial Museum

301 South Main Street
Fort Stockton, Texas 79735
(915) 336-2167

Monday–Saturday, 10:00 A.M.–12:00 P.M., and 1:00–5:00 P.M.; Sunday, 1:30–5:00 P.M.
Seventeen quilts form a regional collection concentrated in Friendship quilts. Nine date after 1900. Principal source: Pioneer Club. Quilts exhibited at all times.
NB: Brand of Pecos County, 1875 to 1910.
Study Services: Contact director to make an appointment giving ten days notice. Accession cards/files.

Fort Worth Museum of Science and History

1501 Montgomery Street
Fort Worth, Texas 76107
(817) 732-1631

Weekdays, 9:00 A.M.–5:00 P.M.
A collection of twenty-four quilts. Eighteen are Texas quilts, two from Virginia, one from Kentucky, one from Nebraska, one from New Jersey, and one from New York. Nine are piecework, four with Log Cabin patterns, eight are crazy quilts (two made of wool), and seven are appliqué quilts. Seven nineteenth century, and three quilts after 1900 can be dated. Quilts are continuously exhibited.
Study Services: Write or call registrar for appointment. Reading room, work tables, accession cards/files, books/journals, photocopy facilities, and microscope.

Log Cabin Village Historical Complex

Log Cabin Village Lane at University Drive
Fort Worth, Texas
(817) 926-5881

Mailing Address:
2222 West Rosedale
Ft. Worth, TX 76110

Weekdays, 8:00 A.M.–4:30 P.M.; Saturday, 11:00
A.M.–4:30 P.M.; Sunday, 12:00–4:30 P.M.
Approximately twenty to twenty-five quilts
are supplemented with information provided
by donors. The collection also includes handwoven coverlets that were brought to Texas.
Quilts are exhibited as part of cabin furnishings.
Study Services: For scholars. Reading room,
work tables, accession cards/files, and books/
journals; photographic reproductions of quilts
are possible.
Public Services: Pioneer crafts demonstration
program for student groups.

Cooke County Heritage Society

Morton Museum of Cooke County
Corner of Dixon and Pecan Streets
Gainesville, Texas
(817) 668-8900

Mailing Address:
P.O. Box 150
Gainesville, TX 76240

Hours not provided.
Collection of approximately twelve quilts.

Rosenberg Library

2310 Sealy
Galveston, Texas 77550
(409) 763-8854

Monday–Saturday, 9:00 A.M.–5:00 P.M.; Sunday,
1:00–5:00 P.M.
The Library has collected ten quilts made in
Galveston, Texas and New England: crazy-
Friendship quilt, Galveston patchwork quilts,
Log Cabin, Sawtooth Star c. 1857, Blazing Star
c. 1850, Jacob's Ladder, 1843 Pineapple
quilted in the 1920s. Eight nineteenth century
quilts, two date after 1900. Principal sources:

Mrs. G.D. Morgan and Mrs. Catharine Davis
Gauss.
NB: Silk crazy quilt made by a group of prominent local women.
Study Services: Make appointment with curator. Reading room, work tables, accession
cards/files, fifty books/journals, and photocopy
facilities.

Somerwell County Museum

Vernon and Elm Streets
Glen Rose, Texas
(817) 897-4529

Mailing Address:
P.O. Box 669
Glen Rose, TX 76043

June–Labor Day: weekdays, 10:00 A.M.–5:00
P.M.; Sunday, 1:00–5:00 P.M. Tuesday after La-
bor Day–May: Saturday, 10:00 A.M.–5:00 P.M.;
Sunday, 1:00–5:00 P.M.
Five quilts from central Texas on continuous
exhibition.

Rusk County Heritage Association

Howard-Dickinson House
501 South Main Street
Henderson, Texas
(214) 657-2411

Mailing Address:
Mrs. Carl Jaggers
207 Fairpark Avenue
Henderson, TX 75652

By appointment, any time.
Seventeen handsewn quilts are accompanied
by information furnished when they were
accessioned. The majority is piecework, some
are appliqué, one is silk with embroidery, and
one is a silk quilt puffed with cotton. Quilts
are exhibited on beds, in glass exhibit cases,
and stored in chests in the restored antebellum Howard-Dickinson House. The collection
also includes woven coverlets.
NB: A Four-Pointed Star or Forgotten Star
quilt, 125 years old when donated.
Study Services: Make appointment. Reading
room, books/journals, and inventory of quilts

and coverlets; some prints may be ordered from negatives.
Public Services: Student tours.

The Bayou Bend Collection
1 Westcott
Houston, Texas
(713) 529-8773

Mailing Address:
P.O. Box 13157
Houston, TX 77219

Tuesday–Friday, 10:00 A.M.–2:45 P.M.; Saturday, half-a-day, by appointment.
Collection includes twenty-three handsewn quilts from the estate of Miss Ima Hogg. Eleven are appliqué quilts, one is trapunto, one is white-on-white, and one is a cotton and penciled work quilt. Seven date from the nineteenth century.
Study Services: Make appointment. Reading room, work tables, accession cards/files, books/journals, and photocopy facilities.

Harris County Heritage Society
1100 Bagby
Houston, Texas 77002
(713) 223-8367

Weekdays, 8:30 A.M.–4:30 P.M.
Twenty quilts are mainly southern; the majority date from the nineteenth century. Most are piecework and several are appliqué, trapunto, and decorative embroidered quilts.
Study Services: Request appointment, subject to curatorial decision. Reading room, work tables, accession cards/files, books/journals, and photocopy facilities; photo reproductions not available at present.

Lyndon B. Johnson National Historic Site
Johnson City, Texas
(512) 868-7128

Mailing Address:
Libby Hulett, Curator
P.O. Box 329
Johnson City, TX 78636
(512) 644-2322

Hours not provided.
Five or more quilts.

John E. Conner Museum
Texas Agricultural & Industrial University
Kingsville, Texas 78363
(512) 595-2819

Mailing Address:
P.O. Box 2172
Kingsville, TX 78363

Weekdays, 8:00 A.M.–5:00 P.M.; Sunday, 2:30–5:00 P.M.
Collection of ten piecework quilts from Texas and one from Nebraska. One is also embroidered. Six are nineteenth century, four date later than 1900, and one is contemporary.
Study Services: For scholars, call for appointment with registrar at (512) 595-2852. Accession cards/files, books/journals, and photocopy facilities.
Public Services: Individuals touring the museum facilities may tour textile storage.

Heard Natural Science Museum and Wildlife Sanctuary
McKinney, Texas
(214) 542-5566

Mailing Address:
Route 6, Box 22
McKinney, TX 75069

Tuesday–Saturday, 9:00 A.M.–5:00 P.M.; Sunday, 1:00–5:00 P.M.
The Museum's twenty-five quilts were made by the family of founder Bessie Heard. All but two of the quilts are handsewn. Eighteen are piecework, six appliqué, and one is printed whole-cloth with quilting. One quilt is dated

in the nineteenth century, twenty-four quilts were made after 1900.

Study Services: Write to curator of cultural collections for appointment. Accession cards/files, and books/journals. Public Services: quilts are exhibited about every two or three years in Museum's activity hall. They are also shown periodically to interested groups.

Roberts County Museum

U.S. Highway 60
Miami, Texas
(806) 868-3291

Mailing Address:
P.O. Box 306
Miami, TX 79059

Weekdays, 1:00–5:00 P.M.; weekends, 2:00–5:00 P.M.
Seven quilts on continuous exhibition.

Stone Fort Museum

Nacogdoches, Texas
(409) 569-2408

Mailing Address:
P.O. Box 6075
Nacogdoches, TX 75962

Tuesday–Saturday, 9:00 A.M.–5:00 P.M.; Sunday, 1:00–5:00 P.M.
Five east Texas quilts on continuous exhibition.

Carson County Square House Museum

Fifth and Elsie
Panhandle, Texas
(806) 537-3118

Mailing Address:
P.O. Box 276
Panhandle, TX 79068

Monday–Saturday, 9:00 A.M.–5:30 P.M.; Sunday, 1:00–5:30 P.M.
The Museum has collected twenty-five quilts from the region, unpublished documentation, and an oral history. There are twelve piecework and thirteen appliqué. Of those dated five date from the nineteenth century, and

eight date after 1900. Quilts are on continuous exhibition.

NB: Tumbling Blocks, c. pre-1900; old appliqués.

Study Services: For scholars, by appointment. Reading room, work tables, accession cards/files, books/journals, and photocopy facilities; slides, and photo prints may be ordered from negatives.

Public Services: Weekly demonstrations and lessons.

Sam Bell Maxey House State Historic Site

810 South Church Street
Paris, Texas 75460
(214) 785-5716

Wednesday and Sunday, hours not provided. Six regional quilts may be seen by appointment.

Governor Hogg Shrine State Historical Park

Park Road
Quitman, Texas
(214) 763-2701

Mailing Address:
Route 3, Box 45
Quitman, TX 75783

Wednesday–Sunday, hours not provided. Closed Christmas and New Year's.
Five nineteenth century quilts may be seen by appointment.

Ralls Historical Museum

801 Main Street
Ralls, Texas
(806) 253-2425

Mailing Address:
P.O. Box 384
Ralls, TX 79357

Weekdays, 8:00 A.M.–5:00 P.M.; Sunday, 2:00–5:00 P.M.
Collection includes twelve handsewn quilts, seventeen quilt patterns or instructions, and one personal narrative by a quiltmaker. Eight are piecework, three embroidered and appli-

qué, and one is an embroidered and piece-work quilt. Five are nineteenth century, four date after 1900, and three are contemporary, including a Bicentennial quilt. Principal source: Prairie Thimble Quilting Club. Quilts are on exhibit at all times.

NB: Ralls 75th Birthday quilt for the Texas Sesquicentennial.

Study Services: Work tables, books and journals.

Public Services: Quilting demonstration in the Museum each second and fourth Tuesday, September through May.

Winedale Historical Center

University of Texas at Austin
Round Top, Texas
(409) 278-3530

Mailing Address:
P.O. Box 11
Round Top, TX 78954

Weekdays, 9:00 A.M.–5:00 P.M. and by appointment. Saturday, 9:00 A.M.–5:00 P.M.; Sunday, 12:00–5:00 P.M.

Approximately ten quilts are on continuous exhibition in restored houses.

Fort Concho National Historic Landmark

213 East Avenue D
San Angelo, Texas 76903
(915) 657-4441

Monday–Saturday, 9:00 A.M.–5:00 P.M.; Sunday, 1:00–5:00 P.M.

Collection of thirty-five quilts: sixteen from Texas, one from Illinois, one from Missouri, and one from Kentucky. The majority is piecework, three appliqué, three crazy quilts with embroidery and decorative quilting, and one Yo-Yo. Those dated are: two pre-1820, sixteen nineteenth century, five post-1900, and one contemporary. Principal source: Mrs. James (Susan) Cockrell.

NB: Triple Irish Chain quilt, Sunburst or Mariner's Compass quilt.

Study Services: Call the curator of collections for appointment. Work tables, accession cards/ files, books/journals, ready-use of collection files.

Public Services: Annual West Texas Quilt Exhibit held at the Museum.

The Institute of Texan Cultures

801 South Bowie
San Antonio, Texas
(512) 226-7651

Mailing Address:
P.O. Box 1226
San Antonio, TX 78294

Tuesday–Sunday, 9:00 A.M.–5:00 P.M.
There are thirteen Texas-made quilts and two transcribed oral history tapes. The majority is on extended loan to the institute. Nine were made by Anglo-Americans in Texas, two by Afro-Americans, and two by Norwegian immigrants. Quilt patterns include Dutch Girl, star, and Ice Cream Cone. Nine are piecework quilts, three appliqué, and one is appliqué and embroidered. Of those dated one is a nineteenth century, four are post-1900, one is contemporary.

NB: Ranch brands quilt.

Study Services: For scholars, make appointment with curator. Reading room, accession cards/files, books/journals, and photocopy facilities; photo prints may be requested from negatives in collection.

Public Services: Continuous quilting demonstration in exhibit. Additional quilting demonstrations during the annual Texas Folklife Festival in August.

San Antonio Museum Association

3801 Broadway
San Antonio, Texas
(512) 226-5544

Mailing Address:
P.O. Box 2601
San Antonio, TX 78299-2601

Tuesday–Sunday, 8:30 A.M.–5:00 P.M.; closed Monday and holidays.

The Association has 120 quilts of regional provenance representing all quilting techniques. Three quilts are from 1820 and before (1746, 1814, and 1820), ninety-six are nineteenth century, seventeen date after 1900, and four are contemporary.

Study Services: For scholars. Limited space and work area make it difficult to accommodate the general public, but every effort is made to assist scholars and serious needleworkers. Reading room, work tables, accession cards/files, twenty-five books/journals, museum records, photocopy facilities, and microscope; photo prints and slides may be requested from negatives.

Public Services: Tours when quilts are exhibited.

Publications: Steinfeldt, Cecilia and Donald L. Stover. *Early Texas Furniture and Decorative Arts* (1973).

Sherman Historical Museum

301 South Walnut
Sherman, Texas 75090
(214) 892-7623

Friday, 9:00 A.M.–12:00 P.M., and 1:00–5:00 P.M.; weekends, 2:00–5:00 P.M.

Collection of nine quilts: one is a Victorian crazy quilt from Denmark, two crazy quilts from Kentucky or Alabama, and six patchwork quilts of Texas origin.

Scurry County Museum

West Texas College
College Avenue
Snyder, Texas
(915) 573-6107

Mailing Address:
West Texas College Campus
P.O. Box 696
Snyder, TX 79549

Weekdays, 8:00 A.M.–5:00 P.M.; Sundays, 1:00–4:00 P.M.

Collection comprises twenty quilts; the majority is from Scurry County, Texas. Six are crazy quilts, two others are pieced, one is a Postage Stamp made from sugar sacks, one Yo-Yo, and one Double Wedding Ring. Of those dated one quilt predates 1820, two are nineteenth

century, four date after 1900, and seven are contemporary.

NB: Bicentennial quilt.

Study Services: Call or write for appointment with curator. Work tables, accession cards/files, books/journals, photocopy machine in the campus administration building.

Publications: Brochure.

Railroad and Pioneer Museum

710 Jack Baskin Street
Temple, Texas
(817) 778-6873

Mailing Address:
P.O. Box 5126
Temple, TX 76501

Tuesday–Friday, 1:00–4:00 P.M.; Saturday, 10:00 A.M.–4:00 P.M.

Five central Texas quilts on continuous exhibition.

Slavonic Benevolent Order of the State of Texas

520 North Main
Temple, Texas
(817) 773-1575

Mailing Address:
P.O. Box 100
Temple, TX 76503

Weekdays, 8:00 A.M.–5:00 P.M.

Five quilts made by Czech Texans on continuous exhibition.

Culberson County Historical Museum

Van Horn, Texas

Mailing Address:
P.O. Box 127
Van Horn, TX 79855

Two days a week, 1:00–5:00 P.M.

Collection that includes eight handsewn regional quilts from local pioneer families and four personal narratives by quiltmakers. Six are piecework and two are appliqué. Six are

nineteenth century, two are later. Quilts are on continuous exhibition.
Study Services: Reading room for scholars.
Public Services: Tours.

Star of the Republic Museum

Washington-on-the-Brazos State Historical Park
Between Brenham and Navasota
Off U.S. Highway 105
Washington, Texas
(409) 878-2461

Mailing Address:
P.O. Box 317
Washington, TX 77880

Daily, 10:00 A.M.–5:00 P.M.
Fourteen quilts in this collection include two Amish, three from Texas, two from Georgia, and one from New York. Ten are pieced, one is tufted or tacked, one is appliqué, one is a combination of pieced, appliqué, and embroidered, and one is a Sunflower or Sunburst quilt with folded points.
NB: Fully documented quilt on loan to the Museum depicting U.S. presidents.
Study Services: Make appointment with curator. Reading room, accession cards/files, photocopy facilities.
Publication: Humphreys, Sherry B. *Quilts and Coverlets* (1975).

UTAH

Along with pioneer and Mormon quilts, there are Hmong and Polynesian examples!

Pioneer Village

375 North Highway 91
Farmington, Utah

Mailing Address:
P.O. Box N
Farmington, UT 84025

Hours not provided.
A collection of fifteen handsewn regional quilts made by Mormons.
NB: Crazy quilt made by a prominent Mormon pioneer.
Study Services: For scholars, make appointment. Work tables, accession cards/files, and photocopy facilities.

Territorial Statehouse

Fillmore, Utah
(801) 743-5316

Mailing Address:
P.O. Box 464
Fillmore, UT 84631

Daily, 8:00 A.M.–5:00 P.M.; summer: daily, 8:00 A.M.–7:00 P.M.
The collection includes twenty-three handsewn quilts and some unpublished documentation. Twelve are piecework, five stuffed, three appliqué, two embroidered, two hand tied, and two are Friendship quilts. Those dated include eight nineteenth century, two contemporary. Continuous exhibit of quilts.
NB: Very old Pioneer quilts, mainly crazy quilts.
Study Services: By appointment. Reading room, work tables, accession cards/files, and books/journals.
Public Services: Interpretive exhibit tours for schools.

Folk Arts Program

Utah Arts Council
617 East South Temple Street
Salt Lake City, Utah 84102
(801) 533-5760

Weekdays, 8:30 A.M.–5:30 P.M.
Ten contemporary Polynesian quilts with documentation, made in Utah by Tongan, Hawaiian, and Tahitian folk artists. Seven are piecework, two appliqué, and one a painted textile quilt.
NB: Tongan pieced polyester quilt, and other Polynesian appliqué cotton quilts.
Public Services: Publications; the Polynesian quilt collection has been organized into a traveling exhibit that tours the state through the council's visual arts program.

Latter Day Saints Museum of Church History and Art

45 North West Temple Street
Salt Lake City, Utah 84150
(801) 531-3587

Weekdays, 9:00 A.M.–9:00 P.M.; weekends, 10:00 A.M.–7:00 P.M. Office: weekdays, 8:30 A.M.–5:00 P.M.
Museum's collection spans 1830 to the present and comprises 220 quilts, three pattern books, and three blocks made by members of the Mormon Church. From the western region 150 quilts, twenty-six midwestern, sixteen Hmong-made, nine Tahitian, five southern, three Hawaiian, and one Tongan. There are 143 piecework, thirty-nine embroidered, twenty-nine appliqué, twenty picture quilts, four Yo-Yo, and three trapunto. Three were made prior to 1820, 110 are nineteenth century, thirty-nine date after 1900, and sixty-eight are contemporary.
NB: Concentration of Pioneer Utah quilts.
Study Services: Contact curator of collections. Reading room, work tables, accession cards/files, books/journals, photocopy facilities, and microscope; photo prints, slides, and prints made from negatives.
Public Services: Tours by appointment.

Pioneer Trail State Park

2601 Sunnyside Avenue
Salt Lake City, Utah 84108
(801) 533-5881

Daily, 8:00 A.M.–5:00 P.M.
There are twenty quilts by Utah Mormons in this collection. Twelve are patchwork, five pieced and tied, two appliqué, and one is printed whole-cloth. Of those dated six are nineteenth century, five post-1900, four are contemporary. Quilts are continuously exhibited as part of household furnishings.
Study Services: Contact park manager or curator of collections. Reading room, accession cards/files, and photocopy facilities.
Public Services: Interpretive demonstrations.

South Center of Utah County

Daughters of Utah Pioneers Museum
Thurber School Building
40 South Main Street
Spanish Fork, Utah 84660

By appointment.
Eight nineteenth century quilts by Mormon pioneers may be seen by appointment.

VERMONT

A quilt sewn of 12,976 pieces, one made by Calvin Coolidge, and quilts from perhaps the largest single collection in the U.S. are part of the state's heritage.

The Bennington Museum
West Main Street
Bennington, Vermont 05201
(802) 447-1571

March 1–November, plus a week at Christmastime: daily, 9:00 A.M.–5:00 P.M.
Of over sixty quilts and a coverlet, the majority was either made or used by the families who donated them. Techniques represented include: patchwork, appliqué, embroidered, and decorative quilting. The collection primarily dates from 1825 to 1900, some mid-1930s quilts, and a Bicentennial quilt of unusual size and composition.
NB: Signed and dated Civil War quilt made by local woman which has been published, particularly in quilt magazines.
Study Services: Quilts are not easily accessible. Write to director outlining research needs. Limited work space, genealogical library has large tables, information on accession cards, photocopy facilities; a few slides, and postcards. Photography is allowed with prior permission.

Orleans County Historical Society
Old Stone House Museum
Browningham, Vermont
(802) 754-2022

Mailing Address:
P.O. Box 27
Orleans, VT 05860

May 15–July 1, and September 1–October 15: Friday–Tuesday, 11:00 A.M.–5:00 P.M.; July 1–September 1: daily, 11:00 A.M.–5:00 P.M.
Twenty handsewn quilts from northern Vermont are predominantly patchwork, with a few examples of appliqué. The majority is tied. Only a few are quilted. Ten are nineteenth century, nine date after 1900, one is contemporary.
Study Services: For scholars, make appointment. Reading room, work tables, and accession cards/files; photo prints and slides made from negatives.

Folklore and Oral History Collection
Bailey/Howe Library
University of Vermont
Burlington, Vermont 05405
(802) 656-2138

Academic year: Monday–Thursday, 8:30 A.M.–9:00 P.M.; Friday, 8:30 A.M.–5:00 P.M.; Saturday, 9:00 A.M.–12:00 P.M. Between semesters (summer): weekdays, 8:30 A.M.–5:00 P.M. Also, July and August: Saturdays, 9:00 A.M.–12:00 P.M.
Three research papers on quilts and quiltmaking, two taped oral histories, three transcriptions, and forty photo prints of area quiltmakers make up the collection.
Study Services: Walk-in basis, although it is advisable to write in advance to request materials. Reading room, work tables, accession cards/files, books/journals, and photocopy facilities; photographic and sound recording duplication services.
Publications: Folklore and Oral History Catalogue, Bailey/Howe Library, University of Vermont (1981).

Chester Historical Society
Main Street
Chester, Vermont 05143

June–September: weekends, 2:00–5:00 P.M., or by appointment.
Society's collection of fourteen New England and some specifically Vermont quilts includes four that are unfinished. Ten are piecework, two homespun, one appliqué, and one embroidered. One quilt predates 1820, seven are

nineteenth century, and six quilts are later than 1900. Quilts are continuously exhibited.
Public Services: Tours, exhibitions, classes, and workshops.

Vermont Historical Society
Pavilion Building
109 State Street
Montpelier, Vermont 05602
(802) 828-2291

Weekdays, 7:45 A.M.–4:30 P.M.
All except three of sixty-seven quilts were either made in Vermont or have a direct Vermont connection. Forty-seven piecework, seventeen crazy quilts, twelve appliqué, four white-on-white, two embroidered, two printed whole-cloth quilts. Two were made prior to 1820, forty-three are nineteenth century, twenty-one were made after 1900, and one is contemporary.
NB: C. 1910 quilt made of 12,976 pieces by Mrs. P.A. Spicer in her 84th year; c. 1900 Star of Bethlehem quilt made by Cynthia Lamoureux Asborn; 1872 brightly colored Log Cabin quilt by Mrs. Vitty; c. 1855 Garden Maze pattern quilt made by Lydia Austin Bemis.
Study Services: Apply at Society to use museum study collection. Work tables, accession cards/files, books/journals, and photocopy facilities; photo prints, slides, prints may be requested from negative collection.

Plymouth Notch Historic District
Birthplace of President Coolidge
Plymouth Notch, Vermont
(802) 828-3226

Mailing Address:
Vermont Division for Historic Preservation
P.O. Box 79
Montpelier, VT 05602

Daily, 9:30 A.M.–5:30 P.M.
Thirty piecework and appliqué quilts made by President Coolidge's mother, stepmother, and grandmother in the nineteenth century, are complemented by ten oral history transcriptions. Quilts are always on exhibition.

NB: Quilt made by former President Calvin Coolidge in his childhood.
Study Services: Contact the office prior to visit. Work tables, and photocopy facilities.
Public Services: Tour through historic houses in village.

The Shelburne Museum
Shelburne Road, U.S. Route 7
Shelburne, Vermont 05482
(802) 985-3346

Office: weekdays, 8:30 A.M.–5:00 P.M. Museum hours not provided.
The Museum has collected more than 630 quilts and 150 woven coverlets from all parts of the United States. There are quilts from Connecticut, Georgia, Indiana, Maine, Massachusetts, Michigan, New Hampshire, New Jersey, New York, Ohio, Pennsylvania, South Carolina, Vermont, Virginia, Wisconsin. One quilt is from Quebec, Canada. There are 135 pieced quilts; 100 appliqué, sixty-five embroidered; sixty-five block printed, painted, dyed, stencilled, or printed fabric; fifty-five white-on-white; forty-four pieced and appliqué, seventy-five chintz; thirty wool; twenty-five crazy quilts; nineteen crib quilts; six bed rugs; and four Hawaiian. Dates range from prior to 1820 to the present. Quilts are always exhibited.
NB: Range and size of collection.
Study Services: Make appointment. Reading room, work tables, accession cards/files, extensive library and files with over fifty books, many articles and pamplets, photocopy services, and microscope; photographs, slides, color transparencies; photo prints may be requested from negatives.
Public Services: Education department kits for docents, visits to schools, and gallery tours.
Publications: Carlisle, Lillian Baker. *Pieced Work and Appliqué Quilts at Shelburne Museum* (1957). Carlisle, Lilian Baker. *Quilts at Shelburne Museum* (1957). Bullard, Lacy Folmar and Betty Jo Shiell. *Chintz Quilts: Unfading Glory* (1983).

The Billings Farm and Museum
River Road
Woodstock, Vermont
(802) 457-2355

Mailing Address:
P.O. Box 627
Woodstock, VT 05091

Seasonal: Monday—Sunday, 10:00 A.M.—4:00 P.M.

The collection of seventy-five quilts is predominantly from eastern central Vermont; and several are from other parts of Vermont or New Hampshire. Sixty-five are piecework, nine appliqué, one white-on-white. Fifty-nine are nineteenth century, sixteen date after 1900. Principal source: Mr. and Mrs. Wentworth Blodgett of Bradford, Vermont.
Study Services: For scholars, make written request. Reading room, work tables, accession cards/files, books/journals, photocopy facilities, and microscope; prints made from negatives of reference photos, partial views only.
Public Services: Lecture series.

VIRGINIA

Quilts associated with Martha Washington or made from her clothing are displayed. The oldest quilts are displayed at historic sites.

Woodlawn Plantation
9000 Richmond Highway
Alexandria, Virginia
(703) 557-7881

Mailing Address:
P.O. Box 37
Mt. Vernon, VA 22121

Daily, 9:30 A.M.—4:30 P.M.; closed Thanksgiving, Christmas and New Year's Day.
The plantation has eighteen quilts. Four are from Pennsylvania, one from New Jersey, one from Kentucky, and one from Virginia. Seven are appliqué, five pieced, three solid color with overall quilting, two trapunto, one crazy quilt. Of those dated fifteen are nineteenth century, one is post-1900.
NB: Baltimore Bride's quilt, Mariner's Compass quilt.
Study Services: Write or phone for appointment with curator. Accession cards/files, and photocopy facilities.
Public Services: Periodic exhibits and displays. Quilt category in annual needlework exhibit. Periodic classes and demonstrations. Special interest tours by reservation.

Division of Historic Preservation
Fairfax County Park Authority
4030 Hummer Road
Annandale, Virginia 22003
(703) 631-1429

Weekdays, 8:30 A.M.—5:00 P.M.
Of approximately thirty-two quilts three are from Fairfax County, Virginia; one from Passiac, New Jersey; one from Long Island, New York; and one from Millerton, Pennsylvania. Twenty-nine are piecework, one appliqué, and

one embroidered. Nineteen are nineteenth century, seven date after 1900, and two are contemporary. Quilts are seasonally exhibited at Sully Plantation; call in advance at (703) 437-1794.

NB: Cavetown quilt and floral fantasy appliqué quilt.

Study Services: Contact collections administrator. Work tables, and accession cards/files; photo prints, slides, and prints made from negatives.

Public Services: Annual (August) Sully Plantation quilt exhibition; quilting workshops.

Southwest Virginia Museum
Historic State Park
Wood Avenue and 1st Street
Big Stone Gap, Virginia
(703) 523-1322

Mailing Address:
Chief Ranger/Interpreter
P.O. Box 742
Big Stone Gap, VA 24219

Tuesday–Sunday, 9:00 A.M.–5:00 P.M.
Twenty to thirty handsewn Appalachian quilts primarily date from the nineteenth century. Log Cabin, Flower Basket, Drunkard's Path, Double Wedding Ring, and Lone Star are some designs represented. The majority of the collection was acquired during the 1930s by C. Bascom Slemp and Janie Slemp. Quilts are continuously on exhibition.

NB: Patchwork quilt made from Martha Washington's petticoat.

Study Services: Visitors to quilt storage must obtain a special permit approved at Museum and at Richmond office (The Division of Parks and Recreation, 1201 Washington Building, Capitol Square, Richmond, Virginia 23219) in advance. Accession cards/files; one slide.

Public Services: Guided tours and self-guided tours of Museum, including quilt exhibitions.

Publications: General brochure on collections.

Thomas Jefferson Memorial Foundation
Monticello
Star Route 53
Charlottesville, Virginia
(804) 295-2657

Mailing Address:
P.O. Box 316
Charlottesville, VA 22902

Daily, 8:00 A.M.–5:00 P.M.
Approximately five nineteenth century Virginia quilts may be seen by scholars by appointment with registrar/curator and director.

Blue Ridge Institute
Ferrum College
Ferrum, Virginia 24088
(703) 365-2121, extension 417

Weekdays, 8:00 A.M.–4:30 P.M.
The Institute has approximately thirty quilts: twenty-three patchwork, four appliqué, three homespun, three with embroidery work, and two are crazy quilts. Of those dated four are nineteenth century, three date after 1900, six are contemporary.

NB: Homespun quilts.

Study Services: Telephone for appointment. Work tables, accession cards/files, and photocopy facilities.

Loudoun Museum, Inc.
16 Loudoun Street, S.W.
Leesburg, Virginia 22075
(703) 777-7427

Monday–Saturday, 10:00 A.M.–5:00 P.M.; Sunday, 1:00–5:00 P.M.
Eight quilts are on continuous exhibition.

Gunston Hall
Lorton, Virginia 22079
(703) 550-9220

Daily, 9:30 A.M.–5:00 P.M.
Six quilts made prior to 1820 are on continuous exhibition.

The Mount Vernon Ladies' Association of the Union

Mount Vernon, Virginia 22121
(703) 780-2000

Weekdays, 9:00 A.M.–5:00 P.M.
Twenty-five American quilts: four are from Virginia, and one is from Kentucky. Ten are piecework, five appliqué, two trapunto, two white-on-white, and two embroidered. Of those dated twelve are pre-1820, five are nineteenth century, and one is contemporary.
NB: Several quilts associated with Martha Washington.
Study Services: For scholars; telephone or write for an appointment. Photocopy facilities; limited number of photo reproductions of quilts.

The Chrysler Museum

Olney Road and Mowbrary Arch
Norfolk, Virginia 23510
(804) 622-1211

Tuesday–Saturday, 10:00 A.M.–4:00 P.M.; Sunday, 1:00–5:00 P.M.; closed Mondays, New Year's Day, Independence Day, Thanksgiving, and Christmas.
The Museum has approximately eighteen handsewn quilts. One predates 1820 and seventeen are nineteenth century. The quilts are exhibited as part of the furnishings of the three historic houses in Norfolk managed by the Museum: Adam Thoroughgood House, Moses Myers House, and the Willoughby-Baylor House.
Study Services: For scholars, by appointment. Reading room, work tables, accession cards/files, books/journals, and photocopy facilities.
Publications: General brochure on Norfolk's Historic Houses.

The Valentine Museum

1015 East Clay Street
Richmond, Virginia 23219
(804) 649-0711

Monday–Saturday, 10:00 A.M.–5:00 P.M.; Sunday, 1:00–5:00 P.M.
In the collection of 130 quilts predominantly with Virginia associations, there are several slave-made quilts from plantations. Eighty-seven quilts are from Virginia, nine are from other parts of the South, three are probably imported from England or India, and two are from New England. Fifty-two are piecework, twenty-two crazy quilts, eighteen pieced and appliqué, ten embroidered, eight appliquéd, seven white-on-white, five stuffed, four Log Cabin, one Yo-Yo, and one corded. Twenty-nine are estimated to predate 1820, eighty-four are nineteenth century, sixteen date after 1900, one is contemporary.
NB: Westover-Berkley coverlet, c. 1780; Robinson Cruso quilt, c. 1800.
Study Services: Call or write curator for appointment. Reading room, work tables, accession cards/files, twenty books/journals; photocopy facilities; photo prints, few negatives available for print orders.
Public Services: Periodic exhibitions with related public programs.

Roanoke Valley Historical Society

Roanoke, Virginia
(703) 342-5772

Mailing Address:
P.O. Box 1904
Roanoke, VA 24008

Tuesday–Saturday, 10:00 A.M.–5:00 P.M.; Sunday, 1:00–5:00 P.M.
The Society's collection comprises twenty handsewn quilts and twelve coverlets. Thirteen are patchwork, five crazy quilts, four pieces of unfinished crazy quilt handwork, two quilt squares, one an off-white tufted candlewick quilt, and one multicolored/multi-fabric embroidered quilt. Of those dated five are nineteenth century, and one dates after 1900.
Study Services: By staff assistance. Reading

room, work tables, accession cards/files with some written information from donors, books/journals, and library concentrating on local and Virginia history.
Public Services: Periodic exhibitions.

Woodrow Wilson Birthplace
70 North Coalter Street
Staunton, Virginia 24401
(703) 885-0897

Monday–Sunday, 9:00 A.M.–5:00 P.M.
Six nineteenth century quilts may be seen by appointment.

The Abby Aldrich Rockefeller Folk Art Center
307 South England Street
Williamsburg, Virginia
(804) 229-1000

Mailing Address:
P.O. Box C
Williamsburg, VA 23187

Monday–Sunday, 11:00 A.M.–7:00 P.M.; office: 8:30 A.M.–5:00 P.M.
Thirty-three American quilts, mainly from the East Coast, form a collection including four Amish and one Mennonite quilt, and several individual object histories. Eighteen are pieced, thirteen are appliqué, two whole-cloth/trapunto/corded, and one stencilled quilt. Two possibly predate 1820, and twenty to twenty-five are nineteenth century. Some quilts are on continuous exhibition.
NB: Several Baltimore Album quilts.
Study Services: Only the most relevant scholarly requests can be accommodated. However, a plan to expand the existing building will facilitate public access to the collection. Scholars may examine data cards of basic information and photographs/slides of many quilts by making written request to registrar. Scholars may study a particular textile by making a second written request to curator or registrar. Small reading room, work tables, accession cards/files, books/journals, and pho-

tocopier; photo prints, slides, and prints made from negatives.
Public Services: Slide lectures are given outside the Museum by request.

Colonial Williamsburg Foundation
Department of Collections
Williamsburg, Virginia 23185
(804) 229-1000

Hours vary; usually, weekdays, 8:30 A.M.–5:00 P.M.
Forty English-American quilts, and an estimated fifteen English quilts form the largest part of a collection of sixty-eight. Thirty-six are worsted whole-cloth quilts, sixteen are corded or stuffed whitework, ten pieced, two appliqué, four to six have miscellaneous techniques. There are quilt fragments. About fifty-eight quilts predate 1820 and ten are nineteenth century. Continuous exhibition of quilts.
NB: A large collection of early American and high style English quilts.
Study Services: Scholars, or groups of three or less can obtain access to the stored collections by written request to the curator of textiles, stating interest and need to see quilts in storage. Reading room, work tables, accession cards/files, approximately seventy-five books/journals, and photocopy facilities; through audio-visual department some photo prints and slides; prints may be ordered.
Public Services: Textile gallery tours by appointment only.

Winchester-Frederick County Historical Society
Winchester, Virginia
(703) 662-6550

Mailing Address:
P.O. Box 97
Winchester, VA 22601-0097

Administers: Abram's Delight Museum (1340 Pleasant Valley Road, Winchester, VA), April 1–October: daily, 10:00 A.M.–5:00 P.M.; Stonewall Jackson's Headquarters; 1861–1862 Civil War Museum (415 North Braddock Street,

Winchester, VA), April 1–October: daily, 10:00
A.M.–5:00 P.M.
Ten nineteenth century handsewn Shenandoah
Valley quilts are housed in Abram's Delight
Museum, Stonewall Jackson's Headquarters
and 1861–1862 Civil War Museum. All are
piecework: Friendship Garden, Sunburst, 1852
Album/Signature, crazy quilt, 1847 quilt, cra-
dle quilt, baby quilt, and 1838 quilt made by a
man. Continuous exhibition of quilts.
NB: Civil War era quilt made from battlefield
shirt scraps by a woman from Winchester.
Study Services: By appointment with execu-
tive director. Facilities can be arranged.
Public Services: Most of the quilts are on permanent exhibit on beds; special guided tours.

Woodstock Museum of Shenandoah County, Inc.
137 West Court Street
Woodstock, Virginia 22664

May–September: Thursday–Saturday, hours
not provided, and by appointment.
Eleven quilts are on exhibit; some are on
loan, and some are in the permanent collection of artifacts pertaining to Shenandoah
County and Woodstock.

WASHINGTON

*Although museums hold a number of
regional quilts, their collections also
include a 1866 Civil War Flag quilt,
Chinese, French, and Canadian quilts.*

Whatcom Museum of History and Art
121 Prospect Street
Bellingham, Washington 98225
(206) 676-6981

Tuesday–Sunday, 12:00–5:00 P.M.
In the total of sixty-six quilts, eight are from
Washington State (seven from Whatcom
County), four from New Jersey, two from Missouri, one from Alabama, one from Iowa, one
from Nebraska and two quilts are from China.
Three are Friendship quilts by church groups.
Thirty are piecework, nineteen crazy quilts,
six Friendship, six appliqué, three embroidered, one batik, and one Biscuit quilt. Of
those dated sixteen are nineteenth century,
eleven date after 1900, and one is contemporary.
NB: Quilt with embroidery on black satin
squares.
Study Services: By appointment. Work tables,
accession cards/files, books/journals, and photocopy facilities.
Public Services: During periodic exhibits
tours, classes, and workshops may be held.

Skagit County Historical Museum
501 South 4th
La Conner, Washington
(206) 466-3365

Mailing Address:
P.O. Box 818
La Conner, WA 98257

Wednesday–Sunday, 1:00–5:00 P.M.; office:
Monday–Thursday, 10:00–4:00 P.M.
The Museum has fifty-eight quilts. Thirty-eight
are local Skagit County quilts. There is one
each from Illinois, Indiana, Iowa, West Vir-

ginia, and Ireland. Twenty-eight are piece-work, seven embroidered, four white-on-white, two appliqué, and two corded. About eighteen are dated as nineteenth century, twenty-three are later than 1900, and three are contemporary. Continuous exhibition of quilts.
Study Services: Write or call office for appointment. Reading room, accession cards/files, and books/journals.

Snoqualmie Valley Museum
320 North Bend Boulevard
North Bend, Washington
(206) 888-3200

Mailing Address:
P.O. Box 179
North Bend, WA 98045

April–October: weekends, 1:00–5:00 P.M.
A collection of sixteen American quilts.
Study Services: No access to stored collections. Reading room, books/journals, and photocopy facilities run by staff only.

Washington State Capital Museum
211 West 21st Avenue
Olympia, Washington 98501
(206) 753-2580

Weekdays, 8:00 A.M.–5:00 P.M.; weekends, 12:00–4:00 P.M.
The collection contains twenty-five quilts and an inventory of community quilts. The collection is being reorganized.
Study Services: Make appointment with curator. Reading room, work tables, and photocopy facilities.
Public Services: Not at present. Future plans include a community quilt exhibit with lectures, demonstrations, classes, and workshops.

Ezra Meeker Historical Society
321 East Pioneer
Puyallup, Washington
(206) 848-1770

Mailing Address:
P.O. Box 103
Puyallup, WA 98372

Wednesday–Sunday, 1:00–5:00 P.M.
Six quilts and various 1930s magazines on quilting.

Henry Art Gallery Textile Collection
University of Washington
Seattle, Washington 98195
(206) 543-1739 or 543-2281

Tuesday–Friday, 8:00 A.M.–5:00 P.M. for research inquiries.
The museum has thirteen quilts: nine from the United States (one from Wisconsin), two from France, and two from Canada. Eight are patchwork, three embroidered, two appliqué, two printed whole-cloth. There are numerous examples of patchwork, decorative quilting, and trapunto on garments and fragments. Of those dated six are nineteenth century quilts, and three date later than 1900.
Study Services: By appointment; researchers can examine detailed index with photographs to select items for study. Reading room, work tables, accession cards/files, on-campus photocopy facilities, and microscope; photo prints for archival purposes, and slides may be reproduced.
Public Services: Study exhibits are arranged upon request for visiting groups. Periodic exhibitions with appropriate programming.

Historical Society of Seattle and King County

Museum of History and Industry
2700 24th Avenue East
Seattle, Washington 98112
(206) 324-1125

Monday–Sunday, 10:00 A.M.–5:00 P.M.
Eighty-five American quilts include twenty-two from the Northwest, eight from the Midwest, four from the East Coast (one from New England), one North Carolina Appalachian quilt; also one Chinese quilt. The forty-one pieced include nine Log Cabin quilts, five crazy quilts, five crazy quilts with embroidery, four with embroidery, two cigar bands, one Postage Stamp, one pieced/tied quilt. Six are appliqué, two are appliqué white-on-white quilts, one appliqué with embroidery, and one woven quilted blue on blue. Three are pre-1820, thirty-nine are nineteenth century, six date after 1900, and one is contemporary.
NB: Historically important quilts made by and/or belonging to founding families of Seattle and King County area.
Study Services: Contact registrar for appointment to see specific types of quilts. M.A. and Ph.D scholars only may study accession cards/files. Twenty-five books/journals, and photocopy facilities; photo prints and slides of some quilts, prints may be requested, photographs may be taken upon request.

Eastern Washington State Historical Society

West 2316 First Avenue
Spokane, Washington 99203
(509) 456-3931

Tuesday–Saturday, 10:00 A.M.–5:00 P.M.; Sunday, 2:00–5:00 P.M.
Sixty-two quilts are American except for one English white-on-white quilt. Fifty-eight are pieced, five appliqué, and two are white-on-white. Two predate 1820, thirty-two are nineteenth century, twenty-one date after 1900, and seven are contemporary.
Study Services: By appointment with curator of collections, state purpose for viewing quilts

in storage. Reading room, work tables, accession cards/files, twenty books/journals, and photocopy facilities; postcard.
Public Services: For special exhibits; lectures and demonstrations.
Publications: "American Coverlets" and "Kaleidoscope: Quilts and Coverlets from the Permanent Collection, May 3–September 3, 1984." Exhibit brochures.

Sumner Historical Society

1228 Main Street
Sumner, Washington
(206) 863-8936

Mailing Address:
P.O. Box 517
Sumner, WA 98390

Weekends, 1:00–4:00 P.M.
Ten quilts form a collection with regional focus; three quilts are from Oregon. Five are piecework, two crazy quilts, two pieced squares, and one appliqué. Three are nineteenth century, six date later than 1900, and one is contemporary.
NB: Crazy quilts; silk and velvet quilt with fancy feather stitching.
Study Services: Contact the curator at (206) 863-5567. Reading room, work tables, accession cards/files, and microfilm machine; photo prints; prints may be requested from file negatives.
Public Services: Annual quilt exhibit in May.

Washington State Historical Society

315 North Stadium Way
Tacoma, Washington 98403
(206) 593-2831

Library: Tuesday–Saturday, 9:30 A.M.–5:00 P.M.
Museum: Tuesday–Saturday, 9:30 A.M.–5:00 P.M.; Sunday, 2:00–5:00 P.M. Closed holidays.
A collection of eighty quilts and patterns/instructions from the United States. The majority dates from the nineteenth century. All techniques are represented. Quilts are on continuous exhibition.
NB: Silk crazy quilt made from tobacco advertising strips. The Rowens collection: twenty

quilts collected from all over the United States.

Study Services: By appointment. Reading room, work tables, accession cards/files, books/journals, photocopy facilities, magnifying glass. Prints made from negatives upon request.

Public Services: Annual exhibition of collection and privately owned quilts.

Yakima Valley Museum and Historical Association

2105 Tieton Drive
Yakima, Washington 98902
(509) 248-0747

Tuesday–Sunday, 10:00 A.M.–5:00 P.M.
The Association has twenty-five quilts and unpublished quilt documentation. Ten are pieced, eight appliqué, three crazy quilts, two embroidered, one whole-cloth corded, and one Yo-Yo. Two quilts predate 1820, fifteen are nineteenth century, six date after 1900, and two are contemporary. Some quilts are on permanent exhibition.

NB: 1805 Linsey-woolsey quilt; 1866 Civil War flag quilt; 1885 Children's handkerchief quilt.

Study Services: By appointment. Work tables, accession cards/files, books/journals, photocopy facilities, and microscope; slides, prints may be made from file negatives.

Public Services: Outside of facility; classes, workshops, exhibitions and workshops are offered.

WEST VIRGINIA

Appalachian regional quilts and Ohio River Valley quilts are the strength of collections.

West Virginia Department of Culture and History

The Cultural Center, Capitol Complex
Charleston, West Virginia 25305
(304) 348-0230

Weekdays, 9:00 A.M.–9:00 P.M.; weekends, 1:00–9:00 P.M.
Forty-two quilts have been made or donated by West Virginians in the Appalachian region. Research papers and other unpublished quilt documentation are also in the collection. Thirty-one are piecework, thirteen embroidered, eight appliqué, two handpainted, one white-on-white, and one knotted. Nineteen are nineteenth century, ten date later than 1900, and thirteen are contemporary.

NB: Two crazy quilts with handpainting and embroidery of family history; Cabin Creek quilts.

Study Services: By appointment. Reading room, work tables, accession cards/files, 500 books/journals, photographic lab, and photocopy facilities; photo prints, slides, and prints may be ordered from file negatives.

Public Services: Juried exhibits, tours, Heritage Trunk filmstrip on quilting for school groups. Annual quilt exhibit from May to September.

Publications: Brochures and posters from previous juried exhibits.

Pearl S. Buck Birthplace Foundation
U. S. Route 219
Hillsboro, West Virginia
(304) 653-4430

Mailing Address:
P.O. Box 126
Hillsboro, WV 24946

April–November: Monday–Saturday, 9:00
A.M.–5:00 P.M.; Sunday, 1:00–5:00 P.M. November–March: by appointment.
Family quilts from the 1890s are on continuous exhibition.

Huntington Galleries
2033 McCoy Road
Huntington, West Virginia 25701
(304) 529-2701

Hours not provided.
Twelve handsewn quilts include four which
are from the Ohio River Valley: a Lily quilt,
crazy quilt, Carpenter's Wheel, and George
Washington's Cherry Tree on loan from the
Museum of American Folk Art. Two quilts are
from Missouri, one is a miniature doll's quilt.
Two are from West Virginia: a Sawtooth quilt
and a Log Cabin variation. One Lone Star quilt
is from North Carolina, Goose Tracks quilt
from North Dakota. Two are other United
States quilts: an Album and a crazy quilt. Five
are cotton piecework quilts in various traditional patterns. Two are piecework primarily
in silk and velvets. One is an appliqué trapunto with embroidery, one is appliqué with
decorative quilting, one is appliqué with
twenty-five blocks bearing bird or plant designs. One is pieced from various materials,
and one is silk and velvet piecework with embroidery. Nine are nineteenth century, two
date later than 1900. Continuous exhibition of
quilts.
NB: Crazy quilt, twelve squares worked in random designs and incorporating clothing, ribbons, campaign and club badges which
belonged to the quiltmaker's husband, General William H. Enochs, Civil War general and
congressman. Made in the Ohio Valley by An-
nis Hamilton Enochs, c. 1895.

Study Services: By appointment only. Reading
room, work tables, accession cards/files,
books/journals, and art research library; photo
prints, slides; prints may be requested from
file negatives.
Public Services: Tour of exhibition *Made in
America*; and workshops offered.

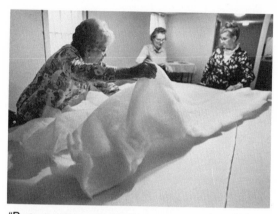

"Putting the filling on the backing." Meadows of Dan Quilters,
Meadows of Dan Baptist Church, Patrick County, Meadows of
Dan, Virginia. American Folklife Center, Blue Ridge Parkway
Project, 1978. Fieldwork by Geraldine Johnson, photo by Lyntha
Eiler, negative number 15-20421, 5. Courtesy of the Archive of
Folk Culture, Library of Congress.

WISCONSIN

Public collections have numerous crazy quilts and early regional examples.

Sauk County Historical Museum

531 4th Avenue
Baraboo, Wisconsin
(608) 356-6549 (Curator's home)

Mailing Address:
321 4th Avenue
Baraboo, WI 53913

May–September: Tuesday–Sunday, 2:00–5:00 P.M.
The Museum has sixteen quilts accompanied by donor's notes. Eight are from Wisconsin, two from Ohio, and one from Pennsylvania. Four are pieced, four crazy quilts, two embroidered, two have decorative quilting, one stuffed linsey-woolsey, one trapunto, one Biscuit, and one pieced and appliqué. One quilt predates 1820, and fifteen are nineteenth century.
NB: Linsey-woolsey quilt; Biscuit quilt.
Study Services: By appointment with curator. Accession cards/files.

Hoard Historical Museum

407 South Merchants Avenue
Ft. Atkinson, Wisconsin 53538
(414) 563-4521

Tuesday–Saturday, 9:30 A.M.–3:30 P.M.
The collection of 124 quilts includes four that predate 1820, nineteen that are nineteenth century, three dating after 1900, and three contemporary quilts.
NB: 1885 Crazy quilt, and 1870 appliqué quilt.
Study Services: Write for appointment. Reading room, work tables, accession cards/files, and photocopy facilities.
Public Services: Tours of periodic exhibitions.

The Rock County Historical Society

10 South High Street
Janesville, Wisconsin
(608) 756-4509

Mailing Address:
P.O. Box 896
Janesville, WI 53545

Weekdays, 9:00 A.M.–5:00 P.M.
The Society has sixty-five piecework quilts of regional provenance. Eighteen date from the nineteenth century.
Study Services: Make written request; appointment depends on staff availability. Reading room, work tables, accession cards/files, photocopy facilities, and microscope.
Public Services: Occasional exhibits until completion of a facility with adequate exhibit space.

LaCrosse County Historical Society

Swarthout Museum
800 Main Street
LaCrosse, Wisconsin 54601
(608) 782-1980

Weekdays, 9:00 A.M.–5:00 P.M.; weekends, 1:00–5:00 P.M.
This collection of twenty-two quilts was made by local Scandinavian or German settlers. Fourteen are pieced, five silk or wool crazy quilts, two appliqué; and two tied, plain fabric comforters. Approximately twelve are nineteenth century, eight or nine date after 1900.
Study Services: By appointment; visit with staff member present. Work tables, accession cards/files, and photocopy facilities.

Helen Allen Textile Collection

University of Wisconsin
1300 Linden Drive
Madison, Wisconsin 53706
(608) 262-1119 or 262-1162

Monday–Friday, 9:00 A.M.–4:00 P.M.; closed December 15–January 15.
A collection that numbers more than 100 quilts. An index to the videodisc visual cata-

log of the collection, now in preparation, will provide more data than is presently available.
Study Services: Write to the curator one week in advance of visit; videodisc available to review collection. Reading room, work tables, accession cards/files, videodisc-computer catalog, about twenty-five books/journals, photocopy facilities, and microscope; photo prints, slides, prints made from negatives; videodisc.
Public Services: Lectures and university classes.
Publications: Brochure.

State Historical Society of Wisconsin
816 State Street
Madison, Wisconsin 53706
(608) 262-0459

Mondays, 8:00 A.M.–5:00 P.M.
The Society has 158 regional quilts (two of which are Canadian), and a large number of 1930s quilt patterns/instructions, scrapbooks, personal narratives by quiltmakers, diaries/journals, research papers, and slides. Two quilts predate 1820, 121 are nineteenth century, thirty later than 1900, and five contemporary.
NB: Linsey-woolsey quilt; several 1830s to 1840s appliqué, silk quilts; silk Tumbling Blocks crib quilt; c. 1870 calico Eagle appliqué doll quilt; Grandmother's Cross reverse variant doll quilt; Nine Patch block quilt made of one-half inch pieces.
Study Services: Make appointment. Reading room, work tables, accession cards/files, books/journals, and photocopy facilities; photocopy facilities, and prints made from negatives.
Public Services: Tours, exhibits, lectures, workshops, and film showings.

Milton Historical Society
Milton House Museum
18 South Janesville Street
Milton, Wisconsin
(608) 868-7772

Mailing Address:
P.O. Box 245
Milton, WI 53563

May 1–June 1, and Labor Day–October 15: weekends. June 1–Labor Day: daily, 11:00 A.M.–4:00 P.M.; Offices: October 15–May 1: weekdays, 9:00 A.M.–12:00 P.M., and 1:00–4:00 P.M.
The thirty-six quilts in this collection include twenty-three pieced quilts, seven crazy quilts with embroidery and made from silk, velvet, wool; more than five unfinished quilts (either quilt tops or quilt squares); and one linen and wool whole-cloth quilt. Four are dated: one pre-1820 and three nineteenth century.
Study Services: Make written request for appointment. Reading room, work tables, accession cards/files, books/journals, and photocopy facilities.
Public Services: Museum tours and programs.

Milwaukee Public Museum
800 West Wells Street
Milwaukee, Wisconsin 53233
(414) 278-2702

Office: weekdays, 8:00 A.M.–4:45 P.M. Museum hours are not specified.
The Museum has assembled fifty-two quilts. Among them are twenty-six pieced, ten appliqué, nine Victorian crazy quilts, three trapunto. In addition there are twenty-eight fragments and squares. Two quilts predate 1820, thirty are nineteenth century, twenty quilts date after 1900.
NB: 1820 Trapunto quilt, 1856 miniature Star of Bethlehem signed and dated quilt, and 1880s silk Log Cabin quilt.
Study Services: Make appointment with curator-in-charge. Library reading room, work tables, accession cards/files, twenty books/journals, and photocopy facilities; prints may

be ordered from file negatives, and quilt exhibition video.
Public Services: In conjunction with exhibits: quilting bee, quiltmaking classes, series of movies on quilts, quilt raffle, lectures, guided tours, and articles in museum journal.
Publications: Hoke, Donald, editor. *Dressing the Bed: Quilts and Coverlets from the Collection of the Milwaukee Public Museum* (1985).

Douglas County Historical Society
906 East 2nd Street
Superior, Wisconsin 54880
(715) 394-5712

Daily, 10:00 A.M.–4:00 P.M.
Collection includes twelve handsewn quilts, one made by a church group, a 1976 women's club history quilt, and a 1976 senior citizen quilt. Four are piecework crazy quilts, three have decorative quilting, two white-on-white, one embroidered with names and events, and one silk, pieced and tied crazy quilt. Six are nineteenth century, three date after 1900, and three are contemporary.
Study Services: Make appointment. Reading room, and work tables.
Public Services: Exhibits.

Waukesha County Historical Museum
101 West Main Street
Waukesha, Wisconsin 53186
(414) 548-7186

Weekdays, 9:00 A.M.–4:30 P.M.; Sunday, 1:00–5:00 P.M.
A collection of thirty-eight quilts predominantly from Waukesha County, and ten quilt patterns/instructions. Seven are midwestern quilts; three are religious designs: Presbyterian and Catholic. Two are European: English and Welsh. One is from New York State. Thirteen are piecework, twelve crazy quilts, two appliqué, two embroidered, and one c. 1800 printed quilt. Those dated are: one pre-1820, seventeen nineteenth century, twelve post-1900, and one contemporary.
NB: 1893 Anti-pipeline quilt; 1885 family

crazy quilt; 1979 Waukesha County quilt made by students.
Study Services: For scholars; make appointment with director and registrar who must accompany visitor. Reading room, accession cards/files, books/journals, research center, and photocopy facilities.
Public Services: Tours, traveling treasure kits, and slide presentations.
Publications: "Quilts and Coverlets: Pioneer Patterns and Piecework," handout/fact sheet.

Marathon County Historical Museum
403 McIndoe
Wausau, Wisconsin 54401
(715) 848-6143

Tuesday–Friday, 9:00 A.M.–5:00 P.M. Weekends, 1:00–5:00 P.M. Closed holidays.
Ten handsewn nineteenth century quilts are in the museum's collection.
Study Services: By appointment. Reading room, work tables, accession cards/files, and photocopy facilities; prints made from negatives; films.

WYOMING

A Name quilt memorializing men who served in the Spanish-American War, crazy quilts, and a Mormon Trail quilt are notable.

Bradford Brinton Memorial Museum
Brinton Road
Big Horn, Wyoming
(307) 672-3173

Mailing Address:
P.O. Box 23
Big Horn, WY 82833

May 1–Labor Day: daily, 9:00 A.M.–5:00 P.M. Thirty American handsewn quilts include one that predates 1820, one nineteenth century quilt, and twenty-three that date after 1900. Continuous exhibition of quilts.
Study Services: For scholars, by special request; prints may be made from file negatives; illustrated catalogs.
Publications: Museum catalog.

Grand Encampment Museum
Encampment, Wyoming
(307) 327-5310

Mailing Address:
P.O. Box 395
Encampment, WY 82325

Hours not provided.
Six nineteenth century quilts on continuous exhibition.

Fort Laramie National Historic Site
Fort Laramie, Wyoming 82212
(307) 837-2221

Daily, 8:00 A.M.–4:30 P.M.
In a collection of twenty nineteenth century quilts seventeen are piecework and three are appliqué. Continuous exhibition of quilts.
Study Services: By appointment and under the supervision of museum staff. Work tables, accession cards/files, books/journals, photocopy facilities, and microscope; slides of room interiors with quilts, prints may be ordered from negatives if available; postcards and posters of quilts on exhibit.

Fremont County Pioneer Museum
630 Lincoln
Lander, Wyoming 82520
(307) 332-4137

Summer: Monday–Saturday, 9:00 A.M.–5:00 P.M., and Sunday, 1:00–5:00 P.M.; winter: Tuesday–Sunday, 1:00–4:00 P.M.
Ten handsewn quilts include eight piecework and two white-on-white. Concentration is in crazy quilts. Those dated are: four nineteenth century and one post-1900. Continuous exhibiting of quilts.
NB: Quilt made on the Mormon Trail depicting sights along the way.
Study Services: Very informal. Reading room, work tables, accession cards/files, and photocopy facilities; prints may be ordered from file negatives.
Public Services: School tours.

Laramie Plains Museum
603 Ivinson
Laramie, Wyoming 82070
(307) 742-4448

Weekdays, 9:00 A.M.–12:00 P.M., and 1:00–
4:00 P.M. Saturday, 1:00–4:00 P.M., and by appointment.

The collection has seventeen quilts and one Yo-Yo pillow top. Eleven are piecework and six embroidered and pieced. Of those dated five are from the nineteenth century, one from 1901 to 1940. Six were made by relatives of a local donor, three by local civic groups, and one is from North Carolina. Quilts are on continuous exhibition.

NB: Name quilt, not a Signature quilt, with the names of local men who served in the Spanish American war.

Study Services: By appointment, with supervision of textiles consultant or director. Reading room, work tables, accession cards/files, photocopy facilities; photographs may be taken by permission.

Canada

Zenna Todd's (Ennice, N. C.)
embroidered one patch echos the shape of her hand.
American Folklife Center, Blue Ridge Parkway Project,
1978. Fieldwork and photo by Geraldine Johnson,
negative number 45-20544, 20. Courtesy of the Archive
of Folk Culture, Library of Congress.

ALBERTA

Calgary and Edmonton institutions hold collections of note including results of a major field project documenting Alberta-made quilts.

Glenbow Museum

130 9th Avenue SE
Calgary, Alberta T2G OP3
(403) 264-8300

Tuesday–Sunday, 10:00 A.M.–6:00 P.M. Office: weekdays, 8:00 A.M.–4:30 P.M.
The Museum has seventy-nine quilts (most are from western Canada), and twelve quilted objects (clothing, tea cozy, etc.). Two quilts are from Scotland, one is a Ontario Mennonite quilt, and one is a Pennsylvania Dutch quilt. Concentration in patchwork, crazy quilts, Log Cabin variations, and Signature quilts. Sixty-five are piecework, twenty crazy quilts, eighteen Log Cabin or Log Cabin variations, eleven appliqué, and four are Signature quilts. Six predate 1820, forty-two are nineteenth century, twenty-eight date after 1900, and three are contemporary.
NB: Quilts using silk cigar bands and commemorative ribbons.
Study Services: Make appointment. Reading room, work tables, accession cards/files, eleven books, and fifty-five issues of *Canada Quilts* from 1974 to the present, and photocopy facilities; Glenbow Archives; photo prints, slides, prints may be made from negatives; films for in-house use only.
Public Services: Tours, and organized programs on quilts have been offered in the past.

Provincial Museum of Alberta

12845-102 Avenue
Edmonton, Alberta T5N OM6
(403) 427-1743

Daily, 10:00 A.M.–8:00 P.M.
A rapidly growing collection of Alberta-made quilts now numbering forty-one, and one set of quilt patterns/instructions are complemented by approximately 300 oral history transcriptions and a slide library created during a major field project documenting Alberta-made quilts. Two-thirds of the quilt collection is from Alberta; the rest is from Ontario, Quebec, New Brunswick, Louisiana, and Montana. Twenty-five are patchwork, twelve embroidered, seven appliqué, five crazy quilts, five quilted cotton prints, two tufted; fifteen are hand quilted, and six machine quilted. Many of the quilts combine two or more techniques. Two are nineteenth century, twenty-nine date later than 1900, and ten are contemporary. Principal donors/sources: seven quilts from the Dutton family, three quilts from the Hess family, and two quilts from the McLean family.
NB: Three utility quilts; five crazy quilts.
Study Services: Make appointment with curator. Work tables, accession cards/files, books/journals, slide library on Alberta-made quilts, photocopy facilities, and microscope by advance notice; photo prints, slides, prints may be ordered from file negatives; posters, and an out-of-print catalog.
Public Services: Exhibitions, fashion shows, lecture series; tours of rolled storage facility.
Publications: Eliot-Los, Elyse. "Alberta Quilts." *Alberta Museums Review* (Spring 1983). Morton, Sandra. "A History of Alberta Quilts." *Material History Bulletin* 18 (Fall 1983). Weizman, Sandra Morton and Elyse Eliot-Los. *Alberta Quilts* (1984).

Historic Costume and Textile Study Collection

Department of Clothing and Textiles
Home Economics Building
University of Alberta
Edmonton, Alberta T6G 2M8
(403) 432-2528

Weekdays, 9:00 A.M.–4:00 P.M.
There are approximately twenty-seven Canadian and American quilts, fifteen interview transcriptions, and five research papers. An estimated twelve quilts are from western Canada (Manitoba, Saskatchewan, Alberta, and British Columbia); eight from central Canada (Ontario); five from the United States (all regions); and two from eastern Canada (Maritimes). Fifteen are piecework, five embroidered, and three appliqué. Five are nineteenth century and twenty-two date from 1901 to 1940.
Study Services: Make appointment. Access to storage is readily available. Reading room, work tables, accession cards/files, university library with books/journals, computer catalog, research reports, textile analysis service, photocopy facilities, and microscope; photo prints, slides, prints may be made from file negatives.
Public Services: Exhibitions, tours, classes, and workshops.

Czar area (Alberta) women admiring a Crazy patch, 1913–19, negative number NA-1534-10. Courtesy of the collection of the Glenbow Museum, Calgary, Alberta, Canada.

BRITISH COLUMBIA

Public collections are small, but diverse.

Matsqui-Sumas-Abbotsford Museum Society

2313 Ware Street
Abbotsford, British Columbia V2S 3C6
(604) 853-0313

Monday–Saturday, 9:00 A.M.–5:00 P.M.; Sunday, 1:00–5:00 P.M.
Nine quilts: one from Peru, Indiana dated 1857, and eight others from southern British Columbia. Quilts may be seen by appointment.

Burnaby Village Museum

4900 Deer Lake Avenue
Burnaby, British Columbia V56 3T6
(604) 294-1231

Tuesday–Sunday, 11:00 A.M.–4:30 P.M.
Less than ten quilts.

Chilliwack Museum and Historical Society

9291 Corbould Street
Chilliwack, British Columbia V2P 4A6
(604) 795-5210

Monday–Saturday, 9:00 A.M.–4:30 P.M.; Thursday until 9:00 P.M.
Five quilts: one from Aurora, Illinois, one from Vancouver Island, and two group-made quilts from Chilliwack, British Columbia.

Kamloops Museum and Archives

207 Seymour Street
Kamloops, British Columbia V2C 2E7
(604) 828-3576

Hours not provided.
Seven handsewn quilts and one Autograph quilt can be seen by appointment.

Mission Historical Society

Mission Museum
33201 Second Avenue
Mission, British Columbia V2V 1J9
(604) 826-1011

Hours not provided.
Quilts in collection; no description provided.

Irving House Historic Centre

302 Royal Avenue
New Westminister, British Columbia V3L 1H7
(604) 521-7656

Mid-September–April 30: weekends, 1:00–
5:00 P.M. May 1–Mid-September: Tuesday–
Sunday, 11:00 A.M.–5:00 P.M. Groups by appointment.
Quilts are on continuous exhibition; no description provided.

British Columbia Provincial Museum

675 Bellville Street
Victoria, British Columbia V8V 1X4
(604) 387-3701

Daily, 10:30 A.M.–5:30 P.M.
A total of twenty-eight quilts includes six
from Ontario, four from British Columbia,
three from Nova Scotia, two from Saskatchewan, one from Alberta; and one from Ohio,
United States. The collection has a concentration in Log Cabin and crazy quilts; there are
twenty-one piecework quilts, three with combined techniques (piecework, appliqué, and
embroidery), two appliqué, and two white-on-white. Of those dated twelve are nineteenth
century, six are post-1900, three are contemporary.
Study Services: For scholars, make appointment with assistant director of collections.
Reading room, work tables, accession cards/
files, books/journals, photocopy facilities, and
microscope by advance notice.

MANITOBA

A collection of twenty-one quilts, including one made of goose feathers.

Manitoba Museum of Man and Nature

190 Rupert Avenue
Winnipeg, Manitoba R3B ON2
(204) 956-2830

Open daily except Christmas day; summer:
10:00 A.M.–9:00 P.M.; winter: 10:00 A.M.–5:00
P.M.
Of the twenty-one quilts in this collection,
eleven are from Manitoba, including one made
by a Mennonite. Six are from Ontario, one
Dutch-Canadian, one from North Dakota, United
States, one from England. Of particular note
are a Dutch-Canadian Tulip appliqué with echo
quilting, c. 1890; appliqué made from bleached
flour sacks; unbleached muslin appliqué and
quilted; one embroidered with names of servicemen killed in World War II; machine made
patchwork by a Manitoba Mennonite; patchwork made from upholstery fabrics; crazy
quilt with added knitted rosettes; Log Cabin Pineapple; Eight-Pointed Star; Steps to the Lighthouse; sheep's wool quilt; and Six Point Stars
with partial flower design quilt top, machine
made in England. Sixteen are piecework quilts,
five embroidered, and three appliqué. Eleven
were made in the nineteenth century, eight
are post-1900, and two are contemporary.
NB: Late 1880s North Dakota quilt constructed of goose down feathers stitched in
rows one centimeter apart, with cotton backing and silk lining. The natural beige down
forms a central free-form design, with two
matching pillow shams. Exhibited at San Francisco World's Fair in 1903.
Study Services: Make appointment with curator. Reading room, work tables, accession
cards/files, catalogs, reference books, photocopy facilities, and microscope.
Public Services: Tour of quilt storage area by
appointment.

NEW BRUNSWICK

A sampler quilt of ninety-nine New Brunswick patterns and one of Canada's oldest quilts belong to collections.

Kings Landing Historical Settlement

Fredericton, New Brunswick
(506) 363-3081

Mailing Address:
P.O. Box 522
Fredericton, NB E3B 5A6

Hours not provided.
A collection of 110 handsewn quilts, of which 103 are from New Brunswick; the others are from Vermont, Nova Scotia, and Ontario Mennonites. Ninety-five are pieced quilts, twelve appliqué, and two are white-on-white. Ten quilts predate 1820, seventy-five are nineteenth century quilts. Continuous exhibit of quilts.
NB: Friendship quilt by Sarah Robbins, age 16, from Perue, Vermont. One quilt with ninety-nine different pattern blocks, an anthology of quilt patterns in New Brunswick.
Study Services: For scholars, make appointment. Reading room, work tables, accession cards/files, thirty books/journals, and photocopy facilities; prints made from negatives in collection.
Public Services: Quilts are displayed as part of the furnishings of ten historical houses.

York-Sunbury Historical Society Museum

Queen Street (Officer's Square)
Fredericton, New Brunswick
(506) 455-6041

Mailing Address:
P.O. Box 1312
Fredericton, NB E3B 5C8

Summer: Monday–Saturday, 10:00 A.M.–6:00 P.M.; winter: Monday, Wednesday, and Friday, 11:00 A.M.–3:00 P.M.
The Museum's twelve handsewn quilts come from the Maritime Provinces of Canada and New England, United States. All made by English-speaking peoples. Five are piecework, two appliqué, two embroidered, two patchwork crazy quilts, and one Signature quilt. Seven are nineteenth century quilts, five are post-1900.
NB: Broderie Perse, or Persanerie marriage quilt.
Study Services: Access to quilts in storage granted with permission from the curator or the society board of directors. Work tables, and accession cards/files; photo prints may be made from museum negatives.
Public Services: Tours of exhibitions.

Kings County Museum

Centennial Building
Hampton, New Brunswick EOG 1ZO
(506) 832-3214

Monday–Saturday, 10:00 A.M.–5:00 P.M.; Sunday, 2:00–5:00 P.M.
Seven quilts.

The New Brunswick Museum

277 Douglas Avenue
Saint John, New Brunswick E2K 1E5
(506) 652-7239

Daily, 10:00 A.M.–5:00 P.M.
The Museum owns a regional collection of thirty-seven handsewn quilts. Fourteen are pieced, seven appliqué, six Log Cabin, two white-on-white, one embroidered, and eight crazy quilts.
NB: C. 1775 white-on-white quilt signed Mary

Morton, 1769, made of woven flax, is one of the oldest surviving Canadian quilts.

Study Services: Make appointment; accession cards/files, and books/journals; prints may be made from museum negatives.

Publications: McNairn, Rosemarie. "Shadows and Sunlight: Quilts from the New Brunswick Museum." *Canadian Collector, A Journal of Antiques and Fine Arts* (March/April 1985).

McLeansboro, Illinois. Southern Illinois farmer (c. 1930s) keeps his car engine warm with an old quilt. RA 10274-E. Microfilm number 2300-2305. Courtesy of the Prints and Photographs Division, Library of Congress.

NOVA SCOTIA

The island province's collections are large and regional in scope.

Nova Scotia Museum
1747 Summer Street
Halifax, Nova Scotia B3H 3A6
(902) 429-4610

Days and hours vary: six or seven days a week, 9:30 A.M.–5:00 P.M.
The scope of this collection of 130 quilts is regional; 120 are from Nova Scotia, and two from Ontario. Documentation includes recent line drawings of a few quilt patterns, and notes by the curator. It is estimated that there are 100 pieced quilts, twenty appliqué, five white-on-white, one stuffed appliqué, one printed whole-cloth, and eight crazy quilts. Two quilts predate 1820, about forty are nineteenth century, seventy date after 1900, and ten are contemporary. Some of the quilts are on continuous display in the historic houses.
Study Services: For scholars, make appointment, initial access through photographs. Accession cards/files, books/journals, and photocopy facilities; limited number of photo prints, slides, prints may be made from negatives.
Public Services: Slides lecture; loan of slide set "Looking at Quilts in Nova Scotia."

Yarmouth County Museum
22 Collins Street
Yarmouth, Nova Scotia
(902) 742-5539

Mailing Address:
P.O. Box 39
Yarmouth, NS B5A 4B1

Hours not provided.
This is a collection of twenty handsewn quilts from Nova Scotia. Sixteen are piecework (three are Signature and two are embroidered) four are appliqué, and one white-on-

white quilt. Approximately seventeen are nineteenth century, and three date after 1900. There is a continuous exhibit of quilts.

NB: Two local Signature quilts.

Study Services: Make appointment with curator, depends on available staff time. Reading room, work tables, accession cards/files, historical research library, books/journals, and photocopy facilities; photo prints, slides, prints made by request.

Publications: Davis, M. *Nova Scotia Workbasket* (1976).

Anna Catherine (Hummel) Markey Garnhart (1773–1860), Frederick, Frederick County, Maryland. In addition to quiltmaking, she was praised for her knowledge and practice of herbal medicine. Courtesy of the Daughters of the American Revolution Museum, Washington, D. C. *See page 67.*

ONTARIO

The province of Ontario is a quilter's haven.

Ameliasburgh Historical Museum
Ameliasburg, Ontario
(613) 968-9678

Mailing Address:
General Delivery
Ameliasburg, ON K0K 1A0

May–September: weekends, 10:00 A.M.–4:30 P.M.
Six quilts are on continuous exhibition.

Region of Peel Museum
9 Wellington Street East
Brampton, Ontario L6W 1Y1
(416) 451-9051

Weekdays, 10:00 A.M.–4:30 P.M.; weekdays, 1:30–4:30 P.M.
Museum has twenty-eight regional quilts, twenty-seven are from the region of Peel in south-central Ontario, and a set of twenty-five different sample blocks prepared by the Peel Women's Institutes for a book. About twenty are piecework, four appliqué, and three embroidered. Two predate 1820, twenty-two are nineteenth century, and four date after 1900.

NB: One Log Cabin quilt that has over 15,120 hand-stitched pieces.

Study Services: Write or phone, giving museum at least three days advanced notice. Work tables, accession cards/files, sample quilt blocks, books/journals, approximately twenty-five patterns published in *Family Herald*, and *Weekly Star*, 1932; photocopy facilities; slides made on request.

Public Services: Slide lectures.

Joseph Brant Museum

1240 North Shore Boulevard
Burlington, Ontario L7S 1C5

Hours not provided.
A collection of fourteen quilts from south-western Ontario that is piecework, two Yo-Yo, and one trapunto. Ten are nineteenth century, three date after 1900, and one is contemporary.
Study Services: Written permission is essential. Reading room, work tables, accession cards/files, books/journals, and photocopy facilities.
Public Services: Programming can be tailored to class or public needs.

Black Creek Pioneer Village

1000 Murray Ross Parkway
Downsview, Ontario M3J 2T3

Hours not provided.
Regional quilts from 1791 to 1867 are on continuous exhibition throughout the restored buildings as part of furnishings.

Wellington County Museum

County Road 18
Fergus, Ontario
(519) 846-5169

Mailing Address:
Rural Route 1
Fergus, ON N1M 2W3

Monday–Saturday, 10:00 A.M.–4:30 P.M.; Sunday, 1:30–4:30 P.M.
The Museum owns fifty-three quilts, most made in Wellington County, and a collection of quilt blocks. Approximately thirty-two are patchwork, nine Signature quilts with embroidery, seven appliqué, seven crazy quilts with embroidery, six whole-cloth, and one white-on-white trapunto. Two are unquilted tops. Thirty-two were made in the nineteenth century, seventeen date after 1900. Four are contemporary quilts: one Yo-Yo, two doll quilts, and one baby quilt.
Study Services: Make request to curator. Reading room, work tables, accession cards/files, books/journals, photocopy facilities, and lighted magnifying lamp.

Muskoka Pioneer Village

Huntsville, Ontario
(705) 789-7576

Mailing Address:
P.O. Box 2802
Huntsville, ON P0A 1K0

Weekdays, 9:00 A.M.–5:00 P.M.
Collection of approximately thirty quilts that date from the 1890s to the 1940s.
Study Services: Make appointment. Work tables, and accession cards/files.

Century Village, Lang

Keene, Ontario
(705) 295-6694

Mailing Address:
Rural Route 3
Keene, ON K0L 3H0

Weekdays, 9:00 A.M.–5:00 P.M.
More than half of this collection of fifty-four quilts is from Peterborough County. There are also fifteen quilt blocks. The collection has about forty-nine patchwork quilts, several are Log Cabin variations, and six appliqué. Approximately sixty-percent of the quilts date from the nineteenth century, and forty-percent are later. Quilts are continuously exhibited.
NB: Natural dyed wool quilts.
Study Services: By formal request and appointment only. Reading room, work tables, accession cards/files, twenty books/journals, and photocopy facilities; photo prints, slides, prints may be requested from negatives in collection.
Public Services: Exhibitions at local craft fairs; annual "Sheep to Shawl" exhibit.

Doon Heritage Crossroads

Corner of Homer Watson Boulevard and
Huron Road
Kitchener, Ontario
(519) 893-4020

Mailing Address:
Rural Route 2
Kitchener, ON N2G 3W5

Office: weekdays, 8:30 A.M.–4:30 P.M. Call for
general hours.
In this collection of about ninety-one quilts,
twenty-two were made by Pennsylvania Germans; and four by Scottish quiltmakers in Waterloo County, Ontario. Eighty-five are
piecework, five appliqué, five embroidered,
and one white-on-white. Eight are nineteenth
century, and eight date after 1900. A limited
number of quilts are on continuous exhibition.
NB: Quilt made from Crimean War uniforms
by convalescing soldier.
Study Services: Write to the curator of collections. Reading room, work tables, accession
cards/files, basic reference books, copy stand
and photographic equipment if needed, photocopy facilities, and microscope; duplication
of slides and photo prints could be arranged
upon request.
Public Services: Periodic public programs.

Joseph Schneider Haus

466 Queen Street South
Kitchener, Ontario N2G 1W7

Labour Day–May 24: Wednesday–Saturday,
10:00 A.M.–5:00 P.M., Sunday, 1:00–5:00 P.M.;
May 24–Labour Day: daily, 10:00 A.M.–5:00
P.M.
A collection of thirty quilts regional in scope.
Twenty-five quilts were made by Germans,
primarily Mennonites, in Waterloo County;
others are from Ontario, and four are Pennsylvania German quilts. Twenty-eight are piecework, one appliqué. Twenty are nineteenth
century quilts, and ten date later. Some quilts
are exhibited on beds as part of furnishings in
historic house.
Study Services: Write for appointment. Re-

search facilities to be expanded in 1986. Computerized documentation (in progress); photo
prints, and slides.
Public Services: Temporary exhibits; annual
quilting bee, quilt block contest.

Fanshawe Pioneer Village

London, Ontario
(519) 451-2800

Mailing Address:
P.O. Box 6278 Station D
London, Ontario N5W 5S1

May to Thanksgiving: daily, 8:30 A.M.–4:30 P.M.
Settlers in southwest Ontario made these fif-
teen nineteenth century quilts. Two are appli-
qué and roughly ten are patchwork.
NB: Local Friendship quilt.
Study Services: Write or call for appointment.
Reading room, work tables, accession cards/
files, books/journals, and photocopy facilities.

London Historical Museums

1017 Western Road
London, Ontario N6G 1G5
(519) 433-6171

Weekdays, 9:00 A.M.–5:00 P.M.
Collection includes fifty-six regional patchwork quilts, forty-nine quilt patterns/instruc-
tions, and information acquired from donors.
Forty-eight are patchwork quilts, three appliqué, two embroidered, one Marseille, one
whole-cloth, and one Bisquit quilt. Eight are
from the nineteenth century, and four quilts
are later.
Study Services: Make appointment with registrar. Reading room, work tables, accession
cards/files, books/journals, photocopy facilities,
and microscope.
Public Services: During periodic quilt exhibits;
tours, programs, and workshops arranged.

Masey Area Museum, Inc.
Massey, Ontario
(705) 865-2266

Mailing Address:
P.O. Box 237
Massey, ON P0P 1P0

May–September: days and hours not provided. Five quilts are on continuous exhibition. One is a Hawaiian quilt of 1896; one Log Cabin, and three crazy quilts.

Upper Canada Village
St. Lawrence Parks Commission
Morrisburg, Ontario
(613) 543-2911

Mailing Address:
P.O. Box 740
Morrisburg, ON K0C 1X0

May–October: daily, 8:15 A.M.–4:30 P.M. October 15–May 15: five days, 8:15 A.M.–4:30 P.M. The village has approximately eighty quilts mainly from eastern Ontario and twelve quilt patterns/instructions. Twenty-two are from other parts of Ontario, eight from Quebec, four from the eastern United States, and one from Alberta. The quilts are piecework, white-on-white, appliqué, embroidered, and some with decorative quilting. Ten can be dataed nineteenth century, two later. Quilts are on exhibit at all times.
Study Services: For scholars, make appointment with registrar and supervisor of domestic interpretation and costuming. Reading room, work tables, accession cards/files, twenty-five books/journals, photocopy facilities; photo prints, slides; and photo prints may be requested.
Public Services: Craft house demonstrations of quiltmaking, and exhibitions; educational programs for schools with quilting as one of the topics.

Black Creek Pioneer Village
1000 Murray Ross Parkway
North York, Ontario M3J 2P3
(416) 661-6600

Daily, except Christmas and New Year's day. March: 9:30 A.M.–4:30 P.M.; April, May, and June: 9:30 A.M.–5:00 P.M.; July and August: 10:00 A.M.–6:00 P.M.; September and October: 9:30 A.M.–5:00 P.M.; November–January: 9:30 A.M.–4:00 P.M.. Weekends and holidays, March: 10:00 A.M.–4:00 P.M.; April–October: 10:00 A.M.–6:00 P.M.; November–January, 10:00 A.M.–4:30 P.M. Village buildings are closed to the public from early January to mid March. The visitor's center remains open year-round. The 151 quilts reflect of the major ethnic groups in this region of Ontario in the mid to late nineteenth and early twentieth centuries: Pennsylvania Germans, Irish, English, and Scottish. The collection concentrates on floral, Log Cabin, geometrics, squares, Sunbursts, and Basket quilts. About 110 are patchwork, twenty-eight appliqué, five crazy quilts, three quilted whole-cloth, two pieced and appliqué, and two tied. Two of the quilts are definitely dated between 1890 and 1900, and another quilt dates to 1885. The museum has a quilting frame, templates, and thread. Quilts are exhibited in most of the restored buildings in the village.
NB: Five quilts made for doll's beds.
Study Services: For research, by appointment only. Reading room, work tables, accession cards/files, books/journals, and photocopy facilities; photo prints, slides; prints may be ordered from file negatives.
Public Services: Quilts and related artifacts can be seen in the village as part of the regular program.

Lundy's Lane Historical Museum
5810 Ferry Street
Niagara Falls, Ontario L2G 1S9
(416) 358-5082

Hours not provided.
Seven handsewn quilts.

Niagara Historical Society Museum

43 Castle Reach Street
Niagara-on-the-Lake, Ontario
(416) 468-3912

Mailing Address:
P.O. Box 208
Niagara-on-the-Lake, ON L0S 1J0

Daily year-round: May–October: 10:00 A.M.–6:00 P.M.; November–April: 1:00–5:00 P.M.
A collection of fourteen quilts includes two Log Cabin, one Barn Raising, one Nine Patch, one crazy quilt, and one embroidered quilt. Of those dated six are nineteenth century, two date later than 1900, and two are contemporary.
Study Services: For people involved in research, exhibitions, publications, or lecture programs. Send for a copy of archival policy statement. Reading room, and accession cards/files.
Public Services: On occasion tours of exhibitions, classes and workshops are offered.

Oshawa Sydenham Museum

6 Henry Street
Oshawa, Ontario
(416) 728-6331

Mailing Address:
P.O. Box 2303
Oshawa, ON L1H 7V5

Five days a week, call for specific days, 9:00 A.M.–5:00 P.M.
The Museum has thirty-five quilts from the Oshawa region, one quilt pattern/instruction. Fifteen are piecework, ten embroidered, five appliqué, and five white-on-white quilts. Fifteen are nineteenth century, five date after 1900.
Study Services: For scholars, make appointment with curator. Reading room, accession cards/files, and photocopy facilities.

Bytown Historical Museum

Ottawa Locks, Rideau Canal
Ottawa, Ontario
(613) 234-4570

Mailing Address:
P.O. Box 523, Station B
Ottawa, ON K1P 5P6

Mid-May to Mid-October. Days and hours not provided.
Eleven quilts from Ontario are all handsewn except one. Nine are nineteenth century, one dates after 1900, one contemporary.
Study Services: For scholars; make appointment. Reading room, work tables, accession cards/files, library, archives, and photocopy facilities.
Public Services: Tours available; exhibits.

Federated Women's Institutes of Canada

46 Elgin Street, Room 28
Ottawa, Ontario
(613) 234-1090

Mailing Address:
Gwen Parker
Chairman Cultural Affairs
5640 Chemin N. Hatley
Rock Forest, PQ J1N 1A4
(819) 562-1687

Office: Monday–Thursday, 9:00 A.M.–4:00 P.M.
This is a collection of seventy-nine slides of quilt blocks, and a book of quilt patterns. The organization is in the process of cataloging holdings in provincial societies.

National Museum of Man

Canadian Centre for Folk Culture Studies
Metcalfe and McLeod Streets
Ottawa, Ontario K1A 0M8
(613) 993-2497

Hours not provided.
Three hundred nineteenth century and contemporary quilts include examples of piecework, appliqué, embroidery, and white-on-white.
Study Services: Make appointment. Reading room, work tables, accession cards/files,

books/journals, and photocopy facilities; slides, prints may be made from file negatives.
Public Services: Exhibitions.

Hutchison House Museum

270 Brock Street
Peterborough, Ontario K9H 2P9
(705) 743-9710

May 1–October 31: Tuesday–Sunday, 1:00 P.M.–5:00 P.M.
This collection contains seventy-nine quilts from Peterborough and the Kawartha region, plus one quilt pattern/instruction. Fifty are piecework, twenty-eight appliqué, one embroidered. One predates 1820, three are nineteenth century, seventy-five are contemporary. Continuous exhibition of quilts.
Study Services: Make appointment with curator, who supervises researchers. Reading room, work tables, accession cards/files, and books/journals.
Public Services: Exhibitions of quilts made by the Kawartha Quiltmakers Guild.

Peterborough Museum and Archives

Hunter Street East on Armour Hill
Peterborough, Ontario
(705) 743-5180

Mailing Address:
P.O. Box 143
Peterborough, ON K9J 6Y5

Summer: daily, 10:00 A.M.–5:00 P.M.; Winter: weekdays, 10:00 A.M.–5:00 P.M.; weekends, 12:00–5:00 P.M.
Twenty-nine quilts and unfinished quilt tops from the Petersborough area form a collection which concentrates in traditional Log Cabin and crazy quilts. Twenty-seven are piecework, two appliqué. Nine are nineteenth century, three date later than 1900.
Study Services: Make appointment with curator. Reading area, work tables, accession cards/files, books/journals, and photocopy facilities.
Public Services: Tours, classes and workshops offered during quilt exhibitions and by special request for groups.

McDougall Mill Museum

Arthur Street
Renfrew, Ontario
(613) 432-8606

Mailing Address:
200 Xavier Street
Renfrew, ON K7V 1L4

June–September: daily, 9:00 A.M.–5:00 P.M.
The Museum has sixteen quilts mostly pieced cotton, one velvet, some wool. Two are nineteenth century, twelve date after 1900, two are contemporary. Continuous exhibition of quilts.
NB: Two Autograph quilts from the area, one made from printed flags in 1900; the other dates from 1908. Log Cabin quilt, over 100 years old.
Public Services: General tours.

Ermatinger Old Stone House

831 Queen Street
Sault Ste. Marie, Ontario
(705) 949-1488

Mailing Address:
P.O. Box 580, Civic Centre
Sault Ste. Marie, ON P6A 5N1

April–September 30: days not provided, 10:00 A.M.–5:00 P.M. October and November: days not provided, 1:00–5:00 P.M.
Six Canadian quilts made in Ontario.

Sombra Township Museum

146 St. Clair Street
Sombra, Ontario
(519) 892-3631

Mailing Address:
P.O. Box 76
Sombra, ON N0P 2H0

May–October: daily, 2:00–5:00 P.M.
This collection of fifteen quilts includes eight that are homespun, two Autograph, one satin and velvet Log Cabin, one crocheted, and one knitted bedspread. Continuous exhibition of quilts.
NB: Homespun quilts.

Study Services: Make appointment to use research facilities. Reading room, and work tables; prints may be made from file negatives. *Public Services:* Tours of exhibitions.

Bruce County Museum
33 Victoria Street North
Southampton, Ontario
(519) 797-3644

Mailing Address:
P.O. Box 180
Southampton, ON N0H 2L0

Weekdays, 9:00 A.M.–5:00 P.M.
Thirty-five quilts represent the museum's region and ethnic settlements. Written information furnished by donors is part of the collection.
Study Services: Research facilities for scholars. Reading room, work tables, accession cards/files, books/journals, and photocopy facilities.

The Adelaide Hunter-Hoodless Homestead
Blue Lake Road, Rural Route #1
St. George, Ontario N0E 1N0
(519) 448-1130

Winter: weekdays, 1:00–5:00 P.M. Spring and summer: daily, hours not provided.
A collection of sixteen Canadian quilts, fifty quilt blocks, patterns and cushions with quilt tops. Twelve date from the nineteenth century, three date from 1901 to 1940, one is contemporary. Two appliqué quilts, fifteen piecework, eleven have embroidery, and one trapunto. A concentration of Log Cabin and crazy quilts. Continuous exhibition of collection.
NB: Original Hunter family quilt; Federated Women's Institutes of Canada Jubilee quilt of 1957. Samples of quilt blocks: thirty-four appliqué, twenty piecework, thirteen embroidered, and three with decorative quilting.
Study Services: Accession cards/files; photo prints and slides made upon request.
Public Services: Guided tours, copies of quilt blocks provided upon request.

Royal Ontario Museum
100 Queen's Park
Toronto, Ontario M5S 2C6
(416) 978-3655

Monday, Wednesday, Friday, and weekends, 10:00 A.M.–5:00 P.M.; Tuesday, and Thursday, 10:00 A.M.–8:00 P.M.
A collection of 133 quilts from international sources: approximately 127 Canadian quilts, seventeen from the United States, sixteen from England, four from eastern India, two from Ireland, one from China, one from France, one from Germany, and one from Portugal. Seventy-seven are pieced, twenty appliqué, fifteen pieced and appliqué, four wholecloth, and one is a glazed quilt.
Study Services: Make appointment to review photographs of artifacts, then arrange with the appropriate curator to see a quilt in storage or to have it brought into the office area for study. Research space is limited and cannot accommodate many people at once. Reading room, work tables, accession cards/files, fifty books/journals, public library, photo and slide file, photocopy facilities, and microscope; photo prints, slides, prints may be ordered from file negatives.
Public Services: During exhibitions: tours, classes, or workshops.
Publications: Burnham, Dorothy K. *Pieced Quilts of Ontario* (1975). Hood, Adrienne D. "Early Canadian Quilts." *Rotunda* 17 (Fall/Winter 1984/5).

Todmorden Mills Historic Site
67 Pottery Road
Toronto, Ontario
(416) 425-2250

Mailing Address:
550 Mortimer Avenue
Toronto, ON M4J 2H2

Tuesday–Friday, 10:00 A.M.–5:00 P.M.; weekends, 11:00 A.M.–5:00 P.M.
Ten or eleven nineteenth century quilts are from metropolitan Toronto: two Log Cabin, one crazy quilt, one Star of Bethlehem, one

Dresden Plate, one Oak Leaf, and one patch-work doll's quilt.

Study Services: For scholars; research facilities available by appointment. Reading room, work tables, accession cards/files, and books/journals.

Meadows of Dan Quilters, Meadows of Dan Baptist Church, Patrick County, Meadows of Dan, Virginia, quilt a Grandmother's Flower Garden. American Folklife Center, Blue Ridge Parkway Project, 1978. Fieldworker: Geraldine Johnson, photo by Lyntha Eiler, negative number 4-20421, 37. Courtesy of the Archive of Folk Culture, Library of Congress.

QUEBEC

Some very early Canadian quilts are part of collections.

Brome County Historical Society

130 Lakeside
Knowlton, Quebec
(514) 243-6782

Mailing Address:
P.O. Box 690
Knowlton, PQ JOE 1VO

During season: daily, 10:00 A.M.–5:00 P.M. Brochure upon request.
This collection of thirty local quilts was made in Brome County, Quebec. Twenty are piecework, eight embroidery/piecework, one appliqué, one trapunto. Twenty-five are nineteenth century, five date later than 1900. Continuous exhibition of quilts.
Study Services: Make appointment. Reading room, work tables, books/journals, and photocopy facilities.

McCord Museum

690 Sherbrooke Street West
Montreal, Quebec H3A 1E9
(514) 392-4763 or 392-4778

Wednesday–Sunday, 11:00 A.M.–5:00 P.M. Office: weekdays, 9:00 A.M.–5:00 P.M.
Forty-two quilts, primarily from Montreal and environs, form a collection of twenty-nine piecework, four appliqué, four crazy quilts, two whole-cloth, one trapunto, one hexagon, and one pieced and appliqué. Four predate 1820; thirty-two date 1821 to 1900; five post-date 1900, and one is contemporary.
NB: Earliest known silk patchwork quilt, 1726: "The McCord Quilt."
Study Services: By appointment. Reading room, work tables, accession cards/files, books/journals, and photocopy facilities; photo prints, slides, prints may be ordered from negatives of some of the quilt collection.

Université Laval
Cité universitaire
Sainte-Foy, Quebec
(418) 656-3330

Mailing Address:
Nicole Bridle
Dép. D'Histoire
Université Laval
Ste.-Foy, PQ G1K 7P4

Weekdays, 9:00 A.M.–5:00 P.M.
Ten French-Canadian quilts are from the twentieth century: seven piecework, three appliqué.
Study Services: For scholars, make appointment. Work tables, accession cards/files, books/journals; slides.

New Madrid County, Missouri. Sharecropper's child reading. Southeast Missouri Farms, May 1938. Photograph by Russell Lee, negative number LC-USF34-31187-D. Courtesy of the Farm Security Administration Collection, Prints and Photographs Division, Library of Congress.

SASKATCHEWAN

Several public institutions display quilts throughout the province.

Broadview Historical and Museum Association
Broadview, Saskatchewan
(306) 696-2612

Mailing Address:
P.O. Box 556
Broadview, Sask. SOG OKO

Hours not provided.
Eight regional quilts are on continuous exhibition.

Jamieson Museum
304 Gertie Street
Moosomin, Saskatchewan
(304) 435-3156

Mailing Address:
P.O. Box 236
Moosomin, Sask. SOG 3NO

Summer only. Days and hours, not provided.
Five Pioneer quilts are on continuous exhibition.

Saskatchewan Western Development Museums
2935 Melville Street
Saskatoon, Saskatchewan
(306) 934-1400

Mailing Address:
P.O. Box 1910
Saskatoon, Sask. S7K 3S5

Winter: daily, 9:00 A.M.–5:00 P.M.; summer: daily, 9:00 A.M.–9:00 P.M.
Seventy-eight quilts have been collected from the Saskatchewan region; it is likely that many of the quilts were brought to the area. These quilts are at the Saskatchewan Western Development Museum branches at Yorkton, Saskatoon, Moose Jaw, North Battleford, and the

Provincial Service Center which has the storage and office facility. Fifteen or more of the total number are from Saskatchewan, and an unknown number are from Ontario. The collection is principally piecework; several quilts are contemporary. Thirty-one of the quilts have embroidery combined with other techniques, twelve are appliqué, nine piecework, six crazy quilts, and one Yo-Yo. Those that have been dated are eight nineteenth century, ten post-1900, thirteen contemporary.

NB: Several quilts made from silk patches offered as premiums by tobacco companies.

Study Services: Make appointment with the collections program of the S.W.D.M. Reading room, work tables, accession cards/files, books/journals, computerized inventory, and photocopy facilities.

QUILTS IN
COLLECTIONS

QUESTIONNAIRE

American Folklife Center
The Library of Congress
Washington, D.C. 20540

September 1985

Institutions with extensive documentation *rather than material quilt collections,* please reply to questions 1, 3, 4, 12, 13, and 15–17.

If you have no collections to report, please fill out and return this page in the enclosed envelope.

1. _____
   Name of institution

   _____
   Street address

   _____
   City   State   Zip Code

   (_____) _____   _____
   Telephone   Days and hours of operation

2. Does the institution have a continuing exhibition of quilts?
   ☐ Yes   ☐ No

3. Is there a procedure for obtaining access to the stored collections?
   a) for the interested public   ☐ Yes   ☐ No
   b) for scholars   ☐ Yes   ☐ No

   _____
   (Describe protocol)
   Does the institution have research facilities for scholars?
   reading room ☐   photocopy facilities ☐
   work tables ☐   microscope ☐
   accession cards, files, etc. ☐

   other facilities _____

4. Are photo reproductions of quilts available?   ☐ Yes   ☐ No
   Please indicate available formats:

   a) photo prints _____   b) slides _____

   c) other _____
            (postcards, posters, catalogs)
   d) prints made from negatives upon request   ☐ Yes   ☐ No

   e) films _____   f) videotapes _____

5. Does the institution have textile conservation facilities?   ☐ Yes   ☐ No
   Do you provide conservation information to the public?   ☐ Yes   ☐ No

6. Does your institution provide public programming (i.e. tours of exhibitions, classes, workshops) for your quilt collection? ☐ Yes ☐ No

   Kinds of programming: _____

   _____

   _____

7. Are there publications based (all or in part) on your quilt collection?
   ☐ Yes ☐ No
   (If yes, please attach a list.)

8. Highlights of the collection:

   Regional, ethnic, or national in scope _____
   _{Concentration on type (technique, pattern, etc.)}

   _____

   Important quilts of special note _____

   _____

   Principal donors, sources _____

   _____   _____

   Other _____

9. Do you categorize your general collections in one or more of the following?
   folk/traditional ☐   contemporary ☐
   fine art ☐   historic ☐

10. What percentage of your collection represents handsewn quilts? _____

11. Number of quilts in the permanent collection: _____

    Number of quilts that can be dated: _____

    a) prior to 1820 _____

    b) 1821 to 1900 _____

    c) 1901 to 1940 _____

    d) 1941 to present _____

12. Does your institution have unpublished documentation on quilts and quilting? ☐ Yes ☐ No
    If yes, indicate type and approximate size of holdings:

    a) quilt patterns and instructions _____
       _{number}

    b) personal narratives by quiltmakers:

       diaries and journals _____
       _{number}

       interviews and oral histories: tapes _____ transcriptions _____
       _{number}   _{number}

    c) research papers _____
       _{number}

    d) other _____

13. Do you have a reference library of published books and/or journals about quilts and quilting?   ☐ Yes   ☐ No

If yes, give approximate number of volumes _____

14. a) Breakdown of collection by ethnic or religious group (e.g. Amish, Afro-American) and state, province, or region (e.g. Appalachian or Oregon).

number	_____
number	_____
number	_____
number	_____
number	_____
number	_____
number	_____

b) range of techniques represented in the collection (e.g. piecework, appliqué, yo-yo or bon-bon, embroidery, trapunto or stuffed or corded quilting, decorative quilting or "all white" quilting, printed whole-cloth with quilting).

number	_____
number	_____
number	_____
number	_____
number	_____
number	_____
number	_____

15. Can you suggest other institutions in your area with quilt collections that are appropriate for inclusion in this survey?

_____

_____

_____

16. Please list quilt organizations with which you are affiliated or know of in your area.

_____

_____

_____

_____

17. Name and title of person filling out questionnaire:

_____

_____

THANK YOU

QUILT DOCUMENTATION PROJECTS IN THE UNITED STATES AND CANADA

ALABAMA

Folk Arts Program Manager
Artists-in-Education Program
Alabama State Council on the Arts and
    Humanities
323 Adams Avenue
Montgomery, Alabama 36130

Decorative Arts Survey of Alabama
Birmingham Museum of Art
2000 8th Avenue North
Birmingham, Alabama 35203

ARIZONA

Arizona Quilt Project
P.O. Box 5062
Mesa, Arizona 85201

CALIFORNIA

California Heritage Quilt Project
P.O. Box 321
Cardiff by the Sea, California 92007

Folk Arts Consultant
California Arts Council
1901 Broadway, Suite A
Sacramento, California 95818

California Heritage Quilt Project
P.O. Box 27231
San Francisco, California 94127

COLORADO

Historical Documentation Committee
Colorado Quilting Council
P.O. Box 2056
Arvada, Colorado 80001-2056

DELAWARE

Delaware Folklife Project
Delaware Quilt Registry
2 Crestwood Place
Wilmington, Delaware 19809

DISTRICT OF COLUMBIA

D.C. Quilt Search
5801 Nebraska Avenue, N.W.
Washington, D.C. 20015

FLORIDA

Florida Quilt Heritage
P.O. Box 4324
Tallahassee, Florida 32315

IDAHO

Idaho Quilt Project
c/o Boise Basin Quilters
P.O. Box 2206
Boise, Idaho 83701

ILLINOIS

Illinois Quilt Research Project
P.O. Drawer 669
Mahomet, Illinois 61853

INDIANA

Indiana Quilt Registry Project, Inc.
Indiana State Museum
202 North Alabama Street
Indianapolis, Indiana 46204

KANSAS

Kansas Quilt Project, Inc.
P.O. Box 7507
Wichita, Kansas 67207

KENTUCKY

The Kentucky Quilt Project
122 River Hill Road
Louisville, Kentucky 40207

LOUISIANA

Louisiana Quilt Search Project
Louisiana State University
Shreveport Library
Archives Department
Shreveport, Louisiana 71105

MAINE

Maine Quilt Heritage
6 Mechanic Street
Bath, Maine 04530

MICHIGAN

Michigan Quilt Project
The Museum
Michigan State University
East Lansing, Michigan 48824-1045

MISSISSIPPI

Mississippi Quilt Project
State Historical Museum
Old Capitol Restoration
Mississippi Department of Archives and
    History
P.O. Box 571
Jackson, Mississippi 39205-0571

MINNESOTA

Minnesota Quilt History Project
P.O. Box 14668
Minneapolis, Minnesotga 55414

MISSOURI

The Missouri Quilt Project
c/o 1004 West Worley
Columbia, Missouri 65201

MONTANA

Historic Quilt and Oral History Project
Jackie Redding
Center on Hardin
204 North Center
Hardin, Montana 59034

NEBRASKA

Nebraska Quilt Project
1820 St. James Road
Lincoln, Nebraska 68506

NEW MEXICO

New Mexico Quilt Survey
Museum of International Folk Art
Museum of New Mexico
P.O. Box 2087
Santa Fe, New Mexico 87503

NEW YORK

Central New York State Quilt Survey
4726 West Lake Road
Cazenovia, New York 13035

The New York Quilt Project
Museum of American Folk Art
444 Park Avenue South
New York, New York 10016

Staten Island Historical Society
Quilt Survey
441 Clark Avenue
Staten Island, New York 10306

The Leatherstocking Country Quilters
Central New York Survey
P.O. Box 234
Stockbridge, New York 13409

NORTH CAROLINA

North Carolina Quilt Project
P.O. Box 2739
Durham, North Carolina 27705

NORTH DAKOTA

The North Dakota Quilt Project
1450 South 8th Street
Fargo, North Dakota 58103

OHIO

The Ohio Quilt Research Project
P.O. Box 13111
Toledo, Ohio 43613

OKLAHOMA

Oklahoma Quilt Heritage Project
1005 South Kings
Stillwater, Oklahoma 74074

SOUTH CAROLINA

South Carolina Quilt Project
McKissick Museums
The University of South Carolina
Columbia, South Carolina 29208

TENNESSEE

Quilts of Tennessee
P.O. Box 4146
Chattanooga, Tennessee 37405

TEXAS

Texas Heritage Quilt Society
P.O. Box 5342
Kingswood, Texas 77325

Texas Sesquicentennial Quilt Project
Great Expectations Quilts
14520 Memorial, #54
Houston, Texas 77079

VIRGINIA

Northern Virginia Quilt Research Project
The Continental Quilting Congress, Inc.
P.O. Box 561
Vienna, Virginia 22180

ALBERTA
CANADA

Alberta Quilts
Department of Social History
Provincial Museum of Alberta
12845 102nd Avenue
Edmonton, Alberta T5N 0M6

SELECTED LISTING OF REGIONAL, NATIONAL, AND INTERNATIONAL QUILT ASSOCIATIONS

UNITED STATES

American/International Quilt Association
(formerly South/Southwest Quilt Association)
P.O. Box 79126
Houston, Texas 77279

American Quilt Study Group
105 Molino Avenue
Mill Valley, California 94941

American Quilter's Society
P.O. Box 3290
Paducah, Kentucky 42001

National Quilting Association
(with regional branches)
P.O. Box 62
Greenbelt, Maryland 20770

New England Quilters Guild
New England Quilt Museum
256 Market Street
Lowell, Massachusetts 01852

The Quilt Conservancy
P.O. Box 22449
Kansas City, Missouri 64113

CANADA

Canadian Quilters' Association
2756 Brimley Road
Agincourt, Ontario M1V 1K2

Fredericton Quilter's Association
258 Church Street
Fredericton, New Brunswick E3B 4E4

Halton Quilters' Guild
P.O. Box 171
Oakville, Ontario L6J 4Z5

Windsor Quilter's Guild
1020 Watson
Windsor, Ontario N8S 3T4

APPENDIX 3

CONSERVATION

Free textile or quilt conservation information is available from many institutions, organizations, and universities. For example, the Smithsonian Institution's Division of Textiles, at the National Museum of American History (Smithsonian Institution, Washington, DC 20560) will provide fact sheets and pamphlets on quilt conservation. In your request for information, describe the materials used in the quilt's construction, i.e., silk, cotton, linen, or wool. The audio-visual loan program at the Office of Museum Programs (Smithsonian Institution, Arts and Industries Building, Washington, DC 20560) has a slide set rental program and brochure. The American Association for State and Local History (708 Berry Road, Nashville, TN 37204) has pamphlets, brochures, and films listed in their annual catalog. "Quilt Conservation" is a pamphlet available from the Cooperative Extension Service, University of Maryland, Home Economics Department, (Room 1200, Symons Hall, College Park, MD 20742). Include a self-addressed stamped letter-size envelope with your request. Many other state college home economics or cooperative extension service departments also can provide conservation information. The Textile Conservation Workshop (Main Street, South Salem, NY 10950) was established in 1978 by Patsy Orlofsky and others to provide high quality conservation services to institutions and individual collectors.

Most of the institutions listed in this directory will provide textile conservation advice. During actual inspection of collections, many institutions require that those handling the textiles wear gloves. Because improper cleaning, wet or dry, can ruin a quilt, it is always best to consult a textile conservator who is knowledgable about fibers before attempting to clean your quilt or other textile.

GLOSSARY

Album Quilt. A quilt constructed of many different units (blocks). Each block is usually signed by its maker. The quilt is given as a gift to a special friend or community figure to commemorate an event. Sometimes called a Friendship Quilt.

Amish Quilt. Originally a quilt made by a member of an Amish (plain people) community and usually characterized by the use of highly stylized and graphic geometric patterns of solid colors, often close in value, in saturated, intense hues, and usually bordered in black or other deep, rich color. Today, a quilt made in the Amish style may also be termed "Amish."

Appliqué. A construction technique involving the sewing of a fabric motif onto a (usually) solid background cloth.

Autograph Quilt. Similar to Album quilt but signed by either the makers or other individuals (e.g., at fund-raisers).

Baby Block. A one-patch diamond-shaped patchwork pattern. Three diamonds sewn together form a small square which appears three-dimensional.

Baltimore Album Quilt. Quilt style attributed to Baltimore, Maryland makers c. 1840–50. Elaborate appliqué blocks of characteristic brilliant colors and types of cloth showing baskets, cornucopia, and sometimes historic buildings and monuments.

Batting. Middle layer or filling of a quilt. Made of cotton, wool, or synthetics. Sometimes old quilts or blankets are used.

Biscuit, Bun. A type of comforter made of stuffed, individually made round or square units sewn together in rows.

Block. Basic unit of a quilt, usually square, and often named for its pattern, such as "Bear's Paw" or "Weathervane." Six thousand piecework patterns have been cataloged.

Blue Resist. Eighteenth-century block or plate printed fabric dyed with indigo in paste form mixed with iron sulphates and thickeners. The cloth was alternately immersed in lime and iron sulphate as many times as needed to obtain the desired shade of blue.

Broderie Perse. An appliqué construction technique begun in the eighteenth century. Motifs are cut from chintz or other printed fabric and applied to a solid ground, often using the buttonhole stitch.

Calamanco. Eighteenth-century (English) glazed wool worsted characterized by crisp, polished surface and clear color.

Candlewick. Nineteenth-century embroidery and/or weaving technique used to decorate bedspreads and pillowshams with coarse white cording. Floral and geometric designs were popular.

Cathedral Window. A type of spread made of

sections of muslin which have been specifically folded and stitched into square units. A "window" shape is formed when two units are joined. A different piece of colored or patterned cloth is set into the windows and covers the joining seam. These secondary units are next set together by rows to form a whole. Because it is not quilted in the usual sense, this textile is properly termed a coverlet. Also the name of a patchwork pattern.

Century of Progress International Exposition. Chicago, Illinois 1933–34. The World's Fair.

Charm Quilt. A one-patch quilt, each piece cut from a different fabric collected by the maker from friends or gathered by trading. Often containing hundreds of pieces, a Charm Quilt is a marvelous record of fabrics of its era. Originally the quilter tried to gather 999 pieces for her quilt.

Chenille. Wool, cotton, silk, or rayon yarn with protruding pile; a pile-face fabric with a filling of this yarn; a bedspread decorated with chenille yarn at first by hand but later by machine.

Chinoiserie. A mid-nineteenth century style of printed fabric reflecting Chinese qualities or motifs.

Chintz. Smooth, often glazed cotton fabric notably with large multicolored flora or fauna designs, originally from India.

Comforter. (United States) A bedcover filled with thick batting held by machine-stitched channels or tied at intervals.

Contained Crazy Quilt. Blocks made in the crazy quilt style are set together with lattice strips forming a grid.

Copperplate Printed Cloth. A mid-eighteenth century cotton or linen cloth printed in England and France, depicting monochromatic scenes or elaborate floral designs.

Coverlet. An elaborate woven bedcover, nineteenth century American, wool and cotton. Also an unquilted top which has been lined with a backing and generally used as a summer bedspread.

Crazy Quilt or Quilting. Patchwork made of irregular (often silk) pieces with no regard to pattern. Usually outlined with decorative embroidery.

Crewel. Decorative embroidery done with yarn on cotton or linen ground.

Decorative Embroidery. Implies elaborate and skillful surface embellishment usually of complex designs.

English Piecing. Patchwork technique whereby design elements are cut of paper or thin cardboard. Cloth is basted over them, and these units are whipstitched together to form the pattern.

Hap. A warm, coarse bedcovering. Term used mainly in Pennsylvania describing a heavy, usually woolen, pieced comforter/blanket, tied or tacked, and generally of a simple geometric pattern in dark colors. The word evolved from northern English dialect.

Hawaiian Quilt. Style begun in Hawaii, late nineteenth century; large intricate appliqué from one piece of fabric ritually folded and cut. Usually of fruit, flowers, or foliage, often only two colors, heavily contour-quilted.

Hawaiian Quilting. A style of quilting involving outlining an elaborate appliqué design in graduated rows of stitching, usually ¼ inch apart, over the entire face of the quilt.

Hewson, John. American textile printer of considerable skill; worked in Philadelphia, Pennsylvania, 1774–1810.

Homespun. A (usually) coarse handloomed fabric of wool or linen handspun yarns.

Linsey-Woolsey. Coarse fabric woven with linen or cotton warp and a wool weft.

Marseilles Quilting. Also known as stuffed or corded work; only two layers are joined.

Material Culture. Refers to the tangible artifacts either manufactured or used by an identifiable group, society, or tribe. Functional objects that contain and reflect the values, aesthetics, and needs of a culture.

Medallion Quilt. A large center design, the focus of the quilt, is surrounded by one or more borders, sometimes very elaborate.

Morning Star Quilt. Variations of a broken star design made by Plains Indians.

One-Patch. A quilt made of units formed from patches all cut the same shape.

Palampore. Eighteenth-century Indian cotton spread richly colored with elaborate designs, often the Tree of Life. These textiles greatly influenced later quilt design.

Patchwork, Piecework. Carefully cut pieces of cloth joined by hand or machine to form a design.

Penciled Blue. Fabric printed with small amounts of indigo dyes, chemicals, and thickeners painted on before oxidation could occur.

Quilt Registry Day. A special day set aside and advertised to encourage individuals to bring quilts to be documented, usually as a state or regional study project.

Reverse Appliqué. Two or more different fabrics are layered; various portions of these are cut away and sewn down forming a design of many colors: notably molas by San Blas Indians.

Roller Fabric. Cloth printed by engraved metal cylinders rather than copperplates; also called cylinder print, beginning about 1810–15.

Sampler Quilt. A block quilt, each one of a different patchwork pattern.

Sara Pierce School. Litchfield, Connecticut, eighteenth-century boarding school for young girls. Curriculum noted for needlework, theorem painting, physical fitness, Christian ethics, and academic subjects.

Saye. A textile, originally silk, then silk and wool (in Europe), finally all wool. Used from the twelfth to the nineteenth century and now obsolete.

Scrap Quilt. A quilt made from many varieties of patterned cloth, not necessarily left-over scraps.

Serial, Quilt Serial. Magazine; quilting magazine.

Sham, also *Pillowsham.* Pillow cover, decorative, usually made to coordinate with a spread or other bed covering.

Slave Quilt. U.S. southern quilts made by or attributed to people held in slavery.

Stencil Quilt. Historically a type of quilt using painted designs applied through a stencil and made mainly in New England 1800–40. Often unquilted, stencilled spreads were both block and whole-cloth. There is a wide range of competence within the style and comparatively few remaining early examples.

String Quilt. A style or technique involving piecing together narrow strips of fabric ("strings") to form either a specific pattern or a random design, usually resulting in a multicolor effect.

Suggan. Also spelled soogan, soogin, and sougan. Quilted bedroll used by cowboys.

Tie, or *Tied.* A technique used to hold together layers of a coverlet or comforter. Yarn or heavy thread is knotted through the three layers at four-to-six inch intervals.

Trapunto. A term used to describe decorative, high relief quilting design worked by outlining the motif in running stitches and then stuffing it from the underside.

White-on-White. A style of quilting whereby a design is quilted in white (or off-white) thread onto a white (or off-white) solid ground.

Whole-Cloth Quilt. Usually made by marking an elaborate design on a large unpieced section of cloth and then quilting that design in matching color thread through top, batting, and back to form quilt.

Yo-Yo, also *Bon Bon.* Coverlet popular in the

1920s and 1930s made of many circular modules tacked together. The module is made by cutting a circle of cloth, stitching around its perimeter with running stitches, drawing it up, and then flattening the ensuing shape. The yo-yo's are sometimes, but not always, lined with a backing.

Anonymous Was A Woman. 30 minutes, 16mm, video, 1977. Producer: Mirra Bank/WNET-TV, New York. Distributor: Films Inc., 5547 North Ravenswood Avenue, Chicago, Illinois, 60640, (312) 878-2600, extension 43.

Before the Industrial Revolution. 17 minutes, 16mm, 1974. Producer: Vincent R. Tortora, Distributor: Vedo Films, 85 Longview Road, Port Washington, NY 11050, (516) 883-7460.

The Folk Way. 60 minutes, video, 1976. Producer and distributor: Maryland Center for Public Broadcasting, Attn: Program Marketing Manager, Owings Mills, MD 21117, (301) 356-5600.

Four Women Artists. 25 minutes, 16mm, video, 1978. Producer and Distributor: Center for Southern Folklore, 1216 Peabody Avenue, Box 40105, Memphis, TN 38104, (901) 726-4205.

The Hardman Quilt: Portrait of an Age. 10 minutes, 16mm, video, 1975. Producer and distributor: Hans Halberstadt, 240 South 13th Street, San Jose, CA 95112, (408) 293-8131.

The Hawaiian Quilt: A Cherished Tradition. 56 minutes, video, 1986. Producers: Elaine Zinn and Richard J. Tibbetts, Jr. Distributor: Hawaii Craftsmen, P.O. Box 22145, Honolulu, HI 96822.

Hearts and Hands: A Social History of Nineteenth-Century Women and Their Quilts. One hour, 16mm, video purchase, 16mm rental, 1987. Producer: Pat Ferrero and Julie Silber. Distributor: for information contact, Ferrero Films, 1259A Folsom Street, San Francisco, CA 94103, (415) 626-FILM.

Images of Country Women: A Patchwork Quilt. 29 minutes, 16mm, 1976. Producer: Lucyann Kerry/Blue Ridge Films. Distributor: The Pennsylvania State University, Audio-Visual Services, Special Services Building, University Park, PA 16802, (814) 865-6315. Order Number 32155.

In Praise of Patchwork. 30 minutes, 16mm, video, 1979. Producer and Distributor: Susan Murphy, 5220 Abbott Avenue South, Minneapolis, MN 55410, (612) 925-0968.

A Jury of Her Peers. 30 minutes, 16mm, video, 1980. Producer: Sally Heckel. Distributor: Films, Incorporated, 5547 Ravenswood Avenue, Chicago, IL 60640, (312) 878-2600, extension 43 or 44.

Kaleidoscope. 3 minutes, 16mm, video, 1978. Producer: Eduardo Darino. Distributor: Darino Films, P.O. Box 5173, New York, NY 10017, (212) 228-4024.

Kathleen Ware, Quiltmaker. 33 minutes, 16mm, 1979. Producer: Sharon Sherman. Distributor: Folklore and Ethnic Studies,

University of Oregon, Eugene, OR 97403, (503) 686-3539/686-3911.

Lap Quilting. Twelve 30 minute programs, hosted by Georgia Bonesteel, video, 1981, 1983, 1985, 1987. Producer and distributor: The University of North Carolina Center for Public Television, 910 Raleigh Road, P.O. Box 3508, Chapel Hill, NC 27515-3508, (919) 962-8191.

*Made in Mississippi: Black Folk Arts and Crafts. 20 minutes, 16mm, 1975. Producer: Bill Ferris/Yale University Media Design Studio in cooperation with Center for Southern Folklore. Distributor: Center for Southern Folklore, 1216 Peabody Avenue, Box 40105, Memphis, TN 38104, (901) 726-4205.

Martha Mitchell of Possum Walk Road: Quiltmaker. 28 minutes, video, 1985. Producer and distributor: Melvin R. Mason, Department of English, Sam Houston State University, Huntsville, TX 77341, (409) 294-1404.

*Missing Pieces: Contemporary Georgia Folk Art. 28 minutes, 16mm, 1976. Producer: Steve Heiser/Georgia Council for the Arts. Distributor: Georgia Council for the Arts, 2082 East Exchange Place, Suite 100, Tucker, GA 30084, (404) 493-5780.

*Mr. and Mrs. Elmer Walls: Craft Traditions Of A Southern Indiana Family. 60 minutes, video, 1976. Producer and distributor: Community Access Cable Channel 3, c/o Monroe County Public Library, 303 E. Kirkwood Avenue, Bloomington, IN 47401, (812) 339-5513.

*Pioneer Living: Education and Recreation. 11 minutes, 16mm, 1971. Producer: Moreland-Latchford Productions, Ltd. Distributor: Coronet M.I.T. Film and Video, 108 Wilmot Road, Deerfield, IL 60015, (800) 621-2131; (312) 940-1260, (IL only: call collect). Order number 3134.

Quilting. (13) 30 minute programs, hosted by Penny McMorris, video, 1981. Producer and distributor: WBGU-TV 27, Bowling Green State University, 245 Troup Street, Bowling Green, OH 43403, (419) 372-2700.

Quilting II. (13) 30 minute programs, hosted by Penny McMorris, video, 1982. Producer and distributor: WBGU-TV 27, Bowling Green State University, 245 Troup Street, Bowling Green, OH 43403, (419) 372-2700.

Quilting Party. 2½ minutes, 16mm, 1981. Producer and distributor: Bill Turner, Trio Films, P.O. Box 737, Mebane, NC 27302, (919) 563-4839.

Quilting: Patterns of Love. 20 minutes, 16mm, 1980. Producer: Lauron Productions, Ltd. Distributor: Cinema Concepts International, 56 Shaftsbury Avenue, Toronto, ON M4T 1A3, Canada, (416) 967-6503.

Quilting Women. 28 minutes, 16mm, 1976. Producer: Elizabeth Barret/Appalshop. Distributor: Appalshop, Box 743, Whitesburg, KY 41858, (800) 545-SHOP.

The Quiltmakers. 17 minutes, Super 8, 1972. Producer and distributor: Pat Mastick Young, Folklore Institute, 540 North Fess Street, Bloomington, IN 47401, (812) 335-3652.

Quiltmakers of Southern Indiana. 60 minutes, video, 1976. Producer and distributor: Community Access Cable Channel 3, c/o Monroe County Public Library, 303 E. Kirkwood Avenue, Bloomington, IN 47401, (812) 339-5513.

Quilts in Women's Lives. 30 minutes, 16mm rental, 16mm and video purchase, 1980. Producer: Pat Ferrero. Distributor: New Day Films, 22 Riverwood Drive, Wayne, NJ 07470, (201) 633-0212.

Threading Through Time. 27 minutes, 16mm rental, video purchase, 1982. Producer: Gloria Rosenberg, Tim Hurson, A Radiant Pictures Production. Distributor: Canadian Filmmakers Distribution Centre, 67A Portland Street, Toronto, Ontario, M5V 2M9, Canada (416) 593-1808.

Traditional Quilting. 29 minutes, 16mm, video, 1970. Producer and distributor: Western Kentucky University, Division of Media Services, College Heights U-147, Bowling Green, KY 42101, (502) 745-3754.

Under the Covers: American Quilts. 11 minutes, 16mm, video, 1976. Producer: Millie Paul. Distributor: Pyramid Films, Box 1048, Santa Monica, CA 90406, (213) 828-7577.

*Films that are not exclusively about quilts or quiltmaking.

SELECTED BIBLIOGRAPHY

The following sources were consulted for the names of quilt collections and documentation listed in pictorial credits and acknowledgments. The Library of Congress call number follows most entries.

Albacete, M.J., Sharon D'Atri, and Jane Reeves. *Ohio Quilts: A Living Tradition.* Canton, OH: Canton Art Institute, 1981. NK9112.A4

Adams, Roman F. *Western Words.* Norman: University of Oklahoma Press, 1968. PE2970.W4A3 1968

Allen, Gloria Seaman. *Old Line Traditions: Maryland Women and Their Quilts.* Washington, DC: DAR Museum, 1985. NK9112.043 1985

Bacon, Lenice Ingram. *American Patchwork Quilts.* New York: William Morrow & Co. 1973. TT835.B23

Bank, Mirra. *Anonymous Was A Woman.* New York: St. Martin's Press, 1979. NK806.A55

Bartis, Peter T. *Arizona Folklife Survey.* Washington, DC: The American Folklife Center, Library of Congress, 1980. GR110.A6B37

_____. *Rhode Island Folklife Resources.* Washington, DC: The American Folklife Center, Library of Congress, 1983. GR110.R4B37 1983

Bartis, Peter T., David S. Cohen, and Gregory Dowd. *Folklife Resources in New Jersey.* Washington, DC: The American Folklife Center, Library of Congress, 1985. GR110.N5B37 1985

Bartis, Peter T., and Barbara C. Fertig. *Folklife Sourcebook.* Washington, DC: The American Folklife Center, Library of Congress, 1986. GR37.B37 1986

Beyer, Jinny. *The Quilter's Album of Blocks and Borders.* McLean, VA: EPM Publications, 1980. TT835.B44

_____. *The Art and Technique of Creating Medallion Quilts.* McLean, VA: EPM Publications, 1982. TT835.B427 1982

Bishop, Robert. *New Discoveries In American Quilts.* New York: E.P. Dutton & Co., 1975. NK9112.B57 1975

_____. *Quilts, Coverlets, Rugs & Samplers.* New York: Alfred A. Knopf, 1982. NK9112.B58 1982

Bishop, Robert, and Elizabeth Safanda. *A Gallery of Amish Quilts: Design Diversity from a Plain People.* New York: E.P. Dutton & Co., 1976. NK9112.B567 1976

Bishop, Robert, and Carter Houck. *All Flags Flying: American Patriotic Quilts As Expressions Of Liberty.* New York: E.P. Dutton & Co. in association with the Museum of American Folk Art, 1986. TT835.B5 1986

Bonfield, Lynn A. "The Production of Cloth, Clothing and Quilts in 19th Century New

England Homes." *Uncoverings 1981* (1982): 77–96.

Brackman, Barbara. *An Encyclopedia of Pieced Quilt Patterns.* 8 Volumes. Lawrence, KS: Prairie Flower Publishing, 1979.

Bresenhan, Karoline Patterson, and Nancy O'Bryant Puentes. *Lone Stars: A Legacy of Texas Quilts, 1836–1936.* Austin: University of Texas Press, 1986. NK9112.B68 1986

Burnham, Dorothy K. *Pieced Quilts of Ontario.* Toronto: Royal Ontario Museum, 1975. TT835.B85

Center for Southern Folklore. *American Folklore Films and Videotapes: An Index.* Memphis, TN: Center for Southern Folklore, 1976. Z5984.U6C45 1976

———. *American Folklore Films and Videotapes: A Catalog.* Volume 2. New York: R.R. Bowker Co., 1982. Z5984.U6A44 1982

Child, Lydia Maria. *The American Frugal Housewife.* Boston: Carter, Hendee, and Co., 1835. TX147.C53 1835

Clarke, Mary Washington. *Kentucky Quilts and Their Makers.* Lexington, KY: University Press of Kentucky, 1976. TT835.C57

Colby, Averil. *Patchwork.* London: B.T. Batsford, 1958. NK9104.C64 Reprint. New York: Charles Scribner's Sons, 1982. TT835.C638 1982

———. *Quilting.* New York: Charles Scribner's Sons, 1972. TT835.C64 1972

Conroy, Mary. *300 Years of Canada's Quilts.* Toronto: Griffin House, 1976. TT835.C65

Cooper, Patricia, and Norma Bradley Buferd. *The Quilters: Women and Domestic Art.* Garden City, NY: Doubleday & Co., 1977. TT835.C66

Craig, Tracey Linton, ed. and comp. *Directory of Historical Societies and Agencies in the United States and Canada.* 12th ed Nashville, TN: American Association for State and Local History, 1982. E172.A538 12th Ed., 1982.

Cross, Mary, ed. *Women's Work: A Study of Quilts.* Portland, OR: Columbia-Willamette Quilt Study Group, 1984.

A Directory of Where To Find Embroidery and other Textile Treasures in the U.S.A. Tulsa, OK: National Standards Council of American Embroiderers, 1977. NK9203.N37

Fanning, Robbie and Tony Fanning. *The Complete Book of Machine Quilting.* Radnor, PA: Chilton Book Co., 1980. TT835.F36 1980

Finley, Ruth E. *Old Patchwork Quilts and the Women Who Made Them.* Philadelphia: J.B. Lippincott Co., 1929. NK9112.F5

Fitzrandolph, Mavis. *Traditional Quilting, Its Story and Its Practice.* London: B.T. Batsford, 1954. NK9144.F58

Fox, Sandi. *Quilts in Utah: A Reflection of the Western Experience.* Salt Lake City, UT: Salt Lake Art Center, 1981. NK9112.F68 1981

———. *Small Endearments: Nineteenth-Century Quilts for Children.* New York: Charles Scribner's Sons, 1985. NK9112.F695 1985

Freeman, Roland L. *Something to Keep You Warm: The Roland Freeman Collection of Black American Quilts from the Mississippi Heartland.* Jackson, MS: Mississippi Department of Archives and History, 1981. NK9112.F73

Gordon, Beverly. *Domestic American Textiles: A Bibliographic Sourcebook.* Pittsburgh, PA: Center for the History of American Needlework, 1978. Z6151.G67

Haders, Phyllis. *The Main Street Pocket Guide to Quilts.* Pittstown, NJ: Main Street Press, 1983. NK9112.H25 1983

———. *Sunshine and Shadow: The Amish and Their Quilts.* New York: Universe Books, 1976. NK9112.H26 Reprint. Pittstown, NJ: The Main Street Press, 1984.

———. *The Warner Collector's Guide to Amer-*

ican Quilts. New York: Warner Books, 1981. NK9112.H27

Hall, Carrie A., and Rose G. Kretsinger. *The Romance of the Patchwork Quilt in America. In Three Parts.* 1935. Reprint. New York: Bonanza Books, 1969. NK9112.H3 1969

Havig, Bettina. *Missouri Heritage Quilts.* Paducah, KY: American Quilter's Society, 1986. NK9112.H38 1986

Hechtlinger, Adelaide. *American Quilts, Quilting, and Patchwork.* Harrisburg, PA: Stackpole Books, 1974. TT835.H38

Hinson, Dolores A. *American Graphic Quilt Designs.* New York: Arco Publishing, 1983. TT835.H46 1983

Holstein, Jonathan. *Abstract Design in American Quilts.* New York: Whitney Museum of American Art, 1971. NK9112.H6

_____. *The Pieced Quilt: An American Design Tradition.* Greenwich, CT: New York Graphic Society, 1973. NK9112.H63

_____. "The Whitney and After . . . What's Happened to Quilts." *The Clarion.* (Spring/Summer 1986): 80–85.

Holstein, Jonathan, and John Finley. *Kentucky Quilts 1800–1900: The Kentucky Quilt Project.* New York: Pantheon Books, 1982. NK9112.H622 1982

Horton, Laurel, and Lynn Robertson Myers. *Social Fabric: South Carolina's Traditional Quilts.* Columbia, SC: McKissick Museum, University of South Carolina, 1985.

Houck, Carter, and Myron Miller. *American Quilts and How to Make Them.* New York: Charles Scribner's Sons, 1975. TT835.H63

Howarth, Shirley Reiff, ed. *Directory of Corporate Art Collections.* Largo, FL: International Art Alliance, 1984. N5207.D57

Ickis, Marguerite. *The Standard Book of Quilt Making and Collecting.* New York: Greystone Press, 1949. TT835.I35

Johnson, Bruce, Susan S. Connor, Josephine Rogers, and Holly Sidford. *A Child's Comfort: Baby and Doll Quilts in American Folk Art.* New York: Harcourt Brace Jovanovich in association with the Museum of American Folk Art, 1977. NK9112.J63 1977

Johnson, Geraldine N. " 'Plain and Fancy': The Socioeconomics of Blue Ridge Quilts." *Appalachian Journal.* 10 (1982): 12–35.

Jones, Stella M. *Hawaiian Quilts.* 1930. Revised ed. Honolulu: Daughters of Hawaii, Honolulu Academy of Arts and Mission Houses Museum, 1973. NK9112.J66 1973

Katzenberg, Dena S. *Baltimore Album Quilts.* Baltimore: The Baltimore Museum of Art, 1981. NK9112.B35 1981

Khin, Yvonne M. *The Collector's Dictionary of Quilt Names and Patterns.* Washington, DC: Acropolis Books, 1980. TT835.K47 1980

Lasansky, Jeannette. *In the Heart of Pennsylvania: 19th and 20th Century Quiltmaking Traditions.* Lewisburg, PA: Oral Traditions Project of the Union County Historical Society, 1985. TT835.L36 1985

_____. *In the Heart of Pennsylvania: Symposium Papers.* Lewisburg, PA: Oral Traditions Project of the Union County Historical Society, 1986. NK9112.I52 1986

_____. *Pieced by Mother: Over 100 Years of Quiltmaking Traditions.* Lewisburg, PA: Oral Traditions Project of the Union County Historical Society, 1987.

Lewis, Alfred Allen. *The Mountain Artisan's Quilting Book.* New York: Macmillan Co., 1973. TT835.L48

Lipsett, Linda Otto. *Remember Me: Women and Their Friendship Quilts.* San Francisco: The Quilt Digest Press, 1985. NK9112.L57

Lithgow, Marilyn. *Quiltmaking and Quiltmakers.* New York: Funk and Wagnalls, 1974. TT835.L57 1974

Lubell, Cecil, ed. *Textile Collections of the World: Volume I, United States and Canada.* New York: Van Nostrand Reinhold Co., 1976. NK8812.U54

Luster, Michael. *Stitches in Time: A Legacy of Ozark Quilts.* Rogers, AR: Rogers Historical Museum, 1986. NK9112.L87 1986

The McCall's Book of Quilts. New York: Simon & Schuster, 1975. TT835.M23

McKendry, Ruth. *Traditional Quilts and Bed Coverings.* New York: Van Nostrand Reinhold Co., 1979. NK9113.A1M32 1979

McKim, Ruby Short. *One Hundred and One Patchwork Patterns.* Independence, MO: McKim Studios, 1931. Reprint. Rev. ed. New York: Dover Publications, 1962. TT835.M3 1962

McMorris, Penny. *Crazy Quilts.* New York: E.P. Dutton & Co., 1984. NK9112.M39 1984

Mainardi, Patricia. *Quilts: The Great American Art.* San Pedro, CA: Miles & Weir, 1978. NK9112.M34

Makowski, Colleen Lahan. *Quilting, 1915– 1983.* Metuchen, NJ: Scarecrow Press, 1985. Z6153.Q54M34 1985

Morgan, Mary and Dee Mosteller. *Trapunto and Other Forms of Raised Quilting.* New York: Charles Scribner's Sons, 1977. TT835.M68

Morris Museum of Arts and Sciences. *New Jersey Quilters: A Timeless Tradition.* Morristown: Morris Museum of Arts and Sciences, 1983. NK9112.N36 1983

Nelson, Cyril I., and Carter Houck. *Treasury of American Quilts.* New York: Greenwich House, 1984. TT835.N44 1984

Newman, Thelma R. *Quilting, Patchwork, Applique, and Trapunto: Traditional Methods and Original Designs.* New York: Crown Publishers, 1974. TT835.N48 1974

Nicoll, Jessica F. *Quilted for Friends: Delaware Valley Signature Quilts, 1840–1855.* Winterthur, DE: The Henry Francis Du Pont Winterthur Museum, 1985.

North Carolina Country Quilts: Regional Variations. Chapel Hill, NC: The Ackland Art Museum, University of North Carolina, 1979. NK9112.N6

The Official Museum Directory, 1986. Washington, DC: American Association of Museums, 1986. AM10.A204

Orlofsky, Patsy, and Myron Orlofsky. *Quilts in America.* New York: McGraw-Hill Book Co., 1974. NK9112.074

Pellman, Rachel T., and Kenneth Pellman. *The World of Amish Quilts.* Intercourse, PA: Good Books, 1984. NK9112.P444 1984

Pellman, Rachel T., and Joanne Ranck. *Quilts Among the Plain People.* Lancaster, PA: Good Books, 1981. NK9112.P44 1981

Peto, Florence. *Historic Quilts.* New York: American Historical Company, 1939. NK9112.P47

———. *American Quilts and Coverlets.* New York: Chanticleer Press, 1949. NK9112.P46 1949

Pottinger, David. *Quilts from the Indiana Amish, A Regional Collection.* New York: E.P. Dutton & Co. in association with the Museum of American Folk Art, 1983. NK9112.P67 1983

The Quilt Digest. San Francisco: Kiracofe and Kile, 1983— . WMLCL 83/142 Serial

The Quilter's Journal. Joyce Gross, editor. Mill Valley, CA: 1983— . WMLC 83/108 Serial

Quilter's Newsletter Magazine. Bonnie Leman, ed. Wheatridge, CO: Leman Publications, 1972— . TT835.Q536

The Quilter's Newsletter Magazine International Quilt Guild Directory, 1984–1985. Marie Shirer, ed. Wheatridge, CO: Leman Publications, 1984.

Ramsey, Bets, and Merikay Waldvogel. *The Quilts of Tennessee: Images of Domestic Life Prior to 1930.* Nashville: Rutledge Hill Press, 1986. NK9112.R36 1986

Robertson, Elizabeth Wells. *American Quilts.*

New York: The Studio Publications, 1948.
NK9112.R6

Robinson, Sharon. *Contemporary Quilting.*
Worcester, MA: Davis Publications, 1982.
TT835.R62 1982

Safford, Carleton L., and Robert Bishop. *America's Quilts and Coverlets.* New York: E.P.
Dutton & Co., 1972. NK9112.S23 1972

Salz, Kay. *Craft Films: An Index of International Films on Crafts.* New York: Neal-
Schuman Publishers, 1979. TT149.S24

Sater, Joel. *The Patchwork Quilt.* Ephrata, PA:
Science Press, 1981. NK9112.S27

Sheldon Memorial Art Gallery. *Quilts from
Nebraska Collections.* Lincoln, NE: The
Gallery, University of Nebraska, 1974.
NK9112.S47 1974

Sink, Susan. *Traditional Crafts and Craftsmanship in America: A Selected Bibliography.* Publications of the American Folklife
Center, no. 11. Washington, DC: The American Folklife Center, Library of Congress,
1983. Z5956.F6S56 1983

Uncoverings. Sally Garoutte, ed. Mill Valley,
CA: American Quilt Study Group, 1980—.
TT835.U52

Webster, Marie Daugherty. *Quilts: Their Story
and How to Make Them.* New York: Doubleday, Doran & Co., 1928. Reprint. New
York: Tudor Publishing Co., 1943.
NK9104.W4 1943. Reprint. Detroit: Gale Research Co., 1972. NK0104.W4 1972

Wilson, Erica. *Quilts of America.* Birmingham,
AL: Oxmoor House, Inc., 1979. TT835.W54

Wiss, Audrey, and Douglas Wiss. *Folk Art
Quilts and How to Recreate Them.* Pittstown, NJ: The Main Street Press, 1983.
TT835.W57 1983

Woodward, Thomas K., and Blanche Greenstein. *Crib Quilts and Other Small Wonders.* New York: E.P. Dutton & Co., 1981.
NK9112.W67 1981

Wooster, Ann-Sargent. *Quiltmaking: The Modern Approach to a Traditional Craft.* New
York: Drake Publishers, 1972. TT835.W66

Yabsley, Suzanne. *Texas Quilts, Texas Women.*
College Station, TX: Texas A&M University
Press, 1984. NK9112.Y32 1984

LIST OF PARTICIPATING INSTITUTIONS

The **A**bby Aldrich Rockefeller Folk Art Center—Williamsburg, Virginia

The Adelaide Hunter-Hoodless Homestead—St. George, Ontario, Canada

Aiken County Historical Museum—Aiken, South Carolina

Alabama Department of Archives and History—Montgomery, Alabama

Alaska State Museum—Juneau, Alaska

Albany Institute of History and Art—Albany, New York

Allaire State Park, Allaire Village—Allaire, New Jersey

Alleghany County Historical Society, History House Museum—Cumberland, Maryland

The Allen County Historical Society—Lima, Ohio

Amana Heritage Society—Amana, Iowa

Ameliasburgh Historical Museum—Ameliasburg, Ontaria, Canada

American Museum of Quilts and Related Arts—San Jose, California

The American Quilt Museum—Marietta, Pennsylvania

American Quilt Study Group—Mill Valley, California

American Telephone and Telegraph Company (AT&T)—New York City, New York

Anchorage Museum of History and Art—Anchorage, Alaska

Annie Riggs Memorial Museum—Fort Stockton, Texas

Annie S. Kemerer Museum—Bethlehem, Pennsylvania

The Antiquarian and Landmarks Society, Inc.—Hartford, Connecticut

Appalachian State University, Appalachian Cultural Center—Boone, North Carolina

Arizona Historical Society—Tucson, Arizona

Arizona State University, University Art Collection—Tempe, Arizona

Arkansas Post County Museum—Gillett, Arkansas

Arkansas State University, Arkansas State University Museum—State University, Arkansas

Arkansas Territorial Restoration—Little Rock, Arkansas

Arlington Heights Historical Society—Arlington Heights, Illinois

Arlington Historical Society—Arlington, Massachusetts

The Art Institute of Chicago, Department of Textiles—Chicago, Illinois

Art of the Plains Indians—Los Altos Hills, California

Atheneum Society of Wilbraham—Wilbraham, Massachusetts

Atlanta Historical Society—Atlanta, Georgia

Aurora Historical Museum—Aurora, Illinois

Aurora History Center—Aurora, California

Baca and Bloom Houses—Trinidad, Colorado

Baker University, Old Castle—Baldwin City, Kansas

Baltimore City Life Museums: Peale Museum, Carroll Mansion, and 1840 House—Baltimore, Maryland

Baltimore County Historical Society—Cockeysville, Maryland

Baltimore Museum of Art, The Jean and Allan Berman Textile Gallery—Baltimore, Maryland

Bank of Boston—Boston, Massachusetts

Bankamerica Corporation Art Program—San Francisco, California

Barclay Farmstead—Cherry Hill, New Jersey

Bartholomew County Historical Society—Columbus, Indiana

The Bayou Bend Collection—Houston, Texas

Belmont County Historical Museum—Barnesville, Ohio

The Bennington Museum—Bennington, Vermont

Berea College, Weatherford-Hammond Mountain Collection and Southern Appalachian Archives, Special Collections—Berea, Kentucky

Bergen County Historical Society—River Edge, New Jersey

Berkshire County Historical Society—Pittsfield, Massachusetts

Bernice P. Bishop Museum—Honolulu, Hawaii

Bethel College, Kauffman Museum—North Newton, Kansas

Bethel Historical Society, Inc.—Bethel, Maine

Beverly Historical Society and Museum—Beverly, Massachusetts

Billings Farm and Museum—Woodstock, Vermont

The Birmingham Museum of Art—Birmingham, Alabama

Bishop Hill Heritage Museum—Bishop Hill, Illinois

Black Creek Pioneer Village—Downsview, Ontario, Canada

Black Creek Pioneer Village—North York, Ontario, Canada

Blue Earth County Historical Society Museum—Mankato, Minnesota

Bluffton College, Mennonite Historical Library—Bluffton, Ohio

Boot Hill Museum, Inc.—Dodge City, Kansas

Boulder Historical Society Museum—Boulder, Colorado

Bowers Museum—Santa Ana, California

Bowne House Historical Society—Flushing, New York

Bradford Brinton Memorial Museum—Big Horn, Wyoming

The Brick Store Museum—Kennebunk, Maine

British Columbia Provincial Museum—Victoria, British Columbia, Canada

Broadview Historical and Museum Association—Broadview, Saskatchewan, Canada

Brome County Historical Society—Knowlton, Quebec, Canada

The Brooklyn Museum—Brooklyn, New York

Bruce County Museum—Southampton, Ontario, Canada

Buffalo and Erie County Historical Society—Buffalo, New York

Burlington County Historical Society—Burlington, New Jersey

Burnaby Village Museum—Burnaby, British Columbia, Canada

Butte County Historical Society—Chico, California

Bytown Historical Museum—Ottawa, Ontario, Canada

Calaveras County Museum and Archives—San Andreas, California

California Department of Parks and Recreation, Office of Interpretive Services—West Sacramento, California

Camden County Historical Society—Camden, New Jersey

Cape Ann Historical Association—Gloucester, Massachusetts

Cape May County Historical & Genealogical Society—Cape May, New Jersey

Carlow College, The Center for the History of American Needlework—Pittsburgh, Pennsylvania

Carrie M. McLain Memorial Museum—Nome, Alaska

Carroll County Farm Museum—Westminster, Maryland

Carson County Square House Museum—Panhandle, Texas

Cascade County Historical Society—Great Falls, Montana

Cass County Historical Society—Harrisonville, Missouri

The Castle and Museum at Inspiration Point—Eureka Springs, Arkansas

Cedar Falls Historical Society—Cedar Falls, Iowa

Center for Southern Folklore Archives—Memphis, Tennessee

Centralia Historical Society—Moberly, Missouri

Centre County Library and Historical Museum—Bellefonte, Pennsylvania

Century Village, Lang—Keene, Ontario, Canada

Champaign County Historical Society—Champaign, Illinois

The Charleston Museum—Charleston, South Carolina

The Chase Manhattan Bank, Art Program—New York City, New York

Cheektowaga Historical Association—Cheektowaga, New York

Chemung County Historical Museum—Elmira, New York

Chenango County Historical Society—Norwich, New York

Cherokee Strip Museum—Arkansas City, Kansas

Chester County Historical Society—West Chester, Pennsylvania

Chester Historical Society—Chester, New Jersey

Chester Historical Society—Chester, Vermont

Chicago Historical Society—Chicago, Illinois

The Children's Museum—Indianapolis, Indiana

Chilliwack Museum and Historical Society—Chilliwack, British Columbia, Canada

Chisholm Trail Museum—Wellington, Kansas

The Chrysler Museum—Norfolk, Virginia

Churchill County Museum and Archive—Fallon, Nevada

Cincinnati Art Museum—Cincinnati, Ohio

City of Greeley Museums—Greeley, Colorado

Clarksville-Montgomery County Historical Museum—Clarksville, Tennessee

Clatsop County Historical Society—Astoria, Oregon

Clausen Memorial Museum—Petersburg, Alaska

Clemson University, Fort Hill, John C. Calhoun Mansion—Clemson, South Carolina

Clinton County Historical Society—Wilmington, Ohio

Clinton County Museum—Frankfort, Indiana

Clinton Historical Museum Village—Clinton, New Jersey

Cole County Historical Society, B. Gratz Brown House—Jefferson City, Missouri

Colonial Williamsburg Foundation, Department of Collections—Williamsburg, Virginia

The Colorado Historical Society—Denver, Colorado

The Columbus Museum—Columbus, Georgia

Concordia Historical Institute—St. Louis, Missouri

The Connecticut Historical Society—Hartford, Connecticut

Cooke County Heritage Society, Morton Museum of Cooke County—Gainesville, Texas

Coos County Historical Museum—North Bend, Oregon

Cornell University, Herbert F. Johnson Museum of Art—Ithaca, New York

Cortland County Historical Society—Cortland, New York

Cowley County Historical Museum—Winfield, Kansas

Crook County Historical Museum, Bowman Museum—Prineville, Oregon

Crosby County Pioneer Memorial—Crosbyton, Texas

Culberson County Historical Museum—Van Horn, Texas

Cumberland County Historical Society—Carlisle, Pennsylvania

Cumberland Museum—Nashville, Tennessee

The Currier Gallery of Art—Manchester, New Hampshire

Dallas County Heritage Center—Dallas, Texas

Dallas Historical Society, Hall of State—Dallas, Texas

Danbury Scott-Fanton Museum and Historical Society, Inc.—Danbury, Connecticut

Darien Historical Society—Darien, Connecticut

Daughters of Hawaii—Honolulu, Hawaii

Daughters of the American Revolution Museum—District of Columbia

Dauphin County Historical Society—Harrisburg, Pennsylvania

Davy Crockett Tavern Museum—Morristown, Tennessee

Dawson County Historical Society—Lexington, Nebraska

Dearborn Historical Museum—Dearborn, Michigan

Delaware County Historical Association—Delhi, New York

Delaware State Museum/Zwaanendael Museum, Bureau of Museums, Division of Historical and Cultural Affairs—Dover, Delaware

The Denver Art Museum—Denver, Colorado

Detroit Historical Museum—Detroit, Michigan

The Detroit Institute of Arts—Detroit, Michigan

Deutschheim, State Historic Site—Hermann, Missouri

DeWitt Historical Society of Tompkins County—Ithaca, New York

Dey Mansion—Wayne, New Jersey

Doon Heritage Crossroads—Kitchener, Ontario, Canada

Douglas County Historical Society—Superior, Wisconsin

Downers Grove Historical Museum—Downers Grove, Illinois

Drake House Museum—Plainfield, New Jersey

Duke University, William R. Perkins Library, The Frank Clyde Brown Papers, Manuscript Department—Durham, North Carolina

Dwight D. Eisenhower Library—Abilene, Kansas

Dyer Memorial Library—Abington, Massachusetts

East Hampton Historical Society—East Hampton, New York

East Tennessee State University, Carroll Reece Museum—Johnson City, Tennessee

East Tennessee State University, The Sherrod Library, Archives of Appalachia—Johnson City, Tennessee

Eastern Washington State Historical Society—Spokane, Washington

The Edison Institute, Greenfield Village, Henry Ford Museum—Dearborn, Michigan

Elkhart County Historical Society—Bristol, Indiana

Ella Sharp Museum—Jackson, Michigan

Elmhurst Historical Museum—Elmhurst, Illinois

Ermatinger Old Stone House—Sault Ste. Marie, Ontario, Canada

The Erpf Catskill Cultural Center—Arkville, New York

Esprit de Corp.—San Francisco, California

Essex Institute—Salem, Massachusetts

Ezra Meeker Historical Society—Puyallup, Washington

Fairbanks Family in America, Inc.—Dedham, Massachusetts

Fairfax County Park Authority, Division of Historic Preservation—Annandale, Virginia

Fairfield County Museum—Winnsboro, South Carolina

Fairfield Historical Society—Fairfield, Connecticut

Fall River Historical Society—Fall River, Massachusetts

Fanshawe Pioneer Village—London, Ontario, Canada

Federated Women's Institutes of Canada—Ottawa, Ontario, Canada

Ferndale Museum—Ferndale, California

Ferrum College, Blue Ridge Institute—Ferrum, Virginia

Fillmore County Historical Society/Center—Preston, Minnesota

The Filson Club—Louisville, Kentucky

The Fine Arts Museums of San Francisco, M. H. de Young Memorial Museum—San Francisco, California

Fitchburg Historical Society—Fitchburg, Masssachusetts

Florida Folklife Programs—White Springs, Florida

Follett House Museum—Sandusky, Ohio

Fort Concho National Historic Landmark—San Angelo, Texas

Fort Davis National Historic Site—Fort Davis, Texas

Fort Delaware/Museum of Colonial History—Narrowsburg, New York

Fort Missoula Historical Museum—Fort Missoula, Montana

Fort Verde State Historical Park—Camp Verde, Arizona

Fort Worth Museum of Science and History—Fort Worth, Texas

Foxfire Fund, Inc.—Rabun Gap, Georgia

Fremont County Pioneer Museum—Lander, Wyoming

Fremont House Museum—Tucson, Arizona

Gage County Historical Museum—Beatrice, Nebraska

Galena/Jo Daviess/County History Museum—Galena, Illinois

Gallier House Museum—New Orleans, Louisiana

Geauga County Historical Society, Burton Century Village—Burton, Ohio

Genesee County Village and Museum—Mumford, New York

Geneva Historical Society—Geneva, New York

Geneva Historical Society Museum—Geneva, Illinois

Georgetown Society, Inc.—Georgetown, Colorado

Gerald R. Ford Museum—Grand Rapids, Michigan

Germantown Historical Society—Philadelphia, Pennsylvania

Gibbs Farm Museum—St. Paul, Minnesota

Glenbow Museum—Calgary, Alberta, Canada

Glensheen—Duluth, Minnesota

Gloucester County Historical Society—Woodbury, New Jersey

Goshen Historical Society—Goshen, Connecticut

Governor Hogg Shrine State Historical Park—Quitman, Texas

Grand Encampment Museum—Encampment, Wyoming

Grand Forks County Historical Society—Grand Lake, Colorado

Grand Rapids Public Museum—Grand Rapids, Michigan

Granny's Quilt House—Cheyenne, Oklahoma

Great Smoky Mountains National Park—Gatlinburg, Tennessee

The Greene County Historical Society—Xenia, Ohio

Greene County Historical Society—Waynesburg, Pennsylvania

Greene County Historical Society, Bronck Museum—Coxsackie, New York

Greensboro Historical Museum—Greensboro, North Carolina

Grout Museum of History and Science—Waterloo, Iowa

Gunston Hall—Lorton, Virginia

The Haggin Museum—Stockton, California

The Hagley Museum—Wilmington, Delaware

Hale Farm and Village—Bath, Ohio

Hancock County Historical Museum—Findlay, Ohio

Harris County Heritage Society—Houston, Texas

Hastings Museum—Hastings, Nebraska

Haverford Township Historical Society—Havertown, Pennsylvania

Heard Natural Science Museum and Wildlife Sanctuary—McKinney, Texas

Hennepin County Historical Society Museum—Minneapolis, Minnesota

The Henry Francis du Pont Winterthur Museum—Winterthur, Delaware

The Henry Francis du Pont Winterthur Museum Library, The Joseph Downs Manuscript and Microfilm Collection—Winterthur, Delaware

Herkimer Home State Historic Site—Little Falls, New York

Hershey Museum of American Life—Hershey, Pennsylvania

Hezekiah Alexander Home Site and History Museum—Charlotte, North Carolina

Hickory County Historical Society—Hermitage, Missouri

The High Museum of Art—Atlanta, Georgia

High Plains Historical Foundation—Clovis, New Mexico

High Point Historical Society, Inc.—High Point, North Carolina

Highland Park Historical Society—Highland Park, Illinois

Hillforest Historical Foundation, Inc.—Aurora, Indiana

Historic Deerfield, Inc.—Deerfield, Massachusetts

Historic Lyme Village Association—Bellevue, Ohio

The Historic New Orleans Collection—New Orleans, Louisiana

Historical Association of Southern Florida—Miami, Florida

Historical Museum of the D. R. Barker Library—Fredonia, New York

Historical Society of Berks County—Reading, Pennsylvania

Historical Society of Centinela Valley—Los Angeles, California

Historical Society of Glastonbury—Glastonbury, Connecticut

Historical Society of Oak Park and River Forest—Oak Park, Illinois

Historical Society of Princeton, Bainbridge House—Princeton, New Jersey

Historical Society of Rockland County—New City, New York

Historical Society of Seattle and King County, Museum of History and Industry—Seattle, Washington

Historical Society of Walden and Wallkill Valley—Walden, New York

Historical Society of York County—York, Pennsylvania

Hoard Historical Museum—Ft. Atkinson, Wisconsin

"Home Sweet Home" Museum—East Hampton, New York

Homestead National Monument—Beatrice, Nebraska

Honolulu Academy of Arts—Honolulu, Hawaii

Hoover-Minthorn House Museum—Newberg, Oregon

Horseheads Cultural Center and Historical Society—Horseheads, New York

Houston Antique Museum—Chattanooga, Tennessee

The Hudson River Museum, Trevor Park-on-Hudson—Yonkers, New York

Huguenot Historical Society of New Paltz—New Paltz, New York

Huntington Galleries—Huntington, West Virginia

Huntington Historical Society—Huntington, New York

Hutchinson House Museum—Peterborough, Ontario, Canada

Idaho State Historical Society—Boise, Idaho

Idaho State Historical Society Library and Archives—Boise, Idaho

Illinois Pioneer Heritage Center, Inc.—Monticello, Illinois

Illinois State Museum—Springfield, Illinois

Illinois State University, The University Museums—Normal, Illinois

Indiana State Museum and Historic Sites—Indianapolis, Indiana

Indianapolis Museum of Art—Indianapolis, Indiana

The Institute of Texan Cultures—San Antonio, Texas

'Iolani Palace—Honolulu, Hawaii

Iowa State Historical Department—Iowa City, Iowa

Irving House Historic Centre—New Westminister, British Columbia, Canada

Isaac Royall House—Medford, Massachusetts

Isanti County Historical Society—Cambridge, Minnesota

Islesboro Historical Society—Islesboro, Maine

The Jackson Homestead—Newton, Massachusetts

Jacksonville Museum of Arts and Sciences—Jacksonville, Florida

Jamieson Museum—Moosomin, Saskatchewan, Canada

Jefferson County Historical Society—Watertown, New York

Jefferson County Historical Society, Hiwan Homestead Museum—Evergreen, Colorado

Jesse Besser Museum—Alpena, Michigan

John Jay Homestead State Historic Site—Katonah, New York

John Muir National Historic Site—Martinez, California

Johnson County Historical Society—Coralville, Iowa

Joseph Brant Museum—Burlington, Ontario, Canada

Joseph Schneider Haus—Kitchener, Ontario, Canada

Joslyn Art Museum—Omaha, Nebraska

Juliette Gordon Low Girl Scout National Center—Savannah, Georgia

Kalona Historical Village—Kalona, Iowa

Kamloops Museum and Archives—Kamloops, British Columbia, Canada

The Kansas City Museum—Kansas City, Missouri

Kansas Museum of History—Topeka, Kansas

Kansas State Historical Society, Manuscript Department—Topeka, Kansas

Kansas State University, Department of Clothing, Textiles, and Interior Design—Manhattan, Kansas

Kaua'i Museum—Lihue, Hawaii

Kennebunkport Historical Society—Kennebunkport, Maine

Kent-Delord House Museum—Plattsburgh, New York

Kentucky Historical Society—Frankfort, Kentucky

Kern County Museum—Bakersfield, California

Kings County Museum—Hampton, New Brunswick, Canada

Kings Landing Historical Settlement—Fredericton, New Brunswick, Canada

Klamath County Museum—Klamath Falls, Oregon

Koochiching County Historical Society—International Falls, Minnesota

LaCrosse County Historical Society, Swarthout Museum—LaCrosse, Wisconsin

Lake County Museum—Wauconda, Illinois

Lake Region Pioneer Daughters Museum—Fort Totten, North Dakota

Lakeview Museum of Arts and Sciences—Peoria, Illinois

Lakewood Historical Society—Lakewood, Ohio

The Landmark Society of Western New York—Rochester, New York

Landmarks Foundation of Montgomery—Montgomery, Alabama

Lane County Historical Museum—Eugene, Oregon

Laramie Plains Museum—Laramie, Wyoming

Latah County Historical Society—Moscow, Idaho

Latter Day Saints Museum of Church History and Art—Salt Lake City, Utah

Lebanon County Historical Society—Lebanon, Pennsylvania

Lenawee County Historical Museum—Adrian, Michigan

Levi Strauss and Company—San Francisco, California

Lexington County Museum—Lexington, South Carolina

Lexington Historical Society—Lexington, Massachusetts

The Library of Congress, American Folklife Center, Archive of Folk Culture; Motion Picture, Broadcasting and Recorded Sound Division; Prints and Photographs Division—District of Columbia

Lightner Museum—St. Augustine, Florida

Lincoln County Cultural and Historical Association—Wiscasset, Maine

Lincoln County Historical Society—Chandler, Oklahoma

Lincoln County Historical Society—Newport, Oregon

Lincoln Home National Historic Site—Springfield, Illinois

Litchfield Historical Society—Litchfield, Connecticut

Living History Farms—Des Moines, Iowa

Log Cabin Village Historical Complex—Fort Worth, Texas

London Historical Museums—London, Ontario, Canada

The Los Angeles County Museum of Art, American Quilt Research Center—Los Angeles, California

Los Angeles County Museum of Natural History—Los Angeles, California

Loudoun Museum, Inc.—Leesburg, Virginia

Louisiana Folklife Program—Baton Rouge, Louisiana

The Louisiana State Museum—New Orleans, Louisiana

Louisiana State University, Rural Life Museum, Burden Research Plantation—Baton Rouge, Louisiana

Loveland Museum and Gallery—Loveland, Colorado

The Luna County Historical Society, Inc., Deming Luna Mimbres Museum—Deming, New Mexico

Lundy's Lane Historical Museum—Niagara Falls, Ontario, Canada

Lycoming County Historical Society and Museum—Williamsport, Pennsylvania

Lyman Allyn Museum—New London, Connecticut

Lyndon B. Johnson National Historic Site—Johnson City, Texas

Lyon County Historical Museum—Emporia, Kansas

McCord Museum—Montreal, Quebec, Canada

McDougall Mill Museum—Renfrew, Ontario, Canada

McHenry County Historical Museum—Union, Illinois

McHenry Museum—Modesto, California

McKinley Museum of History, Science, and Industry—Canton, Ohio

McLean County Historical Society—Bloomington, Illinois

McLoughlin House National Historic Site—Oregon City, Oregon

Madera County Historical Society—Madera, California

Madison County Historical Museum—Edwardsville, Illinois

Madison County Historical Society—Oneida, New York

The Mahoning Valley Historical Society, The Arms Museum—Youngstown, Ohio

Maine Historical Society—Portland, Maine

Maine State Museum—Augusta, Maine

Manitoba Museum of Man and Nature—Winnipeg, Manitoba, Canada

Marathon County Historical Museum—Wausau, Wisconsin

The Margaret Woodbury Strong Museum—Rochester, New York

Marias Museum of History and Art—Shelby, Montana

Marshall County Historical Society—Lacon, Illinois

Marshall County Historical Society, Inc., Marshall County Historical Museum—Holly Springs, Mississippi

Marshall County Historical Society Museum—Plymouth, Indiana

Marshall Historical Society—Marshall, Michigan

The Maryland Historical Society, Enoch Pratt House—Baltimore, Maryland

Masey Area Museum, Inc.—Massey, Ontario, Canada

Mason County Historical Society and White Pine Village, Rose Hawley Museum—Ludington, Michigan

The Massillon Museum—Massillon, Ohio

Matsqui-Sumas-Abbotsford Museum Society—Abbotsford, British Columbia, Canada

Mattatuck Museum—Waterbury, Connecticut

Medina County Historical Society—Medina, Ohio

Memphis Brooks Museum of Art—Memphis, Tennessee

Memphis Pink Palace Museum—Memphis, Tennessee

Mendocino County Museum—Willits, California

Mennonite Heritage Center, Peter Wentz Farmstead—Souderton, Pennsylvania

Menominee County Historical Museum—Menominee, Michigan

Mercer County Historical Museum—Celina, Ohio

The Mercer Museum—Doylestown, Pennsylvania

Merrick County Historical Museum—Central City, Nebraska

The Metropolitan Museum of Art, American Decorative Arts Department—New York, New York

Michigan Historical Museum—Lansing, Michigan

Michigan State University, Michigan State University Museum, Michigan Folk Arts Archive—East Lansing, Michigan

Middlesex County Historical Society—Middletown, Connecticut

Milan Historical Museum—Milan, Ohio

Millard Fillmore House Museum—East Aurora, New York

Milton Historical Society, Milton House Museum—Milton, Wisconsin

Milwaukee Public Museum—Milwaukee, Wisconsin

The Minneapolis Institute of Art—Minneapolis, Minnesota

Minnesota Historical Society, Museum Collections—St. Paul, Minnesota

Mission Historical Society, Mission Museum—Mission, British Columbia, Canada

Mission Houses Museum—Honolulu, Hawaii

Mississippi State Historical Museum, Mississippi Department of Archives and History—Jackson, Mississippi

Missouri Historical Society—St. Louis, Missouri

Missouri State Museum, Missouri State Capitol—Jefferson City, Missouri

Molalla Area Historical Society—Molalla, Oregon

Mondak Heritage Center—Sidney, Montana

Monmouth County Historical Association—Freehold, New Jersey

Monroe County Historical Museum—Bloomington, Indiana

Montana Historical Society—Helana, Montana

Montana State University, Museum of the Rockies—Bozeman, Montana

Montauk—Clermont, Iowa

Monterey County Historical Society—Salinas, California

Montgomery County Historical Society—Rockville, Maryland

Montgomery County Historical Society—Dayton, Ohio

Monticello, Thomas Jefferson Memorial Foundation—Charlottesville, Virginia

Morehead State University, Camden-Carroll Library, Appalachian Collection—Morehead, Kentucky

Morris County Historical Society—Morristown, New Jersey

Morris Museum—Morristown, New Jersey

Morristown National Historical Park—Morristown, New Jersey

The Mount Vernon Ladies' Association of the Union—Mount Vernon, Virginia

Museum of American Folk Art—New York City, New York

Museum of American Textile History—North Andover, Massachusetts

Museum of Appalachia—Norris, Tennessee

Museum of Early Southern Decorative Arts—Winston-Salem, North Carolina

Museum of Early Trades and Crafts—Madison, New Jersey

Museum of Fine Arts, Boston, Department of Textiles—Boston, Massachusetts

Museum of Florida History—Tallahassee, Florida

Museum of International Folk Art, Museum of New Mexico—Santa Fe, New Mexico

Museum of New Mexico, The History Division—Santa Fe, New Mexico

Museum of Our National Heritage—Lexington, Massachusetts

Museum of Ozarks' History—Springfield, Missouri

Museum of San Diego History—San Diego, California

Museum of the Atlantic County Historical Society—Somers Point, New Jersey

Museum of the City of New York—New York City, New York

Museum of Tobacco Art and History—Nashville, Tennessee

Muskegon County Museum—Muskegon, Michigan

Muskoka Pioneer Village—Huntsville, Ontario, Canada

Nantucket Historical Association—Nantucket, Massachusetts

Naperville Heritage Society, Naper Settlement—Naperville, Illinois

Nassau County Museum Collections—Sands Point, New York

National Gallery of Art, Index of American Design—District of Columbia

National Museum of Man, Canadian Centre for Folk Culture Studies—Ottawa, Ontario, Canada

National Trust for Historic Preservation—District of Columbia

Neill Museum—Fort Davis, Texas

Nevada Historical Society—Reno, Nevada

The New Brunswick Museum—Saint John, New Brunswick, Canada

New Canaan Historical Society—New Canaan, Connecticut

New England Quilt Museum—Lowell, Massachusetts

New Hampshire Antiquarian Society, Hopkinton Village—Hopkinton, New Hampshire

New Hampshire Historical Society—Concord, New Hampshire

New Hanover County Museum—Wilmington, North Carolina

The New Jersey Historical Society—Newark, New Jersey

New Jersey State Museum—Trenton, New Jersey

The New York Historical Society—New York City, New York

The New York State Historical Association and the Farmers' Museum—Cooperstown, New York

New York State Office of Parks, Recreation and Historic Preservation, Bureau of Historic Sites—Waterford, New York

New London County Historical Society—New London, Connecticut

The Newark Museum—Newark, New Jersey

Niagara Historical Society Museum—Niagara-on-the-Lake, Ontario, Canada

Noah Webster Foundation—West Hartford, Connecticut

Norman/Cleveland County Historical Museum—Norman, Oklahoma

North Carolina Museum of History—Raleigh, North Carolina

North Dakota State University, Cooperative Extension Service—Fargo, North Dakota

Northampton Historical Society—Northampton, Massachusetts

Northern Arizona University, Arizona Friends of Folklore Archive—Flagstaff, Arizona

The Norwich Free Academy, The Slater Memorial Museum, Norwich Art School—Norwich, Connecticut

Nova Scotia Museum—Halifax, Nova Scotia, Canada

The Oakland Museum—Oakland, California

Oakland Plantation—Bermuda, Louisiana

Oaklands Historic House Museum—Murfreesboro, Tennessee

Ohio Historical Society—Columbus, Ohio

Old Barracks Museum—Trenton, New Jersey

Old Colony Historical Society—Taunton, Massachusetts

Old Economy Village—Ambridge, Pennsylvania

Old Fort Harrod State Park—Harrodsburg, Kentucky

Old Fort Museum—Fort Smith, Arkansas

Old Greer County Museum and Hall of Fame, Inc.—Mangum, Oklahoma

Old Salem, Inc.—Winston-Salem, North Carolina

Old Slave Mart Museum—Charleston, South Carolina

Old State House Museum—Little Rock, Arkansas

Old Sturbridge Village—Sturbridge, Massachusetts

Old York Historical Society—York, Maine

Orange County Historical Museum, Inc.—Hillsborough, North Carolina

Oregon Historical Society—Portland, Oregon

Oregon State University, Horner Museum—Corvallis, Oregon

Orleans County Historical Society—Browningham, Vermont

Oshawa Sydenham Museum—Oshawa, Ontario, Canada

Otter Tail County Historical Society Museum—Fergus Falls, Minnesota

Owensboro Area Museum—Owensboro, Kentucky

Ox Barn Museum, Museum of the Aurora Colony—Aurora, Oregon

Oysterponds Historical Society Museum—Orient, New York

The Packwood House Museum—Lewisburg, Pennsylvania

Pasadena Historical Society—Pasadena, California

Passaic County Historical Society, Lambert Castle—Paterson, New Jersey

Paulson House Museum—Au Train, Michigan

Pearl S. Buck Birthplace Foundation—Hillsboro, West Virginia

Pejepscot Historical Society—Brunswick, Maine

Pennsauken Historical Society, Burrough-Dover House—Pennsauken, New Jersey

Penobscot Marine Museum—Searsport, Maine

Pensacola Historical Museum—Pensacola, Florida

Petersham Historical Society—Petersham, Massachusetts

Pennsylvania Dutch Folk Culture Center—Lenhartsville, Pennsylvania

Pennsylvania Farm Museum—Lancaster, Pennsylvania

Peterborough Museum and Archives—Peterborough, Ontario, Canada

Pettaquamscott Historical Society—Kingston, Rhode Island

Philadelphia College of Textiles and Science, The Goldie Paley Design Center—Philadelphia, Pennsylvania

Philadelphia Museum of Art—Philadelphia, Pennsylvania

Philip Morris Companies, Inc.—New York, New York

Phillips Historical Society—Phillips, Maine

Phoenix Art Museum, Arizona Costume Institute—Phoenix, Arizona

Pike Pioneer Museum—Troy, Alabama

Pioneer Florida Museum—Dade City, Florida

Pioneer Museum—Ashland, Kansas

Pioneer Museum and Art Center—Woodward, Oklahoma

Pioneer Trail State Park—Salt Lake City, Utah

Pioneer Woman Museum—Ponca City, Oklahoma

Pioneer Village—Farmington, Utah

Pioneers' Museum—Colorado Springs, Colorado

Pipestone County Museum—Pipestone, Minnesota

Plainsman Museum—Aurora, Nebraska

Plainville Historic Center—Plainville, Connecticut

Plymouth Notch Historic District, Birthplace of President Coolidge—Plymouth Notch, Vermont

Pocumtuck Valley Memorial Association, Memorial Hall Museum—Deerfield, Massachusetts

Porter-Phelps-Huntington Foundation, Inc.—Hadley, Massachusetts

Potsdam Public Museum—Potsdam, New York

Powers Museum—Carthage, Missouri

Pratt Museum—Homer, Alaska

President Benjamin Harrison Memorial Home—Indianapolis, Indiana

Provincial Museum of Alberta—Edmonton, Alberta, Canada

Putnam County Historical Society—Cold Spring, New York

Railroad and Pioneer Museum—Temple, Texas

Ralls Historical Museum—Ralls, Texas

Rancho Los Cerritos Museum—Long Beach, California

Ravalli County Museum, Old Courthouse—Hamilton, Montana

Raynham Hall Museum—Oyster Bay, New York
Red Clay Historic Park—Cleveland, Tennessee
Red Cloud Indian School, The Heritage Center—Pine Ridge, South Dakota
Redding Museum and Art Center—Redding, California
Region of Peel Museum—Brampton, Ontario, Canada
Rhode Island Historical Society, John Brown House—Providence, Rhode Island
Rhode Island School of Design, Museum of Art—Providence, Rhode Island
Riley County Historical Museum—Manhattan, Kansas
Riverside Municipal Museum—Riverside, California
Roanoke Valley Historical Society—Roanoke, Virginia
Roberson Center for the Arts and Sciences—Binghamton, New York
Roberts County Museum—Miami, Texas
Robinson State Museum—Pierre, South Dakota
Rochester Historical Society—Rochester, New York
Rochester Museum and Science Center—Rochester, New York
The Rock County Historical Society—Janesville, Wisconsin
Rockford Museum Center and Midway Village—Rockford, Illinois
Rocky Mount Historical Association—Bluff City, Tennessee
Rodale Press, Inc.—Emmaus, Pennsylvania
Rogers Historical Museum—Rogers, Arkansas
Ropes Mansion—Salem, Massachusetts
Rosenberg Library—Galveston, Texas
Ross County Historical Museum—Chillicothe, Ohio
Rowe Historical Society, Inc., Helen McCarthy Memorial Museum—Rowe, Massachusetts
Royal Ontario Museum—Toronto, Ontario, Canada
Rusk County Heritage Association, Howard-Dickinson House—Henderson, Texas

Sacramento Valley Museum Association—Williams, California
St. Joseph Museum—St. Joseph, Missouri
The St. Louis Art Museum—St. Louis, Missouri
St. Louis County Historical Society—Duluth, Minnesota
Ste. Genevieve Historical Museum—Ste. Genevieve, Missouri
Salem County Historical Society—Salem, New Jersey
Sam Bell Maxey House State Historic Site—Paris, Texas
Sam Davis Memorial Home—Smyrna, Tennessee
Sam Rayburn House Museum—Bonham, Texas
San Antonio Museum Association—San Antonio, Texas
San Joaquin County Historical Museum—Lodi, California

San Luis Obispo County Historical Society Museum—San Luis Obispo, California
San Mateo County Historical Association and Museum—San Mateo, California
Sanford Museum and Planetarium—Cherokee, Iowa
Santa Cruz City Museum—Santa Cruz, California
Sappington House Foundation—St. Louis, Missouri
Saskatchewan Western Development Museum—Saskatoon, Saskatchewan, Canada
Sauk County Historical Museum—Baraboo, Wisconsin
Schenectady County Historical Society—Schenectady, New York
Schenectady Museum and Planetarium—Schenectady, New York
Schminck Memorial Museum—Lakeview, Oregon
Schuyler Mansion State Historic Site—Albany, New York
Schwenkfelder Library—Pennsburg, Pennsylvania
Scottsboro—Jackson Heritage Center—Scottsboro, Alabama
Seneca Falls Historical Society—Seneca Falls, New York
Senate House State Historical Site—Kingston, New York
The Shadows-on-the-Teche—New Iberia, Louisiana
Shaker Museum—Poland Spring, Maine
Sharlott Hall Museum—Prescott, Arizona
The Shelburne Museum—Shelburne, Vermont
Sherman Historical Museum—Sherman, Texas
Shiloh Museum—Springdale, Arkansas
Sibley House Museum—Mendota, Minnesota
Sierra Historic Sites Association—Oakhurst, California
Siloam Springs Museum—Siloam Springs, Arkansas
Silver City Museum—Silver City, New Mexico
Siouxland Heritage Museums, Old Courthouse Museum—Sioux Falls, South Dakota
Siskiyou County Museum—Yreka, California
Skagit County Historical Museum—La Conner, Washington
Slavonic Benevolent Order of the State of Texas—Temple, Texas
Smithsonian Institution, National Museum of American History, Division of Textiles—District of Columbia
Smithsonian Institution, Office of Folklife Programs, Smithsonian Folklife Program Archives—District of Columbia
Smithtown Valley Museum—North Bend, Washington
Snoqualmie Valley Museum—North Bend, Washington
Sombra Township Museum—Sombra, Ontario, Canada
Somerwell County Museum—Glen Rose, Texas
Sonoma State University, The Ruben Salazar Library—Rohnert Park, California

South Carolina State Museum—Columbia, South Carolina

South Center of Utah County, Daughters of Utah Pioneers Museum—Spanish Fork, Utah

South Dakota State College, Smith-Zimmermann State Museum—Madison, South Dakota

South East Museum—Brewster, New York

Southampton Colonial Society—Southampton, New York

Southern Oregon Historical Society—Jacksonville, Oregon

Southwest Virginia Museum, Historic State Park—Big Stone Gap, Virginia

Spartanburg County Regional Museum—Spartanburg, South Carolina

Spring Valley Community Historical Society, Inc.—Spring Valley, Minnesota

Stamford Historical Society—Stamford, Connecticut

Star of the Republic Museum, Washington-on-the-Bravos State Historical Park—Washington, Texas

Star-Spangled Banner Flag House/1812 Museum—Baltimore, Maryland

State Historical Society of Iowa—Des Moines, Iowa

State Historical Society of North Dakota, North Dakota Heritage Center—Bismarck, North Dakota

State Historical Society of Wisconsin—Madison, Wisconsin

The State Museum of History—Lincoln, Nebraska

State Museum/Oklahoma Historical Society—Oklahoma City, Oklahoma

State Museum of Pennsylvania—Harrisburg, Pennsylvania

State of California Department of Parks and Recreation, Bidwell Mansion State Historic Park—Chico, California

State University of New York at Stony Brook, The Museums—Stony Brook, New York

Staten Island Historical Society, Richmondtown Restoration—Staten Island, New York

Stephenson County Historical Society—Freeport, Illinois

Stone Fort Museum—Schoharie, New York

Stone Fort Museum—Nacogdoches, Texas

The Stowe-Day Foundation—Hartford, Connecticut

Stratford Historical Society—Stratford, Connecticut

Strawberry Banke—Portsmouth, New Hampshire

Stuhr Museum of the Prairie Pioneer—Grand Island, Nebraska

Sul Ross State University, Museum of the Big Bend—Alpine, Texas

Sumner Historical Society—Sumner, Washington

Tallahassee Junior Museum—Tallahassee, Florida

Tehama County Museum Foundation—Tehama, California

Tempe Historical Museum—Tempe, Arizona

The Tennessee State Museum—Nashville, Tennessee

Tennessee Valley Authority, Homeplace-1850—Golden Pond, Kentucky

Tennessee Wesleyan College, McMinn County Living Heritage Museum—Athens, Tennessee

Territorial Statehouse—Fillmore, Utah

Texas Agricultural and Industrial University, John E. Conner Museum—Kingsville, Texas

Texas Folklife Resources—Austin, Texas

The Textile Museum Library—District of Columbia

Thomas Clarke House—Princeton, New Jersey

Thomas County Historical Society and Museum—Colby, Kansas

Tillamook County Pioneer Museum—Tillamook, Oregon

Tioga County Historical Society Museum—Owega, New York

Tippecanoe County Historical Association—Lafayette, Indiana

Todmorden Mills Historic Site—Toronto, Ontario, Canada

Tongass Historical Museum—Ketchikan, Alaska

Torrington Historical Society—Torrington, Connecticut

Traill County Historical Society—Hillsboro, North Dakota

Troy Museum and Historic Village—Troy, Michigan

Union County Historical Society—Lewisburg, Pennsylvania

United Methodist Historical Society, Lovely Lane Museum of the Baltimore Conference—Baltimore, Maryland

Université Laval, Cité universitaire—Sainte-Foy, Quebec, Canada

University of Alabama, Archives of American Minority Cultures, Special Collections—Tuscaloosa, Alabama

University of Alberta, Historic Costume and Textile Study Collection—Edmonton, Alberta, Canada

University of Arkansas, The University Museum—Fayetteville, Arkansas

University of California at Berkeley, Robert E. Lowie Museum of Anthropology—Berkeley, California

University of California at Los Angeles, Museum of Cultural History—Los Angeles, California

University of Chicago, The University Library, Special Collections—Chicago, Illinois

University of Delaware, Folklore and Ethnic Art Center—Newark, Delaware

University of Detroit, Computerized Folklore Archive—Detroit, Michigan

University of Illinois, World Heritage Museum, Textiles Department—Urbana, Illinois

University of Indiana, William Hammond Mathers Museum—Bloomington, Indiana

The University of Kansas, Spencer Museum of Art—Lawrence, Kansas

University of Minnesota, Goldstein Gallery—St. Paul, Minnesota

The University of Mississippi, The University Museums—University, Mississippi

The University of Mississippi, J. D. Williams Library, Department of Archives and Special Collections—University, Mississippi

University of Missouri, Historic Costume and Textile Collection—Columbia, Missouri

University of Nebraska, Sheldon Memorial Art Gallery—Lincoln, Nebraska

University of Oklahoma, Stovall Museum of Science and History—Norman, Oklahoma

University of Oregon, Randall V. Mills Archive of Northwest Folklore—Eugene, Oregon

University of Rhode Island, Historic Textile and Costume Collection—Kingston, Rhode Island

University of South Carolina, McKissick Museum, and South Carolina Folk Art Archive—Columbia, South Carolina

University of South Dakota, W. H. Over State Museum—Vermillion, South Dakota

University of Texas at Austin, Winedale Historical Center—Round Top, Texas

University of Texas, Texas Memorial Museum—Austin, Texas

University of Vermont, Bailey/Howe Library, Folklore and Oral History Collection—Burlington, Vermont

University of Washington, Henry Art Gallery Textile Collection—Seattle, Washington

University of Wisconsin, Helen Allen Textile Collection—Madison, Wisconsin

Upper Canada Village, St. Lawrence Parks Commission—Morrisburg, Ontario, Canada

Upper Snake River Valley Historical Society—Rexburg, Idaho

Utah Arts Council, Folk Arts Program—Salt Lake City, Utah

The **V**alentine Museum—Richmond, Virginia

Van Riper-Hopper House/Wayne Museum—Wayne, New Jersey

Vermilion County Museum Society—Danville, Illinois

Vermont Historical Society—Montpelier, Vermont

Vesterheim, Norwegian-American Museum—Decorah, Iowa

Vigo County Historical Society—Terre Haute, Indiana

Wadsworth Atheneum—Hartford, Connecticut

Warren County Historical and Genealogical Society—Belvidere, New Jersey

Warren County Historical Society—Lebanon, Ohio

Washington County Historical Museum—St. Calhoun, Nebraska

Washington County Historical Society—Stillwater, Minnesota

Washington County Museum—Portland, Oregon

Washington State Capital Museum—Olympia, Washington

Washington State Historical Society—Tacoma, Washington

Waukesha County Historical Museum—Waukesha, Wisconsin

Wayne County Historical Society—Wooster, Ohio

Wayne State University, Purdy Library, Folklore Archives—Detroit, Michigan

Wellington County Museum—Fergus, Ontario, Canada

Wenham Museum—Wenham, Massachusetts

West Texas College, Scurry County Museum—Snyder, Texas

West Texas State University, Panhandle-Plains Historical Museum—Canyon, Texas

West Virginia Department of Culture and History, The Cultural Center—Charleston, West Virginia

Western Hennepin County Pioneers Association, Inc.—Long Lake, Minnesota

Western Heritage Center—Billings, Montana

Western Kentucky University, The Kentucky Library and Museum, Manuscript and Folklore, Folklife Archives Section—Bowling Green, Kentucky

Western Reserve Historical Society—Cleveland, Ohio

Western Rhode Island Civic Historical Society, Paine House—Coventry, Rhode Island

Westfield Athenaeum, Edwin Smith Historical Museum—Westfield, Massachusetts

Westmoreland Museum of Art—Greensburg, Pennsylvania

Westville Historical Handicrafts, Inc.—Lumpkin, Georgia

Wethersfield Historical Society—Wethersfield, Connecticut

Whatcom Museum of History and Art—Bellingham, Washington

Wichita Public Library, Joan O'Bryant Kansas Folklore Collection—Wichita, Kansas

Wichita-Sedgwick County Historical Society—Wichita, Kansas

Wilber Czech Museum—Wilber, Nebraska

William A. Farnsworth Library and Art Museum—Rockland, Maine

Wilson County Historical Society Museum—Fredonia, Kansas

Wilson Historical Society Museum—Wilson, New York

Wilton Heritage Museum—Wilton, Connecticut

Winchester-Frederick County Historical Society—Winchester, Virginia

Winona County Historical Society—Winona, Minnesota

Wise County Heritage Museum—Decatur, Texas

Woodlawn Plantation—Alexandria, Virginia
Woodrow Wilson Birthplace—Stauton, Virginia
The Woodstock Historical Society—Woodstock, Vermont
Woodstock Museum of Shenandoah County, Inc.—Woodstock, Virginia
Wyandotte County Museum—Bonner Springs, Kansas
Wyoming Historical and Geological Society—Wilkes-Barre, Pennsylvania

Yakima Valley Museum and Historical Association—Yakima, Washington
Yamhill County Historical Museum—Lafayette, Oregon
Yarmouth County Museum—Yarmouth, Nova Scotia, Canada
York County Historical Commission Headquarters, Historic Brattonsville—McConnells, South Carolina
York Institute Museum—Saco, Maine
York-Sunbury Historical Society Museum—Fredericton, New Brunswick, Canada
Ypsilanti Historical Museum—Ypsilanti, Michigan

Zoar Village State Memorial, Ohio Historical Society—Zoar, Ohio